AnnualRecipes
2006

INCLUDING PILLSBURY BAKE-OFF CONTEST WINNERS

Pillsbury Annual Recipes 2006

Our recipes have been tested in the Pillsbury Kitchens and meet our standards of easy preparation, reliability and great taste.

For more great recipes, visit pillsbury.com

PUBLISHED BY
Taste of Home Books
Reiman Media Group, Inc.
5400 S. 60ᵗʰ St., Greendale, WI 53129
www.reimanpub.com

This edition published by arrangement with Wiley Publishing, Inc.

Printed in U.S.A.

Library of Congress Cataloging-in-Publication Data is available upon request.

International Standard Book Number:
0-89821-501-3
International Standard Serial Number:
Applied For.

CREDITS
General Mills, Inc.
DIRECTOR, BOOK AND ONLINE PUBLISHING: Kim Walter
MANAGER AND EDITOR, BOOK PUBLISHING: Lois Tlusty
RECIPE DEVELOPMENT AND TESTING: Pillsbury Kitchens
PHOTOGRAPHY: General Mills Photo Studios and Image Center

Reiman Media Group, Inc.
PRESIDENT: Barbara Newton
EDITOR IN CHIEF: Catherine Cassidy
EXECUTIVE EDITOR/BOOKS:
Heidi Reuter Lloyd
EDITOR: Kathy Pohl
CREATIVE DIRECTOR: Ardyth Cope
ART DIRECTOR: Nathan Chow
PROOFREADERS: Julie Blume Benedict, Jean Steiner
GRAPHIC ART ASSOCIATES: Ellen Lloyd, Catherine Fletcher, Anne Baesemann
FOUNDER: Roy Reiman

FRONT COVER PHOTOGRAPHS:
Burgundy Beef and Mushrooms, PG. 255; Turkey-Sweet Potato Pot Pies, PG. 184; Raspberry-Amaretto Tarts, PG. 326; Chicken Enchilada Tortilla Cups, PG. 217; and Orange Cappuccino Tart, PG. 318.

PAGE 5 PHOTOGRAPHS:
Souper Shrimp Bisque, PG. 118; Caribbean Sponge Cake Desserts, PG. 317; Asian Noodle-Chicken Salad, PG. 92; and Chicken and Shrimp Stir-Fry, PG. 162.

BACK COVER PHOTOGRAPHS:
Italian Vegetarian Lasagna, PG. 190; Chicken-Tortellini Soup, PG. 104; Chocolate-Cherry Fantasy Dessert, PG. 336; and Chocolate Chip-Peanut Butter Squares, PG. 306.

contents

"Bringing You the Very Best in a New Annual Cookbook Series!"

introduction

For more than 130 years, good cooks have trusted Pillsbury to make mealtimes special. They've relied on Pillsbury for easy, family-pleasing recipes that are quick to prepare and bursting with homemade flavor in every bite.

That's why we're so excited about this brand-new cookbook! *Pillsbury Annual Recipes 2006* features the best-of-the-best recipes from the popular cooking magazines over the past year, plus dozens of prize-winning recipes from the annual Pillsbury Bake-Off Contests.

In fact, we're so excited about bringing you the best-of-the-best Pillsbury recipes that we've decided to launch a whole new line of cookbooks. This 2006 edition is the first in a series of annual cookbooks we look forward to bringing you year after year.

In this big, colorful 2006 edition, we've compiled 401 mouthwatering recipes, all of them triple-tested by the Pillsbury Test Kitchens. Those experts have sprinkled in handy tips and hints, too, plus simple ingredient substitutions and practical suggestions for rounding out meals so you can get dinner on the table quicker and easier than ever before!

Whether you need a delicious 30-minute dish for dinner tonight, a make-ahead casserole to take to a potluck, a slow-cooked mainstay for a busy day or a memorable dessert for easy entertaining, you're sure to find it here!

There are festive appetizers and fast-to-fix snacks for holiday occasions, grilled burgers for casual gatherings, simple salads and sandwiches for lunch, plus eye-opening breakfast and brunch options. You'll find dishes that are tailor-made for two—or 10! And much more!

We've packed all kinds of appealing meal options into one big book so you'll no longer need to spend precious time trying to decide what's for dinner or searching through old cooking magazines for a long-lost recipe. Take your pick of tasty side dishes, refreshing salads and quick breads to accompany hearty main dishes. And don't forget dessert! The scrumptious sweet treats in this book taste like you fussed—but you'll know otherwise!

Preparing favorite dishes for your family has never been easier, thanks to these simple recipes that use everyday ingredients you likely have on hand or can easily find at your grocery store. Many of the recipes in this book get a head start with brand-name convenience foods you know and trust. Others take advantage of time-saving cooking methods.

What's more, each recipe comes with clear, step-by-step instructions and a gorgeous color photo so you'll know exactly how each dish will look once it's prepared.

AT-A-GLANCE ICONS

Because we know how busy most cooks are these days, we've highlighted the easy recipes in this book with the icon at left, so you can spot them at a glance. These recipes call for 6 ingredients or less OR are ready to cook in 20 minutes or less OR are ready to eat in 30 minutes or less.

At the top of every recipe, we've included "Prep Time" and "Ready in…" times, as well. When you're trying to beat the clock, you'll know exactly how long it takes to prepare each dish.

And because we know good cooks are health-conscious these days, we've also called out the delicious and nutritious low-fat recipes. Look for the symbol at left, which confirms the recipe has 10 grams of fat or less (entrees) or 3 grams of fat or less (all other recipes).

Finally, we've highlighted the Pillsbury Bake-Off Contest Winners—recipes judged to be the very best in the popular Pillsbury Bake-Off Contests over the years. These proven prize-winners from America's best home cooks are bound to be as big a hit with your family as they were with the contest judges. When you're looking for a spectacular dish or a taste-tempting dessert with a "wow" factor, look for the Bake-Off symbol as you're browsing through this book.

HOW TO FIND A RECIPE

We have indexed this cookbook in two helpful ways. If you look under any major ingredient or cooking method in the general index, you'll find a list of the recipes that include it.

For example, if you want to serve chicken to your family tonight, turn to "chicken" in the general index and peruse the many tasty options.

The alphabetical index starts on page 344, so once you and your family have discovered a few favorites, you can easily find them by name the next time you want to make them.

Or you could just page through this book until you find a photo that looks especially appetizing. Of course, you might see so many that whet your appetite that you'll have a hard time deciding on just *one*!

But no matter which recipe you choose, you can be sure it will be a delicious choice for you and your family.

With Pillsbury, you can count on it!

Breakfast & Brunch

Start the day off right—
with these eye-opening delights!

PB & J WAFFLE SANDWICHES
PG. 11

BACON-CHEESE PULL-APARTS
PG. 15

CEREAL S'MORE BARS
PG. 32

Kiwi-Pineapple Yogurt Parfaits

SHERRI KING-RODRIGUES | WARREN, RHODE ISLAND

PREP TIME: 15 MINUTES (READY IN 15 MINUTES)
SERVINGS: 2 (1-1/2 CUPS EACH)

EASY

GRANOLA MIXTURE

4 Nature Valley® Oats 'n Honey Crunchy Granola Bars (2 pouches from 8.9-oz. box), unwrapped, broken into pieces

12 to 14 whole macadamia nuts

YOGURT MIXTURE

1 (6-oz.) container Yoplait® Light Fat Free Very Vanilla Yogurt

1/2 cup frozen (thawed) light whipped topping

1 tablespoon shredded coconut

1 tablespoon finely grated white chocolate baking bar

FRUIT MIXTURE

1/2 cup coarsely chopped peeled kiwifruit (1 1/2 medium)

1/2 cup coarsely chopped drained fresh pineapple or well-drained canned pineapple tidbits

1 1/2 teaspoons honey

GARNISH, (IF DESIRED)

White chocolate baking bar curls or shavings

2 kiwifruit slices

1) In food processor or gallon-size resealable food-storage plastic bag, place granola bars and nuts; process or crush with meat mallet until chopped.

2) In small bowl, mix all yogurt mixture ingredients until well blended; set aside. In another small bowl, gently toss all fruit mixture ingredients until coated; set aside.

3) In each of 2 (12- to 14-oz.) tulip-shaped parfait glasses,* alternately spoon about 3 tablespoons granola mixture, 1/4 cup yogurt mixture and 1/4 cup fruit mixture; repeat layers. Top each parfait with a sprinkle of remaining granola mixture. Garnish each with white chocolate curls and kiwifruit slice. Serve immediately.

*NOTE: Any 12- to 14-oz. tall parfait, dessert or wine glasses can be used.

HIGH ALTITUDE (ABOVE 3500 FT.): No change.

Nutrition Information Per Serving:
Serving Size: 1-1/2 Cups

Calories:	480	From Fat:	200
Total Fat			23g
Saturated			7g
Cholesterol			5mg
Sodium			260mg
Total Carbohydrate			63g
Dietary Fiber			6g
Sugars			41g
Protein			10g

Sausage and Apple Bake

KAREN GULKIN | GREELEY, COLORADO

Pillsbury Bake-Off®

PREP TIME: 40 MINUTES (READY IN 1 HOUR 25 MINUTES)
SERVINGS: 12

- 2 (8-oz.) cans Pillsbury® Refrigerated Crescent Dinner Rolls
- 2 lb. bulk pork or turkey sausage
- 2 cups chopped peeled apples (2 medium)
- 1 medium onion, chopped ($^1\!/_2$ cup)
- Grated peel from 1 medium orange ($1^1\!/_2$ tablespoons)
- 4 eggs
- $^1\!/_2$ cup milk
- 1 teaspoon fennel seed
- 6 oz. ($1^1\!/_2$ cups) shredded Cheddar cheese
- 6 oz. ($1^1\!/_2$ cups) shredded fontina cheese

1) Heat oven to 350°F. Spray 13x9-inch (3-quart) glass baking dish with cooking spray. Unroll 1 can of dough into sprayed dish; firmly press perforations to seal. Bake at 350°F. for 10 to 15 minutes or until light golden brown. Cool while cooking sausage.

2) In 12-inch skillet, cook sausage over medium-high heat for 8 to 10 minutes, stirring frequently, until browned. Drain well; remove sausage from skillet.

3) In same skillet, cook apples, onion and orange peel over medium heat about 5 minutes, stirring occasionally, until onion is translucent. Meanwhile, in small bowl, lightly beat eggs and milk.

4) Stir cooked sausage and fennel seed into apple mixture. Remove from heat. Stir egg mixture into sausage mixture. Sprinkle Cheddar cheese over partially baked crust. Spread sausage mixture evenly over cheese. Sprinkle fontina cheese over top.

5) Unroll second can of dough onto work surface; press to form 13x9-inch rectangle, firmly pressing perforations to seal. Place dough rectangle over cheese; press edges to side of dish.

6) Bake at 350°F. for 25 to 35 minutes or until golden brown. Let stand 10 minutes before serving. Cut into squares.

HIGH ALTITUDE (ABOVE 3500 FT.): No change.

tip

All-purpose apples that are good for baking or eating raw work well in this recipe. Choices include Cortland, Crispin, Criterion, Empire, Fuji, Granny Smith, Jonathan, McIntosh and Winesap.

Nutrition Information Per Serving:
Serving Size: 1/12 of Recipe

Calories:	425	From Fat:	250
Total Fat			28g
Saturated			12g
Cholesterol			130mg
Sodium			1140mg
Total Carbohydrate			24g
Dietary Fiber			1g
Sugars			10g
Protein			19g

Cinnamon French Toast Bake

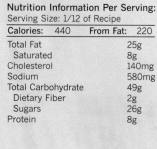

WILL SPERRY | BUNKER HILL, WEST VIRGINIA

PREP TIME: 15 MINUTES (READY IN 1 HOUR)
SERVINGS: 12

FRENCH TOAST BAKE

- ¼ cup butter or margarine, melted
- 2 (12.4-oz.) cans Pillsbury® Refrigerated Cinnamon Rolls with Icing
- 6 eggs
- ½ cup heavy whipping cream
- 2 teaspoons ground cinnamon
- 2 teaspoons vanilla
- 1 cup chopped pecans
- 1 cup maple syrup

GARNISH

- Icing from cinnamon rolls
- Powdered sugar
- ½ cup maple syrup, if desired

1) Heat oven to 375°F. Pour melted butter into ungreased 13x9-inch (3-quart) glass baking dish. Separate both cans of dough into 16 rolls; set icing aside. Cut each roll into 8 pieces; place pieces over butter in dish.

2) In medium bowl, beat eggs. Beat in cream, cinnamon and vanilla until well blended; gently pour over roll pieces. Sprinkle with pecans; drizzle with 1 cup syrup.

3) Bake at 375°F. for 20 to 28 minutes or until golden brown. Cool 15 minutes. Meanwhile, remove covers from icing; microwave on Medium (50%) for 10 to 15 seconds or until drizzling consistency.

4) Drizzle icing over top; sprinkle with powdered sugar. If desired, spoon syrup from dish over individual servings. Serve with the additional ½ cup maple syrup.

HIGH ALTITUDE (ABOVE 3500 FT.): Bake at 375°F. for 25 to 30 minutes.

Nutrition Information Per Serving:
Serving Size: 1/12 of Recipe

Calories:	440	From Fat:	220
Total Fat			25g
Saturated			8g
Cholesterol			140mg
Sodium			580mg
Total Carbohydrate			49g
Dietary Fiber			2g
Sugars			26g
Protein			8g

PB & J Waffle Sandwiches

RENATA STANKO | LEBANON, OREGON

PREP TIME: 15 MINUTES (READY IN 15 MINUTES)
SERVINGS: 8 (1/2 SANDWICH AND 2 TABLESPOONS FRUIT EACH)

❸ EASY

1 (16.3-oz.) can Pillsbury® Grands!® Flaky Layers Refrigerated Original Biscuits

¹/₂ cup peanut butter

¹/₄ cup grape jelly

1 tablespoon powdered sugar

1 cup fresh fruit (such as strawberries, peach slices, grapes)

Nutrition Information Per Serving:
Serving Size: 1/8 of Recipe

Calories:	340	From Fat:	150
Total Fat			17g
Saturated			4g
Cholesterol			0mg
Sodium			770mg
Total Carbohydrate			41g
Dietary Fiber			2g
Sugars			17g
Protein			8g

1) Heat Belgian or regular waffle maker according to manufacturer's directions. Separate dough into 8 biscuits; press or roll each into 4-inch round.

2) Depending on size of waffle maker, place 2 to 4 biscuit rounds at a time in hot waffle maker. Bake 2 minutes or until golden brown. Cool 1 to 2 minutes.

3) Spread peanut butter evenly on 4 of the hot waffles; spread jelly on remaining 4 waffles. Place jelly-spread waffles, jelly down, on peanut butter-spread waffles. Cut sandwiches in half; place on individual plates. Sprinkle with powdered sugar; garnish with fruit.

HIGH ALTITUDE (ABOVE 3500 FT.): No change.

Store peanut butter in a cool, dry place. An unopened jar will stay fresh one year or more. Once opened, regular peanut butter will stay fresh about three months.

Banana-Walnut Brunch Squares

DEBBI BRACKER | CARL JUNCTION, MISSOURI

Pillsbury Bake-Off

PREP TIME: 15 MINUTES (READY IN 1 HOUR)
SERVINGS: 9

3 eggs

1 cup mashed ripe bananas
  (2 to 3 medium)

3 tablespoons granulated sugar

1 (17.5-oz.) can Pillsbury® Grands!®
  Refrigerated Cinnamon Rolls with
  Cream Cheese Icing

1/2 cup all-purpose flour

1/3 cup packed light brown sugar

1/4 cup butter or margarine, softened

3/4 cup coarsely chopped walnuts

1/4 cup maple syrup

   Banana slices, if desired

1) Heat oven to 350°F. Spray 8-inch square (2-quart) glass baking dish with cooking spray. In large bowl, beat eggs, bananas and granulated sugar with wire whisk until well blended.

2) Separate dough into 5 rolls; set icing aside. Cut each roll into 8 equal pie-shaped wedges. Gently stir dough pieces into egg mixture until well coated. Spoon mixture into sprayed dish; spread evenly.

3) In medium bowl, mix flour and brown sugar. With fork, cut in butter until mixture resembles coarse crumbs. Stir in walnuts. Sprinkle mixture over dough mixture in dish.

4) Bake at 350°F. for 35 to 40 minutes or until center is puffed and set and edges are deep golden brown. Cool 10 minutes. Meanwhile, in small bowl, mix icing and syrup until blended.

5) To serve, cut into squares; place on individual serving plates. Drizzle icing mixture over each serving; garnish with banana slices.

HIGH ALTITUDE (ABOVE 3500 FT.): Bake at 375°F. for 35 to 40 minutes.

Nutrition Information Per Serving:	
Serving Size: 1/9 of Recipe	
Calories: 440 From Fat: 190	
Total Fat	21g
Saturated	6g
Cholesterol	95mg
Sodium	510mg
Total Carbohydrate	58g
Dietary Fiber	2g
Sugars	29g
Protein	8g

Make-Ahead Philly Beef Strata

PREP TIME: 20 MINUTES
(READY IN 9 HOURS 20 MINUTES)
SERVINGS: 8

- 7 cups cubed (1 inch) French bread

- 1 bag (1 lb.) frozen bell pepper and onion stir-fry

- 1/2 lb. thinly sliced cooked roast beef (from deli), cut into bite-sized strips (1 1/2 cups)

- 2 cups shredded Monterey Jack cheese (8 oz.)

- 8 eggs

- 2 1/4 cups milk

- 2 tablespoons Dijon mustard

- 1/2 teaspoon salt

- 1/2 teaspoon pepper

1) Spray 13x9-inch (3-quart) glass baking dish or 3-quart oval casserole with cooking spray. Spread 1/3 of the bread cubes in baking dish. Top evenly with 1/3 of the bell pepper and onion stir-fry and 1/3 of the beef. Sprinkle with 1/3 of the cheese. Repeat layers twice, ending with cheese.

2) In large bowl, beat eggs. Stir in all remaining ingredients; pour evenly over cheese. Cover tightly with foil; refrigerate at least 8 hours or overnight.

3) When ready to bake, heat oven to 350°F. Uncover baking dish; bake 40 to 50 minutes or until puffed, top is golden brown and center is set. Let stand 10 minutes before serving.

HIGH ALTITUDE (3500-6000 FT.): Spray sheet of foil with cooking spray; cover baking dish with foil, sprayed side down. Bake covered at 350°F. 30 minutes. Uncover; bake 20 to 30 minutes longer or until top is golden brown and center is set.

Nutrition Information Per Serving:
Serving Size: 1/8 of Recipe

Calories:	350	From Fat:	155
Total Fat			17g
Saturated			8g
Cholesterol			255mg
Sodium			960mg
Total Carbohydrate			25g
Dietary Fiber			1g
Sugars			6g
Protein			24g

Creamy Apple-Raisin Oatmeal

| PREP TIME: | 10 MINUTES (READY IN 10 MINUTES) |
| SERVINGS: | 1 (3/4 CUP) |

 EASY LOW FAT

1/3 cup quick-cooking oats

1 tablespoon raisins

2/3 cup apple juice

2 tablespoons Yoplait® Original French vanilla yogurt (from 6-oz. container)

2 teaspoons packed brown sugar, if desired

Nutrition Information Per Serving:
Serving Size: 3/4 Cup

Calories:	240	From Fat:	20
Total Fat		2g	
Saturated		1g	
Cholesterol		0mg	
Sodium		25mg	
Total Carbohydrate		51g	
Dietary Fiber		4g	
Sugars		28g	
Protein		6g	

1) In 2-cup microwavable cereal bowl, stir oats, raisins and apple juice until well blended.

2) Microwave on High 1 1/2 to 2 minutes, stirring every 30 seconds, until thickened. Top with yogurt; sprinkle with brown sugar.

HIGH ALTITUDE (ABOVE 3500 FT.): No change.

Oatmeal contains soluble fiber, which can help reduce blood cholesterol levels.

Overnight Cranberry-Orange French Toast

| PREP TIME: | 15 MINUTES (READY IN 4 HOURS 45 MINUTES) |
| SERVINGS | 8 |

3/4 cup sweetened dried cranberries

3 tablespoons finely chopped pecans

16 slices (3x2 1/2 inches) soft French bread, 1 inch thick

6 eggs

1 tablespoon grated orange peel

2 cups milk

1 1/2 cups orange juice

3 tablespoons butter or margarine, melted

1 cup maple-flavored or real maple syrup

Nutrition Information Per Serving:
Serving Size: 1/8 of Recipe

Calories:	520	From Fat:	125
Total Fat		14g	
Saturated		5g	
Cholesterol		175mg	
Sodium		590mg	
Total Carbohydrate		85g	
Dietary Fiber		2g	
Sugars		32g	
Protein		14g	

1) Grease 13x9-inch (3-quart) glass baking dish with shortening or spray with cooking spray. Sprinkle cranberries and pecans evenly into dish; arrange bread slices tightly in single layer over top.

2) In large bowl with wire whisk, beat eggs. Stir in orange peel, milk, orange juice and butter until smooth. Pour egg mixture over bread. Cover tightly with foil; refrigerate at least 4 hours or overnight.

3) When ready to bake, heat oven to 425°F. Uncover baking dish; bake 25 to 30 minutes or until bread is puffy and edges are golden brown. Serve with syrup.

HIGH ALTITUDE (3500-6000 FT.): No change.

Bacon-Cheese Pull-Aparts

TERRI BARTON | SALT LAKE CITY, UTAH

PREP TIME: 15 MINUTES (READY IN 45 MINUTES)
SERVINGS: 8

1 egg

2 tablespoons milk

1 (16.3-oz.) can Pillsbury® Grands!® Flaky Layers Refrigerated Original Biscuits

1 (2.1-oz.) pkg. precooked bacon, cut into 1/2-inch pieces

3 oz. (3/4 cup) shredded Cheddar cheese

1/4 cup finely chopped green onions (4 medium)

Nutrition Information Per Serving:
Serving Size: 1/8 of Recipe

Calories:	300	From Fat:	150
Total Fat			16g
Saturated			6g
Cholesterol			45mg
Sodium			890mg
Total Carbohydrate			28g
Dietary Fiber			1g
Sugars			9g
Protein			10g

1) Heat oven to 350°F. Spray 11x7- or 12x8-inch (2-quart) glass baking dish with cooking spray. In large bowl, beat egg and milk with wire whisk until smooth.

2) Separate dough into 8 biscuits; cut each into quarters. Gently stir biscuit pieces into egg mixture to coat evenly. Fold in bacon, cheese and onions. Spoon mixture into sprayed dish; arrange biscuit pieces in single layer.

3) Bake at 350°F. for 23 to 28 minutes or until golden brown. Cut into squares.

HIGH ALTITUDE (ABOVE 3500 FT.): Bake at 350°F. for 28 to 33 minutes.

Whole-Grain Waffles

PREP TIME:	15 MINUTES (READY IN 15 MINUTES)
SERVINGS:	3 (TWO 4-INCH WAFFLES EACH)

 EASY   LOW FAT

½ cup all-purpose flour

½ cup whole wheat flour

½ cup quick-cooking oats

1 teaspoon baking powder

1¼ cups fat-free (skim) milk

¼ cup fat-free egg product or 1 egg

1 tablespoon vegetable oil

Powdered sugar, if desired

Nutrition Information Per Serving:
Serving Size: 2 Waffles

Calories:	270	From Fat:	60
Total Fat			6g
Saturated			1g
Cholesterol			0mg
Sodium			260mg
Total Carbohydrate			45g
Dietary Fiber			5g
Sugars			5g
Protein			13g

1) Heat nonstick waffle maker. In large bowl, mix all-purpose flour, whole wheat flour, oats and baking powder.

2) In small bowl, mix milk, egg product and oil until well blended. Add to flour mixture all at once; stir just until large lumps disappear.

3) Spread batter in hot waffle maker; bake until waffle is golden brown and steaming stops. Sprinkle with powdered sugar.

HIGH ALTITUDE (ABOVE 3500 FT.): Add up to ¼ cup additional milk if batter is too thick.

tip

If you haven't used your waffle iron for quite some time, use a pastry brush to lightly coat the grids with vegetable oil; use a paper towel to wipe off excess oil.

Greek Egg Scramble

PREP TIME: 10 MINUTES (READY IN 10 MINUTES)
SERVINGS: 4 (1/2 CUP EACH)

 EASY LOW FAT

1 cup frozen bell pepper and onion stir-fry (from 1-lb. bag), coarsely chopped

6 eggs or 1$\frac{1}{2}$ cups fat-free egg product

$\frac{1}{4}$ teaspoon salt

$\frac{1}{8}$ teaspoon pepper

1 medium Italian plum tomato, seeded, chopped

$\frac{1}{4}$ cup crumbled feta cheese with garlic and herbs (2 oz.)

Nutrition Information Per Serving: Serving Size: 1/2 Cup		
Calories: 150	From Fat:	90
Total Fat		10g
Saturated		4g
Cholesterol		325mg
Sodium		350mg
Total Carbohydrate		5g
Dietary Fiber		0g
Sugars		2g
Protein		11g

1) Heat 10-inch nonstick skillet over medium-high heat. Add bell pepper and onion stir-fry; cook 2 to 3 minutes, stirring frequently, until vegetables are crisp-tender.

2) Meanwhile, in medium bowl, beat eggs, salt and pepper. Pour egg mixture over vegetables in skillet. Reduce heat to medium; cook 4 to 6 minutes, stirring frequently, until eggs are set but still moist.

3) Divide egg mixture evenly onto 4 serving plates; top each with tomato and cheese.

HIGH ALTITUDE (ABOVE 3500 FT.): No change.

Hot Irish Creme Mocha

PREP TIME: 10 MINUTES (READY IN 10 MINUTES)
SERVINGS: 8 (1 CUP EACH)

 EASY

6 cups hot strong brewed coffee

4 envelopes (1.25 oz. each) Irish creme instant cocoa mix

$\frac{1}{4}$ cup powdered sugar

2 cups half-and-half

$\frac{1}{4}$ cup Irish creme-flavored syrup, if desired

Sweetened whipped cream, if desired

Chocolate shavings, if desired

Nutrition Information Per Serving: Serving Size: 1 Cup		
Calories: 170	From Fat:	70
Total Fat		8g
Saturated		4g
Cholesterol		20mg
Sodium		90mg
Total Carbohydrate		22g
Dietary Fiber		0g
Sugars		20g
Protein		2g

1) In 3-quart saucepan, mix hot coffee, cocoa mix and powdered sugar until blended. Stir in half-and-half and syrup. Cook over medium heat about 5 minutes, stirring occasionally, until hot.

2) Serve in mugs; top with whipped cream and chocolate shavings.

HIGH ALTITUDE (3500-6000 FT.): No change.

Bacon and Potato Breakfast Pizza

RICHARD MCHARGUE | RICHMOND, KENTUCKY

PREP TIME: 15 MINUTES (READY IN 40 MINUTES)
SERVINGS: 8

1 (8-oz.) can Pillsbury® Refrigerated Crescent Dinner Rolls

1 (9-oz.) box Green Giant® Frozen Roasted Potatoes with Garlic & Herbs

4 eggs

1/3 cup milk

8 slices precooked bacon, cut into 1-inch pieces

6 oz. (1 1/2 cups) shredded Cheddar cheese

Salt and pepper, if desired

2 tablespoons chopped fresh parsley

Nutrition Information Per Serving:
Serving Size: 1/8 of Recipe

Calories:	320	From Fat:	180
Total Fat			20g
Saturated			8g
Cholesterol			135mg
Sodium			570mg
Total Carbohydrate			21g
Dietary Fiber			1g
Sugars			5g
Protein			13g

1) Heat oven to 350°F. Spray 13x9-inch pan with cooking spray. Unroll dough into sprayed pan; press in bottom and 1/2 inch up sides to form crust; press perforations to seal. Bake at 350°F. for 5 minutes.

2) Meanwhile, cut small slit in center of roasted potatoes pouch; microwave on High for 2 to 3 minutes or until thawed. Remove potatoes from pouch; cut larger pieces in half.

3) In medium bowl, beat eggs. Stir in milk, bacon, 1 cup of the cheese, the thawed potatoes, salt and pepper.

4) Remove partially baked crust from oven. Spoon potato mixture evenly over crust. Sprinkle remaining 1/2 cup cheese and the parsley over top.

5) Return to oven; bake an additional 20 to 25 minutes or until set and edges are golden brown. Cut into squares.

HIGH ALTITUDE (ABOVE 3500 FT.): Bake crust at 350°F. for 7 minutes. Bake pizza 25 to 30 minutes.

Ham and Veggie Strata

PREP TIME: 30 MINUTES (READY IN 7 HOURS 30 MINUTES)
SERVINGS: 10

2 tablespoons olive oil

3 medium onions, chopped (about 1½ cups)

1 medium green bell pepper, chopped (1 cup)

1 tablespoon minced garlic

1 package (8 oz.) sliced cooked ham, cut into small pieces

3 medium tomatoes, seeded, chopped

12 slices day-old English muffin or sourdough bread (about 1½ lb.), torn into pieces

8 eggs

3 cups milk

1½ teaspoons salt

¼ teaspoon pepper

1 cup shredded Cheddar cheese (4 oz.)

1) In 12-inch nonstick skillet, heat oil over medium heat. Add onions, bell pepper and garlic; cook 6 to 8 minutes, stirring frequently, until tender. Stir in ham and tomatoes. Cook 2 minutes longer.

2) Meanwhile, spray 13x9-inch (3-quart) glass baking dish with cooking spray. Place torn bread in baking dish. In large bowl, beat eggs, milk, salt and pepper until well blended.

3) Spoon ham mixture over bread. Pour egg mixture over top. Cover; refrigerate at least 6 hours or overnight.

4) When ready to bake, heat oven to 350°F. Uncover baking dish; bake 30 minutes. Sprinkle with cheese; bake 30 minutes longer or until knife inserted in center comes out clean. Cut into squares.

HIGH ALTITUDE (3500-6000 FT.): Prepare as directed. Bake covered at 350°F. 50 minutes. Uncover; add cheese. Bake 20 minutes longer or until knife inserted in center comes out clean.

Nutrition Information Per Serving:
Serving Size: 1/10 of Recipe

Calories:	370	From Fat:	130
Total Fat			14g
Saturated			5g
Cholesterol			200mg
Sodium			1120mg
Total Carbohydrate			40g
Dietary Fiber			3g
Sugars			15g
Protein			21g

tip

This make-the-day-before casserole can be toted in a cooler and baked at the home of a potluck gathering. Be sure to ask the hostess if her oven is available.

Turkey and Egg Brunch Bake

PREP TIME: 40 MINUTES (READY IN 10 HOURS)
SERVINGS: 12

 LOW FAT

EGG BAKE

1¼ lb. bulk Italian-seasoned
   lean ground turkey

5 cups frozen country-style
   shredded hash-brown potatoes
   (from 30-oz. bag)

½ cup sliced green onions
   (8 medium)

2 jars (4.5 oz. each) Green Giant®
   sliced mushrooms, drained

1 can (2¼ oz.) sliced ripe olives,
   drained

1 tablespoon chopped fresh or 1
   teaspoon dried basil leaves

3 cups shredded reduced-fat
   Cheddar cheese (12 oz.)

8 eggs

1½ cups fat-free (skim) milk

½ teaspoon salt

TOPPING

1 clove garlic, minced

6 medium Italian plum tomatoes,
   chopped (about 2 cups)

¼ teaspoon salt

2 tablespoons chopped fresh or
   2 teaspoons dried basil leaves

Nutrition Information Per Serving:
Serving Size: 1/12 of Recipe

Calories:	280	From Fat:	90
Total Fat			10g
Saturated			3g
Cholesterol			180mg
Sodium			840mg
Total Carbohydrate			22g
Dietary Fiber			2g
Sugars			4g
Protein			25g

1) Spray 13x9-inch (3-quart) glass baking dish and 10-inch nonstick skillet with cooking spray. In skillet, cook ground turkey over medium-high heat, stirring frequently, until no longer pink. Remove turkey from skillet; drain on paper towels.

2) In large bowl, mix potatoes, onions, mushrooms, olives, 1 tablespoon basil and 2 cups of the cheese. Stir in turkey; spoon evenly into baking dish. Sprinkle with remaining 1 cup cheese.

3) In large bowl, beat eggs. Stir in milk and ½ teaspoon salt; pour over potato mixture in baking dish. Cut sheet of foil large enough to cover baking dish; spray with cooking spray. Cover baking dish with foil, sprayed side down. Refrigerate at least 8 hours or overnight.

4) When ready to bake, heat oven to 350°F. Bake covered 45 minutes. Uncover; bake 20 to 25 minutes longer or until center is set. Let stand 10 minutes before serving.

5) Meanwhile, spray 8-inch nonstick skillet with cooking spray. Add garlic; cook and stir over medium heat 1 minute. Stir in tomatoes and ¼ teaspoon salt; cook about 5 minutes, stirring occasionally, until tomatoes are tender. Stir in 2 tablespoons basil.

6) To serve, cut egg bake into squares; serve with warm topping.

HIGH ALTITUDE (3500-6000 FT.): Bake covered at 350°F. 45 minutes. Uncover; bake 25 to 30 minutes longer. Continue as directed above.

Breakfast Banana Sundaes

ERIN RENOUF MYLROIE | ST. GEORGE, UTAH

Pillsbury
Bake-Off

| PREP TIME: | 15 MINUTES (READY IN 15 MINUTES) |
| SERVINGS: | 4 |

e EASY

1 teaspoon butter or margarine

¼ cup chopped walnuts

2 tablespoons packed brown sugar

2 firm, ripe large bananas, sliced

¼ cup orange juice

¼ teaspoon rum extract,
if desired

4 Nature Valley® Oats 'n Honey
Crunchy Granola Bars (2 pouches
from 8.9-oz. box), unwrapped

4 (6-oz.) containers Yoplait® Light
Fat Free Very Vanilla Yogurt

4 teaspoons chopped walnuts

Nutrition Information Per Serving:
Serving Size: 1/4 of Recipe

Calories:	330	From Fat:	100
Total Fat			11g
Saturated			2g
Cholesterol			5mg
Sodium			170mg
Total Carbohydrate			49g
Dietary Fiber			4g
Sugars			33g
Protein			11g

1) In 8-inch skillet, melt butter over medium heat. Add ¼ cup walnuts and
the brown sugar; stir until sugar is melted. Add bananas; cook 1 to 2 minutes,
stirring gently, until bananas are coated.

2) Stir in orange juice and rum extract. Cook an additional minute or until liquid
is thick and syrupy. Remove from heat. Reserve 4 banana slices for garnish.

3) Spoon about ⅓ cup remaining banana mixture into each 10-oz. dessert bowl.
Chop 1 granola bar; reserve 2 teaspoons for garnish. Sprinkle remaining
chopped granola over banana mixture. Spoon 1 container yogurt over granola.

4) Garnish each serving with 1 teaspoon walnuts, reserved 2 teaspoons chopped
granola and 1 reserved banana slice. Serve immediately.

HIGH ALTITUDE (ABOVE 3500 FT.): No change.

tip
To ripen bananas, keep
them uncovered at room
temperature (about 70°F.).
To speed up the process,
place the bananas in a
perforated brown paper
bag with a ripe apple.

Ham 'n Cheese Omelet Bake

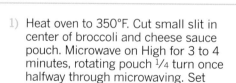

JULIE AMBERSON | BROWNS POINT, WASHINGTON

PREP TIME: 15 MINUTES (READY IN 1 HOUR 15 MINUTES)
SERVINGS: 8

1 (10-oz.) box Green Giant® Frozen Broccoli & Cheese Flavored Sauce

1 (10.2-oz.) can (5 biscuits) Pillsbury® Grands!® Flaky Layers Refrigerated Original Biscuits

10 eggs

1½ cups milk

1 teaspoon dry ground mustard

Salt and pepper, if desired

2 cups diced cooked ham

⅓ cup chopped onion

4 oz. (1 cup) shredded Cheddar cheese

4 oz. (1 cup) shredded Swiss cheese

1 (4.5-oz.) jar Green Giant® Sliced Mushrooms, drained

1) Heat oven to 350°F. Cut small slit in center of broccoli and cheese sauce pouch. Microwave on High for 3 to 4 minutes, rotating pouch ¼ turn once halfway through microwaving. Set aside to cool slightly.

2) Meanwhile, spray bottom only of 13x9-inch (3-quart) glass baking dish with cooking spray. Separate dough into 5 biscuits. Cut each biscuit into 8 pieces; arrange evenly in sprayed dish.

3) In large bowl, beat eggs, milk, mustard, salt and pepper with wire whisk until well blended. Stir in ham, onion, both cheeses, mushrooms and cooked broccoli and cheese sauce. Pour mixture over biscuit pieces in dish. Press down with back of spoon, making sure all biscuit pieces are covered with egg mixture.

4) Bake at 350°F. for 40 to 50 minutes or until edges are deep golden brown and center is set. Let stand 10 minutes before serving. Cut into squares.

HIGH ALTITUDE (ABOVE 3500 FT.): Bake at 375°F. for 40 to 50 minutes.

Nutrition Information Per Serving: Serving Size: 1/8 of Recipe		
Calories: 450	From Fat: 240	
Total Fat		27g
Saturated		12g
Cholesterol		320mg
Sodium		1360mg
Total Carbohydrate		24g
Dietary Fiber		2g
Sugars		10g
Protein		30g

Monkey Cereal Bars

SITA L. WILLIAMS | BLACKSBURG, VIRGINIA

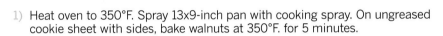

PREP TIME: 15 MINUTES (READY IN 45 MINUTES)
SERVINGS: 12

1 cup coarsely chopped walnuts

¼ cup flaked coconut

¼ cup butter or margarine

1 (10-oz.) bag marshmallows

2 tablespoons unsweetened baking cocoa

6 cups Cocoa Puffs® Cereal

1 cup coarsely crushed dried banana chips

Nutrition Information Per Serving:
Serving Size: 1 Bar

Calories:	295	From Fat:	125
Total Fat			14g
Saturated			5g
Cholesterol			10mg
Sodium			130mg
Total Carbohydrate			39g
Dietary Fiber			2g
Sugars			22g
Protein			3g

1) Heat oven to 350°F. Spray 13x9-inch pan with cooking spray. On ungreased cookie sheet with sides, bake walnuts at 350°F. for 5 minutes.

2) Remove cookie sheet from oven. Stir coconut into walnuts. Return to oven; bake an additional 4 to 6 minutes or until coconut is light golden brown, stirring twice during baking. Set aside to cool.

3) In 4-quart saucepan or Dutch oven, melt butter over medium heat. Add marshmallows; cook 4 to 6 minutes, stirring constantly, until melted. Stir in cocoa until well blended. Remove from heat.

4) Stir in cereal, banana chips, toasted walnuts and coconut until evenly coated; pour into sprayed pan. Spread mixture evenly, pressing down slightly. Cool 30 minutes. Cut into bars.

HIGH ALTITUDE (ABOVE 3500 FT.): No change.

Breakfast Parfait for One

PREP TIME: 10 MINUTES (READY IN 10 MINUTES)
SERVINGS: 1 (1 CUP)

 EASY (f) LOW FAT

1 container (6 oz.) Yoplait® Original yogurt (any fruit-flavored)

⅓ cup Oatmeal Crisp® or Whole Grain Total® cereal, slightly crushed

½ cup blueberries, sliced strawberries and/or raspberries

In tall narrow glass, place ⅓ of the yogurt. Top with ⅓ of the cereal and ⅓ of the fruit. Repeat layers twice.

HIGH ALTITUDE (ABOVE 3500 FT.): No change.

Nutrition Information Per Serving:
Serving Size: 1 Cup

Calories:	280	From Fat:	25
Total Fat			3g
Saturated			1g
Cholesterol			5mg
Sodium			180mg
Total Carbohydrate			58g
Dietary Fiber			4g
Sugars			39g
Protein			10g

Grands!® Breakfast Brûlées

GAIL SINGER | CALABASAS, CALIFORNIA

PREP TIME: 15 MINUTES (READY IN 1 HOUR)
SERVINGS: 8

2 eggs

¼ cup heavy whipping cream

⅛ teaspoon ground nutmeg

2 (6-oz.) containers Yoplait® Original 99% Fat Free French Vanilla Yogurt

1 (16.3-oz.) can Pillsbury® Grands!® Flaky Layers Refrigerated Original Biscuits

⅓ cup sugar

3 tablespoons butter or margarine, melted

1) Heat oven to 375°F. Spray 8 (6-oz.) ramekins or custard cups with cooking spray; place on cookie sheet with sides. In medium bowl, beat eggs, cream, nutmeg and yogurt with electric mixer on medium speed until well blended.

2) Separate dough into 8 biscuits; separate each evenly into 2 layers, making 16 dough rounds. Place sugar in shallow dish. Brush both sides of each dough round with melted butter; coat both sides with sugar. Place 1 dough round in bottom of each sprayed ramekin.

3) Spoon ¼ cup yogurt mixture over dough round in each ramekin. Top with remaining dough rounds.

4) Bake at 375°F. for 20 to 26 minutes or until tops are deep golden brown. Cool 15 minutes before serving.

HIGH ALTITUDE (ABOVE 3500 FT.): Bake at 375°F. for 26 to 32 minutes.

Nutrition Information Per Serving:
Serving Size: 1/8 of Recipe

Calories:	360	From Fat:	150
Total Fat			17g
Saturated			7g
Cholesterol			75mg
Sodium			770mg
Total Carbohydrate			44g
Dietary Fiber			1g
Sugars			24g
Protein			8g

Southwestern Brunch Eggs

PREP TIME: 40 MINUTES (READY IN 4 HOURS 40 MINUTES)
SERVINGS: 12 (3/4 CUP EACH)

5 cups frozen shredded hash-brown potatoes (from 30-oz. bag)

1 can (15 oz.) black beans, drained, rinsed

16 eggs

1 cup half-and-half

½ teaspoon salt

¼ teaspoon pepper

2 tablespoons butter or margarine

1 can (10 ¾ oz.) condensed cream of mushroom soup

2 cups shredded Colby-Monterey Jack cheese blend (8 oz.)

1 cup Old El Paso® Thick 'n Chunky salsa

Nutrition Information Per Serving:
Serving Size: 3/4 Cup

Calories:	360	From Fat:	170
Total Fat			19g
Saturated			9g
Cholesterol			315mg
Sodium			740mg
Total Carbohydrates			31g
Dietary Fiber			4g
Sugars			5g
Protein			19g

1) In medium bowl, microwave potatoes on High 3½ to 4 minutes, stirring once, until thawed. Stir in beans. With back of spoon, press mixture in bottom and 2 to 3 inches up side of 3- to 4-quart slow cooker; set aside.

2) In large bowl, beat eggs, half-and-half, salt and pepper with wire whisk until well blended. In 10-inch nonstick skillet, melt butter over medium heat. Add egg mixture; cook, stirring occasionally, until eggs are almost set.

3) Spoon half of egg mixture into slow cooker; top with half each of the soup, cheese and salsa. Layer with remaining egg mixture, soup, cheese and salsa.

4) Cover; cook on Low setting 3 to 4 hours.

HIGH ALTITUDE (ABOVE 3500 FT.): No change.

Garden Variety Omelet

| PREP TIME. | 25 MINUTES (READY IN 25 MINUTES) |
| SERVINGS: | 2 |

 EASY   LOW FAT

FILLING

- ¼ cup sliced (¼-inch-thick) zucchini
- ¼ cup thinly sliced onion
- ¼ cup chopped red bell pepper (¼ medium)
- ¼ cup chopped yellow or green bell pepper (¼ medium)
- ¼ cup sliced fresh mushrooms
- ¼ teaspoon salt
- Dash pepper

OMELET

- 1 carton (8 oz.) fat-free egg product (1 cup) or 4 eggs
- 1 tablespoon fat-free (skim) milk

TOPPINGS

- ¼ cup shredded reduced-fat Swiss cheese (1 oz.)
- 1 small Italian plum tomato, sliced

1) Cut zucchini slices into quarters. Heat 10- to 8-inch nonstick skillet with sloping sides (omelet pan) over medium heat. Add zucchini and all remaining filling ingredients; cook 4 to 6 minutes, stirring occasionally, until tender. Remove cooked vegetables from skillet; place on plate and cover to keep warm. Cool skillet 1 minute; wipe clean with paper towel.

2) In small bowl, mix egg product and milk. Heat same skillet over medium heat. Pour egg mixture into skillet; cook 4 to 5 minutes without stirring, but lifting edges occasionally to allow uncooked egg mixture to flow to bottom of skillet, until mixture is set but top is still moist.

3) Spoon cooked vegetables onto half of omelet; sprinkle with cheese. With wide spatula, loosen edge of omelet and fold over vegetables. Arrange tomato slices on top of omelet.

HIGH ALTITUDE (ABOVE 3500 FT.): No change.

Nutrition Information Per Serving:
Serving Size: 1/2 of Recipe

Calories:	130	From Fat:	30
Total Fat			3g
Saturated			2g
Cholesterol			10mg
Sodium			550mg
Total Carbohydrate			9g
Dietary Fiber			2g
Sugars			6g
Protein			17g

Easy Oatmeal Pancakes with Mixed Berry Topping

PREP TIME: 20 MINUTES (READY IN 20 MINUTES)
SERVINGS: 5 (2 PANCAKES AND 1/4 CUP TOPPING EACH)

 EASY · LOW FAT

TOPPING
- 1¼ cups frozen unsweetened mixed berries (from 14-oz. bag)
- ½ cup blueberry syrup

PANCAKES
- ¾ cup quick-cooking oats
- 1 tablespoon packed brown sugar
- 1 cup fat-free (skim) milk
- ½ teaspoon vanilla
- 1 egg
- 1 cup reduced-fat all-purpose baking mix

Nutrition Information Per Serving:
Serving Size: 1/5 of Recipe

Calories:	280	From Fat:	35
Total Fat			4g
Saturated			1g
Cholesterol			45mg
Sodium			340mg
Total Carbohydrate			57g
Dietary Fiber			3g
Sugars			21g
Protein			7g

1) In 2-quart saucepan, cook topping ingredients over medium heat, stirring occasionally, until berries are thawed and mixture is warm. Remove from heat; set aside.

2) In medium bowl, mix oats, brown sugar, milk and vanilla; set aside.

3) Heat 12-inch nonstick skillet or griddle over medium-high heat, or heat to 375°F. Add egg and baking mix to oat mixture; stir just until all ingredients are moistened.

4) For each pancake, pour scant ¼ cup batter into hot skillet; cook 1 to 1½ minutes or until bubbly. Turn; cook 1 minute longer or until browned. Serve pancakes with topping.

HIGH ALTITUDE (ABOVE 3500 FT.): Add up to 1/4 cup additional milk if batter is too thick.

tip

Instead of maple syrup, try berries on your pancakes, like this recipe calls for. Berries provide fiber, vitamin C, and antioxidants that may help maintain health.

Strawberry-Key Lime Smoothie

PREP TIME: 10 MINUTES (READY IN 10 MINUTES)
SERVINGS: 1 (1-3/4 CUPS)

 EASY · LOW FAT

- ½ medium banana
- ½ cup frozen strawberries (not in syrup)
- ½ cup orange juice with calcium
- 1 container (6 oz.) Yoplait® Original Key lime pie yogurt

Nutrition Information Per Serving:
Serving Size: 1-3/4 Cups

Calories:	310	From Fat:	25
Total Fat			3g
Saturated			1g
Cholesterol			5mg
Sodium			105mg
Total Carbohydrate			66g
Dietary Fiber			5g
Sugars			55g
Protein			9g

In blender container, place all ingredients. Cover; blend 1 to 2 minutes or until smooth and frothy.

HIGH ALTITUDE (ABOVE 3500 FT.): No change.

Chai Crunch

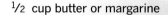

CAROL THORESON | ROCKFORD, ILLINOIS

Bake-Off

PREP TIME: 10 MINUTES (READY IN 1 HOUR 25 MINUTES)
SERVINGS: 22 (1/2 CUP EACH)

- 1/2 cup butter or margarine
- 1/2 cup honey
- 1 teaspoon instant nonfat dry milk or non-dairy original-flavor creamer, if desired*
- 1/2 teaspoon ground cardamom
- 1/2 teaspoon ground ginger
- 1/2 teaspoon ground cinnamon
- 1/2 teaspoon ground nutmeg
- 1/2 teaspoon ground cloves
- 1/2 teaspoon dried orange peel
- 1 teaspoon vanilla
- 3 cups Corn Chex® Cereal
- 3 cups Wheat Chex® Cereal
- 3 cups Honey Nut Cheerios® Cereal
- 1 cup dried banana chips
- 1 1/2 cups sliced almonds

1) Heat oven to 300°F. In 1-quart saucepan, melt butter over medium heat. Remove from heat. Stir in honey, dry milk, cardamom, ginger, cinnamon, nutmeg, cloves, orange peel and vanilla until well mixed.

2) In 15x11-inch roasting pan, mix all remaining ingredients. Pour butter mixture over cereal mixture; toss until evenly coated.

3) Bake at 300°F. for 45 to 60 minutes or until golden brown, stirring every 15 minutes. Pour mixture onto waxed paper or paper towels. Cool 15 minutes before serving. Store in tightly covered container.

*NOTE: For spicy flavor, omit dried milk or creamer. If dried milk is used, flavor will be less spicy and a little sweeter.

HIGH ALTITUDE (ABOVE 3500 FT.): No change.

Nutrition Information Per Serving:
Serving Size: 1/2 Cup

Calories:	180	From Fat:	80
Total Fat		9g	
Saturated		4g	
Cholesterol		10mg	
Sodium		170mg	
Total Carbohydrate		22g	
Dietary Fiber		2g	
Sugars		10g	
Protein		3g	

Tex-Mex Breakfast Bake

LYNNE MILLIRON | AUSTIN, TEXAS

Bake-Off

PREP TIME: 20 MINUTES (READY IN 1 HOUR 15 MINUTES)
SERVINGS: 6

¼ lb. bulk lean breakfast sausage

1 (10-oz.) can Old El Paso® Red
  Enchilada Sauce

2½ oz. (½ cup) crumbled queso fresco
  (Mexican cheese) or farmer cheese

⅓ cup sour cream

¼ cup chopped green onions
  (4 medium)

1 (16.3-oz.) can Pillsbury® Grands!®
  Flaky Layers Refrigerated Original
  or Buttermilk Biscuits

5 oz. (1¼ cups) shredded
  Colby-Monterey Jack cheese blend

¼ cup chopped fresh cilantro

1) Heat oven to 350°F. Spray 8x8- or 11x7-inch (2-quart) glass baking dish with cooking spray. In 10-inch skillet, cook sausage over medium-high heat, stirring frequently, until no longer pink.

2) Meanwhile, in small bowl, mix ¼ cup of the enchilada sauce, the queso fresco, sour cream and onions; set aside. Pour remaining enchilada sauce into medium bowl. Separate dough into 8 biscuits; cut each into 8 pieces. Gently stir dough pieces into enchilada sauce to coat. Spoon mixture into sprayed dish; spread evenly.

3) Drain sausage on paper towels. Sprinkle sausage evenly on top of biscuit pieces. Spread sour cream mixture evenly over top.

4) Bake at 350°F. for 30 to 35 minutes or until center is set and edges are deep golden brown. Remove from oven. Sprinkle Colby-Monterey Jack cheese over top.

5) Return to oven; bake an additional 10 minutes or until cheese is bubbly. Sprinkle with cilantro. Let stand 5 minutes before serving. Cut into squares.

HIGH ALTITUDE (ABOVE 3500 FT.): Use 11x7-inch (2-quart) glass baking dish. Bake at 375°F. for 45 to 50 minutes. Sprinkle Colby-Monterey Jack cheese over top; bake an additional 5 minutes.

Nutrition Information Per Serving:
Serving Size: 1/6 of Recipe

Calories:	450	From Fat:	230
Total Fat		25g	
Saturated		11g	
Cholesterol		40mg	
Sodium		1400mg	
Total Carbohydrate		41g	
Dietary Fiber		2g	
Sugars		13g	
Protein		15g	

tip

Before using green onions, trim off the roots. Discard the outer white layer of the onion. The entire onion—both the white and green parts—is edible. The green stems have a milder flavor than the white onions.

Quesadilla Quiche

LAURIE KEANE | ESCONDIDO, CALIFORNIA

PREP TIME: 25 MINUTES (READY IN 1 HOUR 25 MINUTES)
SERVINGS: 6

CRUST

1 box (15 oz.) Pillsbury®
refrigerated pie crusts,
softened as directed on box

FILLING

1 cup coarsely chopped onions

1 tablespoon butter or margarine

1 cup coarsely chopped tomato
(1 medium), drained

1 can (3.8 oz.) sliced ripe olives,
drained

1/4 teaspoon garlic powder or garlic salt

1/4 teaspoon ground cumin

1/8 teaspoon pepper

1 can (4.5 oz.) Old El Paso® chopped
green chiles, drained

2 eggs, beaten

2 to 3 drops red pepper sauce

1 cup shredded Monterey Jack
cheese (4 oz.)

1 cup shredded Cheddar cheese (4 oz.)

Sour cream, if desired

Old El Paso® Thick 'n Chunky salsa
or picante sauce, if desired

1) Make pie crust as directed on box for Two-Crust Pie using 10-inch tart pan with removable bottom or 9-inch glass pie pan. Place 1 crust in pan; press in bottom and up sides. Trim edges if necessary.

2) Place oven rack in lowest rack position; heat oven to 375°F. In 8-inch skillet, melt butter over medium heat. Add onions; cook and stir until tender. Reserve 1 tablespoon each chopped tomato and sliced olives; stir remaining tomato and olives, the garlic powder, cumin, pepper and chiles into cooked onion.

3) In small bowl with fork, beat eggs and red pepper sauce; reserve 2 teaspoons mixture. Stir in 1/2 cup of the Monterey Jack cheese and 1/2 cup of the Cheddar cheese. Sprinkle remaining cheeses in bottom of pie crust-lined pan. Spoon onion mixture evenly over cheese. Carefully pour egg mixture over onion mixture; spread to cover.

4) Top with second pie crust; seal edges. Cut slits in crust in decorative design in several places. Brush with reserved egg mixture.

5) Place pie on lowest oven rack; bake 45 to 55 minutes or until golden brown. Let stand 5 minutes; remove sides of pan. Serve warm with sour cream, salsa and reserved chopped tomatoes and sliced olives.

HIGH ALTITUDE (3500-6500 FT.): Bake on lowest oven rack at 375°F. 50 to 55 minutes.

Nutrition Information Per Serving:
Serving Size: 1/6 of Recipe

Calories:	540	From Fat:	330
Total Fat			36g
Saturated			16g
Cholesterol			120mg
Sodium			1010mg
Total Carbohydrate			41g
Dietary Fiber			3g
Sugars			6g
Protein			14g

Florentine Eggs on English Muffins

PREP TIME: 15 MINUTES (READY IN 15 MINUTES)
SERVINGS: 2

 EASY  LOW FAT

¼ cup Yoplait® Original plain yogurt
(from 6-oz. container)

1 tablespoon light mayonnaise

½ teaspoon Dijon mustard

2 eggs

1 English muffin, split, toasted

½ cup fresh baby spinach leaves

Dash pepper

Nutrition Information Per Serving:
Serving Size: 1/2 of Recipe

Calories:	190	From Fat:	80
Total Fat		8g	
Saturated		2g	
Cholesterol		215mg	
Sodium		300mg	
Total Carbohydrate		17g	
Dietary Fiber		1g	
Sugars		7g	
Protein		11g	

1) In small microwavable bowl, mix yogurt, mayonnaise and mustard. Microwave on High 20 to 40 seconds or until warm. Stir; set aside.

2) In 10-inch skillet, heat 1 ½ to 2 inches water to boiling. Reduce heat to medium-low. Break each egg into shallow dish; carefully slide egg into hot water. Quickly spoon hot water over each egg until film forms over yolk. Simmer 3 to 5 minutes or until eggs are desired doneness.

3) Meanwhile, spread about 2 tablespoons sauce on each English muffin half. Top each with half of the spinach leaves.

4) With slotted spoon, remove eggs from water; place over spinach. Top each with half of remaining sauce; sprinkle with pepper.

HIGH ALTITUDE (ABOVE 3500 FT.): No change.

Spinach is an excellent source of the important nutrients folic acid and vitamin C. Spinach is also a good source of iron.

Cereal S'more Bars

BARBARA STYLES | ST. CLOUD, MINNESOTA

Pillsbury Bake-Off

PREP TIME: 15 MINUTES (READY IN 45 MINUTES)
SERVINGS: 24

3 cups Cocoa Puffs® Cereal

3 cups Golden Grahams® Cereal

1 cup peanuts

½ cup peanut butter

1 (10.5-oz.) bag miniature marshmallows

2 tablespoons milk

Nutrition Information Per Serving:
Serving Size: 1 Bar

Calories:	140	From Fat:	50
Total Fat		6g	
Saturated		1g	
Cholesterol		0mg	
Sodium		125mg	
Total Carbohydrate		20g	
Dietary Fiber		1g	
Sugars		11g	
Protein		4g	

1) Spray bottom and sides of 13x9-inch pan with cooking spray or grease with shortening. In large bowl, mix both cereals and peanuts.

2) In 3-quart saucepan, heat peanut butter, marshmallows and milk over low heat, stirring occasionally, until peanut butter and marshmallows are melted and mixture is smooth.

3) Pour peanut butter mixture over cereal mixture; stir to coat well. Press mixture in greased pan. Cool at least 30 minutes before serving. Cut into bars.

HIGH ALTITUDE (ABOVE 3500 FT.): No change.

Sausage Breakfast Cups

MARY K. BUCHER | FENTON, MISSOURI

Bake-Off
Pillsbury

PREP TIME: 25 MINUTES (READY IN 55 MINUTES)
SERVINGS: 8

1/3 lb. bulk pork sausage

1 tablespoon all-purpose flour

3/4 cup milk

1/8 teaspoon salt

1/2 teaspoon coarse ground
black pepper

2 eggs

1 tablespoon half-and-half

1/2 teaspoon dried parsley flakes

1/8 teaspoon California-style
garlic salt or garlic salt

1 tablespoon butter or margarine

1/2 cup frozen southern-style cubed
hash-brown potatoes
(from 32-oz. bag)

1 (16.3-oz.) can Pillsbury® Grands!®
Homestyle Refrigerated Buttermilk
Biscuits

Fresh parsley, if desired

1) Heat oven to 375°F. In 10-inch nonstick skillet, cook sausage over medium heat, stirring frequently, until thoroughly cooked. Drain; return sausage to skillet. Stir flour into sausage. Over medium heat, gradually add milk, cooking and stirring until bubbly and thickened. Stir in salt and 1/4 teaspoon of the pepper. Remove from heat; set aside.

2) In small bowl, beat eggs, half-and-half, parsley flakes, garlic salt and remaining 1/4 teaspoon pepper with wire whisk until well blended; set aside.

3) In another 10-inch nonstick skillet, melt 1/2 tablespoon of the butter over medium-high heat. Stir in potatoes. Cook about 5 minutes, stirring frequently, until lightly browned and almost fork-tender. Reduce heat to medium-low; stir remaining 1/2 tablespoon butter into potatoes. Pour egg mixture over potatoes; cook, folding potatoes into egg mixture, just until firm and moist. Remove from heat; set aside.

4) Separate dough into 8 biscuits; place each biscuit in ungreased 2 3/4x1 1/4-inch muffin cup. Firmly press dough in bottom and up side of each cup, forming 1/2-inch rim. Spoon potato mixture evenly into dough-lined cups. Spoon sausage mixture evenly over potato mixture (cups will be very full).

5) Bake at 375°F. for 17 to 22 minutes or until edges of biscuits are deep golden brown. Cool 5 minutes. Remove from muffin cups. If desired, garnish each with fresh parsley.

HIGH ALTITUDE (ABOVE 3500 FT.): No change.

Nutrition Information Per Serving:
Serving Size: 1/8 of Recipe

Calories:	290	From Fat:	130
Total Fat			15g
Saturated			5g
Cholesterol			65mg
Sodium			900mg
Total Carbohydrate			32g
Dietary Fiber			1g
Sugars			10g
Protein			8g

Ham and Eggs Frittata Biscuits

SANDY BRADLEY | BOLINGBROOK, ILLINOIS

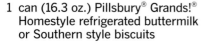

PREP TIME: 15 MINUTES (READY IN 35 MINUTES)
SERVINGS: 8

1 can (16.3 oz.) Pillsbury® Grands!® Homestyle refrigerated buttermilk or Southern style biscuits

3 eggs

1¼ to 1½ teaspoons Italian seasoning

½ cup diced cooked ham

1 cup shredded Italian cheese blend (4 oz.)

¼ cup roasted red bell peppers (from a jar), drained, chopped

½ cup diced seeded plum (Roma) tomatoes (1 to 2 medium)

2 tablespoons thinly sliced fresh basil leaves

Fresh basil sprigs, if desired

Cherry tomatoes, if desired

Nutrition Information Per Serving:
Serving Size: 1 Biscuit

Calories:	290	From Fat:	140
Total Fat		16g	
Saturated		6g	
Cholesterol		95mg	
Sodium		900mg	
Total Carbohydrate		25g	
Dietary Fiber		0g	
Sugars		5g	
Protein		12g	

1) Heat oven to 375°F. Spray large cookie sheet with cooking spray. Separate dough into 8 biscuits; place 3 inches apart on cookie sheet. Press out each biscuit into 4-inch round with ¼-inch-high rim around outside edge.

2) In small bowl with fork, beat 1 of the eggs; brush over tops and sides of biscuits. Sprinkle with 1 teaspoon of the Italian seasoning.

3) In another small bowl, beat remaining 2 eggs and remaining ¼ to ½ teaspoon Italian seasoning until well blended. Spoon egg mixture evenly into indentations in each biscuit. Top with ham, ½ cup of the cheese, the roasted peppers, tomatoes, sliced basil and remaining ½ cup cheese.

4) Bake 15 to 20 minutes or until biscuits are golden brown and eggs are set. Garnish with basil sprigs and cherry tomatoes.

HIGH ALTITUDE (3500-6500 FT.): No change.

Bacon Quiche Biscuit Cups

DORIS GEIST | BETHLEHEM, PENNSYLVANIA

PREP TIME: 35 MINUTES (READY IN 1 HOUR 5 MINUTES)
SERVINGS: 10

5 slices bacon

1 package (8 oz.) cream cheese, softened

2 tablespoons milk

2 eggs

$\frac{1}{2}$ cup shredded Swiss cheese (2 oz.)

2 tablespoons chopped green onions (2 medium)

1 can (12 oz.) Pillsbury® Golden Layers® refrigerated buttermilk biscuits

1) Heat oven to 375°F. Spray 10 regular-size muffin cups with cooking spray. In 8-inch skillet, cook bacon until crisp; drain on paper towels. Crumble bacon; set aside.

2) Meanwhile, in small bowl with electric mixer, beat cream cheese on medium speed until smooth. Gradually beat in milk and eggs on low speed until well blended. Stir in Swiss cheese and onions; set aside.

3) Separate dough into 10 biscuits; press or roll each into 5-inch round. Place 1 biscuit round in each muffin cup; firmly press in bottom and up sides, forming $\frac{1}{4}$-inch rim over edge of cup. Place half of bacon in bottoms of muffin cups. Spoon cheese mixture evenly over bacon in cups.

4) Bake 21 to 26 minutes or until filling is set and edges of biscuits are golden brown. Sprinkle each with remaining bacon; lightly press into filling. Remove biscuit cups from pan; serve immediately.

HIGH ALTITUDE (3500-6500 FT.): No change.

Nutrition Information Per Serving:
Serving Size: 1 Biscuit Cup

Calories:	260	From Fat:	170
Total Fat			19g
Saturated			9g
Cholesterol			75mg
Sodium			510mg
Total Carbohydrate			15g
Dietary Fiber			0g
Sugars			4g
Protein			8g

tip

Buy bacon that's firm and well-colored. Always check the date stamp on packages of vacuum-packed bacon to make sure the meat you buy is fresh. The stamp reflects the last date of sale.

Appetizers, Snacks & Beverages

Appealing munchies and sparkling
punches add pizzazz to parties.

GREEK SPINACH-TURKEY WRAPS
PG. 63

MARGARITA SLUSH
PG. 40

ITALIAN SPINACH TORTA
PG. 56

Antipasto Appetizer Pizza

BRANDY KOPROSKI | OSWEGO, NEW YORK

Bake-Off

| PREP TIME: | 20 MINUTES (READY IN 40 MINUTES) |
| SERVINGS: | 16 APPETIZERS |

1½ teaspoons all-purpose flour

1 (13.8-oz.) can Pillsbury® Refrigerated Pizza Crust

1 (7.5-oz.) jar roasted red bell peppers, drained, chopped

1 (6-oz.) jar marinated artichoke hearts, drained, chopped

¾ cup drained pitted ripe olives, chopped

3 oz. thinly sliced Genoa salami, cut into ½-inch pieces

3 oz. thinly sliced provolone cheese, cut into ½-inch pieces

4 oz. (1 cup) crumbled feta cheese

½ teaspoon dried Italian seasoning, if desired

1) Heat oven to 400°F. Sprinkle flour evenly over cookie sheet. Unroll dough; place on floured cookie sheet. Starting at center, press into 14x10-inch rectangle.

2) Sprinkle roasted peppers, artichokes and olives evenly over dough. Top with salami, provolone cheese and feta cheese. Sprinkle with Italian seasoning.

3) Bake at 400°F. for 15 to 20 minutes or until provolone cheese is melted and edge of crust is golden brown. Cut into squares. Serve warm.

Nutrition Information Per Serving:
Serving Size: 1 Appetizer

Calories:	140	From Fat:	60
Total Fat			7g
Saturated			3g
Cholesterol			15mg
Sodium			490mg
Total Carbohydrate			15g
Dietary Fiber			1g
Sugars			3g
Protein			6g

Dilly Veggie Dip

PREP TIME: 10 MINUTES (READY IN 2 HOURS 10 MINUTES)
SERVINGS: 6 (2 TABLESPOONS EACH); YIELD: 3/4 CUP

 EASY LOW FAT

¼ cup chopped green onions

2 tablespoons chopped fresh dill
or 2 teaspoons dried dill weed

⅛ teaspoon garlic salt

⅛ teaspoon pepper

½ cup light sour cream

¼ cup plain nonfat yogurt

1) In small bowl, combine all ingredients; mix well. Cover; refrigerate 1 to 2 hours to blend flavors.

2) Stir dip before serving. Serve with assorted cut-up fresh vegetables. Store in refrigerator.

HIGH ALTITUDE (ABOVE 3500 FT.): No change.

Nutrition Information Per Serving:
Serving Size: 2 Tablespoons

Calories:	35	From Fat:	10
Total Fat			1g
Saturated			1g
Cholesterol			10mg
Sodium			50mg
Total Carbohydrate			4g
Dietary Fiber			0g
Sugars			3g
Protein			2g

Fresh Tomato Salsa

PREP TIME: 20 MINUTES (READY IN 1 HOUR 20 MINUTES)
SERVINGS: 24 (2 TABLESPOONS EACH); YIELD: 3 CUPS

 LOW FAT

4 medium tomatoes, seeded, chopped (2 cups)

1 medium onion, chopped (½ cup)

½ cup chopped green bell pepper (½ medium)

½ cup chopped fresh cilantro

2 tablespoons lemon juice

1 tablespoon lime juice

1 jalapeño chile, seeded, finely chopped (2 tablespoons)

Tortilla chips

Nutrition Information Per Serving:
Serving Size: 2 Tablespoons

Calories:	10	From Fat:	0
Total Fat			0g
Saturated			0g
Cholesterol			0mg
Sodium			5mg
Total Carbohydrate			2g
Dietary Fiber			0g
Sugars			1g
Protein			0g

In medium nonmetal bowl, combine all ingredients; mix well. Cover; refrigerate 1 to 2 hours to blend flavors. Serve with tortilla chips. Salsa can be stored covered in refrigerator for up to 5 days.

HIGH ALTITUDE (ABOVE 3500 FT.): No change.

Margarita Slush

PREP TIME: 15 MINUTES (READY IN 5 HOURS 15 MINUTES)
SERVINGS: 6 (ABOUT 1 CUP EACH)

 EASY

2 (10-oz.) cans frozen margarita concentrate

1 cup tequila

1/3 cup fresh lime juice (2 to 3 medium limes)

1 medium lime, cut into 6 slices

Margarita salt for glass rims, if desired

1 (12-oz.) can lemon-lime carbonated beverage

Nutrition Information Per Serving:	
Serving Size: About 1 Cup	
Calories: 220	From Fat: 0
Total Fat	0g
Saturated 0g	0g
Cholesterol	0mg
Sodium	550mg
Total Carbohydrate	55g
Dietary Fiber	0g
Sugars	49g
Protein	0g

1) In medium bowl, combine margarita concentrate, tequila and lime juice; mix well. Spread mixture in 8-inch square (2-quart) glass baking dish. Freeze at least 5 hours or until set.

2) To serve, run lime wedge around rim of each glass; dip in margarita salt. For each drink, spoon 2/3 cup frozen mixture into glass; pour 1/4 cup carbonated beverage over top. Garnish with lime wedges.

High Altitude (ABOVE 3500 FT.): No change.

 tip Look for flavored, colored salts in the beverage aisle of the grocery store or in gourmet shops. Garnish with lime slices, if desired.

Italian BLT Pinwheels

PREP TIME: 30 MINUTES (READY IN 1 HOUR 30 MINUTES)
SERVINGS: 24 APPETIZERS

4 oz. cream cheese, softened

1/2 cup mayonnaise

1/4 cup finely chopped sun-dried tomatoes in oil

6 slices bacon, crisply cooked, crumbled

3 spinach- or tomato-flavored flour tortillas (9-inch diameter)

1 cup chopped seeded Italian plum tomatoes (about 3 medium)

1 1/2 cups shredded romaine lettuce

Nutrition Information Per Serving:	
Serving Size: 1 Appetizer	
Calories: 90	From Fat: 65
Total Fat	7g
Saturated	2g
Cholesterol	10mg
Sodium	100mg
Total Carbohydrate	5g
Dietary Fiber	0g
Sugars	1g
Protein	2g

1) In small bowl, mix cream cheese, mayonnaise and sun-dried tomatoes until well blended. Gently stir in bacon.

2) Spread mayonnaise mixture evenly over tortillas. Top each evenly with plum tomatoes and lettuce; roll up tightly. Wrap each tortilla roll in plastic wrap; refrigerate 1 hour.

3) To serve, with serrated knife, cut each roll into about 1-inch-thick slices.

HIGH ALTITUDE (3500-6000 FT.): No change.

Bean and Bacon Fiesta Dip

MADELEINE BERGQUIST | SYRACUSE, NEW YORK

PREP TIME:	20 MINUTES (READY IN 35 MINUTES)
SERVINGS:	22 (1/4 CUP DIP AND 6 CHIPS EACH)

8 slices bacon*

1 (16-oz.) can Old El Paso® Refried Beans

1 (4.5-oz.) can Old El Paso® Chopped Green Chiles, drained

1 cup Green Giant® Niblets® Frozen Corn (from 1-lb. bag)

1 (15-oz.) can Progresso® Black Beans, drained, rinsed

1 (16-oz.) jar Old El Paso® Thick 'n Chunky Salsa

6 oz. (1½ cups) shredded Mexican cheese blend

Sour cream, if desired

Corn tortilla chips, if desired

1) Cook bacon until crisp; drain on paper towel. Set 2 slices of bacon aside; crumble remaining 6 slices.

2) Spray 8-inch square (2-quart) microwavable dish with cooking spray. In medium bowl, mix refried beans, green chiles and crumbled bacon. Spread mixture evenly in sprayed dish. Sprinkle frozen corn and black beans evenly over refried bean mixture. Pour salsa over top. Sprinkle cheese over salsa. Crumble remaining 2 slices of bacon; sprinkle over cheese.

3) Microwave on High for 10 to 15 minutes or until cheese is bubbly and mixture is thoroughly heated. Garnish with spoonfuls of sour cream. Serve warm dip with tortilla chips.

*NOTE: Eight slices precooked bacon from 2.1-oz. package, chopped, can be substituted for the cooked bacon.

HIGH ALTITUDE (ABOVE 3500 FT.): No change.

Nutrition Information Per Serving:
Serving Size: 1/22 of Recipe

Calories:	105	From Fat:	35
Total Fat			4g
Saturated			2g
Cholesterol			10mg
Sodium			330mg
Total Carbohydrate			11g
Dietary Fiber			3g
Sugars			2g
Protein			6g

Caramel Apple Baked Brie

PREP TIME: 20 MINUTES (READY IN 1 HOUR 40 MINUTES)
SERVINGS: 12 (1/12 BRIE AND 4 BREAD SLICES EACH)

1 tablespoon butter

½ cup chopped peeled firm apple (Braeburn, Gala or Granny Smith)

¼ cup sweetened dried cranberries

¼ cup packed brown sugar

2 tablespoons chopped shelled pistachios or pecans

2 tablespoons brandy or apple juice

1 round (8 oz.) Brie cheese

Baguette French bread slices, assorted crackers or fresh apple slices

1) Heat oven to 350°F. In 8-inch skillet, melt butter over low heat. Add apple, cranberries, brown sugar, pistachios and brandy; cook 3 minutes or just until apples are tender, stirring frequently.

2) Cut Brie round in half horizontally; place bottom half in ungreased 9-inch pie pan. Spoon half of fruit mixture over cheese; place top half of cheese over fruit. Top with remaining fruit mixture. Secure with 3 toothpicks.

3) Bake 15 to 20 minutes or until cheese is soft. With broad spatula, slide Brie from pie pan onto serving platter. Spoon any syrup and fruit from pan over top. Serve warm with baguette bread slices.

HIGH ALTITUDE (3500-6000 FT.): No change.

Nutrition Information Per Serving:
Serving Size: 1/12 of Recipe

Calories:	180	From Fat:	70
Total Fat			8g
Saturated			4g
Cholesterol			20mg
Sodium			300mg
Total Carbohydrate			22g
Dietary Fiber			1g
Sugars			7g
Protein			7g

Creamy Spinach-Artichoke Mini Pizzas

HEATHER HALONIE | WEBSTER, WISCONSIN

PREP TIME: 15 MINUTES (READY IN 40 MINUTES)
SERVINGS: 10 PIZZAS

4 oz. cream cheese
(from 8-oz. pkg.), softened

2 tablespoons sour cream

¾ cup Green Giant® Frozen
Spinach (from 1-lb. bag),
thawed, squeezed to drain*

½ cup artichoke hearts
(from 14-oz. can), drained,
patted dry with paper towels

1 (10.6-oz.) box Pillsbury®
Refrigerated Garlic Breadsticks

1 oz. (¼ cup) shredded
Parmesan cheese

1) Heat oven to 350°F. In medium bowl, mix cream cheese, sour cream, thawed spinach and artichoke hearts until well blended, breaking up artichokes during stirring.

2) Unroll dough into 1 large rectangle. Spread garlic mixture from box evenly over dough. Separate dough into 10 breadsticks. Reroll each breadstick, coiling dough into spiral shape with garlic mixture inside; place 2 inches apart on ungreased cookie sheet.

3) Starting at center, press out each coil into 3½-inch round (edges will curl up slightly). Spoon and spread cream cheese mixture on top of each round. Sprinkle with cheese.

4) Bake at 350°F. for 17 to 22 minutes or until cheese is melted and edges are golden brown. Immediately remove from cookie sheet. Serve warm.

*NOTE: To quickly thaw frozen spinach, place in colander; rinse with cool water until thawed. Drain well; squeeze dry with paper towels.

HIGH ALTITUDE (ABOVE 3500 FT.): No change.

Nutrition Information Per Serving:
Serving Size: 1 Pizza

Calories:	155	From Fat:	80
Total Fat			9g
Saturated			4g
Cholesterol			15mg
Sodium			400mg
Total Carbohydrate			14g
Dietary Fiber			1g
Sugars			2g
Protein			5g

Creole Shrimp and Cheese Tart

STEVE GRIEGER | EL CAJON, CALIFORNIA

PREP TIME: 15 MINUTES (READY IN 1 HOUR 5 MINUTES)
SERVINGS: 16

½ lb. cooked deveined shelled shrimp or crawfish, tail shells removed, shrimp coarsely chopped

1 to 2 teaspoons dried Creole seasoning

4 oz. (1 cup) shredded hot pepper-Monterey Jack cheese

¼ cup finely chopped green onions (4 medium)

2 eggs, slightly beaten

1 tablespoon butter or margarine, melted

1 Pillsbury® Refrigerated Pie Crust (from 15-oz. box), softened as directed on box

Red pepper sauce, if desired

1) Heat oven to 375°F. In medium bowl, toss shrimp and Creole seasoning to coat. Stir in all remaining ingredients except pie crust and pepper sauce.

2) Remove pie crust from pouch; place crust flat on ungreased cookie sheet. If necessary, press out folds or creases. Spread filling over crust to within 1 inch of edge. Carefully fold 1-inch edge of crust up over filling, pleating crust as necessary.

3) Bake at 375°F. for 32 to 37 minutes or until set in center and crust is golden brown. Cool 10 minutes. Cut into wedges. Serve warm with pepper sauce.

HIGH ALTITUDE (ABOVE 3500 FT.): Bake at 375°F. for 35 to 40 minutes.

Nutrition Information Per Serving:
Serving Size: 1/16 of Recipe

Calories:	110	From Fat:	60
Total Fat			7g
Saturated			3g
Cholesterol			65mg
Sodium			150mg
Total Carbohydrate			7g
Dietary Fiber			0g
Sugars			1g
Protein			6g

Strawberry-Citrus Slush

PREP TIME: 5 MINUTES (READY IN 6 HOURS 5 MINUTES)
SERVINGS: 16 (1 CUP EACH)

EASY   **LOW FAT**

1 (46-oz.) can (about 6 cups) pink grapefruit juice

1 (12-oz.) can frozen lemonade concentrate, thawed

½ cup sugar

1 (.14-oz.) pkg. strawberry-flavored drink mix

1 (1-liter) bottle (8 cups) ginger ale, chilled

Nutrition Information Per Serving:	
Serving Size: 1 Cup	
Calories: 130	From Fat: 0
Total Fat	0g
Saturated	0g
Cholesterol	0mg
Sodium	15mg
Total Carbohydrate	31g
Dietary Fiber	0g
Sugars	27g
Protein	1g

1) In 2-quart nonmetal freezer container, combine all ingredients except ginger ale; stir until sugar is dissolved. Freeze 4 to 6 hours or until slush consistency.

2) To serve, spoon ½ cup slush mixture into each glass.* Pour ½ cup ginger ale over each.

*NOTE: If slush is frozen solid, let stand at room temperature for about 30 minutes before serving.

HIGH ALTITUDE (ABOVE 3500 FT.): No change.

Game-Time Nachos

PREP TIME: 15 MINUTES (READY IN 15 MINUTES)
SERVINGS: 8

EASY

6 oz. light pasteurized prepared cheese product loaf, cubed

¼ cup shredded reduced-fat sharp Cheddar cheese (1 oz.)

3 tablespoons fat-free (skim) milk

1½ teaspoons Old El Paso® 40% less-sodium taco seasoning mix (from 1.25-oz. package)

3 oz. baked bite-size tortilla chips (about 64 chips)

1½ cups finely chopped Italian plum tomatoes (about 5 medium)

¼ cup chopped fresh cilantro

Nutrition Information Per Serving:	
Serving Size: 1/8 of Recipe	
Calories: 120	From Fat: 35
Total Fat	4g
Saturated	2g
Cholesterol	10mg
Sodium	440mg
Total Carbohydrate	14g
Dietary Fiber	1g
Sugars	3g
Protein	7g

1) In 1-quart saucepan, mix cubed cheese product, Cheddar cheese, milk and taco seasoning mix. Cook over medium-low heat, stirring frequently, until cheeses are melted and mixture is smooth.

2) Meanwhile, on large serving platter, arrange chips.

3) Pour warm cheese mixture over chips. Top with tomatoes and cilantro. Serve immediately.

HIGH ALTITUDE (3500-6000 FT.): No change.

tip For a fun presentation, vary the color of tortilla chips you use. Choose among red, green white, yellow and blue tortilla chips.

Spicy Shrimp Pot Stickers

WENDY P. OSBORNE | SYRACUSE, NEW YORK

PREP TIME: 30 MINUTES (READY IN 45 MINUTES)
SERVINGS: 10 (2 POT STICKERS & 2 TEASPOONS SAUCE EACH)

POT STICKERS

1 egg white

1 tablespoon water

¼ lb. (½ cup) cooked cocktail shrimp, tails removed

¼ cup sliced peeled carrot

1 medium green onion, cut into pieces

2 tablespoons teriyaki sauce

1 teaspoon ground ginger

¼ teaspoon crushed red pepper flakes

1 (12-oz.) can Pillsbury® Golden Layers® Refrigerated Flaky Original or Buttermilk Biscuits

DIPPING SAUCE

⅓ cup orange marmalade

3 tablespoons teriyaki sauce

1) Heat oven to 400°F. Line large cookie sheet with parchment paper. In small bowl, mix egg white and water until foamy; set aside.

2) In food processor, process shrimp, carrot and onion until finely chopped. In medium bowl, mix shrimp mixture and all remaining pot sticker ingredients except biscuits with fork until well blended.

3) Separate dough into 10 biscuits; separate each evenly into 2 layers, making 20 biscuit rounds. Press or roll each into 3½-inch dough round. Place 1 rounded teaspoon shrimp filling in a line about ½ inch up from bottom of each dough round.

4) For each pot sticker, bring sides of dough round up slightly over filling; bring bottom edge of dough up over filling. Brush top edge with egg white mixture; continue rolling up to seal. Place sealed side down on paper-lined cookie sheet. Brush rolls with remaining egg mixture.

5) Bake at 400°F. for 10 to 14 minutes or until golden brown. Meanwhile, in small bowl, mix dipping sauce ingredients with wire whisk or fork. Serve warm pot stickers with dipping sauce.

HIGH ALTITUDE (ABOVE 3500 FT.): No change.

Nutrition Information Per Serving:
Serving Size: 1/10 of Recipe

Calories:	170	From Fat:	45
Total Fat			5g
Saturated			1g
Cholesterol			20mg
Sodium			790mg
Total Carbohydrate			26g
Dietary Fiber			0g
Sugars			11g
Protein			6g

Chicken-Chutney-Cucumber Cups

PREP TIME: 20 MINUTES (READY IN 20 MINUTES)
SERVINGS: 36 APPETIZERS

 EASY

1½ cups finely chopped cooked chicken

¼ cup finely chopped unpeeled red apple

¼ cup chopped peanuts

½ cup mango chutney, chopped

3 medium English (seedless) cucumbers

Nutrition Information Per Serving:
Serving Size: 1 Appetizer

Calories: 25	From Fat: 10
Total Fat	1g
Saturated	0g
Cholesterol	5mg
Sodium	10mg
Total Carbohydrate	2g
Dietary Fiber	0g
Sugars	2g
Protein	2g

1) In medium bowl, mix all ingredients except cucumbers.

2) Cut tapered ends from cucumbers. Draw tines of fork lengthwise through cucumber peel to score; cut into ³⁄₄-inch-thick slices.

3) With small melon baller, scoop and discard center portion of each slice; do not go through bottom. Fill each with 1 tablespoon chicken mixture.

HIGH ALTITUDE (3500-6000 FT.): No change.

Happy Trails Mix

PREP TIME: 5 MINUTES
SERVINGS: 4 (1/2 CUP EACH); YIELD: 2 CUPS

 EASY

1 cup Chex Mix® Snack (any flavor)

½ cup frosted animal cookies

¼ cup candy-coated chocolate peanut pieces

¼ cup raisins

Ice cream cones, if desired

Nutrition Information Per Serving:
Serving Size: 1/2 Cup

Calories: 185	From Fat: 55
Total Fat	6g
Saturated	2g
Cholesterol	0mg
Sodium	210mg
Total Carbohydrate	30g
Dietary Fiber	2g
Sugars	16g
Protein	3g

In resealable quart-sized food storage plastic bag, combine all ingredients; shake to mix.

HIGH ALTITUDE (ABOVE 3500 FT.): No change.

 This is a fun mixture to serve kids for a sleepover snack or while watching a favorite video with the family. Make eating it extra fun by serving the mix in ice cream cones.

Chiles Rellenos Puffs

SUE TYNER | TUSTIN, CALIFORNIA

| PREP TIME: | 25 MINUTES (READY IN 1 HOUR) |
| SERVINGS: | 24 PUFFS |

1½ cups water

½ cup butter or margarine

1 cup all-purpose flour

½ cup cornmeal

1 teaspoon salt

6 eggs, beaten

3 oz. (¾ cup) shredded Monterey Jack cheese

3 oz. (¾ cup) shredded sharp Cheddar cheese

2 (4.5-oz.) cans Old El Paso® Chopped Green Chiles, drained

1) Heat oven to 400°F. Spray 24 regular-size muffin cups with cooking spray.* In 3-quart saucepan, heat water and butter over high heat to a full rolling boil. Remove from heat.

2) Stir in flour, cornmeal and salt until mixture forms a dough and all lumps have disappeared. Gradually stir in beaten eggs until well blended. Stir in both cheeses and the chiles. Spoon dough evenly into sprayed muffin cups, filling each ¾ full.

3) Bake at 400°F. for 25 to 29 minutes or until golden brown. Cool 2 minutes; remove from muffin cups. Serve warm.

*NOTE: If 2 (12-cup) muffin pans are unavailable, spoon dough into pan; refrigerate remaining dough while baking first pan. Spoon refrigerated dough into pan; bake 28 to 35 minutes.

HIGH ALTITUDE (ABOVE 3500 FT.): No change.

Nutrition Information Per Serving:
Serving Size: 1 Puff

Calories:	110	From Fat:	70
Total Fat			8g
Saturated			4g
Cholesterol			70mg
Sodium			220mg
Total Carbohydrate			7g
Dietary Fiber			0g
Sugars			1g
Protein			4g

Smoked Salmon Wraps

PREP TIME: 30 MINUTES (READY IN 30 MINUTES)
SERVINGS: 20 APPETIZERS

 EASY

4 oz. thinly sliced smoked
salmon (lox)

¼ cup whipped cream cheese
(from 8-oz. container)

20 small sprigs fresh dill

20 fresh sugar snap peas

1) Carefully separate slices of salmon;
place individually on work surface.
Spread slices with thin layer of
cream cheese.

2) Cut each slice of salmon into about
3x1-inch strips (because salmon
slices are irregular shape, some strips
may need to be cut in one direction
and some in another direction). Top
each strip with dill. Place 1 sugar
snap pea crosswise on each strip;
roll up.

HIGH ALTITUDE (3500-6000 FT.): No change.

Nutrition Information Per Serving:
Serving Size: 1 Appetizer

Calories:	15	From Fat:	10
Total Fat			1g
Saturated			0g
Cholesterol			5mg
Sodium			50mg
Total Carbohydrate			0g
Dietary Fiber			0g
Sugars			0g
Protein			1g

The sprigs of dill
will vary in size. If
they are small or
if you like dill, use
2 sprigs in each
roll instead of 1.

Hot Cheesy Artichoke Dip

PREP TIME: 15 MINUTES (READY IN 15 MINUTES)
SERVINGS: 22 (2 TABLESPOONS DIP AND 2 BREAD SLICES EACH)

 EASY

1 cup milk

¾ cup canned artichoke hearts, drained, chopped

1 slice bacon, crisply cooked, crumbled, or 1 tablespoon cooked real bacon pieces

4 teaspoons all-purpose flour

2 teaspoons Dijon mustard

¼ teaspoon garlic powder

⅛ teaspoon pepper

1½ cups shredded Cheddar cheese (6 oz.)

1 box (8 oz.) pasteurized prepared cheese product, cubed

Baguette French bread slices or Melba bagel chips

1) In 2-quart saucepan, mix milk, artichoke hearts, bacon, flour, mustard, garlic powder and pepper. Cook over medium-low heat 4 to 6 minutes, stirring constantly, until hot and thickened, but not boiling.

2) Gradually stir in cheeses. Cook about 2 minutes, stirring constantly, until cheeses are melted.

3) Transfer mixture to fondue pot. Adjust flame or heat so mixture stays hot but does not boil. Serve warm with baguette bread slices.

HIGH ALTITUDE (3500-6000 FT.): No change.

Nutrition Information Per Serving:
Serving Size: 1/22 of Recipe

Calories:	110	From Fat:	50
Total Fat			6g
Saturated			3g
Cholesterol			15mg
Sodium			320mg
Total Carbohydrate			10g
Dietary Fiber			0g
Sugars			2g
Protein			6g

Holiday Appetizer Wreath

PREP TIME: 20 MINUTES (READY IN 55 MINUTES)
SERVINGS: 16

6 slices bacon

2 cans (8 oz. each) Pillsbury®
refrigerated crescent dinner rolls

½ cup chive-and-onion cream cheese
spread (from 8-oz. container)

2 cups Green Giant Select® frozen
broccoli florets (from 14-oz. bag),
thawed, finely chopped and patted
dry with paper towel

⅓ cup diced red bell pepper

1 egg, beaten

1 teaspoon sesame seed

Fresh rosemary, if desired

1) Heat oven to 375°F. Cook bacon until
crisp; drain. Crumble and set aside.

2) Unroll both cans of dough; separate into
16 triangles. On ungreased large cookie
sheet, arrange triangles with shortest
sides toward center, overlapping in
wreath shape and leaving 5-inch round
circle open in center (see diagram
below right). Crescent dough points may
overlap edge of cookie sheet. Press
overlapping dough to flatten and form a
4-inch circle in center.

3) Spread cream cheese spread on dough
to within 1 inch of points. In small bowl,
mix bacon, broccoli and bell pepper;
spoon onto widest part of dough. Pull
end points of triangles over broccoli
mixture and tuck under dough to form
ring (filling will be visible). Brush
dough with beaten egg; sprinkle with
sesame seed.

4) Bake 25 to 30 minutes or until deep
golden brown. Cool 5 minutes. With
broad spatula, carefully loosen wreath
from cookie sheet; slide onto serving
platter. Garnish with fresh rosemary.
Serve warm. Store in refrigerator.

HIGH ALTITUDE (3500-6000 FT.): Heat oven to 350°F.
Use 1/3 cup cheese spread. Bake 30 to 35 minutes.

Nutrition Information Per Serving:
Serving Size: 1/16 of Recipe

Calories:	160	From Fat:	90
Total Fat		10g	
Saturated		4g	
Cholesterol		25mg	
Sodium		320mg	
Total Carbohydrate		12g	
Dietary Fiber		0g	
Sugars		3g	
Protein		4g	

Keep the crescent
dough refrigerated
until you are ready
to work with it.
Chilled dough is
much easier to work
with than dough
warmed to room
temperature.

Shaping the wreath

Mediterranean Cheese Foldovers

LYNETTE RUSSELL | SUN PRAIRIE, WISCONSIN

Pillsbury Bake-Off

PREP TIME: 25 MINUTES (READY IN 50 MINUTES)
SERVINGS: 16 APPETIZERS

BUNDLES

1 (6-oz.) container (1¼ cups) crumbled garlic-and-herb feta cheese

2 oz. (½ cup) finely shredded Romano cheese

¼ cup finely chopped green onions (4 medium)

2 tablespoons finely chopped ripe olives

1 egg

1 egg, separated

1 (16.3-oz.) can Pillsbury® Grands!® Flaky Layers Refrigerated Buttermilk Biscuits

1 teaspoon water

2 teaspoons sesame seed

GARNISH, (IF DESIRED)

Sprigs fresh parsley

Whole ripe olives

1) Heat oven to 350°F. Lightly grease large cookie sheet with shortening or spray with cooking spray. In medium bowl, mix both cheeses, onions and olives. Mash with fork to break up any large chunks of cheese. Stir in 1 egg and 1 egg white with fork until well combined.

2) Separate dough into 8 biscuits; separate each evenly into 2 layers, making 16 biscuit rounds. Press each into 3½-inch dough round. Spoon about 1 rounded tablespoon cheese mixture onto center of each dough round. Fold dough in half over filling; press edges to seal. Place on greased cookie sheet.

3) In small bowl, beat egg yolk and water with fork until well blended; brush over dough foldovers. Sprinkle sesame seed over each.

4) Bake at 350°F. for 16 to 20 minutes or until golden brown. Cool 5 minutes. Remove from cookie sheet; place on serving platter. Garnish platter with parsley and several olives. Serve warm.

HIGH ALTITUDE (ABOVE 3500 FT.): No change.

Nutrition Information Per Serving:
Serving Size: 1 Appetizer

Calories:	155	From Fat:	70
Total Fat			8g
Saturated			3g
Cholesterol			25mg
Sodium			550mg
Total Carbohydrate			15g
Dietary Fiber			1g
Sugars			5g
Protein			6g

Buffalo-Style Chicken Bites

PREP TIME: 20 MINUTES (READY IN 20 MINUTES)   EASY
SERVINGS: 20

¼ cup butter or
margarine, melted

¼ cup chili sauce

¼ cup hot pepper sauce

1¼ lb. boneless skinless
chicken breast halves,
cut into 1-inch cubes

1 cup chunky blue cheese
salad dressing

Nutrition Information Per Serving:
Serving Size: 1/20 of Recipe

Calories:	110	From Fat:	80
Total Fat			8g
Saturated			2g
Cholesterol			25mg
Sodium			200mg
Total Carbohydrate			2g
Dietary Fiber			0g
Sugars			2g
Protein			7g

1) In small bowl, mix butter, chili sauce and hot pepper sauce.

2) In large bowl, mix chicken and half of the chili sauce mixture. In 10-inch nonstick skillet, cook chicken over medium-high heat 8 to 10 minutes, stirring frequently, until well browned and no longer pink in center.

3) Add remaining half of chili sauce mixture; toss to coat. Serve chicken with toothpicks and blue cheese dressing for dipping.

HIGH ALTITUDE (3500-6000 FT.): No change.

Layered Pizza Dip

PREP TIME: 10 MINUTES (READY IN 25 MINUTES)   EASY
SERVINGS: 16 (2 TABLESPOONS DIP AND 4 BAGEL CHIPS EACH)

tip

Layer the dip ingredients in a microwave-safe dish. Microwave on HIGH for 1 to 2 minutes or just until hot.

1 container (8 oz.) chives-and-onion cream cheese spread

½ cup pizza sauce

½ cup chopped green bell pepper (½ medium)

⅓ cup finely chopped pepperoni (1¾ oz.)

½ cup shredded mozzarella cheese (2 oz.)

½ cup shredded Cheddar cheese (2 oz.)

Bagel chips or crackers

Nutrition Information Per Serving:
Serving Size: 1/16 of Recipe

Calories:	120	From Fat:	80
Total Fat			9g
Saturated			5g
Cholesterol			25mg
Sodium			200mg
Total Carbohydrate			5g
Dietary Fiber			0g
Sugars			1g
Protein			4g

1) Heat oven to 350°F. In ungreased 9-inch glass pie pan or 1-quart shallow baking dish, layer cream cheese spread, pizza sauce, bell pepper, pepperoni, mozzarella and Cheddar cheese.

2) Bake 10 to 15 minutes or until dip is hot and cheese is melted. Serve warm with bagel chips.

HIGH ALTITUDE (3500-6000 FT.): No change.

Crab and Asparagus Dip

PREP TIME: 15 MINUTES (READY IN 40 MINUTES)
SERVINGS: 22 (2 TABLESPOONS DIP AND 4 CRACKERS EACH)

½ cup sour cream

1 package (8 oz.) cream cheese, softened

1 can (15 oz.) Green Giant® extra long tender green asparagus spears, drained, chopped

½ cup shredded Parmesan cheese (2 oz.)

2 tablespoons sliced green onions (2 medium)

1 teaspoon prepared horseradish

1 teaspoon Dijon mustard

1 can (6 oz.) crabmeat, drained

⅓ cup sliced almonds

1 package (9.75 oz.) assorted crackers

1) Heat oven to 375°F. In medium bowl, mix sour cream, cream cheese and asparagus. Add cheese, onions, horseradish, mustard and crabmeat; mix well.

2) Spread evenly in ungreased 1-quart baking dish. Sprinkle with almonds.

3) Bake 20 to 25 minutes or until thoroughly heated. Serve warm with crackers or cut-up vegetables.

HIGH ALTITUDE (3500-6000 FT.): No change.

Nutrition Information Per Serving:
Serving Size: 1/22 of Recipe

Calories:	140	From Fat:	80
Total Fat			9g
Saturated			4g
Cholesterol			25mg
Sodium			260mg
Total Carbohydrate			11g
Dietary Fiber			1g
Sugars			2g
Protein			6g

Jalapeño-Chicken Crescent Pinwheels

LUPE CORTES | FOREST, VIRGINIA

PREP TIME: 20 MINUTES (READY IN 40 MINUTES)
SERVINGS: 32 APPETIZERS

4 oz. cream cheese (from 8-oz. pkg.), softened

½ cup chopped cooked chicken

¼ cup chopped fresh cilantro

2 to 3 tablespoons finely chopped sliced jalapeño chiles (from 12-oz. jar)

2 tablespoons finely chopped green onions (2 medium)

⅛ teaspoon salt

1 (8-oz.) can Pillsbury® Refrigerated Crescent Dinner Rolls

1) Heat oven to 375°F. In small bowl, mix all ingredients except dough until well combined; set aside.

2) Unroll dough; separate into 2 long rectangles. Place 1 rectangle on long cutting board; press perforations to seal. Spread half of cream cheese mixture on dough rectangle to within ½ inch of edges.

3) Starting with one long side, roll up rectangle; press seam to seal. Cut roll into 16 slices; place slices, cut side down, on ungreased cookie sheet. Repeat with remaining dough rectangle.

4) Bake at 375°F. for 14 to 16 minutes or until light golden brown. Immediately remove from cookie sheet. Serve warm.

HIGH ALTITUDE (ABOVE 3500 FT.): No change.

Nutrition Information Per Serving:
Serving Size: 1 Appetizer

Calories:	40	From Fat:	20
Total Fat			2g
Saturated			1g
Cholesterol			5mg
Sodium			115mg
Total Carbohydrate			4g
Dietary Fiber			0g
Sugars			1g
Protein			1g

Italian Spinach Torta

LARRY ELDER | CHARLOTTE, NORTH CAROLINA

Pillsbury Bake-Off

PREP TIME: 15 MINUTES (READY IN 1 HOUR 15 MINUTES)
SERVINGS: 12

CRUST

1 box (15 oz.) Pillsbury® refrigerated pie crusts, softened as directed on box

FILLING

1 box (9 oz.) Green Giant® frozen spinach, thawed, squeezed to drain

1 cup ricotta cheese

1/2 cup grated Parmesan cheese

1/4 to 1/2 teaspoon garlic salt

1/4 teaspoon pepper

1 egg, separated

1 teaspoon water

1) Make pie crusts as directed on box for Two-Crust Pie using 10-inch tart pan with removable bottom or 9-inch glass pie pan. Place 1 pie crust in pan; press in bottom and up sides of pan. Trim edges if necessary.

2) Place oven rack in lowest rack position; heat oven to 400°F. In medium bowl, mix spinach, ricotta cheese, Parmesan cheese, garlic salt, pepper and egg yolk until well blended; spread evenly in crust-lined pan.

3) To make lattice top, cut remaining pie crust into 3/4-inch-wide strips; arrange in lattice design over spinach mixture. Trim and seal edges. In small bowl with fork, beat egg white and water; gently brush over lattice.

4) Bake on lowest oven rack 45 to 50 minutes or until dark golden brown. If necessary, cover torta with foil during last 5 to 10 minutes of baking to prevent excessive browning. Cool 10 minutes; remove sides of pan.

HIGH ALTITUDE (3500-6500 FT.): No change.

Nutrition Information Per Serving:
Serving Size: 1/12 of Recipe

Calories:	200	From Fat:	100
Total Fat		11g	
Saturated		4.5g	
Cholesterol		30mg	
Sodium		290mg	
Total Carbohydrate		20g	
Dietary Fiber		0g	
Sugars		3g	
Protein		6g	

Shrimp and Pancetta Pizza

LINDA DIANE WRIGHT-SMITH | MANASSAS, VIRGINIA

PREP TIME: 20 MINUTES (READY IN 30 MINUTES)
SERVINGS: 16 APPETIZERS

🄴 EASY

¼ lb. frozen cooked salad shrimp, thawed

1 tablespoon extra-virgin olive oil

1 clove garlic, minced

1 (13.8-oz.) can Pillsbury® Refrigerated Pizza Crust

3 oz. sliced pancetta or 3 slices bacon

½ cup Alfredo pasta sauce

5 oz. (1¼ cups) shredded mozzarella cheese

1 medium Italian plum tomato

3 tablespoons fresh Italian (flat-leaf) parsley leaves

1) Heat oven to 400°F. Spray cookie sheet with cooking spray. In medium bowl, mix thawed shrimp, oil and garlic until coated; set aside.

2) Unroll dough; place on sprayed cookie sheet. Starting at center, press out dough into 14x9-inch rectangle. Bake at 400°F. for 6 to 8 minutes or until edges are light golden brown.

3) Meanwhile, in 8-inch skillet, cook pancetta over medium heat until crisp; drain on paper towels.

4) Remove partially baked crust from oven. Spread Alfredo sauce over crust. Sprinkle with mozzarella cheese. Return to oven; bake 6 to 10 minutes or until cheese is melted and edges are golden brown. Meanwhile, chop pancetta, seed and finely chop tomato, and chop parsley.

5) Remove pizza from oven. Top pizza evenly with shrimp, pancetta and tomato. Return to oven; bake an additional 3 minutes or until shrimp is thoroughly heated. Sprinkle with parsley. Cut into squares. Serve warm.

HIGH ALTITUDE (ABOVE 3500 FT.): No change.

Nutrition Information Per Serving:
Serving Size: 1 Appetizer

Calories:	150	From Fat:	60
Total Fat			6g
Saturated			3g
Cholesterol			70mg
Sodium			340mg
Total Carbohydrate			13g
Dietary Fiber			0g
Sugars			2g
Protein			11g

Baked Club Sandwich Rounds

PHIL CAPALDI | SAUNDERSTOWN, RHODE ISLAND

Pillsbury Bake-Off

PREP TIME: 35 MINUTES (READY IN 1 HOUR 5 MINUTES)
SERVINGS: 12

1 lb. bacon

1 can (11 oz.) Pillsbury® refrigerated crusty French loaf

1 cup shredded sharp Cheddar cheese (4 oz.)

2 oz. thinly sliced cooked turkey

2 oz. thinly sliced cooked ham

1) Heat oven to 350°F. Spray cookie sheet with cooking spray. Cook bacon until crisp; drain on paper towel. Crumble; set aside.

2) Unroll dough. Sprinkle cheese over dough; top with turkey, ham and bacon. Starting with one long side, roll up dough; press edges to seal. Cut 3 or 4 slits in top of loaf; place on cookie sheet.

3) Bake 23 to 28 minutes or until golden brown. Cool 5 minutes. Remove from cookie sheet. Cut into 1-inch diagonal slices; serve warm. Serve with mustard, if desired.

HIGH ALTITUDE (3500-6500 FT.): No change.

Nutrition Information Per Serving:
Serving Size: 1/12 of Recipe

Calories:	170	From Fat:	90
Total Fat			10g
Saturated			4g
Cholesterol			25mg
Sodium			450mg
Total Carbohydrate			11g
Dietary Fiber			0g
Sugars			1g
Protein			10g

Kicked-Up Crab Bites

LAURIE MCGRAW | RAEFORD, NORTH CAROLINA

PREP TIME: 30 MINUTES (READY IN 45 MINUTES)
SERVINGS: 32 APPETIZERS

1 (3-oz.) pkg. cream cheese, softened

¼ cup wasabi-horseradish flavored light mayonnaise

½ teaspoon prepared horseradish

1 tablespoon finely chopped onion

1½ teaspoons lemon juice

1 (6-oz.) can crabmeat, drained

2 (8-oz.) cans Pillsbury® Refrigerated Crescent Dinner Rolls

Paprika, if desired

Chopped fresh parsley, if desired

1) Heat oven to 375°F. In medium bowl, mix cream cheese, mayonnaise and horseradish until creamy. Stir in onion, lemon juice and crabmeat until well blended.

2) Unroll 1 can of the dough; separate into 4 rectangles. Press each into 8x4-inch rectangle, firmly pressing perforations to seal. With pizza cutter, cut each into 8 squares. Spoon about 1 rounded measuring teaspoon crab mixture onto center of each square.

3) Unroll second can of dough; separate into 4 rectangles. Press or roll each into 8x4-inch rectangle, firmly pressing perforations to seal. Cut each into 8 squares. Place squares on top of crab mixture. Press edges with fork to seal; place on ungreased cookie sheets.

4) Bake at 375°F. for 10 to 14 minutes or until golden brown. Remove from oven. Sprinkle each with paprika and parsley; remove from cookie sheet. Serve warm.

HIGH ALTITUDE (ABOVE 3500 FT..): No change.

Nutrition Information Per Serving:
Serving Size: 1 Appetizer

Calories:	70	From Fat:	35
Total Fat			4g
Saturated			1g
Cholesterol			10mg
Sodium			210mg
Total Carbohydrate			7g
Dietary Fiber			0g
Sugars			2g
Protein			2g

Mango-Mint Fruit Dip

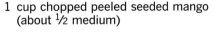

PREP TIME: 10 MINUTES (READY IN 10 MINUTES)
SERVINGS: 18 (2 TABLESPOONS DIP AND 2/3 CUP FRUIT EACH)

EASY

1 cup chopped peeled seeded mango (about ½ medium)

1 teaspoon chopped fresh mint leaves

1 cup marshmallow creme

1 package (8 oz.) cream cheese

Assorted cut-up fresh fruit

Nutrition Information Per Serving:
Serving Size: 1/18 of Recipe

Calories:	130	From Fat:	45
Total Fat			5g
Saturated			3g
Cholesterol			15mg
Sodium			40mg
Total Carbohydrate			22g
Dietary Fiber			2g
Sugars			19g
Protein			2g

1) In food processor bowl with metal blade, process mango and mint until smooth, about 10 seconds.

2) Add marshmallow creme and cream cheese; process until well blended, about 10 seconds. Serve with cut-up fresh fruit. Garnish with mint leaf, if desired.

HIGH ALTITUDE (3500-6000 FT.): No change.

Ham and Asparagus Squares

PREP TIME: 20 MINUTES (READY IN 40 MINUTES)
SERVINGS: 24 APPETIZERS

 EASY

½ lb. fresh thin asparagus spears

1 can (8 oz.) Pillsbury® refrigerated crescent dinner rolls

1½ cups finely shredded Swiss cheese (6 oz.)

1½ oz. thinly sliced prosciutto or deli ham, cut into 1-inch strips

2 teaspoons olive oil

¼ teaspoon crushed red pepper flakes

1) Heat oven to 375°F. In 10-inch skillet, heat ½ inch water to boiling. Add asparagus; reduce heat to medium-low. Cover; simmer 2 to 3 minutes or until crisp-tender. Drain. Plunge asparagus into bowl of ice water to cool; drain on paper towels.

2) Unroll dough on ungreased cookie sheet; press into 11x8-inch rectangle, firmly pressing perforations to seal. With fork, prick crust generously. Bake 6 to 9 minutes or until light golden brown.

3) Remove partially baked crust from oven. Sprinkle with ½ cup of the cheese; top with prosciutto strips. Sprinkle with remaining 1 cup cheese. Arrange cooked asparagus spears in rows over cheese, alternating tips. Brush with oil; sprinkle with pepper flakes.

4) Return to oven; bake 5 to 7 minutes longer or until edges of crust are deep golden brown and cheese is melted. Cool 5 minutes. With serrated knife, cut into squares. Serve warm.

HIGH ALTITUDE (3500-6000 FT.): Bake untopped crust at 375°F. 8 to 11 minutes. Continue as directed above.

Nutrition Information Per Serving:
Serving Size: 1 Appetizer

Calories:	70	From Fat:	35
Total Fat			4g
Saturated			2g
Cholesterol			5mg
Sodium			150mg
Total Carbohydrate			5g
Dietary Fiber			0g
Sugars			1g
Protein			3g

Mexican Chili Dip

PREP TIME: 15 MINUTES (READY IN 15 MINUTES)
SERVINGS: 24 (2 TABLESPOONS DIP AND 6 CELERY STICKS EACH)

 EASY

¼ cup chopped onion (½ medium)

1 garlic clove, minced

2 tablespoons water

1 can (14.5 oz.) stewed tomatoes, undrained

1 can (4.5 oz.) Old El Paso® chopped green chiles, drained

½ teaspoon salt

½ teaspoon chili powder

Dash ground red pepper (cayenne) or red pepper sauce

½ cup shredded Monterey Jack cheese (2 oz.)

1 package (8 oz.) ⅓-less-fat cream cheese (Neufchâtel), cut into small cubes

Chili powder, if desired

Assorted cut-up fresh vegetables or tortilla chips

1) In 2-quart saucepan, cook onion, garlic and water over medium heat 2 to 4 minutes, stirring occasionally, until onion is tender and water has evaporated.

2) Stir in tomatoes, chiles, salt, chili powder and ground red pepper. Cook about 2 minutes until hot, stirring occasionally.

3) Reduce heat to medium-low. Add cheeses; cook, stirring constantly, just until melted. Sprinkle with chili powder. Serve with cut-up fresh vegetables.

*NOTE: To make dip in microwave, in 1½-quart microwavable bowl, microwave onion, garlic and water on High 2 to 3 minutes or until onion is tender and water has evaporated. Stir in cheeses; microwave on High 1½ to 2 minutes or until cheeses are melted. Stir in tomatoes, chiles, salt, chili powder and ground red pepper. Microwave on High 2 minutes or until mixture is hot.

HIGH ALTITUDE (3500-6000 FT.): No change.

Nutrition Information Per Serving:
Serving Size: 1/24 of Recipe

Calories:	45	From Fat:	25
Total Fat			3g
Saturated			2g
Cholesterol			10mg
Sodium			190mg
Total Carbohydrate			3g
Dietary Fiber			0g
Sugars			2g
Protein			2g

For a festive touch, tie a ribbon with a small ornament around a serving dish.

Greek Layered Dip with Pita Crisps

PREP TIME: 20 MINUTES (READY IN 20 MINUTES)
SERVINGS: 18 (2 TABLESPOONS DIP AND 1 PITA CRISP EACH)

 EASY

PITA CRISPS

3 pita (pocket) breads (6 inch)

Cooking spray

½ teaspoon garlic powder

DIP

1 container (8 oz.) chives and onion cream cheese spread

1 container (8 oz.) hummus

1 medium cucumber, peeled, seeded and chopped

3 medium Italian plum tomatoes, seeded, chopped

1 can (2¼ oz.) sliced ripe olives, drained

1 container (4 oz.) crumbled feta cheese

¼ cup chopped green onions (4 medium)

1) Heat oven to 350°F. Carefully split each pita bread into 2 rounds. Cut each round into 6 wedges; place on ungreased cookie sheets. Spray wedges lightly with cooking spray; sprinkle with garlic powder.

2) Bake 5 to 7 minutes or until crisp and golden brown. Cool while making dip.

3) Meanwhile, in 10-inch plate or pie pan, spread cream cheese spread. Drop small spoonfuls of hummus evenly over cream cheese; spread evenly. Top with remaining ingredients in order listed.

4) Serve dip with pita crisps.

*NOTE: To make ahead, dip can be refrigerated up to 2 hours.

HIGH ALTITUDE (3500-6000 FT.): No change.

Nutrition Information Per Serving:
Serving Size: 1/18 of Recipe

Calories:	120	From Fat:	70
Total Fat			8g
Saturated			4g
Cholesterol			20mg
Sodium			240mg
Total Carbohydrate			9g
Dietary Fiber			1g
Sugars			1g
Protein			4g

tip If you're taking this to a party, layer the ingredients on a decorative plastic plate or tray from a party store—no risk of breaking your favorite serving plate.

Hot Artichoke and Spinach Dip

PREP TIME: 20 MINUTES (READY IN 4 HOURS 20 MINUTES)
SERVINGS: 24 (2 TABLESPOONS DIP AND 4 SLICES BREAD EACH)

2 cups Green Giant® frozen cut leaf spinach (from 1-lb. bag)

1 can (14 oz.) quartered artichoke hearts, drained, chopped

½ cup refrigerated Alfredo pasta sauce (from 10-oz. container)

½ cup mayonnaise

¾ teaspoon garlic salt

¼ teaspoon pepper

1 cup shredded Swiss cheese (4 oz.)

3 loaves (16 inches each) baguette French bread, each cut into 32 slices

Nutrition Information Per Serving: Serving Size: 1/24 of Recipe		
Calories: 180	From Fat:	70
Total Fat		8g
Saturated		3g
Cholesterol		10mg
Sodium		360mg
Total Carbohydrate		21g
Dietary Fiber		2g
Sugars		1g
Protein		6g

1) Cook spinach as directed on bag. Drain spinach, pressing with fork to remove excess liquid. Finely chop spinach.

2) In 1- to 2-quart slow cooker, mix chopped spinach and all remaining ingredients except bread.

3) Cover; cook on Low setting 3 to 4 hours. Serve dip with sliced French bread.

HIGH ALTITUDE (ABOVE 3500 FT.): No change.

Greek Spinach–Turkey Wraps

PREP TIME: 20 MINUTES (READY IN 1 HOUR 20 MINUTES)
SERVINGS: 24 APPETIZERS

 EASY

½ cup chives-and-onion cream cheese spread (from 8-oz. container)

½ cup crumbled feta cheese (2 oz.)

¼ cup chopped pitted Kalamata olives

4 spinach-flavor flour tortillas (8 inch)

4 oz. thinly sliced cooked turkey (from deli)

1 cup loosely packed fresh spinach leaves

Nutrition Information Per Serving: Serving Size: 1 Appetizer		
Calories: 50	From Fat:	25
Total Fat		3g
Saturated		2g
Cholesterol		10mg
Sodium		140mg
Total Carbohydrate		4g
Dietary Fiber		0g
Sugars		0g
Protein		2g

1) In small bowl, mix cream cheese spread, feta cheese and olives. Spread evenly over tortillas, covering completely.

2) Arrange turkey over cream cheese mixture, covering half of each tortilla. Top turkey with spinach leaves.

3) Starting with topped side, roll up each tightly. Wrap individually in plastic wrap. Refrigerate until completely chilled, at least 1 hour.

4) To serve, trim off ends of each roll; cut each into 3 sections. Cut each section in half on a slight diagonal.

HIGH ALTITUDE (3500-6000 FT.): No change.

Pepper Biscuit Pull-Apart

JULIE ANN HALVERSON | BIG LAKE, MINNESOTA

PREP TIME: 10 MINUTES (READY IN 25 MINUTES)
SERVINGS: 10

EASY

¼ teaspoon garlic powder

¼ teaspoon salt, if desired

¼ teaspoon dried basil leaves, crushed

¼ teaspoon dried oregano leaves, crushed

1 can (12 oz.) Pillsbury® Golden Layers® refrigerated buttermilk biscuits

4½ teaspoons olive oil

¼ cup chopped green bell pepper

¼ cup chopped red bell pepper

¼ cup shredded mozzarella cheese (1 oz.)

2 tablespoons grated Romano or Parmesan cheese

1) Heat oven to 400°F. In small bowl, mix garlic powder, salt, basil and oregano; set aside.

2) Separate dough into 10 biscuits. Place 1 biscuit in center of ungreased cookie sheet; arrange remaining biscuits in circle, edges slightly overlapping, around center biscuit. Gently press out into 10-inch round. Brush with oil; top with bell peppers and cheeses. Sprinkle garlic powder mixture over top.

3) Bake 12 to 15 minutes or until golden brown. Pull apart into warm biscuits to serve.

HIGH ALTITUDE (3500-6500 FT.): No change.

Nutrition Information Per Serving:
Serving Size: 1/10 of Recipe

Calories:	150	From Fat:	80
Total Fat			9g
Saturated			2.5g
Cholesterol			0mg
Sodium			390mg
Total Carbohydrate			15g
Dietary Fiber			0g
Sugars			3g
Protein			3g

Tomato-Topped Onion Bread Wedges

SANDRA J. BANGHAM | ROCKVILLE, MARYLAND

PREP TIME: 30 MINUTES (READY IN 50 MINUTES)
SERVINGS: 6

SALAD

1 tablespoon olive or vegetable oil

2 large tomatoes, chopped (about 2 cups)

1 medium red bell pepper, chopped (1 cup)

1 tablespoon chopped fresh parsley

1 tablespoon tarragon vinegar

1/2 teaspoon dried basil leaves

1/2 teaspoon dried oregano leaves

1/8 teaspoon pepper

BREAD

1/3 cup olive or vegetable oil

1/3 cup chopped onion

1 clove garlic, minced

1 can (13.8 oz.) Pillsbury® refrigerated pizza crust

1/4 cup grated Parmesan cheese

1) In 10-inch skillet, heat 1 tablespoon oil over medium heat. Add tomatoes and bell pepper; cook 10 to 15 minutes, stirring occasionally, until most of liquid has evaporated. Remove from heat. Stir in remaining salad ingredients; place in medium bowl and set aside to cool. Wipe skillet clean with paper towel.

2) Heat oven to 400°F. In same skillet, heat 1/3 cup oil over medium heat. Add onion and garlic; cook and stir 2 to 3 minutes or until onion is tender. Set onion mixture aside. With 1 tablespoon of the oil from onion mixture, grease 9-inch round pan.

3) Unroll dough; fold in half. Place dough in pan; gently press evenly in pan. With fork, poke holes in dough every 2 inches. Spread onion mixture evenly over dough. Sprinkle Parmesan cheese over top.

4) Bake 18 to 20 minutes or until golden brown and slightly puffed. Cool slightly, about 10 minutes. Remove from pan; place on serving plate. Top warm bread with salad.

HIGH ALTITUDE (3500-6500 FT.): Bake at 400°F. 20 to 22 minutes.

Nutrition Information Per Serving:
Serving Size: 1/6 of Recipe

Calories:	330	From Fat:	160
Total Fat			18g
Saturated			3.5g
Cholesterol			0mg
Sodium			550mg
Total Carbohydrate			36g
Dietary Fiber			2g
Sugars			7g
Protein			8g

For color variation in the salad, substitute 1 medium green bell pepper for the red bell pepper.

Jerk Chicken Wings with Creamy Dipping Sauce

PREP TIME: 10 MINUTES (READY IN 1 HOUR 55 MINUTES)
SERVINGS: 12

CHICKEN WINGS

2 tablespoons dried thyme leaves

1 tablespoon packed brown sugar

1 tablespoon minced garlic
(3 to 4 medium cloves)

3 teaspoons ground allspice

1 teaspoon salt

2 tablespoons cider vinegar

2 tablespoons hot pepper sauce

1 package (3 lb.) frozen chicken
wing drummettes, thawed

DIPPING SAUCE

½ cup chopped green onions
(8 medium)

½ cup sour cream

½ cup mayonnaise

1) In large nonmetal bowl, mix thyme, brown sugar, garlic, allspice, salt, vinegar and hot pepper sauce. Add chicken drummettes; toss to coat evenly. Cover; refrigerate 1 hour to marinate.

2) Heat oven to 425°F. Line two 15x10x1-inch pans with foil; spray foil with cooking spray. Place chicken drummettes in pans; discard any remaining marinade.

3) Bake 45 minutes or until chicken is no longer pink next to bone.

4) Meanwhile, in small bowl, mix all dipping sauce ingredients.

5) Serve chicken wings with sauce.

*NOTE: To make ahead, make and bake drummettes as directed in recipe. Place in covered container; refrigerate up to 24 hours. To reheat, place in foil-lined 15x10x1-inch pan; heat at 350°F. until thoroughly heated, about 20 minutes.

HIGH ALTITUDE (3500-6000 FT.): No change.

Nutrition Information Per Serving:
Serving Size: 1/12 of Recipe

Calories:	170	From Fat:	120
Total Fat			13g
Saturated			3g
Cholesterol			50mg
Sodium			140mg
Total Carbohydrate			1g
Dietary Fiber			0g
Sugars			1g
Protein			13g

Zesty Margarita Shrimp Cocktail

PREP TIME: 10 MINUTES (READY IN 10 MINUTES)
SERVINGS: 32 (1 SHRIMP AND 1 TEASPOON DIP EACH)

 EASY

½ cup mayonnaise

2 tablespoons refrigerated honey mustard salad dressing

1 teaspoon grated lime peel

1 tablespoon fresh lime juice

1 tablespoon tequila, if desired

32 deveined shelled cooked extra-large shrimp with tails on (about 2 lb.)

In medium bowl, mix all ingredients except shrimp. Serve as dip for shrimp.

HIGH ALTITUDE (3500-6000 FT.): No change.

Nutrition Information Per Serving:
Serving Size: 1/32 of Recipe

Calories: 35	From Fat: 30
Total Fat	3g
Saturated	0g
Cholesterol	20mg
Sodium	45mg
Total Carbohydrate	0g
Dietary Fiber	0g
Sugars	0g
Protein	2g

Pepper-Jack Crescent Twists with Salsa-Ranch Dip

ELIZABETH DELL | GRAYSLAKE, ILLINOIS

PREP TIME: 15 MINUTES (READY IN 30 MINUTES)
SERVINGS: 12 (1 TWIST AND 2 TABLESPOONS DIP EACH)

 EASY

DIP

1 cup Old El Paso® Thick 'n Chunky salsa

½ cup ranch dressing

TWISTS

2 cans (8 oz. each) Pillsbury® refrigerated crescent dinner rolls

1 cup shredded hot pepper Monterey Jack cheese (4 oz.)

2 tablespoons sesame seed

Nutrition Information Per Serving:
Serving Size: 1/12 of Recipe

Calories: 240	From Fat: 150
Total Fat	16g
Saturated	5g
Cholesterol	10mg
Sodium	600mg
Total Carbohydrate	18g
Dietary Fiber	0g
Sugars	4g
Protein	5g

1) In small bowl, mix salsa and dressing. Cover; refrigerate at least 1 hour.

2) Heat oven to 375°F. Lightly grease cookie sheets with shortening. Unroll 1 can of dough into 11x8-inch rectangle, firmly pressing perforations to seal. Sprinkle evenly with cheese to within ½ inch of long sides. Unroll remaining can of dough; place over cheese and seal perforations. Sprinkle with sesame seed.

3) With rolling pin, lightly roll dough to press layers together. Cut crosswise through both layers of dough into 12 strips; place strips on cookie sheets. Press 1 end of each strip to cookie sheet. Gently twist strip 3 to 4 times; press remaining end to cookie sheet.

4) Bake 10 to 15 minutes or until golden brown. Remove from cookie sheet; serve warm with dip.

HIGH ALTITUDE (3500-6500 FT.): No change.

Sensational
Salads

Take your pick from this
fresh-from-the-garden salad bar!

ASIAN CUCUMBER-ZUCCHINI SALAD
PG. 86

TORTELLINI-SPINACH SALAD
PG. 78

MANDARIN ORANGE-CORN SLAW
PG. 70

Mandarin Orange-Corn Slaw

JYL LEININGER | SEATTLE, WASHINGTON

Pillsbury Bake-Off

PREP TIME: 10 MINUTES (READY IN 10 MINUTES)
SERVINGS: 8 (1/2 CUP EACH)

SALAD

3 cups three-color coleslaw blend*

3 tablespoons chopped green onions (3 medium), reserving 1 green top for garnish

1 can (11 oz.) Green Giant® Mexicorn® whole kernel corn with red and green peppers, drained

1 can (11 oz.) mandarin orange segments, drained, reserving 6 to 8 segments for garnish

DRESSING

½ cup light mayonnaise

2 tablespoons sugar

1 tablespoon red wine vinegar

1 tablespoon lime juice

1) In large bowl, mix salad ingredients except onion top and reserved orange segments.

2) In small bowl, mix dressing ingredients until well blended. Add dressing to salad; toss to coat. Serve immediately, or cover and refrigerate until serving time.

3) To make flower garnish, in reserved green onion top, cut lengthwise slits ⅔ of the way down; curve strips to resemble leaves and place on salad. Arrange reserved mandarin orange segments on top of leaves to resemble flower petals.

*NOTE: If three-color coleslaw blend is not available, substitute 2 cups coleslaw blend and 1 cup shredded red cabbage.

HIGH ALTITUDE (3500-6500 FT.): No change.

Nutrition Information Per Serving:
Serving Size: 1/2 Cup

Calories:	120	From Fat:	50
Total Fat			5g
Saturated			1g
Cholesterol			5mg
Sodium			230mg
Total Carbohydrate			17g
Dietary Fiber			2g
Sugars			10g
Protein			2g

Minted Peas and Pasta Salad

VIRGINIA MOON | HARVEST, ALABAMA

PREP TIME: 30 MINUTES (READY IN 1 HOUR 30 MINUTES)
SERVINGS: 5 (1 CUP EACH)

DRESSING

- ¼ cup reduced-fat or regular mayonnaise
- ¼ cup reduced-fat or regular sour cream
- 2 tablespoons basil pesto
- 1 tablespoon chopped fresh mint or 1 teaspoon dried mint leaves
- ½ teaspoon salt
- ⅛ teaspoon coarsely ground black pepper

SALAD

- 1 package (9 oz.) refrigerated cheese-filled tortellini
- 2 cups Green Giant Select® LeSueur® Frozen Baby Early Peas (from 1-lb. bag)
- 4 oz. mozzarella cheese, cubed (1 cup)
- 2 thinly sliced green onions (2 tablespoons)
- Red leaf lettuce, if desired
- Fresh mint leaves, if desired

1) In small bowl, mix dressing ingredients until well blended. Cover; refrigerate while cooking tortellini and peas.

2) Cook tortellini as directed on package. Drain; rinse with cold water. Drain well; cool 15 minutes. Meanwhile, cook peas as directed on bag; drain.

3) In large bowl, mix cooked tortellini and peas, cheese and onions. Pour dressing over salad; toss lightly to coat. Refrigerate at least 1 hour before serving to blend flavors. Serve on lettuce-lined plates; garnish with fresh mint.

HIGH ALTITUDE (3500-6500 FT.): No change.

Nutrition Information Per Serving:
Serving Size: 1 Cup

Calories:	280	From Fat:	150
Total Fat			17g
Saturated			7g
Cholesterol			65mg
Sodium			570mg
Total Carbohydrate			19g
Dietary Fiber			2g
Sugars			5g
Protein			13g

Tri-Berry Spinach Salad

PREP TIME:	15 MINUTES		EASY
SERVINGS:	4 (1 CUP EACH)		

DRESSING

¼ cup oil

1 tablespoon sugar

3 tablespoons frozen raspberry-lemonade concentrate

2 tablespoons vinegar

¼ teaspoon Dijon mustard

SALAD

1 (6-oz.) pkg. prewashed fresh baby spinach (about 7 cups)

⅓ cup sliced fresh strawberries

⅓ cup fresh blueberries

⅓ cup fresh raspberries

¼ cup sliced red onion, separated into rings

1) In small bowl, combine all dressing ingredients; mix well.

2) In large serving bowl, combine all salad ingredients. Pour dressing over salad; toss gently to coat.

HIGH ALTITUDE (ABOVE 3500 FT.): No change.

Nutrition Information Per Serving:
Serving Size: 1 Cup

Calories:	200	From Fat:	125
Total Fat			14g
Saturated			2g
Cholesterol			0mg
Sodium			45mg
Total Carbohydrate			16g
Dietary Fiber			2g
Sugars			12g
Protein			2g

tip

You can make the dressing the night before, refrigerating it in a jar or container with a lid. Just before serving, shake the jar until the dressing is well-combined.

Broccoli, Bacon and Cheddar Toss

PREP TIME: 15 MINUTES
SERVINGS: 8 (1/2 CUP EACH)

✦ EASY

SALAD

3 cups fresh small broccoli florets

2 oz. (½ cup) shredded reduced-fat Cheddar cheese

⅓ cup raisins

¼ cup chopped red onion

4 slices purchased precooked bacon or ⅓ cup real bacon pieces

DRESSING

½ cup fat-free mayonnaise or salad dressing

2 tablespoons sugar

2 teaspoons lemon juice

Nutrition Information Per Serving:
Serving Size: 1/2 Cup

Calories: 80	From Fat: 20
Total Fat	2g
Saturated	1g
Cholesterol	5mg
Sodium	250mg
Total Carbohydrate	12g
Dietary Fiber	1g
Sugars	9g
Protein	4g

1) In large bowl, combine all salad ingredients except bacon.

2) In small bowl, combine all dressing ingredients; mix well. Pour dressing over salad; toss gently to coat.

3) Just before serving, heat bacon slices as directed on package until crisp. Drain on paper towels; crumble. Stir bacon into salad.

HIGH ALTITUDE (ABOVE 3500 FT.): No change.

Tuna with Mixed Greens And Balsamic Dressing

PREP TIME: 15 MINUTES
SERVINGS: 4 (2 CUPS EACH)

✦ EASY

1 (8-oz.) pkg. prewashed spring mix salad greens (5 cups)

20 pitted kalamata olives

12 cherry tomatoes, halved

2 hard-cooked eggs (from deli), cut into wedges

2 (6-oz.) cans albacore tuna, drained, flaked

½ cup purchased balsamic vinaigrette dressing

Nutrition Information Per Serving:
Serving Size: 2 Cups

Calories: 300	From Fat: 170
Total Fat	19g
Saturated	3g
Cholesterol	130mg
Sodium	810mg
Total Carbohydrate	6g
Dietary Fiber	2g
Sugars	3g
Protein	26g

1) Divide salad greens evenly onto individual serving plates. Top each evenly with olives, tomatoes, eggs and tuna.

2) Drizzle vinaigrette dressing evenly over salads.

HIGH ALTITUDE (ABOVE 3500 FT.): No change.

Grilled Shrimp and Wild Rice Salad

PREP TIME: 30 MINUTES (READY IN 1 HOUR 30 MINUTES)
SERVINGS: 2

1 (10-oz.) pkg. Green Giant® Frozen White & Wild Rice (with green beans)

½ cup sliced fresh mushrooms

¼ cup sliced green onions (4 medium)

¼ cup shredded carrot

¼ cup oil

1 teaspoon grated lime peel

2 tablespoons lime juice

1 tablespoon rice vinegar

1½ teaspoons honey

½ teaspoon Dijon mustard

6 oz. shelled deveined uncooked medium shrimp (about 12 shrimp), tails removed

1 tablespoon oil

3 cups lightly packed torn romaine lettuce

1) Cook rice as directed on package. In medium bowl, combine cooked rice, mushrooms, onions and carrot; mix well. Cover; refrigerate 1 hour or until cool.

2) In small bowl, combine ¼ cup oil, lime peel, lime juice, vinegar, honey and mustard; mix well. Pour lime mixture over rice mixture; toss gently to coat. Return to refrigerator.

3) Heat gas or charcoal grill. In medium bowl, combine shrimp and 1 tablespoon oil; toss to coat. Let stand at room temperature for 10 minutes to marinate.

4) When grill is heated, place shrimp in grill basket (grill "wok"). Place grill basket on gas grill over medium heat or on charcoal grill 4 to 6 inches from medium coals. Cook 4 to 6 minutes or until shrimp turn pink, stirring occasionally.

5) Divide lettuce evenly onto individual serving plates. Gently stir rice mixture; spoon evenly onto lettuce. Top each with shrimp.

HIGH ALTITUDE (ABOVE 3500 FT.): No change.

Nutrition Information Per Serving:
Serving Size: 1/2 of Recipe

Calories:	560	From Fat:	340
Total Fat			38g
Saturated			6g
Cholesterol			120mg
Sodium			860mg
Total Carbohydrate			37g
Dietary Fiber			4g
Sugars			9g
Protein			18g

Five-Layer Salad

PREP TIME: 10 MINUTES
SERVINGS: 4 (1-3/4 CUPS EACH)

 EASY

1 (5-oz.) pkg. mixed salad greens

1 medium cucumber, peeled, seeded and coarsely chopped

½ cup purchased three-cheese ranch salad dressing

¼ cup cooked real bacon pieces (from 2.5-oz. pkg.)

2 oz. (½ cup) finely shredded Cheddar-Monterey Jack cheese blend

Nutrition Information Per Serving: Serving Size: 1-3/4 Cups	
Calories: 225	From Fat: 180
Total Fat	20g
Saturated	6g
Cholesterol	25mg
Sodium	480mg
Total Carbohydrate	4g
Dietary Fiber	1g
Sugars	4g
Protein	7g

Layer all ingredients on large serving platter. Serve immediately.

HIGH ALTITUDE (ABOVE 3500 FT.): No change.

Wild Rice and Bean Salad

PREP TIME: 20 MINUTES
SERVINGS: 10 (1/2 CUP EACH)

 EASY

SALAD

1 (10-oz.) pkg. frozen cooked wild rice, thawed, or 2 cups cooked wild rice

1 (15.8-oz.) can great northern beans, drained, rinsed

1 (15-oz.) can black beans, drained, rinsed

1 (4.5-oz.) can Old El Paso® Chopped Green Chiles

½ cup sliced celery (1 medium stalk)

⅓ cup chopped onion (1 small)

¼ cup chopped fresh cilantro

DRESSING

¼ cup olive oil

¼ cup vinegar

1 teaspoon dry mustard

½ teaspoon salt

½ teaspoon pepper

2 garlic cloves, minced

Nutrition Information Per Serving: Serving Size: 1/2 Cup	
Calories: 185	From Fat: 55
Total Fat	6g
Saturated	1g
Cholesterol	0mg
Sodium	440mg
Total Carbohydrate	30g
Dietary Fiber	6g
Sugars	3g
Protein	9g

1) In large bowl, combine all salad ingredients; stir gently to combine.

2) In small bowl, combine all dressing ingredients; mix well.

3) Pour dressing over salad; toss gently to coat. Serve immediately, or cover and refrigerate until serving time.

HIGH ALTITUDE (ABOVE 3500 FT.): No change.

Grilled Turkey-Spinach Salad

PREP TIME: 25 MINUTES (READY IN 25 MINUTES)
SERVINGS: 2

EASY

2 slices bacon

1 medium yellow summer squash, cut into ½-inch-thick slices

1 small red bell pepper, cut into thin bite-size strips

½ cup balsamic vinaigrette dressing

1 turkey tenderloin (½ to ¾ lb.), cut crosswise into ½-inch-thick slices

4 cups fresh baby spinach leaves

1) Heat closed contact grill 5 minutes. When grill is heated, place bacon on bottom grill surface. Close grill; cook 4 to 6 minutes, turning once, until crisp. Drain on paper towels. Coarsely chop bacon.

2) In medium bowl, mix squash, bell pepper and ¼ cup of the vinaigrette dressing to coat. With slotted spoon, place vegetables on bottom grill surface; reserve dressing. Close grill; cook 3 to 5 minutes or until crisp-tender. Remove vegetables from grill.

3) Add turkey to reserved dressing in bowl; toss to coat. Place turkey on bottom grill surface; discard dressing. Close grill; cook 3 to 5 minutes or until turkey is no longer pink in center.

4) Arrange spinach on individual serving plates; top each with vegetables and turkey. Drizzle with remaining ¼ cup vinaigrette dressing; sprinkle with bacon.

HIGH ALTITUDE (3500-6000 FT.): Cook bacon in closed grill 7 to 9 minutes. Continue as directed above.

Nutrition Information Per Serving:
Serving Size: 1/2 of Recipe

Calories:	380	From Fat:	220
Total Fat			25g
Saturated			4g
Cholesterol			80mg
Sodium			650mg
Total Carbohydrate			10g
Dietary Fiber			4g
Sugars			5g
Protein			31g

Spicy Broccoli–Mango Salad

Pillsbury
Bake-Off

DEBORAH PHINNEY | LAKEWOOD, OHIO

PREP TIME:	25 MINUTES (READY IN 25 MINUTES)
SERVINGS:	6 (1 CUP EACH)

 EASY

SWEET-HOT PECANS

4 teaspoons sugar

¼ to ½ teaspoon ground red pepper (cayenne)

½ cup pecan halves, broken into coarse pieces

DRESSING

2 containers (6 oz. each) Yoplait® Original 99% Fat Free Orange Crème Yogurt

⅓ cup light mayonnaise

1 tablespoon cider vinegar

⅛ teaspoon salt

SALAD

5 cups fresh broccoli florets and cut-up stems (1 small bunch)

1½ cups diced peeled seeded mango (2 medium)

¼ cup finely chopped red onion

1) Lightly spray 8-inch skillet with cooking spray. Add sugar and ground red pepper; mix well. Stir in pecans. Cook over low heat, stirring occasionally, until sugar mixture is melted and pecans are coated. Remove from heat; set aside to cool.

2) In small bowl, mix all dressing ingredients with wire whisk until smooth. In large bowl, mix all salad ingredients.

3) Add dressing to salad; toss gently to mix. Just before serving, stir in cooled pecans. Store in refrigerator.

HIGH ALTITUDE (3500-6500 FT.): No change.

Nutrition Information Per Serving:
Serving Size: 1 Cup

Calories:	250	From Fat:	110
Total Fat			12g
Saturated			2g
Cholesterol			5mg
Sodium			190mg
Total Carbohydrate			29g
Dietary Fiber			4g
Sugars			22g
Protein			6g

tip

If you can't find fresh mangoes, substitute 1½ cups fresh peaches or frozen peaches thawed.

Tortellini-Spinach Salad

PREP TIME: 40 MINUTES
SERVINGS: 6 (1-1/3 CUPS EACH)

1 (9-oz.) pkg. refrigerated cheese-filled tortellini

1 medium yellow bell pepper, coarsely chopped (about 1 cup)

14 cherry tomatoes, cut in half

½ cup pitted kalamata olives

1 (10-oz.) pkg. prewashed fresh baby spinach (about 8 cups)

¾ cup purchased Italian salad dressing

1 oz. (¼ cup) shredded fresh Parmesan cheese

Nutrition Information Per Serving:
Serving Size: 1-1/3 Cups

Calories:	255	From Fat:	160
Total Fat			18g
Saturated			3g
Cholesterol			45mg
Sodium			520mg
Total Carbohydrate			16g
Dietary Fiber			2g
Sugars			6g
Protein			7g

1) Cook tortellini as directed on package. Drain. Rinse with cold water to cool; drain well.

2) Meanwhile, in large serving bowl, combine bell pepper, tomatoes, olives and spinach.

3) Add cooked tortellini to vegetable mixture. Pour dressing over salad; toss gently to coat. Sprinkle with cheese.

HIGH ALTITUDE (ABOVE 3500 FT.): No change.

Garden Bean and Onion Salad

PREP TIME: 25 MINUTES (READY IN 1 HOUR 25 MINUTES)
SERVINGS: 6 (1/2 CUP EACH)

SALAD
½ lb. fresh green beans, trimmed

½ lb. fresh yellow wax beans, trimmed

½ cup finely chopped red onion

DRESSING
¼ cup olive oil

1 tablespoon balsamic vinegar

1 teaspoon sugar

2 teaspoons Dijon mustard

½ teaspoon salt

½ teaspoon coarsely ground black pepper

Nutrition Information Per Serving:
Serving Size: 1/2 Cup

Calories:	110	From Fat:	80
Total Fat			9g
Saturated			1g
Cholesterol			0mg
Sodium			240mg
Total Carbohydrate			6g
Dietary Fiber			2g
Sugars			3g
Protein			1g

1) If desired, cut beans in half crosswise. Place beans in 2-quart microwave-safe bowl. Add ½ cup water; cover with microwave-safe waxed paper. Microwave on High for 10 to 12 minutes or until crisp-tender. Drain. Rinse with cold water to cool; drain well.

2) Meanwhile, in medium bowl, combine all dressing ingredients; mix well.

3) Add beans and onion to dressing; toss to coat. Cover; refrigerate at least 1 hour before serving to blend flavors.

HIGH ALTITUDE (ABOVE 3500 FT.): Cut beans in half crosswise.

Santa Fe Nectarine Salad

PREP TIME:	15 MINUTES
SERVINGS:	6 (1 CUP EACH)

EASY

DRESSING

- ½ cup peach preserves
- ¼ cup lime juice
- 2 tablespoons oil
- ¼ teaspoon ground ginger
- ¼ teaspoon salt

SALAD

- 2 cups purchased finely shredded coleslaw blend (from 16-oz. pkg.)
- 2 cups purchased torn mixed romaine and leaf lettuce (from 10-oz. pkg.)
- 2 medium nectarines or peaches, pitted, thinly sliced
- 1 cup seedless red grapes
- 1 to 2 jalapeño chiles, finely chopped, if desired
- 2 tablespoons chopped fresh cilantro, if desired

1) In small bowl, combine all dressing ingredients; mix well.

2) In large bowl, combine all salad ingredients. Just before serving, add dressing; toss gently to mix.

HIGH ALTITUDE (ABOVE 3500 FT.): No change.

Nutrition Information Per Serving:
Serving Size: 1 Cup

Calories:	175	From Fat:	45
Total Fat			5g
Saturated			1g
Cholesterol			0mg
Sodium			115mg
Total Carbohydrate			31g
Dietary Fiber			2g
Sugars			23g
Protein			1g

PREP TIME: 15 MINUTES
SERVINGS: 4 (2 CUPS EACH)   **e** EASY **f** LOW FAT

½ lb. extra-lean (at least 90%) ground beef

½ teaspoon peppered seasoned salt

1 (15-oz.) can Green Giant® Three Bean Salad, drained, reserving 2 tablespoons liquid

1 cup cherry tomatoes, halved

½ cup purchased light Italian salad dressing

4 cups (about 6½ oz.) torn mixed salad greens

2 tablespoons finely chopped red onion

1) In 10-inch nonstick skillet, break up ground beef; sprinkle with peppered seasoned salt. Cook over medium-high heat for 5 to 7 minutes or until beef is thoroughly cooked, stirring frequently. Drain.

2) Stir in bean salad, reserved 2 tablespoons liquid from salad, the tomatoes and salad dressing.

3) Arrange salad greens in 2-quart shallow serving bowl or on individual plates. Spoon beef mixture over greens; sprinkle with onion.

HIGH ALTITUDE (ABOVE 3500 FT.): No change

Pick up some fresh sourdough bread at the bakery to slice and serve with this tasty salad.

Nutrition Information Per Serving:
Serving Size: 2 Cups

Calories:	210	From Fat:	65
Total Fat			7g
Saturated			2g
Cholesterol			35mg
Sodium			830mg
Total Carbohydrate			20g
Dietary Fiber			4g
Sugars			8g
Protein			17g

Rice Salad with Toasted Pecans

PREP TIME: 25 MINUTES   (READY IN 4 HOURS 25 MINUTES)
SERVINGS: 8 (2/3 CUP EACH)

2 boxes (10 oz. each) Green Giant® frozen white & wild rice (with green beans)

1 cup chopped celery (2 to 3 stalks)

1/3 cup sliced green onions (5 to 6 medium)

1 can (11 oz.) mandarin orange segments, drained

1 container (6 oz.) Yoplait® Original 99% Fat Free mandarin orange yogurt

1/2 cup coarsely chopped pecans

1 tablespoon butter or margarine

Nutrition Information Per Serving:
Serving Size: 2/3 Cup

Calories:	180	From Fat:	70
Total Fat			8g
Saturated			1.5g
Cholesterol			0mg
Sodium			400mg
Total Carbohydrate			25g
Dietary Fiber			2g
Sugars			10g
Protein			3g

1) Microwave rice as directed on box; place in large serving bowl. Cool 15 minutes.

2) Add celery, onions and mandarin orange segments to cooled rice; mix lightly. Add yogurt; stir gently just until coated. Cover; refrigerate at least 4 hours or until thoroughly chilled.

3) Meanwhile, in 8-inch skillet, cook pecans in butter over medium heat about 4 minutes, stirring occasionally, until toasted and browned; set aside.

4) Before serving, stir toasted pecans into salad.

HIGH ALTITUDE (3500-6500 FT.): No change.

Southwestern Caesar Salad With Chicken

PREP TIME: 10 MINUTES
SERVINGS: 4 (2 CUPS EACH)   ⊖ EASY

DRESSING
1/2 cup purchased Caesar salad dressing

2 teaspoons Old El Paso® Taco Seasoning Mix (from 1.25-oz. pkg.)

SALAD
1 (10-oz.) pkg. chopped romaine lettuce (about 9 cups)

1/2 cup croutons

1 oz. (1/4 cup) shredded fresh Parmesan cheese

1 (9-oz.) pkg. frozen cooked chicken breast strips, thawed

Nutrition Information Per Serving:
Serving Size: 2 Cups

Calories:	270	From Fat:	145
Total Fat			16g
Saturated			4g
Cholesterol			70mg
Sodium			770mg
Total Carbohydrate			7g
Dietary Fiber			1g
Sugars			3g
Protein			25g

1) In small bowl, combine dressing ingredients; mix well.

2) In large bowl, combine lettuce, croutons and cheese; toss to mix. Add dressing; mix well.

3) Divide lettuce mixture evenly onto individual serving plates. Top each evenly with chicken. If desired, sprinkle with additional shredded Parmesan cheese.

HIGH ALTITUDE (ABOVE 3500 FT.): No change.

Fennel Slaw

| PREP TIME: | 20 MINUTES | EASY |
| SERVINGS: | 4 (3/4 CUP EACH) | |

1 large bulb fennel with greens (about 13 oz.)

1 medium red apple, unpeeled, finely chopped (1 cup)

1 small carrot, shredded (about 1/3 cup)

1/2 cup dried cherries or cranberries

1/2 cup refrigerated coleslaw salad dressing

1) Cut outer stalks and feathery greens from fennel bulb; chop feathery greens to make 2 tablespoons and set aside. Cut bulb into quarters; cut core from each quarter and discard. Thinly slice bulb quarters crosswise into shreds. Reserve outer stalks and any remaining greens for a future use or discard.

2) In medium bowl, combine shredded fennel, reserved fennel greens, apple, carrot and cherries.

3) Pour salad dressing over salad; toss gently to coat. Serve immediately, or cover and refrigerate until serving time.

HIGH ALTITUDE (ABOVE 3500 FT.): No change.

Nutrition Information Per Serving:
Serving Size: 3/4 Cup

Calories:	225	From Fat:	100
Total Fat			11g
Saturated			2g
Cholesterol			15mg
Sodium			450mg
Total Carbohydrate			30g
Dietary Fiber			3g
Sugars			24g
Protein			1g

Cucumber and Tomato Salad Caprese

PREP TIME: 20 MINUTES EASY
SERVINGS: 6

1 large red tomato, sliced

1 large yellow tomato, sliced

1 medium cucumber, sliced

8 oz. fresh mozzarella cheese, sliced

2 tablespoons extra-virgin olive oil

1 tablespoon lemon juice

⅛ teaspoon salt

⅛ teaspoon freshly ground black pepper

⅓ cup coarsely chopped fresh basil or lemon basil

Nutrition Information Per Serving:
Serving Size: 1/6 of Recipe

Calories:	165	From Fat:	100
Total Fat			11g
Saturated			5g
Cholesterol			20mg
Sodium			260mg
Total Carbohydrate			5g
Dietary Fiber			1g
Sugars			3g
Protein			11g

1) On large serving platter, arrange slices of tomatoes, cucumber and mozzarella cheese overlapping in a single layer.

2) In small bowl, combine oil, lemon juice, salt and pepper; mix well. Drizzle over salad. Sprinkle with basil.

HIGH ALTITUDE (ABOVE 3500 FT.): No change.

Grilled Chicken Summer Salad

PREP TIME: 30 MINUTES EASY
SERVINGS: 8 (2 CUPS EACH)

8 boneless skinless chicken breast halves

½ teaspoon salt

½ teaspoon pepper

8 cups salad greens (from 10-oz. pkg.)

2 medium nectarines, pitted, sliced (about 1½ cups)

1 red onion, thinly sliced

1 cup pecan halves, toasted

½ cup fresh blueberries

1 cup purchased raspberry-poppy seed or poppy seed salad dressing

Nutrition Information Per Serving:
Serving Size: 2 Cups

Calories:	400	From Fat:	215
Total Fat			24g
Saturated			3g
Cholesterol			70mg
Sodium			290mg
Total Carbohydrate			19g
Dietary Fiber			4g
Sugars			11g
Protein			27g

1) Heat gas or charcoal grill. When grill is heated, sprinkle both sides of chicken with salt and pepper; place on gas grill over medium heat or on charcoal grill 4 to 6 inches from medium coals. Cook 10 to 15 minutes or until chicken is fork-tender and juices run clear, turning once.

2) Divide salad greens evenly onto individual serving plates. Top each with nectarines, onion, pecans and blueberries.

3) Cut chicken into slices; arrange in center of each plate. Drizzle each with 2 tablespoons salad dressing.

HIGH ALTITUDE (ABOVE 3500 FT.): Cook chicken on grill over medium heat.

Chile Taco Salad

| PREP TIME: | 15 MINUTES |
| SERVINGS: | 4 (3 CUPS EACH) |

⊖ EASY 🍴 LOW FAT

½ cup Old El Paso® Thick 'n Chunky Salsa

½ cup chili sauce

1 teaspoon cumin

1 teaspoon chili powder

1 lb. extra-lean (at least 90%) ground beef

½ teaspoon garlic salt

1 (11-oz.) can Green Giant® Mexicorn® Whole Kernel Corn, Red and Green Peppers

1 (10-oz.) pkg. (6 cups) torn mixed salad greens

1 medium tomato, chopped (½ cup)

1 cup small corn chips

1) In small bowl, combine salsa, chili sauce, cumin and chili powder; mix well. Set aside.

2) In 12-inch nonstick skillet, break up ground beef; sprinkle with garlic salt. Cook over medium-high heat for 5 to 7 minutes or until beef is thoroughly cooked, stirring frequently. Drain.

3) Add corn and ¼ cup of the salsa mixture; cook and stir 1 minute.

4) On individual serving plates, layer salad greens, beef mixture and tomato. Drizzle with some of the salsa mixture; sprinkle each serving with ¼ cup corn chips. Drizzle with remaining salsa mixture.

HIGH ALTITUDE (ABOVE 3500 FT.): No change.

Nutrition Information Per Serving:
Serving Size: 3 Cups

Calories:	315	From Fat:	80
Total Fat			9g
Saturated			3g
Cholesterol			70mg
Sodium			790mg
Total Carbohydrate			33g
Dietary Fiber			5g
Sugars			13g
Protein			31g

Texas Two-Step Slaw

BETTY SCHROEDL | JEFFERSON, WISCONSIN

PREP TIME: 15 MINUTES (READY IN 2 HOURS)
SERVINGS: 8

SALAD

- 4 cups shredded green cabbage
- 1 cup shredded red cabbage
- ¼ cup chopped red onion
- 2 jalapeño chiles, seeded, finely chopped*
- 2 tablespoons chopped fresh cilantro
- 1 can (11 oz.) Green Giant® Mexicorn® whole kernel corn with red and green peppers, drained
- 1 cup shredded Cheddar cheese (4 oz.)
- Fresh cilantro sprigs

DRESSING

- ¾ cup ranch dressing
- 1 tablespoon fresh lime juice
- 1 teaspoon ground cumin

Nutrition Information Per Serving:
Serving Size: 1/8 of Recipe

Calories:	210	From Fat:	150
Total Fat			16g
Saturated			5g
Cholesterol			20mg
Sodium			400mg
Total Carbohydrate			12g
Dietary Fiber			2g
Sugars			5g
Protein			6g

1) In large bowl, mix salad ingredients.

2) In small bowl, mix dressing ingredients until well blended. Pour dressing over salad; toss to coat. Cover; refrigerate at least 2 hours or overnight to blend flavors. Before serving, garnish with fresh cilantro sprigs.

*NOTE: When handling jalapeño chiles, wear plastic or rubber gloves, or cover hands with plastic wrap to protect hands. Do not touch face or eyes.

HIGH ALTITUDE (3500-6500 FT.): No change.

Speedy Honey-Lime Fruit Salad

PREP TIME: 5 MINUTES (READY IN 5 MINUTES)
SERVINGS: 8 (1 CUP EACH)

 EASY

- ½ cup refrigerated coleslaw dressing
- 3 tablespoons honey
- 1 teaspoon grated lime peel
- 1½ teaspoons fresh lime juice
- 2 quarts (8 cups) fresh fruit salad (from deli)

Nutrition Information Per Serving:
Serving Size: 1 Cup

Calories:	205	From Fat:	70
Total Fat			8g
Saturated			1g
Cholesterol			5mg
Sodium			85mg
Total Carbohydrate			32g
Dietary Fiber			3g
Sugars			29g
Protein			1g

1) In small bowl, mix coleslaw dressing, honey, lime peel and lime juice until well blended.

2) Just before serving, in large serving bowl, gently mix fruit salad and dressing mixture to coat.

HIGH ALTITUDE (3500-6000 FT.): No change.

Asian Cucumber-Zucchini Salad

PREP TIME: 15 MINUTES
SERVINGS: 5 (1/2 CUP EACH)

 EASY LOW FAT

1 tablespoon sesame seed

1 medium seedless cucumber

1 medium zucchini

2 tablespoons soy sauce

1 tablespoon rice vinegar

½ teaspoon sugar

1) Spread sesame seed in 8-inch skillet; cook and stir over medium-low heat for about 5 minutes or until golden brown, stirring constantly. Remove seed from skillet; set aside.

2) Quarter cucumber and zucchini lengthwise; cut into ½-inch thick slices.

3) In small bowl, combine soy sauce, vinegar and sugar; mix well. Add cucumbers and zucchini; toss gently until well coated. Sprinkle with sesame seed.

HIGH ALTITUDE (ABOVE 3500 FT.): No change.

Nutrition Information Per Serving:
Serving Size: 1/2 Cup

Calories: 35	From Fat: 10
Total Fat	1g
Saturated	0g
Cholesterol	0mg
Sodium	470mg
Total Carbohydrate	5g
Dietary Fiber	1g
Sugars	2g
Protein	2g

This light Asian salad tastes great served with julienne carrots and sliced roast beef.

Pesto-Chicken-Potato Salad

PREP TIME: 20 MINUTES (READY IN 2 HOURS 35 MINUTES)
SERVINGS: 6 (1-1/2 CUPS EACH)

- 2 lb. Yukon Gold potatoes (about 6 medium), cut into ³⁄₄-inch cubes (6 cups)
- 1 (7-oz.) container refrigerated pesto
- ½ cup mayonnaise
- 2 tablespoons cider vinegar
- 2 teaspoons Dijon mustard
- ³⁄₄ teaspoon salt
- 2 cups chopped deli rotisserie-cooked chicken (without skin)
- 1 cup sliced celery (2 medium stalks)
- ½ cup sliced green onions (8 medium)
- 2 medium tomatoes, chopped (1 cup)
- Boston leaf lettuce, if desired

1) In 3½-quart saucepan, combine potatoes and enough water to cover potatoes by 1 inch. Bring to a boil over medium-high heat. Reduce heat to medium; cover and cook 10 to 15 minutes or until tender. Drain; cool 15 minutes or until slightly cooled.

2) Meanwhile, in large serving bowl, combine pesto, mayonnaise, vinegar, mustard and salt; mix well.

3) Add cooked potatoes and all remaining ingredients except lettuce to pesto mixture; toss gently until evenly coated. Cover; refrigerate at least 2 hours or overnight to blend flavors. If desired, serve salad on lettuce-lined plates.

HIGH ALTITUDE (ABOVE 3500 FT.): No change.

Nutrition Information Per Serving:
Serving Size: 1-1/2 Cups

Calories:	515	From Fat:	325
Total Fat			36g
Saturated			7g
Cholesterol			55mg
Sodium			880mg
Total Carbohydrate			33g
Dietary Fiber			5g
Sugars			4g
Protein			20g

Fiesta Chicken Taco Salad

PREP TIME: 10 MINUTES
SERVINGS: 4 (2-1/4 CUPS EACH)

 EASY

DRESSING

- ²/₃ cup French salad dressing
- ²/₃ cup Old El Paso® Thick 'n Chunky Salsa
- 1 tablespoon Old El Paso® taco seasoning mix (from 1.25 oz. package)

SALAD

- 1 (10-oz.) pkg. chopped romaine lettuce (about 9 cups)
- 1 (9-oz.) pkg. frozen cooked chicken breast strips, thawed
- 2 cups (4 oz.) crushed taco-flavored tortilla chips
- 4 oz. (1 cup) shredded Cheddar cheese
- 2 medium tomatoes, cut into wedges or diced
- 1 (2¼-oz.) can sliced ripe olives, drained
- ½ cup sour cream

   Taco-flavored tortilla chips, if desired

1) In small bowl, combine dressing ingredients; blend well.

2) In large bowl, combine lettuce, chicken, crushed tortilla chips, cheese, tomatoes and olives.

3) Pour dressing over salad; toss gently to coat.

4) Divide salad evenly onto individual serving plates; top each with a dollop of sour cream. Arrange tortilla chips around edge of each plate, if desired.

Nutrition Information Per Serving:
Serving Size: 2-1/4 Cups

Calories: 650	From Fat: 360

Total Fat	40g
Saturated	13g
Cholesterol	105mg
Sodium	1580mg
Total Carbohydrate	39g
Dietary Fiber	5g
Sugars	16g
Protein	33g

Pilgrim Corn Salad

MARGO SCOFIELD | FAIR OAKS, CALIFORNIA

e EASY

PREP TIME: 10 MINUTES (READY IN 20 MINUTES)
SERVINGS: 8 (1/2 CUP EACH)

2 cans (11 oz. each) Green Giant® white shoepeg corn, drained

¾ cup sweetened dried cranberries

¼ cup chopped pecans

2 tablespoons balsamic vinegar

2 tablespoons olive oil

1 tablespoon apricot preserves

1 teaspoon Dijon mustard

1 teaspoon Worcestershire sauce

2 tablespoons finely chopped fresh basil

Fresh basil sprigs

8 pecan halves

Nutrition Information Per Serving:
Serving Size: 1/2 Cup

Calories:	170	From Fat:	70
Total Fat			8g
Saturated			1g
Cholesterol			0mg
Sodium			180mg
Total Carbohydrate			25g
Dietary Fiber			3g
Sugars			12g
Protein			2g

1) In medium bowl, mix corn, cranberries and chopped pecans.

2) In small bowl with wire whisk, mix vinegar, oil, preserves, mustard and Worcestershire sauce until smooth. Add vinegar mixture and chopped basil to corn mixture; toss to coat well. Let stand at room temperature 10 minutes to blend flavors.

3) Gently stir salad before serving; garnish with basil sprigs and pecan halves.

HIGH ALTITUDE (3500-6500 FT.): No change.

Veggie Thai Noodle Salad

PREP TIME: 30 MINUTES (READY IN 30 MINUTES)
SERVINGS: 8 (3/4 CUP EACH)

e EASY

1 package (7 oz.) vermicelli, broken in half

1 medium carrot, shredded

1 cup sliced quartered cucumber

1 cup coarsely chopped red bell pepper

⅓ cup sliced green onions

¼ cup chopped fresh cilantro

½ cup Thai peanut stir-fry and dipping sauce

Nutrition Information Per Serving:
Serving Size: 3/4 Cup

Calories:	150	From Fat:	40
Total Fat			4.5g
Saturated			1g
Cholesterol			0mg
Sodium			135mg
Total Carbohydrate			23g
Dietary Fiber			3g
Sugars			3g
Protein			6g

1) Cook vermicelli as directed on package. Drain in colander or strainer; rinse with cold water until cold. Drain well.

2) In large bowl, toss drained cold vermicelli and all remaining ingredients to coat evenly with sauce.

HIGH ALTITUDE (3500-6500 FT.): No change.

Turkey Clubhouse Salad

PREP TIME: 15 MINUTES   **e** EASY   **f** LOW FAT
SERVINGS: 6

DRESSING

- $\frac{1}{3}$ cup chopped fresh chives
- $\frac{1}{3}$ cup light mayonnaise
- $\frac{1}{3}$ cup buttermilk
- $\frac{1}{4}$ teaspoon salt
- $\frac{1}{8}$ teaspoon pepper

SALAD

- 6 slices purchased precooked bacon or $\frac{1}{4}$ cup real bacon pieces
- 1 (10-oz.) pkg. chopped romaine lettuce (about 9 cups)
- 1$\frac{1}{2}$ cups cubed cooked turkey breast (about $\frac{1}{2}$ lb.)
- 2 medium tomatoes, cut into thin wedges

1) In small bowl, combine all dressing ingredients; mix well. Set aside.

2) If using bacon slices, heat as directed on package until crisp. Drain on paper towels; crumble.

3) In large bowl, combine lettuce and turkey. Pour dressing over salad; toss gently to coat. Arrange salad on serving platter. Arrange tomatoes and bacon over top.

HIGH ALTITUDE (ABOVE 3500 FT.):
No change.

Nutrition Information Per Serving:
Serving Size: 1/6 of Recipe

Calories:	165	From Fat:	80
Total Fat			9g
Saturated			2g
Cholesterol			40mg
Sodium			430mg
Total Carbohydrate			7g
Dietary Fiber			1g
Sugars			4g
Protein			14g

tip

If you don't have buttermilk on hand, replace it with 1 teaspoon vinegar mixed with $\frac{1}{3}$ cup milk.

Layered Caribbean Chicken Salad

BARBARA JANSKY | ESTERO, FLORIDA

PREP TIME: 30 MINUTES (READY IN 30 MINUTES)
SERVINGS: 6 (1-1/2 CUPS EACH)

 EASY

DRESSING

1 (6-oz.) container Yoplait® Original 99% Fat Free Piña Colada Yogurt

1½ to 2 tablespoons lime juice

1 teaspoon Caribbean jerk seasoning

SALAD

3 cups shredded romaine lettuce

2 cups cubed cooked chicken

4 oz. (1 cup) shredded Monterey Jack cheese

1 (15-oz.) can Progresso® Black Beans, drained, rinsed

1½ cups diced peeled ripe fresh mango

½ cup chopped seeded Italian plum tomatoes (1 to 2 medium)

4 oz. (1 cup) shredded Cheddar cheese

½ cup thinly sliced green onions (8 medium)

½ cup cashews

Fresh edible flowers, if desired

1) In small bowl, mix all dressing ingredients until well blended.

2) In 3- or 4-quart clear glass serving bowl, layer all salad ingredients in order listed, except cashews and flowers. Spoon dressing evenly over salad; sprinkle cashews over top. Garnish with flowers.

HIGH ALTITUDE (ABOVE 3500 FT.): No change.

Nutrition Information Per Serving:
Serving Size: 1-1/2 Cups

Calories:	450	From Fat:	190
Total Fat			21g
Saturated			10g
Cholesterol			80mg
Sodium			630mg
Total Carbohydrate			37g
Dietary Fiber			7g
Sugars			15g
Protein			33g

If you don't have cashews, you can substitute almonds or pine nuts in this salad.

Asian Noodle-Chicken Salad

PREP TIME: 10 MINUTES
SERVINGS: 5 (1-1/4 CUPS EACH)

 EASY   LOW FAT

1 (16-oz.) pkg. 3-color coleslaw blend

2 tablespoons sliced green onions

1 (9-oz.) pkg. frozen cooked chicken breast strips, thawed

⅓ cup purchased citrus-flavored vinaigrette dressing

1 (3-oz.) pkg. chicken or oriental-flavor ramen noodle soup mix

1) In large bowl, combine coleslaw blend, onions, chicken and salad dressing.

2) Discard seasoning packet from soup mix; coarsely crush noodles. Add noodles to salad; stir gently to mix. Serve immediately.

HIGH ALTITUDE (ABOVE 3500 FT.): No change.

Nutrition Information Per Serving:
Serving Size: 1-1/4 Cups

Calories:	210	From Fat:	55
Total Fat			6g
Saturated			2g
Cholesterol			45mg
Sodium			420mg
Total Carbohydrate			20g
Dietary Fiber			2g
Sugars			7g
Protein			19g

Spinach and Cabbage Slaw

PREP TIME:	10 MINUTES (READY IN 25 MINUTES)
SERVINGS:	6 (1/2 CUP EACH)

 EASY　　LOW FAT

2　cups coleslaw blend (from 1-lb. bag)

2　cups torn fresh spinach leaves

½　cup thin bite-size strips red bell pepper

¼　cup light ranch salad dressing

¼　teaspoon dried dill weed

In large bowl, toss all salad ingredients. Refrigerate at least 15 minutes to blend flavors.

HIGH ALTITUDE (ABOVE 3500 FT.): No change.

Nutrition Information Per Serving:
Serving Size: 1/2 Cup

Calories:	35	From Fat:	20
Total Fat			2g
Saturated			0g
Cholesterol			0mg
Sodium			115mg
Total Carbohydrate			3g
Dietary Fiber			0g
Sugars			2g
Protein			1g

Beef Garden Salad with Tangy Vinaigrette

PREP TIME:	20 MINUTES
SERVINGS:	4 (2 CUPS EACH)

 EASY

SALAD

4　cups mixed salad greens

½　cup sliced seedless cucumber

⅓　cup sliced red onion, separated into rings

2　medium tomatoes, cut into wedges

1　medium green bell pepper, cut into thin bite-sized strips

1　(9-oz.) pkg. frozen cooked seasoned beef strips, thawed

DRESSING

¼　cup olive oil

2　tablespoons white balsamic vinegar

1　tablespoon lime juice

½　teaspoon sugar

¼　teaspoon dry mustard

1　garlic clove, minced

Nutrition Information Per Serving:
Serving Size: 2 Cups

Calories:	270	From Fat:	160
Total Fat			18g
Saturated			3g
Cholesterol			40mg
Sodium			340mg
Total Carbohydrate			10g
Dietary Fiber			2g
Sugars			5g
Protein			17g

1) In large bowl, combine all salad ingredients except beef strips.

2) In small bowl, combine all dressing ingredients; mix well.

3) Pour dressing over salad; toss gently to coat. Divide salad evenly onto individual serving plates. Top each evenly with beef strips.

HIGH ALTITUDE (ABOVE 3500 FT.): No change.

Salmon-Apple Salad

| PREP TIME: | 20 MINUTES |
| SERVINGS: | 4 (1-3/4 CUPS EACH) |

 EASY

SALAD

- 2 (4.5-oz.) pkg. smoked salmon, skin removed, broken into bite-sized pieces
- 1 medium green apple, unpeeled, chopped (1 cup)
- 1 medium seedless cucumber, unpeeled, chopped (1 cup)
- ¼ cup chopped red onion
- 4 cups mixed salad greens

DRESSING

- 2 tablespoons sour cream
- 2 tablespoons mayonnaise
- 1 tablespoon cider vinegar
- 1 teaspoon Dijon mustard
- ½ teaspoon sugar
- ⅛ teaspoon white pepper
- ¼ cup whipping cream, whipped

1) In medium bowl, combine all salad ingredients except salad greens; stir gently to mix.

2) In small bowl, combine all dressing ingredients except whipped cream; mix well. Gently fold in whipped cream until well blended.

3) Pour dressing over salad mixture; toss gently to coat. Divide salad greens evenly onto individual serving plates. Spoon salmon mixture evenly onto greens. If desired, garnish with edible flowers.

HIGH ALTITUDE (ABOVE 3500 FT.): No change.

Nutrition Information Per Serving:
Serving Size: 1-3/4 Cups

Calories:	230	From Fat:	135
Total Fat			15g
Saturated			5g
Cholesterol			40mg
Sodium			590mg
Total Carbohydrate			10g
Dietary Fiber			2g
Sugars			7g
Protein			14g

Spicy Chicken and Bow Tie Pasta Salad

PREP TIME: 25 MINUTES
SERVINGS: 5 (1-1/3 CUPS EACH)

 EASY

8 oz. (3½ cups) uncooked bow tie pasta (farfalle)

1 cup mayonnaise

1 (4.5-oz.) can Old El Paso® Chopped Green Chiles

1 (9-oz.) pkg. frozen southwestern-flavored cooked chicken breast strips, thawed, cut into bite-sized pieces

2 medium tomatoes, chopped (1 cup)

1 medium red bell pepper, chopped (1 cup)

2 oz. (½ cup) shredded taco-flavored cheese blend

3 medium green onions, sliced (about ¼ cup)

Nutrition Information Per Serving:
Serving Size: 1-1/3 Cups

Calories: 655	From Fat:	380
Total Fat		42g
Saturated		8g
Cholesterol		80mg
Sodium		830mg
Total Carbohydrate		43g
Dietary Fiber		3g
Sugars		7g
Protein		26g

1) Cook pasta as directed on package. Drain. Rinse with cold water to cool; drain well.

2) Meanwhile, in large serving bowl, combine mayonnaise and green chiles; mix well. Add chicken, tomatoes, bell pepper and cheese.

3) Add cooked pasta to chicken mixture; toss gently to coat. Serve immediately, or cover and refrigerate until serving time. Sprinkle with green onions.

HIGH ALTITUDE (ABOVE 3500 FT.): No change.

Tortellini Toss Salad

PREP TIME: 15 MINUTES
SERVINGS: 2 (1-1/2 CUPS EACH)

 EASY

6 oz. (1¼ cups) frozen uncooked tortellini

6 cherry tomatoes, halved

¼ cup sliced green onions

1 (6 oz.) jar marinated artichoke hearts, drained, cut up

¼ cup purchased creamy Italian dressing

Nutrition Information Per Serving:
Serving Size: 1-1/2 Cups

Calories: 430	From Fat:	180
Total Fat		20g
Saturated		5g
Cholesterol		25mg
Sodium		630mg
Total Carbohydrate		47g
Dietary Fiber		5g
Sugars		9g
Protein		15g

1) Cook tortellini as directed on package. Drain; rinse with cold water until cool.

2) Meanwhile, in medium bowl, mix tomatoes, onions and artichoke hearts. Add cooked tortellini and dressing; toss gently to coat. Serve immediately.

Soups & Sandwiches

Serve your family a hearty soup or
sandwich every day of the week.

CHICKEN SOUP PROVENÇAL
PG. 102

OPEN-FACED VEGGIE BURGER MELTS
PG. 101

CHICKEN AND BROWN RICE SOUP
PG. 111

Ciabatta Ham Sandwiches

PREP TIME:	10 MINUTES	EASY
SERVINGS:	4 SANDWICHES	

- 1 (1-lb.) loaf ciabatta bread
- 3 tablespoons honey-raspberry Dijon mustard
- ¾ lb. sliced cooked Virginia ham (from deli)
- 8 leaves Bibb or Boston lettuce
- ¼ cup thinly sliced red onion

1) Cut bread in half lengthwise. Spread cut side of each half with mustard.

2) On bottom half of bread, layer ham, lettuce and onion. Cover with top half of bread. Cut filled loaf into 4 sandwiches.

HIGH ALTITUDE (ABOVE 3500 FT.): No change.

Nutrition Information Per Serving:
Serving Size: 1 Sandwich

Calories:	490	From Fat:	110
Total Fat			12g
Saturated			4g
Cholesterol			50mg
Sodium			2080mg
Total Carbohydrate			65g
Dietary Fiber			3g
Sugars			7g
Protein			30g

tip

Honey-mustard can be substituted for the honey-raspberry mustard. Or, make your own flavored mustard by adding 1 tablespoon seedless raspberry jam to 2 tablespoons honey-mustard.

Curried Pumpkin-Vegetable Soup

PREP TIME: 20 MINUTES (READY IN 20 MINUTES)
SERVINGS: 4 (1-1/2 CUPS EACH)

 EASY  LOW FAT

1 teaspoon olive oil

1 medium onion, chopped (¹/₂ cup)

1 clove garlic, minced

2 cups Green Giant® frozen mixed vegetables (from 1-lb. bag)

1 can (15 oz.) pumpkin

1 can (14.5 oz.) diced tomatoes, undrained

1 can (14 oz.) fat-free chicken broth with 33% less sodium

¹/₂ cup water

¹/₂ teaspoon sugar

1¹/₂ teaspoons curry powder

1 teaspoon paprika

Nutrition Information Per Serving:
Serving Size: 1-1/2 Cups

Calories:	125	From Fat:	20
Total Fat			2g
Saturated			1g
Cholesterol			0mg
Sodium			400mg
Total Carbohydrate			29g
Dietary Fiber			9g
Sugars			11g
Protein			7g

1) In 3-quart saucepan, heat oil over medium-high heat. Add onion and garlic; cook 1 to 2 minutes, stirring frequently, until onion is crisp-tender.

2) Stir in all remaining ingredients. Heat to boiling. Reduce heat to low; cover and simmer 10 to 12 minutes, stirring occasionally, until vegetables are tender. If desired, season to taste with pepper.

HIGH ALTITUDE (ABOVE 3500 FT.): No change.

Cheesy Barbeque Pork Sandwiches

PREP TIME: 20 MINUTES
SERVINGS: 4 SANDWICHES

 EASY

1 tablespoon butter or margarine

1 medium onion, thinly sliced

1 (18-oz.) tub Lloyd's® Refrigerated Shredded Pork in Honey Hickory Barbeque Sauce

4 (³/₄-oz.) slices pasteurized prepared cheese product, cut in half

4 hoagie buns, split

Nutrition Information Per Serving:
Serving Size: 1 Sandwich

Calories:	595	From Fat:	160
Total Fat			18g
Saturated			8g
Cholesterol			60mg
Sodium			1890mg
Total Carbohydrate			81g
Dietary Fiber			3g
Sugars			33g
Protein			27g

1) Melt butter in medium skillet over medium heat. Add onion; cook 3 to 4 minutes or until onion is tender, stirring frequently. Add pork in barbeque sauce; cook 3 to 4 minutes or until thoroughly heated, stirring frequently.

2) Place hoagie buns, cut side up, on ungreased cookie sheet. Broil 4 to 6 inches from heat for 3 to 4 minutes or until toasted.

3) Spoon pork mixture onto bottom halves of toasted buns. Top with cheese slice. Cover with top halves of buns.

HIGH ALTITUDE (ABOVE 3500 FT.): No change.

Smothered Bistro Burgers

PREP TIME:	20 MINUTES (READY IN 20 MINUTES)
SERVINGS:	2 SANDWICHES

e EASY

1½ cups sliced fresh mushrooms (4 oz.)

1 small onion, thinly sliced

2 tablespoons Worcestershire sauce

½ teaspoon garlic-pepper blend

2 frozen ground beef patties (4 oz. each), thawed

2 slices (about ¾ oz. each) sharp Cheddar cheese

2 sandwich buns, split, toasted if desired

1 to 2 tablespoons creamy mustard-mayonnaise sauce

1) Heat closed contact grill 5 minutes. In medium bowl, mix mushrooms, onion, 1 tablespoon of the Worcestershire sauce and ¼ teaspoon of the garlic-pepper blend.

2) When grill is heated, place mushroom mixture on bottom grill surface. Close grill; cook 3 to 4 minutes or until mushrooms are tender. Remove from grill; cover to keep warm.

3) Brush both sides of beef patties with remaining tablespoon Worcestershire sauce; sprinkle with remaining ¼ teaspoon garlic-pepper blend. Place patties on bottom grill surface. Close grill; cook 4 to 6 minutes or until thoroughly cooked. Top each patty with cheese slice (do not close grill); cook until melted.

4) Spread bottom halves of buns with mustard-mayonnaise sauce. Top each with cheese-topped beef patty, mushroom mixture and top half of bun.

Nutrition Information Per Serving:
Serving Size: 1 Sandwich

Calories:	500	From Fat:	260
Total Fat			28g
Saturated			12g
Cholesterol			90mg
Sodium			640mg
Total Carbohydrate			31g
Dietary Fiber			3g
Sugars			9g
Protein			32g

Make your own creamy mustard-mayonnaise sauce by mixing half Dijon mustard and half mayonnaise.

Vegetable, Bean and Ham Soup

PREP TIME: 20 MINUTES (READY IN 20 HOURS 20 MINUTES)   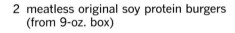 LOW FAT
SERVINGS: 4 (1-1/2 CUPS EACH)

1 cup dried navy beans
(from 16-oz. bag)

1 cup diced cooked ham (about 6 oz.)

1 cup sliced celery
(about 2 medium stalks)

1 cup sliced carrots (about 2 medium)

2 cans (14 oz. each) fat-free chicken
broth with 33% less sodium

3/4 cup water

1/4 teaspoon garlic powder

1/4 teaspoon pepper

2 dried bay leaves

Nutrition Information Per Serving:
Serving Size: 1-1/2 Cups

Calories:	240	From Fat:	35
Total Fat			4g
Saturated			2g
Cholesterol			20mg
Sodium			960 mg
Total Carbohydrate			37g
Dietary Fiber			9g
Sugars			6g
Protein			23g

1) Sort beans; rinse well and drain. Soak beans at least 8 hours or overnight as directed on bag; drain.

2) In 3- to 4-quart slow cooker, mix beans and all remaining ingredients.

3) Cover; cook on Low setting 8 to 12 hours. Before serving, remove and discard bay leaves.

HIGH ALTITUDE (ABOVE 3500 FT.): No change.

Open-Faced Veggie Burger Melts

PREP TIME: 20 MINUTES (READY IN 20 MINUTES)   EASY
SERVINGS: 2 OPEN-FACED SANDWICHES

2 meatless original soy protein burgers
(from 9-oz. box)

4 medium fresh broccoli spears
(about 2 1/2 oz.)

2 slices whole-grain bread, toasted

2 teaspoons sweet honey mustard

2 tomato slices

2 slices Swiss cheese (3/4 oz. each),
cut into 6 strips

Nutrition Information Per Serving:
Serving Size: 1 Open-Faced Sandwich

Calories:	250	From Fat:	90
Total Fat			10g
Saturated			4g
Cholesterol			20mg
Sodium			560mg
Total Carbohydrate			23g
Dietary Fiber			4g
Sugars			6g
Protein			21g

1) Cook frozen protein burgers as directed on box.

2) Meanwhile, in small microwavable bowl, combine broccoli and 1/4 cup water; cover with microwavable plastic wrap. Microwave on High 2 to 3 minutes or until broccoli is crisp-tender. Drain.

3) Place toasted bread slices on ungreased cookie sheet; spread each with mustard. Place protein burgers on bread; top with tomato slices and broccoli. Arrange cheese slices on top of broccoli.

4) Broil 3 to 4 inches from heat 1 to 2 minutes or until cheese is melted.

HIGH ALTITUDE (ABOVE 3500 FT.): No change.

Chicken Soup Provençal

PREP TIME: 15 MINUTES (READY IN 25 MINUTES)   **EASY**   **LOW FAT**
SERVINGS: 2 (2 CUPS EACH)

2 teaspoons olive oil

½ lb. chicken breast strips for stir-frying

½ cup sliced onions or leeks

1 can (14.5 oz.) diced tomatoes with basil, garlic and oregano, undrained

1 can (14 oz.) fat-free chicken broth with ⅓ less sodium

2 oz. angel hair pasta (capellini), broken

Shredded Parmesan cheese, if desired

Nutrition Information Per Serving:
Serving Size: 2 Cups

Calories:	355	From Fat:	80
Total Fat			9g
Saturated			2g
Cholesterol			70mg
Sodium			790mg
Total Carbohydrate			34g
Dietary Fiber			3g
Sugars			6g
Protein			35g

1) In 2-quart saucepan, heat oil over medium-high heat. Add chicken and onions; cook 5 minutes, stirring frequently.

2) Stir in tomatoes and broth. Heat to boiling. Reduce heat to medium-low; simmer uncovered 10 minutes.

3) Stir in pasta. Simmer uncovered 3 to 5 minutes, stirring occasionally, until pasta is tender and chicken is no longer pink in center. Sprinkle individual servings with Parmesan cheese.

Sloppy Joe Burgers

PREP TIME: 30 MINUTES   **EASY**
SERVINGS: 6 SANDWICHES

1½ lb. lean (at least 80%) ground beef

¼ cup ketchup

1 (1.31 to 1.5-oz.) pkg. sloppy Joe seasoning mix

6 (¾-oz.) slices American cheese or American pasteurized prepared cheese product

6 burger buns, split

Nutrition Information Per Serving:
Serving Size: 1 Sandwich

Calories:	440	From Fat:	200
Total Fat			22g
Saturated			10g
Cholesterol			90mg
Sodium			1130mg
Total Carbohydrate			29g
Dietary Fiber			1g
Sugars			11g
Protein			31g

1) Heat gas or charcoal grill. In large bowl, combine ground beef, ketchup and sloppy Joe seasoning mix; mix gently. Shape mixture into 6 patties, ½ inch thick.

2) When grill is heated, carefully oil grill rack. Place patties on gas grill over medium heat or on charcoal grill 4 to 6 inches from medium coals. Cover grill; cook 13 to 15 minutes or until meat thermometer inserted in center of patties reads 160°F., turning once. During last 1 to 2 minutes of cooking time, place cheese on patties; cook until melted. Serve patties in buns.

*NOTE: To broil patties, place on broiler pan; broil 3 to 4 inches from heat for 10 to 12 minutes or until meat thermometer inserted in center of patties reads 160°F., turning once. During last 30 to 60 seconds of broiling time, place cheese on patties; broil until melted.

HIGH ALTITUDE (ABOVE 3500 FT.): Cook on grill over medium-low heat.

Chicken BLT Sandwiches

| PREP TIME: | 20 MINUTES (READY IN 20 MINUTES) | EASY |
| SERVINGS: | 2 SANDWICHES | |

4 slices bacon

2 boneless skinless chicken breasts

½ teaspoon dried Italian seasoning

4 slices sourdough or Vienna bread, toasted

2 tablespoons mayonnaise

2 lettuce leaves

1 small tomato, sliced

tip

Add a spark of flavor to these BLTs by using a flavored mayo. Chipotle chile and sun-dried tomato are two of the fun flavors available.

1) Heat closed contact grill 5 minutes. When grill is heated, place bacon on bottom grill surface. Close grill; cook 4 to 6 minutes, turning once, until crisp. Drain on paper towels.

2) Meanwhile, place 1 chicken breast, boned side up, between 2 sheets of plastic wrap or waxed paper. With flat side of meat mallet or rolling pin and working from center, gently pound chicken until ¼ inch thick; remove wrap. Repeat with remaining chicken breast. Sprinkle chicken with Italian seasoning.

3) Place chicken on bottom grill surface. Close grill; cook 4 to 6 minutes or until fork-tender and juices run clear.

4) Spread toasted bread slices with mayonnaise. Layer lettuce, tomato, chicken and bacon between toast slices.

HIGH ALTITUDE (3500-6000 FT.): Cook bacon in closed grill 7 to 11 minutes. Continue as directed above.

Nutrition Information Per Serving:
Serving Size: 1 Sandwich

Calories:	490	From Fat:	210
Total Fat			23g
Saturated			6g
Cholesterol			90mg
Sodium			730mg
Total Carbohydrate			35g
Dietary Fiber			2g
Sugars			2g
Protein			37g

Chicken-Tortellini Soup

PREP TIME: 1 HOUR 20 MINUTES (READY IN 1 HOUR 20 MINUTES)
SERVINGS: 10 (1-1/2 CUPS EACH)

 LOW FAT

1 box (9 oz.) Green Giant® frozen cut broccoli

6 cups water

½ cup dry vermouth or water

3 cans (10½ oz. each) condensed chicken broth

1 can (10¾ oz.) condensed cream of chicken soup

2 cups cubed cooked chicken

1 cup chopped onions (2 medium)

1 cup sliced carrots (2 medium)

½ teaspoon dried basil leaves

½ teaspoon dried oregano leaves

2 cloves garlic, minced

1 package (7 oz.) dry cheese tortellini

¼ cup grated Parmesan cheese, if desired

1) Remove broccoli from freezer; let stand at room temperature to thaw. In 5-quart saucepan or Dutch oven, mix all remaining ingredients except tortellini and cheese. Heat to boiling.

2) Stir in tortellini. Reduce heat; simmer uncovered 30 minutes, stirring occasionally.

3) Stir in thawed broccoli; simmer 5 to 10 minutes longer or until broccoli is crisp-tender. Sprinkle individual servings with cheese.

HIGH ALTITUDE (3500-6000 FT.): No change.

Nutrition Information Per Serving:
Serving Size: 1-1/2 Cups

Calories:	165	From Fat:	65
Total Fat			7g
Saturated			2g
Cholesterol			45mg
Sodium			890mg
Total Carbohydrate			11g
Dietary Fiber			1g
Sugars			2g
Protein			15g

Light Chicken-Wild Rice Soup

| PREP TIME: | 20 MINUTES (READY IN 20 MINUTES) |
| SERVINGS: | 6 (1-1/2 CUPS EACH) |

 EASY **if** LOW FAT

4 slices bacon

3 boneless skinless chicken breast halves, cut into ³⁄₄-inch pieces

1 box (6.2 oz.) quick-cooking long-grain and wild rice mix (with seasoning packet)

2 cans (14 oz. each) fat-free chicken broth with 33% less sodium

4 cups fat-free (skim) milk

³⁄₄ cup all-purpose flour

1¹⁄₂ teaspoons diced pimientos

1 tablespoon dry sherry, if desired

Nutrition Information Per Serving:
Serving Size: 1-1/2 Cups

Calories:	260	From Fat:	50
Total Fat			5g
Saturated			2g
Cholesterol			45mg
Sodium			580mg
Total Carbohydrate			28g
Dietary Fiber			0g
Sugars			8g
Protein			26g

1) Cook bacon until crisp. Drain on paper towel; crumble and set aside.

2) In nonstick Dutch oven or 4-quart saucepan, mix chicken, rice with contents of seasoning packet and broth. Heat to boiling. Reduce heat to low; cover and simmer 5 to 10 minutes or until rice is tender.

3) In small jar with tight-fitting lid, shake 1 cup of the milk and the flour until well blended.

4) Add flour mixture, remaining 3 cups milk, the bacon, pimientos and sherry to rice mixture; cook over medium heat, stirring constantly, until soup is bubbly and thickened and chicken is no longer pink in center. If desired, season to taste with salt and pepper.

HIGH ALTITUDE (ABOVE 3500 FT.): No change.

To round out the meal, serve this soup with tossed salad and breadsticks.

Carolina Reuben Sandwiches

KEVIN DELL | FAIRPORT, NEW YORK

PREP TIME: 30 MINUTES (READY IN 30 MINUTES)
SERVINGS: 4 (1 SANDWICH AND 1 PICKLE EACH)

EASY

¼ cup butter or margarine, softened

8 slices marble rye bread

¼ cup Russian dressing

4 (1-oz.) slices Swiss cheese

1 cup Lloyd's® Refrigerated Original Barbeque Sauce with Shredded Pork (from 18-oz. container)

1 cup creamy coleslaw (from deli)

4 dill pickle spears

Nutrition Information Per Serving:	
Serving Size: 1 Sandwich and Pickle	
Calories: 590	From Fat: 320
Total Fat	36g
Saturated	15g
Cholesterol	80mg
Sodium	1540mg
Total Carbohydrate	49g
Dietary Fiber	5g
Sugars	18g
Protein	20g

1) Spread butter on one side of each slice of bread. Spread other side of each bread slice with Russian dressing.

2) On each of 2 slices of bread, salad dressing side up, layer 1 slice cheese, ¼ cup barbeque sauce with shredded pork and ¼ cup coleslaw. Top with 2 bread slices, salad dressing side down.

3) Heat 12-inch skillet or griddle over medium heat until hot. Cook 2 sandwiches in hot skillet 4 to 8 minutes, turning once, until golden brown. Meanwhile, make remaining 2 sandwiches. Cook remaining 2 sandwiches as directed. Serve hot sandwiches with dill pickle spears.

HIGH ALTITUDE (ABOVE 3500 FT.): No change.

Bean and Barley Vegetable Soup

PREP TIME: 35 MINUTES (READY IN 35 MINUTES)
SERVINGS: 4 (1-3/4 CUPS EACH)

LOW FAT

2 teaspoons olive oil

2 cups ready-to-eat baby-cut carrots, thinly sliced

2 medium celery stalks, thinly sliced (about 1 cup)

1 medium onion, chopped (½ cup)

½ cup uncooked quick-cooking barley

1 can (15.8 oz.) Great Northern beans, drained, rinsed

1 can (14.5 oz.) diced tomatoes with basil, garlic and oregano, undrained

1 can (8 oz.) no-salt-added tomato sauce

2½ cups water

Nutrition Information Per Serving:	
Serving Size: 1-3/4 Cups	
Calories: 310	From Fat: 30
Total Fat	3g
Saturated	1g
Cholesterol	0mg
Sodium	220mg
Total Carbohydrate	66g
Dietary Fiber	16g
Sugars	10g
Protein	16g

1) In 3-quart saucepan, heat oil over medium-high heat. Add carrots, celery and onion; cook 3 minutes, stirring frequently, until vegetables are crisp-tender.

2) Stir in all remaining ingredients. Heat to boiling. Reduce heat to medium; cover and cook 15 to 20 minutes, stirring occasionally, until vegetables and barley are tender.

HIGH ALTITUDE (ABOVE 3500 FT.): Increase water to 3 cups.

Inside-Out Taco Salad Wraps

KAREN HARRIS | CASTLE ROCK, COLORADO

| PREP TIME: | 30 MINUTES (READY IN 30 MINUTES) |
| SERVINGS: | 6 (2 WRAPS AND 4 TABLESPOONS SAUCE EACH) |

e EASY

DIPPING SAUCE

- 1 cup Old El Paso® Thick 'n Chunky Salsa
- ½ cup peach preserves
- ½ teaspoon Liquid Smoke
- ½ teaspoon Worcestershire sauce

WRAPS

- ⅔ cup diced peeled jicama
- 2 teaspoons fresh lime juice
- 1 ripe large avocado, pitted, peeled and coarsely chopped
- 1 (18-oz.) container Old El Paso® Refrigerated Taco Sauce with Seasoned Ground Beef
- 1¾ cups coarsely crushed tortilla chips
- ¼ cup chopped green onions (4 medium)
- 1 (2.25-oz.) can sliced ripe olives, drained
- 2 oz. (½ cup) finely shredded sharp Cheddar cheese
- ¼ cup coarsely chopped fresh cilantro
- 12 large leaves Bibb lettuce, rinsed, patted dry with paper towel

1) In small bowl, mix all dipping sauce ingredients; set aside. In another small bowl, mix jicama with 1 teaspoon of the lime juice. In third small bowl, mix avocado with remaining teaspoon lime juice. Heat taco sauce with ground beef in microwave as directed on container.

2) On large serving platter, layer crushed chips, warm taco sauce with ground beef, jicama, avocado, onions, olives and cheese. Sprinkle cilantro over top. On large plate, arrange lettuce leaves.

3) To serve, spoon about ⅓ cup layered fillings onto each lettuce leaf; wrap lettuce around filling. Serve with dipping sauce.

HIGH ALTITUDE (ABOVE 3500 FT.): Heat taco sauce with ground beef in microwave following High Altitude directions on container.

Nutrition Information Per Serving:
Serving Size: 1/6 of Recipe

Calories:	430	From Fat:	190
Total Fat		21g	
Saturated		6g	
Cholesterol		30mg	
Sodium		1110mg	
Total Carbohydrate		48g	
Dietary Fiber		5g	
Sugars		20g	
Protein		15g	

tip

If your family prefers traditional tacos, roll up filling in flour tortillas instead of in lettuce leaves, and serve with dipping sauce.

Barbeque Black Bean Chili

PAULA MURPHY | RICHMOND, VIRGINIA

| PREP TIME: | 30 MINUTES (READY IN 30 MINUTES) |
| SERVINGS: | 6 (1-1/3 CUPS EACH) |

 EASY

CHILI

- 1 (18-oz.) container Lloyd's® Refrigerated Original Barbeque Sauce with Shredded Pork or Chicken
- 2 (15-oz.) cans Progresso® Black Beans, drained, rinsed
- 1 (28-oz.) can Progresso® Crushed Tomatoes, undrained
- 1 (14-oz.) can beef broth
- 1 (1.25-oz.) pkg. Old El Paso® Taco Seasoning Mix
- 1 teaspoon ground cumin
- 1 teaspoon chili powder

TOPPINGS, (IF DESIRED)

Sour cream

Grated cheese (such as Colby-Monterey Jack or Cheddar)

Old El Paso® Thick 'n Chunky Salsa

Old El Paso® Pickled Jalapeño Slices and/or Chopped Green Chiles

Red pepper sauce

Tortilla chips

1) In 4½-quart Dutch oven or 4-quart saucepan, mix all chili ingredients. Heat over medium-high heat to boiling, stirring occasionally.

2) Reduce heat; simmer uncovered 20 minutes, stirring occasionally.* Serve with choice of toppings.

*NOTE: For a thicker consistency and more flavor, simmer longer. If time does not permit longer cooking, mix 1 tablespoon cornstarch and ¼ cup cold water until blended. Stir into chili; return to boiling and cook until desired consistency.

HIGH ALTITUDE (ABOVE 3500 FT.): Add ¼ cup water to all chili ingredients. Continue as directed above.

Nutrition Information Per Serving:
Serving Size: 1⅓ Cups, No Toppings

Calories:	380	From Fat:	50
Total Fat		6g	
Saturated		2g	
Cholesterol		25mg	
Sodium		1870mg	
Total Carbohydrate		64g	
Dietary Fiber		11g	
Sugars		23g	
Protein		24g	

Smoked Turkey-Potato Chowder

PREP TIME: 30 MINUTES (READY IN 30 MINUTES)
SERVINGS: 4 (1-1/2 CUPS EACH)

  EASY   LOW FAT

1 tablespoon butter or margarine

1 cup sliced celery (2 medium stalks)

2 tablespoons all-purpose flour

⅛ teaspoon pepper

1 can (14 oz.) fat-free chicken broth with 33% less sodium

3 cups frozen potatoes O'Brien with onions and peppers (from 28-oz. bag)

6 oz. smoked turkey breast, cut into cubes (1⅓ cups)

1 cup Green Giant® frozen sweet peas (from 1-lb. bag)

2 cups fat-free (skim) milk

¼ cup chopped fresh parsley

Nutrition Information Per Serving:
Serving Size: 1-1/2 Cups

Calories:	300	From Fat:	45
Total Fat			5g
Saturated			3g
Cholesterol			30mg
Sodium			890mg
Total Carbohydrate			47g
Dietary Fiber			5g
Sugars			10g
Protein			19g

1) In 3-quart saucepan, melt butter over medium heat. Add celery; cook 2 to 3 minutes, stirring frequently, until crisp-tender.

2) Stir in flour and pepper until well blended. Increase heat to medium-high; gradually stir in broth, cooking and stirring until bubbly and thickened.

3) Stir in potatoes, turkey breast, peas and milk. Heat to boiling. Reduce heat to low; cover and simmer 8 to 10 minutes, stirring occasionally, until potatoes are tender. During last 2 minutes of cooking time, stir in parsley.

HIGH ALTITUDE (ABOVE 3500 FT.): No change.

Caesar Chicken Wraps

PREP TIME: 10 MINUTES
SERVINGS: 4 WRAPS

 EASY

1 (7.5-oz.) pkg. complete Caesar salad mix

1 cup chopped cooked chicken

4 (8 to 9-inch) garden vegetable flour tortillas

2 tablespoons shredded fresh Parmesan cheese

Nutrition Information Per Serving:
Serving Size: 1 Wrap

Calories:	295	From Fat:	115
Total Fat			13g
Saturated			3g
Cholesterol			50mg
Sodium			450mg
Total Carbohydrate			27g
Dietary Fiber			2g
Sugars			1g
Protein			17g

1) Crush croutons from salad mix; set aside. In large bowl, combine remaining Caesar salad mix, dressing and chicken; mix well.

2) Wrap tortillas in moist paper towels. Microwave on High for 15 to 20 seconds or until warm.

3) Spoon salad mixture evenly onto center of warm tortillas; spread to within 1 inch of edges. Sprinkle each with shredded cheese and crushed croutons. Fold bottom of each tortilla up over filling; fold sides over.

HIGH ALTITUDE (ABOVE 3500 FT.): No change.

Grilled Chicken Panzanellas

PREP TIME: 30 MINUTES
SERVINGS: 4 SANDWICHES

 EASY

4 boneless skinless chicken breast halves

1 medium red bell pepper, cut in half, seeds removed

½ cup purchased Italian salad dressing

4 slices frozen Texas garlic toast

1 tablespoon coarsely chopped fresh chives

1) Heat gas or charcoal grill. When grill is heated, place chicken breast halves and bell pepper pieces on gas grill over medium heat or on charcoal grill 4 to 6 inches from medium coals. Cover grill; cook bell pepper 10 to 15 minutes or until tender, turning once; cook chicken 12 to 15 minutes or until fork-tender and juices run clear, turning once and brushing frequently with half of the salad dressing.

2) During last 6 minutes of cooking time, place garlic toast on grill; cook 4 to 6 minutes or until light golden brown, turning and rearranging several times.

3) Cut chicken and bell pepper into thin strips; place in medium bowl. Add chives and remaining salad dressing; stir gently to coat. Divide chicken mixture evenly onto garlic toast. Serve with knife and fork.

HIGH ALTITUDE (ABOVE 3500 FT.): No change.

Nutrition Information Per Serving:
Serving Size: 1 Sandwich

Calories:	515	From Fat:	235
Total Fat			26g
Saturated			4g
Cholesterol			80mg
Sodium			800mg
Total Carbohydrate			37g
Dietary Fiber			2g
Sugars			5g
Protein			33g

Chicken and Brown Rice Soup

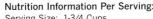

PREP TIME: 25 MINUTES (READY IN 25 MINUTES)
SERVINGS: 4 SERVINGS (1-3/4 CUPS EACH)

✎ EASY ❿ LOW FAT

2 cups cubed cooked chicken

1 cup uncooked instant brown rice

¼ cup chopped red bell pepper

¼ cup chopped green onions (4 medium)

½ teaspoon dried basil leaves

¼ teaspoon pepper

2 cans (14 oz. each) fat-free chicken broth with 33% less sodium

1½ cups water

2 cups Green Giant Select® frozen broccoli florets (from 14-oz. bag)

Nutrition Information Per Serving:
Serving Size: 1-3/4 Cups

Calories: 330	From Fat: 55
Total Fat	6g
Saturated	2g
Cholesterol	60mg
Sodium	500mg
Total Carbohydrate	40g
Dietary Fiber	4g
Sugars	2g
Protein	29g

1) In 3-quart saucepan, mix all ingredients except broccoli. Heat to boiling. Reduce heat to low; cover and simmer 5 minutes.

2) Add broccoli; return to boiling over medium-high heat. Reduce heat to low; cover and simmer 5 to 8 minutes, stirring occasionally, until vegetables and rice are tender.

HIGH ALTITUDE (ABOVE 3500 FT.): No change.

Turkey and Cheese Packet Sandwiches

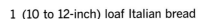

PREP TIME: 30 MINUTES
SERVINGS: 6 SANDWICHES

✎ EASY

1 (10 to 12-inch) loaf Italian bread

⅓ cup chive and onion cream cheese spread (from 8-oz. container)

6 (1-oz.) slices Cheddar cheese, each cut in half

¾ lb. shaved cooked turkey (from deli)

4 medium Italian plum tomatoes, each cut into 3 lengthwise slices

Nutrition Information Per Serving:
Serving Size: 1 Sandwich

Calories: 405	From Fat: 160
Total Fat	18g
Saturated	10g
Cholesterol	70mg
Sodium	1280mg
Total Carbohydrate	37g
Dietary Fiber	2g
Sugars	3g
Protein	24g

1) Heat gas or charcoal grill. Cut six 15x12-inch sheets of nonstick foil. (DO NOT USE REGULAR FOIL.) Cut off rounded ends from loaf of bread. Cut loaf crosswise into 12 slices, each about ¾-inch thick. Spread one side of each slice of bread with rounded teaspoon cream cheese.

2) For each sandwich, top 1 bread slice, cream cheese side up, with half slice of cheese, ⅙ of the turkey, 2 tomato slices, remaining half slice of cheese and second bread slice, cream cheese side down. Place sandwich on 1 foil sheet; wrap securely using double-fold seals, allowing room for heat expansion.

3) When grill is heated, place foil-wrapped sandwiches on gas grill over low heat or on charcoal grill 4 to 6 inches from low coals. Cover grill; cook 10 to 12 minutes or until cheese is melted and sandwiches are thoroughly heated, turning sandwiches over every 2 minutes. To serve, open wrapped sandwiches carefully to allow steam to escape.

HIGH ALTITUDE (ABOVE 3500 FT.): No change.

Curry-Crab Chowder

NANCY J. PEART | LONDON, OHIO

PREP TIME: 30 MINUTES (READY IN 30 MINUTES)
SERVINGS: 6 (1-1/3 CUPS EACH)

e EASY

1 (8.25-oz.) box Betty Crocker® Tuna Helper® Creamy Pasta

1 (12-oz.) can evaporated milk

5 cups water

1 medium carrot, thinly sliced (¾ cup)

3 tablespoons clam juice

1 teaspoon salt

1 teaspoon curry powder

¼ teaspoon white pepper

1 (6-oz.) can lump crabmeat, drained

1 (4.5-oz.) jar Green Giant® Sliced Mushrooms, drained

Nutrition Information Per Serving:
Serving Size: 1-1/3 Cups

Calories:	270	From Fat:	60
Total Fat		7g	
Saturated		3g	
Cholesterol		70mg	
Sodium		1570mg	
Total Carbohydrate		38g	
Dietary Fiber		2g	
Sugars		13g	
Protein		15g	

1) In 4½-quart Dutch oven, mix uncooked Pasta and contents of Sauce Mix packet, evaporated milk and water. Stir in all remaining ingredients.

2) Heat over medium-high heat to boiling, stirring occasionally. Reduce heat; simmer uncovered 10 to 13 minutes, stirring occasionally, until pasta and carrots are tender.

HIGH ALTITUDE (ABOVE 3500 FT.): Simmer chowder uncovered 12 to 15 minutes.

Two-Potato Vegetable Soup

PREP TIME: 20 MINUTES (READY IN 12 HOURS 35 MINUTES)
SERVINGS: 4 (1-1/2 CUPS EACH)

e EASY   f LOW FAT

1 large dark-orange sweet potato, peeled, cut into ½-inch cubes (1¼ cups)

1 medium russet or baking potato, cut into ½-inch cubes (1 cup)

¼ cup chopped onion (½ medium)

1 can (14.5 oz.) diced tomatoes with basil, garlic and oregano, undrained

2½ cups water

¾ teaspoon salt

2 vegetarian vegetable bouillon cubes

2 cups frozen peas and carrots (from 1-lb. bag), thawed*

Nutrition Information Per Serving:
Serving Size: 1-1/2 Cups

Calories:	120	From Fat:	5
Total Fat		1g	
Saturated		0g	
Cholesterol		0mg	
Sodium		1220mg	
Total Carbohydrate		27g	
Dietary Fiber		5g	
Sugars		11g	
Protein		5g	

1) In 3- to 4-quart slow cooker, mix all ingredients except peas and carrots.

2) Cover; cook on Low setting 8 to 12 hours.

3) About 15 minutes before serving, stir thawed peas and carrots into soup. Cover; cook on Low setting 15 minutes longer or until peas and carrots are thoroughly heated.

*NOTE: To quickly thaw frozen peas and carrots, place in colander or strainer; rinse with warm water until thawed. Drain well.

HIGH ALTITUDE (ABOVE 3500 FT.): No change.

Italian Burgers Supreme

PREP TIME: 45 MINUTES
SERVINGS: 4 SANDWICHES

½ lb. lean (at least 80%)
  ground beef

½ lb. bulk hot Italian pork sausage

¼ cup tomato pasta sauce

2 (¾-oz.) slices provolone or
  mozzarella cheese, cut in half

1 teaspoon olive or vegetable oil

¼ cup green bell pepper strips
  (1½x¼x¼-inch)

¼ cup red bell pepper strips
  (1½x¼x¼-inch)

¼ cup thinly sliced onion

4 burger buns, split, toasted if desired

¼ cup tomato pasta sauce, heated

1) Heat gas or charcoal grill. In large bowl,
   combine ground beef, sausage and ¼
   cup pasta sauce; mix gently. Shape
   mixture into 4 patties, ½ inch thick.

2) When grill is heated, place patties on gas
   grill over medium heat or on charcoal
   grill 4 to 6 inches from medium coals.
   Cover grill; cook 11 to 13 minutes or until
   meat thermometer inserted in center of
   patties reads 160°F., turning once. During
   last 1 to 2 minutes of cooking time, place
   cheese on patties; cook until melted.

3) Heat oil in 8-inch nonstick skillet over
   medium heat until hot. Add bell peppers
   and onion; cook 4 to 5 minutes or until
   tender, stirring frequently.

4) Place patties on bottom halves of buns.
   Top each with ¼ of bell pepper mixture
   and top half of bun. Serve with warm
   pasta sauce.

*NOTE: To broil patties, place on broiler pan; broil 3 to
   4 inches from heat for 10 to 12 minutes or until
   meat thermometer inserted in center of patties
   reads 160°F., turning once. During last 30 to
   60 seconds of broiling time, place cheese on
   patties; broil until melted.

HIGH ALTITUDE (ABOVE 3500 FT.): Cook on grill over
medium-low heat.

Nutrition Information Per Serving:
Serving Size: 1 Sandwich

Calories:	445	From Fat:	215
Total Fat			24g
Saturated			9g
Cholesterol			75mg
Sodium			900mg
Total Carbohydrate			30g
Dietary Fiber			1g
Sugars			9g
Protein			27g

Luau Tacos

TORI JOHNSON | GILBERT, ARIZONA

PREP TIME: 30 MINUTES (READY IN 30 MINUTES)
SERVINGS: 6 (2 TACOS EACH)

 EASY

1 (18-oz.) container Lloyd's® Refrigerated Honey Hickory Barbeque Sauce with Shredded Pork

1 (15.25-oz.) can pineapple tidbits, drained

1 (10.5-oz.) pkg. (12 tortillas) Old El Paso® Flour Tortillas for Soft Tacos & Fajitas

12 oz. (3 cups) shredded Monterey Jack cheese or Mexican 4-cheese blend

¼ cup chopped fresh cilantro

3 cups shredded iceberg or green leaf lettuce

1 large tomato, diced (1 cup)

Sour cream, if desired

1) In 1½-quart saucepan, cook barbeque sauce with shredded pork and ⅔ cup of the pineapple tidbits over medium-high heat for 6 to 8 minutes, stirring occasionally, until thoroughly heated.

2) In 10-inch skillet, cook each tortilla over medium-high heat for 20 to 30 seconds, turning once, until thoroughly heated.

3) Onto each warm tortilla, spoon about 3 tablespoons pork mixture, ¼ cup cheese, 1 teaspoon cilantro, ¼ cup lettuce, heaping tablespoon tomato and scant tablespoon remaining pineapple tidbits. Top each with sour cream.

HIGH ALTITUDE (ABOVE 3500 FT.): No change.

Nutrition Information Per Serving:
Serving Size: 2 Tacos

Calories:	560	From Fat:	230
Total Fat			25g
Saturated			13g
Cholesterol			75mg
Sodium			1130mg
Total Carbohydrate			58g
Dietary Fiber			3g
Sugars			26g
Protein			28g

To add a little more zip to the tacos, substitute pepper-Jack cheese for the Monterey Jack cheese.

Havarti Burgers in Pitas

PREP TIME: 30 MINUTES
SERVINGS: 4 SANDWICHES

 EASY

1 medium tomato, sliced

½ medium cucumber, thinly sliced

¼ cup purchased balsamic vinaigrette

1 lb. lean (at least 80%) ground beef

½ cup finely chopped onion (1 medium)

½ teaspoon dried Italian seasoning

½ teaspoon garlic-pepper blend

½ teaspoon salt

4 (1-oz.) thin slices Havarti cheese

2 (8-inch) pita (pocket) breads, halved

1) Heat gas or charcoal grill. In shallow bowl, mix tomato, cucumber and vinaigrette. Let stand while preparing patties.

2) In medium bowl, combine ground beef, onion, Italian seasoning, garlic-pepper blend and salt; mix well. Shape mixture into 4 oblong patties, about ½ inch thick.

3) When grill is heated, place patties on gas grill over medium heat or on charcoal grill 4 to 6 inches from medium coals. Cover grill; cook 11 to 13 minutes or until meat thermometer inserted in center of patties reads 160°F., turning once. During last 1 to 2 minutes of cooking time, place cheese on patties; cook until melted.

4) Place cheese-topped patties in pita bread halves. Spoon tomato-cucumber mixture into bread halves with patties.

*NOTE: To broil patties, place on broiler pan; broil 3 to 4 inches from heat for 10 to 12 minutes or until meat thermometer inserted in center of patties reads 160°F., turning once. During last 30 to 60 seconds of broiling time, place cheese on patties; broil until melted.

HIGH ALTITUDE (ABOVE 3500 FT.): Cook on grill over medium-low heat.

Nutrition Information Per Serving:
Serving Size: 1 Sandwich

Calories:	535	From Fat:	280
Total Fat			31g
Saturated			13g
Cholesterol			100mg
Sodium			960mg
Total Carbohydrate			30g
Dietary Fiber			2g
Sugars			3g
Protein			34g

Blue Cheese and Tomato Hamburgers

PREP TIME: 35 MINUTES (READY IN 35 MINUTES)
SERVINGS: 4 SANDWICHES

1 lb. lean (at least 80%) ground beef

¼ cup oil-packed sun-dried tomatoes, drained, chopped

½ teaspoon dried basil leaves

3 tablespoons mayonnaise

½ teaspoon Dijon mustard

3 tablespoons crumbled blue cheese

4 burger buns, split

4 lettuce leaves

1) Heat gas or charcoal grill. In medium bowl, gently mix ground beef, tomatoes and basil until well blended. Shape mixture into 4 patties, 4 inches in diameter.

2) Meanwhile, in small bowl, mix mayonnaise, mustard and cheese; set aside.

3) When grill is heated, place patties on gas grill over medium heat or on charcoal grill over medium coals; cover grill. Cook 11 to 13 minutes, turning once, until thermometer inserted in center of patties reads 160°F.

4) Place buns, cut sides down, on grill; cover grill. Cook 1 to 2 minutes or until buns are heated.

5) Place lettuce leaves on bottom halves of buns. Top with patties; spoon cheese mixture evenly onto patties. Cover with top halves of buns.

HIGH ALTITUDE (3500-6500 FT.): Place patties on gas grill over medium-low heat or on charcoal grill over medium-low coals; cover grill. Cook using times above as a guide, turning once.

Nutrition Information Per Serving:	
Serving Size: 1 Sandwich	
Calories: 430 From Fat: 230	
Total Fat	26g
Saturated	8g
Cholesterol	80mg
Sodium	470mg
Total Carbohydrate	24g
Dietary Fiber	1g
Sugars	3g
Protein	25g

tip

Kitchen scissors make quick work of "chopping" sun-dried tomatoes. Leftover tomatoes can be refrigerated and added to favorite pasta dishes, sauces or vegetables.

Caesar Chicken Sandwiches

PREP TIME:	20 MINUTES (READY IN 20 MINUTES)	EASY
SERVINGS:	2 SANDWICHES	

2 boneless skinless chicken breast halves

¼ cup Caesar dressing

1 tablespoon chopped fresh chives

2 kaiser rolls, split

2 slices (1 oz. each) provolone cheese

2 leaves romaine lettuce

2 slices tomato

1 tablespoon Caesar dressing

1) Heat gas or charcoal grill. Between 2 pieces of plastic wrap or waxed paper, place 1 chicken breast half. With flat side of meat mallet or rolling pin and working from center, gently pound chicken until about ¼ inch thick; remove wrap. Repeat with remaining chicken breast half.

2) In shallow dish, mix ¼ cup Caesar dressing and chives. Place chicken breasts in mixture; turn to coat all sides.

3) When grill is heated, place chicken on gas grill over medium heat or on charcoal grill over medium coals; cover grill. Cook 8 to 10 minutes, turning once and brushing occasionally with remaining dressing mixture, until chicken is fork-tender and juices run clear. Discard any remaining dressing mixture.

4) To toast buns, place cut sides down on grill during last 1 to 2 minutes of cooking time. Place cheese slice on each chicken breast half; cover grill. Cook just long enough to melt.

5) Top bottom halves of each roll with lettuce, tomato and cheese-topped chicken breast half. Spread inside of each roll top with 1 tablespoon dressing. Cover chicken with top halves of rolls.

HIGH ALTITUDE (3500-6500 FT.): Place chicken on gas grill over medium-low heat or on charcoal grill over medium-low coals; cover grill. Cook using times above as a guide, turning once and brushing occasionally with reserved marinade. Toast buns as directed above.

Nutrition Information Per Serving:
Serving Size: 1 Sandwich

Calories:	510	From Fat:	210
Total Fat			23g
Saturated			8g
Cholesterol			95mg
Sodium			780mg
Total Carbohydrate			37g
Dietary Fiber			8g
Sugars			8g
Protein			45g

Grilled Beef and Provolone Sandwiches

PREP TIME: 10 MINUTES (READY IN 10 MINUTES)
SERVINGS: 2 SANDWICHES

 EASY

4 slices Italian or Vienna bread

2 tablespoons refrigerated basil pesto

¼ lb. thinly sliced cooked roast beef (from deli)

¼ cup thin slices roasted red bell peppers (from a jar)

2 slices (¾ oz. each) provolone cheese

1 tablespoon butter or margarine, melted

Nutrition Information Per Serving:
Serving Size: 1 Sandwich

Calories:	380	From Fat:	200
Total Fat			23g
Saturated			10g
Cholesterol			60mg
Sodium			1180mg
Total Carbohydrate			23g
Dietary Fiber			2g
Sugars			3g
Protein			21g

1) Heat closed contact grill 5 minutes. Spread one side of each slice of bread with pesto. On 2 slices of the bread, layer beef, roasted peppers and cheese; top with remaining slices of bread, pesto side down. Brush outside of sandwiches with butter.

2) When grill is heated, place sandwiches on bottom grill surface. Close grill; cook 3 to 5 minutes or until bread is toasted and cheese is melted.

Souper Shrimp Bisque

NINA PAJAK | LONGWOOD, FLORIDA

Pillsbury Bake-Off

PREP TIME: 20 MINUTES (READY IN 20 MINUTES)
SERVINGS: 4 (3/4 CUP EACH)

EASY

8 oz. cooked deveined shelled shrimp, tail shells removed

1 (19-oz.) can Progresso® Vegetable Classics Hearty Tomato Soup

2 teaspoons Worcestershire sauce

¾ teaspoon seafood seasoning

⅓ cup whipping cream

Purchased or homemade croutons, if desired*

¼ to ⅓ cup chopped fresh basil, if desired

Nutrition Information Per Serving:
Serving Size: 3/4 Cup

Calories:	170	From Fat:	70
Total Fat			8g
Saturated			4g
Cholesterol			135mg
Sodium			970mg
Total Carbohydrate			11g
Dietary Fiber			0g
Sugars			5g
Protein			13g

1) In blender, process half of the shrimp with on/off pulses until chopped. Add half of the soup; process until smooth. Pour into 2-quart saucepan. Repeat with remaining half of shrimp and soup.

2) Stir Worcestershire sauce and seafood seasoning into soup. Heat over medium heat to boiling. Reduce heat; simmer 2 to 3 minutes, stirring frequently, until thoroughly heated. Stir in cream. Heat about 1 minute or just until thoroughly heated.

3) Ladle soup into individual soup bowls. Top each with croutons and basil.

*NOTE: To make homemade croutons, heat oven to 325°F. Trim crusts from 3 slices of white bread; cut bread into 3/4-inch cubes. Place on ungreased cookie sheet. Bake at 325°F. for 3 to 4 minutes or until crisp.

HIGH ALTITUDE (ABOVE 3500 FT.): No change.

Cheesy Mushroom Burgers

PREP TIME: 20 MINUTES
SERVINGS: 4 SANDWICHES

 EASY

¼ cup mayonnaise

2 teaspoons purchased balsamic vinaigrette salad dressing

4 (4 to 5-inch) portobello mushroom caps, cleaned

¼ teaspoon salt

¼ teaspoon pepper

4 kaiser rolls, split

¼ cup purchased balsamic vinaigrette salad dressing

4 (1-oz.) slices provolone cheese

1) Heat gas or charcoal grill. In small bowl, combine mayonnaise and 2 teaspoons salad dressing; blend well. Set aside. Sprinkle mushroom caps with salt and pepper.

2) When grill is heated, place mushrooms on gas grill over medium heat or on charcoal grill 4 to 6 inches from medium coals. Cover grill; cook 5 to 8 minutes or until thoroughly heated, turning once.

3) Meanwhile, brush cut sides of rolls with ¼ cup salad dressing. During last 1 to 2 minutes of cooking time, place cheese on mushrooms and place rolls, cut side down, on grill to toast.

4) Spread toasted rolls with mayonnaise mixture. Serve cheese-topped mushrooms in rolls.

HIGH ALTITUDE (ABOVE 3500 FT.) No change.

Nutrition Information Per Serving:
Serving Size: 1 Sandwich

Calories:	435	From Fat:	260
Total Fat			29g
Saturated			8g
Cholesterol			25mg
Sodium			920mg
Total Carbohydrate			30g
Dietary Fiber			1g
Sugars			2g
Protein			14g

Greek Quesadillas

JENNIFER MCCUSKER-ORTH | KINGSPORT, TENNESSEE

PREP TIME: 30 MINUTES (READY IN 30 MINUTES)
SERVINGS: 8 (1 QUESADILLA AND 1-1/2 TABLESPOONS SAUCE EACH)

e EASY

DIPPING SAUCE

- 1 (6-oz.) container Yoplait® Original Fat Free Plain Yogurt
- 1 tablespoon chopped fresh dill
- 1 teaspoon extra-virgin olive oil
- 1 teaspoon lemon juice
- 1 clove garlic, minced

QUESADILLAS

- 4 oz. (1 cup) crumbled feta cheese
- 4 oz. (1 cup) shredded mozzarella cheese
- 1 cup diced peeled cucumber (1 small)
- 1 cup finely chopped tomato (1 large)
- 1/2 cup chopped pitted kalamata olives
- 1/8 teaspoon salt
- 1/8 teaspoon pepper
- 1 (11.5-oz.) pkg. (8 tortillas) Old El Paso® Flour Tortillas for Burritos

1) In small bowl, mix all dipping sauce ingredients; set aside. In large bowl, mix feta cheese, mozzarella cheese, cucumber, tomato, olives, salt and pepper.

2) Heat 12-inch nonstick skillet over medium heat until hot. Sprinkle 1/2 cup cheese mixture onto half of each tortilla. Fold untopped half of each tortilla over cheese mixture; gently press down with pancake turner.

3) Cook quesadillas, 3 at a time, in hot skillet about 2 minutes on each side, gently pressing down with pancake turner, until tortillas are lightly browned and crisp and cheese is melted. Remove from skillet; place on cutting board. Cut each quesadilla in half. Serve warm with dipping sauce.

Nutrition Information Per Serving:
Serving Size: 1/8 of Recipe

Calories:	240	From Fat:	90
Total Fat			10g
Saturated			5g
Cholesterol			20mg
Sodium			560mg
Total Carbohydrate			28g
Dietary Fiber			2g
Sugars			3g
Protein			11g

tip

For a milder flavor, substitute black olives for the kalamata olives in this recipe.

Old-Fashioned Beef-Vegetable Soup

PREP TIME: 45 MINUTES (READY IN 4 HOURS)
SERVINGS: 14 (1-1/2 CUPS EACH)

LOW FAT

3 lb. meaty cross-cut beef shank bones, cut into 3-inch pieces

10 cups water

3 tablespoons beef-flavor instant bouillon

1½ teaspoons salt

½ teaspoon pepper

½ teaspoon dried thyme leaves

2 dried bay leaves

4 cups vegetable juice

3 cups cubed potatoes (3 medium)

3 cups coarsely chopped cabbage

2 cups frozen small whole onions (from 16-oz. bag)

2 cups cubed peeled rutabaga (1½ medium)

2 cups Green Giant® frozen cut green beans (from 1-lb. bag)

4 medium carrots, sliced (2 cups)

3 medium stalks celery, sliced (1½ cups)

1) In 8-quart stockpot or Dutch oven, place beef bones and water. Heat to boiling. Reduce heat; cover and simmer 30 minutes. Skim off and discard any residue that rises to surface.

2) Stir in bouillon, salt, pepper, thyme and bay leaves. Return to boiling. Reduce heat; cover and simmer 2 to 2½ hours longer or until meat is tender.

3) Remove beef bones and bay leaves from broth. Skim and discard fat from broth. When bones are cool enough to handle, remove meat from bones; cut into bite-size pieces.

4) Return meat to broth. Stir in all remaining ingredients. Heat to boiling. Reduce heat; cover and simmer 30 minutes or until vegetables are tender.

HIGH ALTITUDE (3500-6000 FT.): No change.

Nutrition Information Per Serving:
Serving Size: 1-1/2 Cups

Calories:	160	From Fat:	25
Total Fat			3g
Saturated			1g
Cholesterol			30mg
Sodium			850mg
Total Carbohydrate			18g
Dietary Fiber			4g
Sugars			7g
Protein			15g

Breads&Pastries

Easy-to-make baked goods that taste like you fussed.

CREAMY APPLE PUFFS
PG. 131

STRAWBERRY ROLY-POLIES
PG. 139

CHERRY-CINNAMON CRISPS
PG. 134

Strawberry-Cream Cheese Pastries

BECKY KOYLE | BOISE, IDAHO

PREP TIME: 20 MINUTES (READY IN 50 MINUTES)
SERVINGS: 8 PASTRIES

1 (8-oz.) pkg. cream cheese, softened

½ cup sugar

1 tablespoon whipping cream

½ teaspoon ground cinnamon

½ teaspoon grated lemon peel

1 teaspoon lemon juice

8 rolls Betty Crocker® Fruit Roll-Ups® Strawberry Fruit Snack (from 5-oz. box)

2 (8-oz.) cans Pillsbury® Refrigerated Crescent Dinner Rolls

1 tablespoon milk

2 tablespoons sugar

1) Heat oven to 375°F. In medium bowl, beat cream cheese and ½ cup sugar with electric mixer on medium speed until creamy. Beat in cream, cinnamon, lemon peel and lemon juice.

2) Remove fruit snack rolls from wrappers; fold each in half lengthwise.

3) Unroll both cans of dough; separate into 8 rectangles, firmly pressing perforations to seal. Place 1 folded fruit roll lengthwise down center of each dough rectangle.

4) Spoon 2 rounded tablespoons cream cheese mixture onto one half of each fruit snack roll; spread slightly. Fold dough rectangle in half crosswise. Place on ungreased cookie sheet; press edges with fork to seal. Brush tops with milk; sprinkle with 2 tablespoons sugar. With sharp knife, cut 3 diagonal slits in top of each square.

5) Bake at 375°F. for 13 to 18 minutes or until deep golden brown. Cool on cookie sheet 10 minutes. Remove from cookie sheet. Serve warm.

Nutrition Information Per Serving:
Serving Size: 1 Pastry

Calories:	420	From Fat:	180
Total Fat			20g
Saturated			9g
Cholesterol			35mg
Sodium			820mg
Total Carbohydrate			55g
Dietary Fiber			1g
Sugars			32g
Protein			6g

Twelfth Night Scones

PREP TIME: 20 MINUTES (READY IN 45 MINUTES)
SERVINGS: 8 SCONES

SCONES

1¾ cups all-purpose flour

¼ cup sugar

2 teaspoons baking powder

¼ teaspoon baking soda

¼ teaspoon salt

¼ cup butter, softened

½ cup sweetened dried cranberries

½ cup white vanilla chips

1 teaspoon grated orange peel

½ cup vanilla low-fat yogurt

⅓ cup buttermilk*

TOPPING

1 to 2 tablespoons buttermilk or milk

1 tablespoon sugar

½ teaspoon grated orange peel

1) Heat oven to 375°F. Grease cookie sheet with shortening. In large bowl, stir together flour, ¼ cup sugar, the baking powder, baking soda and salt. With pastry blender or fork, cut in butter until mixture resembles coarse crumbs.

2) Stir in cranberries, vanilla chips and 1 teaspoon orange peel. Add yogurt and ⅓ cup buttermilk; stir just until dry ingredients are moistened.

3) Shape dough into ball; place on cookie sheet. With floured fingers, press or roll dough into 8-inch round. Cut into 8 wedges; do not separate.

4) Brush dough with 1 to 2 tablespoons buttermilk. In small bowl, mix 1 tablespoon sugar and ½ teaspoon orange peel. Sprinkle over dough.

5) Bake 15 to 20 minutes or until edges are light golden brown. Immediately remove from cookie sheet; place on serving tray. Cool 5 minutes. Cut into wedges. Serve warm.

*NOTE: To substitute for buttermilk, use 1 teaspoon vinegar or lemon juice plus milk to make ⅓ cup.

HIGH ALTITUDE (3500-6000 FT.): Increase flour to 2 cups. Continue as directed above.

Nutrition Information Per Serving:		
Serving Size: 1 Scone		
Calories: 325	From Fat:	110
Total Fat		12g
Saturated		7g
Cholesterol		20mg
Sodium		310mg
Total Carbohydrate		49g
Dietary Fiber		1g
Sugars		27g
Protein		5g

Poppin' Fresh® Citrus-Glazed Crullers

ERIKA COUCH | BALLSTON SPA , NEW YORK

PREP TIME: 15 MINUTES (READY IN 40 MINUTES)
SERVINGS: 12 SWEET ROLLS

ROLLS

¼ cup butter or margarine, melted

½ cup granulated sugar

1 can (11 oz.) Pillsbury® refrigerated breadsticks

GLAZE

⅔ cup powdered sugar

¼ teaspoon grated orange peel

¼ teaspoon grated lemon peel

1 tablespoon orange juice

1 teaspoon lemon juice

1) Heat oven to 375°F. Line cookie sheet with parchment paper or spray with cooking spray. In shallow dish, place melted butter; in another shallow dish, place granulated sugar.

2) Unroll dough; separate into breadsticks. Dip both sides of each breadstick in butter; coat with sugar. Twist each breadstick; place on cookie sheet, pressing ends down firmly.

3) Bake 13 to 17 minutes or until golden brown. Meanwhile, in small bowl, stir together all glaze ingredients until smooth.

4) Remove rolls from oven. Immediately drizzle glaze over rolls. Remove from cookie sheet; cool 5 minutes before serving.

HIGH ALTITUDE (3500-6500 FT.): No change.

Nutrition Information Per Serving:
Serving Size: 1 Sweet Roll

Calories:	160	From Fat:	45
Total Fat			5g
Saturated			2g
Cholesterol			10mg
Sodium			210mg
Total Carbohydrate			28g
Dietary Fiber			0g
Sugars			16g
Protein			2g

Giant Cinnamon-Cheese Danish

BETTY NICOSON | TERRE HAUTE, INDIANA

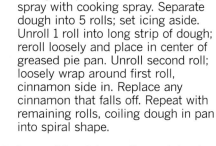

PREP TIME: 15 MINUTES (READY IN 55 MINUTES)
SERVINGS: 6

1 (17.5-oz.) can Pillsbury® Grands!®
Refrigerated Cinnamon Rolls
with Icing

1 (8-oz.) pkg. cream cheese, softened

½ cup sugar

2 teaspoons sour cream

1 teaspoon lemon juice

1 teaspoon vanilla

1) Heat oven to 350°F. Lightly grease 9-inch glass pie pan with shortening or spray with cooking spray. Separate dough into 5 rolls; set icing aside. Unroll 1 roll into long strip of dough; reroll loosely and place in center of greased pie pan. Unroll second roll; loosely wrap around first roll, cinnamon side in. Replace any cinnamon that falls off. Repeat with remaining rolls, coiling dough in pan into spiral shape.

2) In small bowl, beat all remaining ingredients with electric mixer on medium speed until smooth. Spoon cream cheese mixture into decorating bag with tip or gallon-size resealable food-storage plastic bag with ½-inch hole cut in bottom corner. With tip or corner of bag about halfway down into rolls, pipe mixture between strips of dough, starting at center and working to edge of pan, using all of mixture.

3) Bake at 350°F. for 25 to 35 minutes or until center is thoroughly baked and edges are deep golden brown. Cool 5 minutes. Meanwhile, remove cover from icing; microwave on Medium (50%) for 10 to 15 seconds or until drizzling consistency.

4) Drizzle icing over warm coffee cake. Cut into wedges. Serve warm.

HIGH ALTITUDE (ABOVE 3500 FT.): No change.

Nutrition Information Per Serving:
Serving Size: 1/6 of Recipe

Calories:	480	From Fat:	220
Total Fat			24g
Saturated			12g
Cholesterol			60mg
Sodium			790mg
Total Carbohydrate			59g
Dietary Fiber			1g
Sugars			29g
Protein			8g

Heat leftover Danish in the microwave on Medium for a few seconds before serving.

Crescent Walnut-Raisin Potica

MIKKI GOTTWALT | NEW BRIGHTON, MINNESOTA

PREP TIME: 15 MINUTES (READY IN 55 MINUTES)
SERVINGS: 16

BREAD

1 cup chopped walnuts

½ cup raisins

2 tablespoons packed brown sugar

½ teaspoon ground cinnamon

1 tablespoon butter or margarine, melted

1 tablespoon half-and-half

1 tablespoon honey

1 egg

1 (8-oz.) can Pillsbury® Refrigerated Crescent Dinner Rolls

ICING

½ cup powdered sugar

⅛ teaspoon almond extract

1½ to 2 teaspoons milk or half-and-half

1) Heat oven to 375°F. Grease cookie sheet with shortening or spray with cooking spray. In food processor, grind all bread ingredients except dough; set aside.

2) On lightly floured surface, unroll dough into 1 large rectangle; press or roll into 14x10-inch rectangle, firmly pressing perforations to seal. Spread nut mixture evenly over dough to within ½ inch of long sides.

3) Starting with one long side of rectangle, tightly roll up dough, carefully stretching roll until 17 inches long; press edge and ends to seal. Place on greased cookie sheet; loosely coil into spiral shape.

4) Bake at 375°F. for 28 to 33 minutes or until deep golden brown. Cover loosely with foil if bread is browning too quickly. Cool 10 minutes. Meanwhile, in small bowl, blend powdered sugar, almond extract and enough milk for desired drizzling consistency until smooth.

5) Drizzle icing over warm bread. Cut into wedges. Serve warm.

HIGH ALTITUDE (ABOVE 3500 FT.): No change.

Nutrition Information Per Serving:
Serving Size: 1/16 of Recipe

Calories:	150	From Fat:	70
Total Fat			8g
Saturated			2g
Cholesterol			15mg
Sodium			180mg
Total Carbohydrate			18g
Dietary Fiber			0g
Sugars			12g
Protein			3g

Blueberry-Pistachio Biscuits for Two

SHIRLEY DESANTIS | BETHLEHEM, PENNSYLVANIA

PREP TIME: 15 MINUTES (READY IN 55 MINUTES)
SERVINGS: 2

2 Pillsbury® Oven Baked Classics® Extra Large Easy Split™ frozen biscuits (from 31.8-oz. bag)*

3 tablespoons butter or margarine, melted

2 tablespoons caramel ice cream topping

1/3 cup fresh or frozen blueberries (do not thaw)

4 teaspoons chopped pistachios

3 tablespoons sugar

1/4 teaspoon vanilla powder, if desired

1/4 teaspoon ground cinnamon

Yoplait® Light Fat Free very vanilla yogurt, whipped cream or ice cream, if desired

1) Heat oven to 375°F. On microwavable plate, microwave biscuits, uncovered, on Medium (50%) for 50 to 60 seconds, turning biscuits over halfway through microwaving, until thawed.

2) Into each of 2 ovenproof 10-oz. custard cups or ramekins, spoon 1 teaspoon of the melted butter; tilt cups to completely coat bottom with butter. Place 1 tablespoon caramel topping in each cup. Top each evenly with blueberries and pistachios.

3) In small bowl or resealable food-storage plastic bag, mix sugar, vanilla powder and cinnamon. Cut each thawed biscuit into 6 pieces. Lightly dip each piece into remaining melted butter; roll or shake in sugar mixture to coat. Place 6 coated biscuit pieces in each custard cup. Drizzle with any remaining butter; sprinkle with any remaining sugar mixture.

4) Bake 21 to 26 minutes or until biscuits are golden brown and edges are bubbly. Cool 10 minutes. Run knife around inside edge of custard cups; invert onto individual plates. Serve with yogurt.

*NOTE: If Extra Large Easy Split™ frozen biscuits are unavailable, use 3 Pillsbury® Oven Baked Classics® frozen buttermilk biscuits (from 25-oz. bag). Cut each biscuit into quarters; continue as directed above.

HIGH ALTITUDE (3500-6500 FT.): Bake at 375°F. for 24 to 29 minutes.

Nutrition Information Per Serving:
Serving Size: 1 Biscuit

Calories:	610	From Fat:	290
Total Fat			33g
Saturated			13g
Cholesterol			45mg
Sodium			1060mg
Total Carbohydrate			71g
Dietary Fiber			3g
Sugars			34g
Protein			8g

Raspberry Crescent Twists

MARY ANN MARIOTTI | PLAINFIELD, ILLINOIS

PREP TIME:	15 MINUTES (READY IN 35 MINUTES)
SERVINGS:	8 TWISTS

TWISTS

1 (8-oz.) can Pillsbury® Refrigerated Regular or Reduced Fat Crescent Dinner Rolls

¼ cup red raspberry filling (from 12-oz. can)

¼ cup sliced almonds, finely chopped

GLAZE

½ cup powdered sugar

½ teaspoon almond extract

1 to 2 teaspoons water

GARNISH

Additional sliced almonds, if desired

1) Heat oven to 375°F. Line 15x10-inch pan with sides or large cookie sheet with parchment paper. Unroll dough on cutting board into 2 long rectangles; press each into 12x3½-inch rectangle, firmly pressing perforations to seal.

2) Spread raspberry filling on 1 dough rectangle to within ½ inch of all edges. Sprinkle evenly with chopped almonds. Place second dough rectangle over almonds; gently press top and long edges to seal. Cut crosswise into 8 strips. Twist each strip twice; place 2 inches apart in paper-lined pan.

3) Bake at 375°F. for 11 to 13 minutes or until deep golden brown. Remove twists from pan; place on wire rack. Cool 10 minutes. Meanwhile, in small bowl, blend powdered sugar, almond extract and enough water for desired spreading consistency until smooth.

4) Spread glaze over cooled twists. If desired, sprinkle with additional sliced almonds.

HIGH ALTITUDE (ABOVE 3500 FT.): Bake at 375°F. for 13 to 15 minutes.

Nutrition Information Per Serving:
Serving Size: 1 Twist

Calories:	160	From Fat:	50
Total Fat			6g
Saturated			1g
Cholesterol			0mg
Sodium			340mg
Total Carbohydrate			24g
Dietary Fiber			0g
Sugars			13g
Protein			3g

Creamy Apple Puffs

LAUREL HATFIELD | PRIEST RIVER, IDAHO

Bake-Off

PREP TIME: 15 MINUTES (READY IN 35 MINUTES)
SERVINGS: 8 ROLLS

PUFFS

4 oz. cream cheese (from 8-oz. pkg.), softened

1/4 cup powdered sugar

1 (17.3-oz.) can Pillsbury® Grands!® Homestyle Refrigerated Extra Rich Biscuits

1 cup loosely packed shredded unpeeled apple (about 1 large), drained on paper towels

1/4 cup chopped dates

ICING

1/2 cup powdered sugar

2 to 3 teaspoons milk

1) Heat oven to 350°F. In small bowl, mix cream cheese and 1/4 cup powdered sugar until well blended; set aside.

2) Separate dough into 8 biscuits; separate each evenly into 2 rounds. Place 8 rounds on ungreased cookie sheet. Spread each biscuit round on cookie sheet with 1 tablespoon cream cheese mixture to within 1/2 inch of edge.

3) Top each with 1 rounded tablespoon loosely packed apple and 1 rounded teaspoon dates. Press remaining 8 biscuits halves out slightly. Place each on apple-topped biscuit round; press edges to seal.

4) Bake at 350°F. for 14 to 18 minutes or until golden brown. Meanwhile, blend 1/2 cup powdered sugar with enough milk for desired drizzling consistency until smooth.

5) Immediately remove rolls from cookie sheet. Drizzle icing over warm rolls.

HIGH ALTITUDE (ABOVE 3500 FT.): No change.

Nutrition Information Per Serving: Serving Size: 1 Roll	
Calories: 330	From Fat: 130
Total Fat	14g
Saturated	5g
Cholesterol	15mg
Sodium	780mg
Total Carbohydrate	47g
Dietary Fiber	2g
Sugars	26g
Protein	5g

Braided Pumpkin Wreaths

PREP TIME: 50 MINUTES (READY IN 3 HOURS 45 MINUTES)
SERVINGS: 24 SLICES EACH WREATH; YIELD: 2 WREATHS

BREAD

5¾ to 6½ cups all-purpose flour

⅓ cup sugar

1½ teaspoons salt

2 packages regular active dry yeast

1 cup canned pumpkin
(not pie filling mix)

¼ cup butter or margarine

1½ cups apple cider or apple juice

TOPPING

1 egg

1 tablespoon water

2 teaspoons sesame seed, if desired

2 teaspoons poppy seed, if desired

1) In large bowl, stir 2 cups of the flour, sugar, salt and yeast. In 2-quart saucepan, heat pumpkin, butter and cider over medium heat, until 120°F. to 130°F. Add to flour mixture; beat on medium speed 3 minutes, scraping bowl occasionally.

2) Stir in enough of the remaining flour to make a soft dough. On floured surface, knead until smooth and elastic, 3 to 5 minutes. Place dough in greased bowl, turning to grease top. Cover with plastic wrap and cloth towel; let rise in warm place until double in size, about 1 hour.

3) Grease large cookie sheet. Punch down dough. Divide in half; divide each half into 3 pieces. On lightly floured surface, roll each piece into 24-inch-long rope. On cookie sheet, place 3 ropes close together. Braid loosely; pinch ends together, forming a circle. Repeat with remaining dough. Cover; let rise in warm place until almost double in size, 20 to 30 minutes.

4) Heat oven to 375°F. In small bowl, beat egg and water until well blended; brush over braids; sprinkle with sesame and poppy seed.

5) Bake 18 to 24 minutes or until golden brown. Remove from cookie sheet to wire racks. Cool about 1 hour.

HIGH ALTITUDE (3500-6000 FT.): Use 1 package regular active dry yeast. Bake at 375°F. 22 to 26 minutes.

Nutrition Information Per Serving: Serving Size: 1 Slice		
Calories: 75	From Fat:	10
Total Fat		1g
Saturated		1g
Cholesterol		5mg
Sodium		80mg
Total Carbohydrate		14g
Dietary Fiber		0g
Sugars		3g
Protein		2g

Lemon Poppy Seed Muffins

PREP TIME: 10 MINUTES (READY IN 40 MINUTES)
SERVINGS: 15 MUFFINS

e EASY

1 box (15.8 oz.) lemon-poppy seed premium muffin mix (with glaze)

¾ cup milk

¼ cup vegetable oil

2 eggs

⅓ cup lemon curd (from 10 or 11¼-oz. jar)

1) Heat oven to 425°F. Line 15 standard-size muffin cups with paper baking cups. In medium bowl, stir muffin mix, milk, oil and eggs with spoon just until blended (batter may be lumpy).

2) Spoon about 2 tablespoons batter into each muffin cup. Place about 1 teaspoon lemon curd on batter in each cup. Top with remaining batter, dividing evenly among cups.

3) Bake 14 to 17 minutes or until golden brown. Cool in pan on wire rack 10 minutes. Remove from pan.

4) Squeeze Glaze packet from muffin mix about 10 seconds (do not microwave). With scissors, cut off tip of 1 corner of packet. Drizzle glaze over warm muffins. Serve warm or cool.

HIGH ALTITUDE (3500-6000 FT.): Add 1 tablespoon flour to dry muffin mix. Bake at 425°F. 12 to 15 minutes. Continue as directed above.

Lemon curd is a thick pudding-like product usually found alongside the jams and jellies in the supermarket. Lemon pie filling can be used instead of the lemon curd.

Nutrition Information Per Serving:
Serving Size: 1 Muffin

Calories:	180	From Fat:	55
Total Fat		6g	
Saturated		5g	
Cholesterol		30mg	
Sodium		190mg	
Total Carbohydrate		29g	
Dietary Fiber		0g	
Sugars		15g	
Protein		3g	

Cherry-Cinnamon Crisps

PREP TIME: 20 MINUTES (READY IN 40 MINUTES)
SERVINGS: 6 ROLLS

 EASY

1 can (8 oz.) Pillsbury® refrigerated crescent dinner rolls

⅓ cup chopped dried cherries

¼ cup butter or margarine, melted

¼ cup sugar

1 teaspoon ground cinnamon

The easiest way to flatten these melt-in-your-mouth pastries is with a rolling pin.

1) Heat oven to 375°F. Grease 2 cookie sheets with shortening or spray with cooking spray. Separate dough into 2 rectangles, about 7x6 inches each; press perforations to seal. Sprinkle cherries evenly over dough, pressing into dough. Brush rectangles with half of the butter.

2) In small bowl, mix sugar and cinnamon. Sprinkle half of sugar mixture evenly over dough.

3) Starting with one short side of each rectangle, roll up; pinch edge to seal. With serrated knife, cut each roll into 3 slices. Place each slice, cut side down, between 2 sheets of plastic wrap or waxed paper; roll or press each into 5-inch round. Remove plastic wrap; place 2 inches apart on cookie sheets.

4) Brush rounds with remaining butter; sprinkle with remaining sugar mixture. Cover rounds with plastic wrap or waxed paper; press or roll sugar mixture into dough.

5) Bake 14 to 16 minutes or until golden brown. Immediately remove from cookie sheets. Serve warm or cool.

HIGH ALTITUDE (3500-6000 FT.): No change.

Nutrition Information Per Serving:
Serving Size: 1 Roll

Calories:	255	From Fat:	115
Total Fat			13g
Saturated			6g
Cholesterol			20mg
Sodium			510mg
Total Carbohydrate			32g
Dietary Fiber			1g
Sugars			19g
Protein			3g

Candy Cane Coffee Cake

PREP TIME: 20 MINUTES (READY IN 1 HOUR 15 MINUTES)
SERVINGS: 12

COFFEE CAKE

- 1 package (3 oz.) cream cheese, softened
- 2 tablespoons granulated sugar
- 1 teaspoon almond extract
- ¼ cup sliced almonds
- ¼ cup chopped maraschino cherries, well drained
- 1 can (8 oz.) Pillsbury® refrigerated crescent dinner rolls

GLAZE

- ½ cup powdered sugar
- 2 teaspoons milk

1) Heat oven to 375°F. Grease cookie sheet with shortening. In small bowl, beat cream cheese and granulated sugar until light and fluffy. Stir in almond extract, almonds and cherries; set aside.

2) Unroll dough onto cookie sheet; press into 13x7-inch rectangle, firmly pressing perforations to seal. Spoon cream cheese mixture down center ⅓ of rectangle.

3) On each long side of dough rectangle, make cuts 1 inch apart to edge of filling. Fold opposite strips of dough over filling and cross in center to form a braided appearance; seal ends. Curve one end to form candy cane shape.

4) Bake 18 to 22 minutes or until golden brown. Remove from cookie sheet; place on wire rack. Cool completely, about 30 minutes.

5) In small bowl, mix glaze ingredients until smooth; drizzle over coffee cake. If desired, garnish with additional sliced almonds and cherries. Store in refrigerator.

HIGH ALTITUDE (3500-6000 FT.): No change.

Nutrition Information Per Serving:
Serving Size: 1/12 of Recipe

Calories:	135	From Fat:	55
Total Fat		6g	
Saturated		2g	
Cholesterol		10mg	
Sodium		250mg	
Total Carbohydrate		18g	
Dietary Fiber		0g	
Sugars		11g	
Protein		2g	

Cheese-Filled Parmesan Biscuit Loaves

EILEEN M. WATSON | OVIEDO, FLORIDA

Pillsbury Bake-Off

PREP TIME: 15 MINUTES (READY IN 50 MINUTES)
SERVINGS: 8 BISCUITS

¾ cup grated Parmesan cheese

⅓ cup finely chopped walnuts

2 oz. cream cheese, softened

1½ tablespoons finely chopped fresh basil

1 clove garlic, minced

1 can (16.3 oz.) Pillsbury® Grands!® Homestyle refrigerated buttermilk biscuits

¼ cup butter or margarine, melted

1) Heat oven to 350°F. Lightly grease 2 (9x5- or 8x4-inch) loaf pans with shortening. In small bowl, mix Parmesan cheese and walnuts. In another small bowl, mix cream cheese, basil and garlic until well blended.

2) Separate dough into 8 biscuits. Spoon 1 teaspoon cream cheese mixture onto half of each biscuit. Fold biscuit over cream cheese; press edges to seal.

3) Dip each biscuit in melted butter; coat with cheese-walnut mixture. Arrange 4 biscuits, seam side down, in each loaf pan. Drizzle any remaining butter over biscuits; sprinkle with any remaining cheese mixture.

4) Bake 25 to 35 minutes or until golden brown. Immediately remove from pan; serve warm. Store in refrigerator.

HIGH ALTITUDE (3500-6500 FT.): Heat oven to 375°F. Bake as directed above.

Nutrition Information Per Serving:
Serving Size: 1 Biscuit

Calories:	350	From Fat:	210
Total Fat			23g
Saturated			10g
Cholesterol			30mg
Sodium			840mg
Total Carbohydrate			25g
Dietary Fiber			0g
Sugars			4g
Protein			9g

Cookies 'n Crescent Sweet Rolls

ROBERT HOLT | MENDOTA HEIGHTS, MINNESOTA

PREP TIME: 15 MINUTES (READY IN 1 HOUR 5 MINUTES)
SERVINGS: 12 SWEET ROLLS

ROLLS

1 can (8 oz.) Pillsbury® refrigerated crescent dinner rolls

6 inches Pillsbury® refrigerated chocolate chip cookies (from 18-oz. roll)

¼ cup chopped pecans

GLAZE

⅔ cup powdered sugar

¼ teaspoon vanilla

3 to 4 teaspoons milk

1) Heat oven to 350°F. Lightly spray 9-inch round pan or glass pie pan with cooking spray.

2) Separate crescent dough into 2 long rectangles. Overlap long sides ½ inch to form 1 large rectangle; press seam and perforations to seal. Spoon small amounts of cookie dough evenly over crescent dough; press or pat to evenly cover. Sprinkle with pecans.

3) Starting with one long side, roll up dough; pinch seam to seal. Cut into 12 pieces; arrange cut side up in pan.

4) Bake 28 to 35 minutes or until crescent dough is golden brown. Cool 15 minutes.

5) In small bowl, stir together all glaze ingredients until smooth, adding enough milk for desired drizzling consistency; drizzle over warm rolls. Serve warm.

HIGH ALTITUDE (3500-6500 FT.): Bake at 350°F. 35 to 40 minutes. Continue as directed above.

Nutrition Information Per Serving:
Serving Size: 1 Sweet Roll

Calories:	250	From Fat:	110
Total Fat			13g
Saturated			3.5g
Cholesterol			0mg
Sodium			240mg
Total Carbohydrate			31g
Dietary Fiber			1g
Sugars			18g
Protein			3g

Orange-Glazed Cranberry Crowns

CLAUDIA SHEPARDSON | LOUDONVILLE, NEW YORK

PREP TIME: 15 MINUTES (READY IN 40 MINUTES)
SERVINGS: 6 SWEET ROLLS

6 tablespoons frozen (thawed) orange juice concentrate

¼ cup sweetened dried cranberries

¼ cup coarsely chopped walnuts

½ cup butter, melted (do not use margarine or spread)

½ cup sugar

1 teaspoon ground cinnamon

1 can (16.3 oz.) Pillsbury® Grands!® Flaky Layers refrigerated original or buttermilk biscuits

1) Heat oven to 350°F. Spray 6 miniature fluted tube cups generously with cooking spray. Place 1 tablespoon orange juice concentrate in each cup. Sprinkle evenly with cranberries and walnuts.

2) In shallow bowl, place melted butter; in another shallow bowl, mix sugar and cinnamon. Separate dough into 8 biscuits; cut each into 3 wedge-shaped pieces. Dip each biscuit piece into butter; lightly coat with sugar mixture. Place 4 biscuit pieces, point side down, over mixture in each cup; press lightly. Drizzle any remaining butter evenly over rolls.

3) Bake 18 to 23 minutes or until golden brown. Invert pan onto serving platter or cookie sheet; leave pan over rolls for 1 minute. Carefully remove pan. If any topping remains in pan, spoon over rolls. Serve warm.

*NOTE: To make in 12-cup fluted tube pan, generously spray with cooking spray. Place orange juice concentrate in bottom of pan. Sprinkle with cranberries and walnuts. Make biscuit pieces as directed above; place rounded side down over mixture in pan. Bake 23-33 minutes.

HIGH ALTITUDE (3500-6500 FT.): For miniature fluted tube cups, bake at 350°F. 23 to 28 minutes; for 12-cup fluted tube pan, bake at 350°F. 33 to 38 minutes.

Nutrition Information Per Serving:
Serving Size: 1 Sweet Roll

Calories:	540	From Fat:	280
Total Fat			31g
Saturated			12g
Cholesterol			40mg
Sodium			920mg
Total Carbohydrate			61g
Dietary Fiber			0g
Sugars			32g
Protein			7g

Strawberry Roly-Polies

CATHY FREY | LOCK HAVEN, PENNSYLVANIA

Pillsbury Bake-Off®

PREP TIME: 15 MINUTES (READY IN 40 MINUTES)
SERVINGS: 12 (1 ROLL, 1 BERRY AND 1 ORANGE SLICE EACH)

ROLLS

1 (11-oz.) can Pillsbury® Refrigerated Breadsticks

3 rolls Betty Crocker® Fruit by the Foot® Strawberry Fruit Snack (from 4.5-oz. box)

¼ to ⅓ cup sugar

1 egg white, beaten

GARNISH

12 fresh strawberries

12 orange slices

1) Heat oven to 375°F. Grease cookie sheet with shortening or spray with cooking spray. Unroll dough; separate into 12 breadsticks. Stretch each breadstick until about 9 inches long.

2) Unroll all fruit snack rolls. With scissors, cut each evenly into 4 (about 8-inch-long) pieces. Place 1 piece on each breadstick. Roll up each breadstick, coiling dough into spiral shape; press ends to seal. Place sugar in shallow dish. Brush top and side of each coil with beaten egg white; roll in sugar. Place sugar side up on greased cookie sheet.

3) Bake at 375°F. for 11 to 16 minutes or until light golden brown. Immediately remove from cookie sheet. Cool 5 minutes. Serve warm with strawberries and orange slices.

HIGH ALTITUDE (ABOVE 3500 FT.): No change.

Nutrition Information Per Serving: Serving Size: 1/12 of Recipe	
Calories: 120	From Fat: 15
Total Fat	2g
Saturated	0g
Cholesterol	0mg
Sodium	200mg
Total Carbohydrate	24g
Dietary Fiber	1g
Sugars	11g
Protein	3g

Pineapple-Orange Blossoms

Pillsbury Bake-Off

SHARON HENDERSON | ELLETTSVILLE, INDIANA

PREP TIME: 15 MINUTES (READY IN 45 MINUTES)
SERVINGS: 8 ROLLS

1 (12.4-oz.) can Pillsbury® Refrigerated Cinnamon Rolls with Icing

½ cup crushed pineapple (from 8-oz. can), well drained on paper towels

⅓ cup orange marmalade

4 oz. cream cheese (from 8-oz. pkg.), softened

1) Heat oven to 350°F. Spray 8 (2³⁄₄x1¹⁄₄-inch) muffin cups with cooking spray. Separate dough into 8 rolls; set icing aside. Cut each roll into quarters; place 4 quarters, points up and separated slightly, in each sprayed muffin cup.

2) In small bowl, mix pineapple, marmalade and cream cheese. Place 2 tablespoons mixture into center of dough in each cup.

3) Bake at 350°F. for 17 to 22 minutes or until light golden brown. Cool in pan on wire rack 5 minutes. Run knife around edge of muffin cups; remove rolls from cups and place on serving plate.

4) Remove cover from icing; microwave on Medium (50%) for 10 to 15 seconds or until drizzling consistency. Drizzle icing over warm rolls. Serve warm.

HIGH ALTITUDE (ABOVE 3500 FT.): Bake at 375°F. for 20 to 23 minutes.

Nutrition Information Per Serving:
Serving Size: 1 Roll

Calories:	240	From Fat:	90
Total Fat			11g
Saturated			5g
Cholesterol			25mg
Sodium			410mg
Total Carbohydrate			34g
Dietary Fiber			0g
Sugars			15g
Protein			4g

Maple Cream Coffee Treat

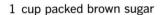

RETA EBBINK | TORRANCE, CALIFORNIA

PREP TIME: 15 MINUTES (READY IN 50 MINUTES)
SERVINGS: 20 SWEET ROLLS

1 cup packed brown sugar

½ cup chopped nuts

⅓ cup maple-flavored syrup or dark corn syrup

¼ cup butter or margarine, melted

1 package (8 oz.) cream cheese, softened

¼ cup powdered sugar

2 tablespoons butter or margarine, softened

½ cup coconut

2 cans (12 oz. each) Pillsbury® Golden Layers® refrigerated buttermilk biscuits

1) Heat oven to 350°F. In ungreased 13x9-inch pan, mix brown sugar, nuts, syrup and ¼ cup butter; spread evenly in bottom of pan. In small bowl with spoon, beat cream cheese, powdered sugar and 2 tablespoons butter until smooth. Stir in coconut.

2) Separate dough into 20 biscuits; press or roll each into 4-inch round. Spoon 1 tablespoon cream cheese mixture down center of each biscuit round to within ¼ inch of edge. Overlap sides of dough over filling, forming finger-shaped rolls; arrange seam side down in 2 rows of 10 rolls each over brown sugar mixture in pan.

3) Bake 25 to 30 minutes or until deep golden brown. Cool 5 minutes. Invert pan onto sheet of foil or waxed paper, or serving platter; remove pan. Serve warm. Store in refrigerator.

HIGH ALTITUDE (3500-6500 FT.): Bake at 350°F. 30 to 35 minutes.

Nutrition Information Per Serving:
Serving Size: 1 Sweet Roll

Calories:	280	From Fat:	140
Total Fat			16g
Saturated			6g
Cholesterol			20mg
Sodium			420mg
Total Carbohydrate			32g
Dietary Fiber			0g
Sugars			18g
Protein			3g

Wondering what kind of nuts to use in this recipe? Try chopped walnuts, pecans or macadamia nuts.

Lemon-Almond Breakfast Pastry

SHARON RICHARDSON | DALLAS, TEXAS

PREP TIME: 20 MINUTES (READY IN 1 HOUR 10 MINUTES)
SERVINGS: 16

FILLING

½ cup butter or margarine, softened

1 roll (7 oz.) almond paste, broken into small pieces

2 eggs

5 teaspoons Pillsbury BEST® all-purpose flour

1 to 2 teaspoons grated lemon peel

CRUST

1 box (15 oz.) Pillsbury® refrigerated pie crusts, softened as directed on box

1 egg, beaten

1 tablespoon milk

2 tablespoons sugar

1) In small bowl with spoon or food processor, beat or process butter and almond paste until smooth. Add 2 eggs; beat or process until well blended. By hand, stir in flour and lemon peel just until blended. Cover; place in freezer until mixture is thick, 20 to 30 minutes.

2) Remove 1 pie crust from pouch; place crust flat on work surface. If necessary, press out folds or creases. Cut 1-inch circle from center of crust. With very sharp knife, and curving motions, decoratively score crust in pinwheel design (do not cut through crust or filling will leak out).

3) Heat oven to 400°F. Remove remaining pie crust from pouch; place crust flat on work surface. If necessary, press out folds or creases. Place crust on ungreased 12-inch pizza pan or cookie sheet.

4) Spread cold filling over crust to within 2 inches of edge. Brush edge with beaten egg. Carefully place scored crust over filled bottom crust. Press edges to seal; flute. In small bowl, mix remaining beaten egg and milk; brush over pastry. Sprinkle with sugar.

5) Bake 22 to 27 minutes or until golden brown. Cut into wedges; serve warm. Store in refrigerator.

HIGH ALTITUDE (3500-6500 FT.): Bake at 400°F. 24 to 29 minutes.

Nutrition Information Per Serving:
Serving Size: 1/16 of Recipe

Calories:	240	From Fat:	150
Total Fat			16g
Saturated			6g
Cholesterol			60mg
Sodium			150mg
Total Carbohydrate			21g
Dietary Fiber			0g
Sugars			8g
Protein			3g

Cherry-Almond Swirls

JENNY RIEGSECKER | DELTA, OHIO

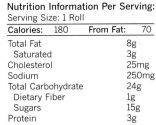

PREP TIME: 20 MINUTES (READY IN 40 MINUTES)
SERVINGS: 12 ROLLS

¼ cup granulated sugar

½ cup slivered almonds

1 (3-oz.) pkg. cream cheese

¼ teaspoon vanilla

⅛ teaspoon almond extract

1 egg yolk

1 (8-oz.) can Pillsbury® Refrigerated Crescent Dinner Rolls

¼ cup cherry preserves

½ cup powdered sugar

2 teaspoons water

1) Heat oven to 375°F. Spray 12 regular-size muffin cups with cooking spray. In food processor, place granulated sugar and almonds; process about 30 seconds or until almonds are finely ground. Add cream cheese, vanilla, almond extract and egg yolk; process about 10 seconds or until combined.

2) On lightly floured surface, unroll dough into 1 large rectangle. With floured rolling pin or fingers, roll or press dough into 12x9-inch rectangle, firmly pressing perforations to seal.

3) Spread cream cheese mixture evenly over dough. Starting with 1 long side of dough rectangle, roll up dough into log (filling will be soft). With serrated knife, cut log into 12 slices; place slices, cut side up, in sprayed muffin cups.

4) Bake at 375°F. for 11 to 15 minutes or until light golden brown. Remove from oven. With handle of wooden spoon, make indentation in center of each roll. Spoon 1 teaspoon preserves into each indentation.

5) Return to oven; bake an additional 2 to 4 minutes or until golden brown. Run knife around edge of muffin cups to loosen; remove rolls from cups and place on wire racks.

6) In small bowl, blend powdered sugar and water until smooth; drizzle over warm rolls. Serve warm or at room temperature. Store in refrigerator.

HIGH ALTITUDE (ABOVE 3500 FT.): No change.

Nutrition Information Per Serving:
Serving Size: 1 Roll

Calories:	180	From Fat:	70
Total Fat			8g
Saturated			3g
Cholesterol			25mg
Sodium			250mg
Total Carbohydrate			24g
Dietary Fiber			1g
Sugars			15g
Protein			3g

Crunchy Banana-Colada Bread

SUSAN ADAMS | NAPERVILLE, ILLINOIS

PREP TIME: 15 MINUTES (READY IN 3 HOURS 40 MINUTES)
SERVINGS: 16 SLICES; YIELD: 1 LOAF

3/4 cup sugar

1/2 cup unsalted or regular butter, softened

2 eggs

1 cup mashed very ripe bananas (2 medium)

1 (6-oz.) container Yoplait® Original 99% Fat Free Piña Colada Yogurt

1 1/2 cups all-purpose flour

1 teaspoon baking soda

1 teaspoon salt

4 Nature Valley® Banana Nut Crunchy Granola Bars (2 pouches from 8.9-oz. box), coarsely crushed*

1/4 cup flaked coconut

1) Heat oven to 350°F. (If using dark pan, decrease oven temperature to 325°F.) Generously grease 9x5-inch loaf pan with shortening or spray with cooking spray. In large bowl, beat sugar and butter with electric mixer on medium speed until well blended. Beat in eggs, bananas and yogurt.

2) Add flour, baking soda and salt; beat until combined. Stir in 1/2 cup of the crushed granola bars until well combined. Pour batter into greased pan.

3) In small bowl, mix remaining 1/4 cup crushed granola bars and the coconut. Sprinkle evenly over batter in pan; press in lightly.

4) Bake at 350°F. for 60 to 70 minutes or until toothpick inserted in center comes out clean, covering with foil during last 15 to 20 minutes of baking to prevent excessive browning. Cool in pan on wire rack 15 minutes. Remove loaf from pan; place on rack. Cool completely, about 2 hours. Wrap tightly and store in refrigerator.

*NOTE: To easily crush granola bars, do not unwrap. Use rolling pin to crush bars.

HIGH ALTITUDE (ABOVE 3500 FT.): Bake at 350°F. for 65 to 70 minutes.

Nutrition Information Per Serving:
Serving Size: 1 Slice

Calories:	195	From Fat:	70
Total Fat			8g
Saturated			4g
Cholesterol			40mg
Sodium			260mg
Total Carbohydrate			28g
Dietary Fiber			1g
Sugars			15g
Protein			3g

Country Apple Coffee Cake

SUSAN F. PORUBCAN | JEFFERSON, WISCONSIN

PREP TIME: 20 MINUTES (READY IN 1 HOUR 10 MINUTES)
SERVINGS: 8

COFFEE CAKE

2 tablespoons butter or margarine, softened

1½ cups chopped peeled apples (1 to 2 medium)

1 can (12 oz.) Pillsbury® Golden Layers® refrigerated buttermilk biscuits

⅓ cup packed brown sugar

¼ teaspoon ground cinnamon

⅓ cup light corn syrup

1½ teaspoons whiskey, if desired

1 egg

½ cup pecan halves or pieces

GLAZE

⅓ cup powdered sugar

¼ teaspoon vanilla

1 to 2 teaspoons milk

1) Heat oven to 350°F. Using 1 tablespoon of the butter, generously grease 9-inch round or 8-inch square pan. Spread 1 cup of the apples in pan.

2) Separate dough into 10 biscuits. Cut each into quarters; arrange points up over apples. Top with remaining ½ cup apples.

3) In small bowl with electric mixer, beat remaining 1 tablespoon butter, the brown sugar, cinnamon, corn syrup, whiskey and egg on medium speed 2 to 3 minutes or until sugar is partially dissolved. Stir in pecans. Spoon over biscuit pieces and apples.

4) Bake 35 to 45 minutes or until deep golden brown. Cool 5 minutes. Meanwhile, in small bowl, stir together all glaze ingredients until smooth, adding enough milk for desired drizzling consistency.

5) If desired, remove coffee cake from pan. Drizzle glaze over warm cake. Serve warm or cool. Store in refrigerator.

HIGH ALTITUDE (3500-6500 FT.): No change.

Nutrition Information Per Serving:
Serving Size: 1/8 of Recipe

Calories:	320	From Fat:	130
Total Fat			14g
Saturated			4g
Cholesterol			35mg
Sodium			490mg
Total Carbohydrate			46g
Dietary Fiber			1g
Sugars			25g
Protein			4g

Main Dishes

Fill 'em up with comforting classics, casseroles and stews.

SPICY MANGO CHICKEN
PG. 160

ITALIAN VEGETARIAN LASAGNA
PG. 190

MINT MARINATED LAMB CHOPS
PG. 211

Italian Cheese-Stuffed Meat Loaf

PREP TIME:	30 MINUTES (READY IN 1 HOUR 40 MINUTES)
SERVINGS:	8

2 eggs

1½ lb. lean (at least 80%) ground beef

2 cups soft French bread crumbs

½ cup shredded Parmesan cheese (2 oz.)

¼ cup chopped fresh basil or 1½ teaspoons dried basil leaves

½ teaspoon salt

¼ teaspoon pepper

4 cloves garlic, minced

1 can (8 oz.) pizza sauce

1½ cups shredded provolone cheese (6 oz.)

1 jar (7.25 oz.) roasted red bell peppers, drained, chopped

¼ cup chopped ripe olives

1) Heat oven to 375°F. Line 15x10x1-inch pan with foil; spray foil with cooking spray. In large bowl, beat eggs. Stir in ground beef, bread crumbs, Parmesan cheese, basil, salt, pepper, garlic and ½ cup of the pizza sauce until well combined.

2) On large sheet of foil, shape beef mixture into 12x10-inch rectangle. Top evenly with provolone cheese, roasted peppers and olives to within ½ inch of edges. Starting with one 10-inch side, roll up; press seam to seal. Place seam side down in pan.

3) Bake 40 minutes. Remove from oven; spoon remaining pizza sauce over loaf. Insert meat thermometer so bulb reaches center of loaf.

4) Return to oven; bake 15 to 20 minutes longer or until loaf is thoroughly cooked in center and thermometer reads 160°F. Let stand 10 minutes before slicing.

HIGH ALTITUDE (3500-6000 FT.): In Step 3, bake at 375°F. 50 minutes. In Step 4, bake 10 to 15 minutes or until loaf is thoroughly cooked in center and thermometer reads 160°F.

Nutrition Information Per Serving:
Serving Size: 1/8 of Recipe

Calories:	330	From Fat:	190
Total Fat			21g
Saturated			10g
Cholesterol			120mg
Sodium			780mg
Total Carbohydrate			11g
Dietary Fiber			1g
Sugars			3g
Protein			25g

Southwest Nacho Casserole

PREP TIME: 20 MINUTES (READY IN 1 HOUR 10 MINUTES)
SERVINGS: 10

2 lb. lean (at least 80%) ground beef

1 cup water

2 envelopes (1.25 oz. each) Old El Paso® 40% less-sodium taco seasoning mix

1 can (4.5 oz.) Old El Paso® chopped green chiles

2 cans (16 oz. each) Old El Paso® fat-free refried beans

2 cups shredded reduced-fat Cheddar cheese (8 oz.)

1 cup chopped tomato (1 large)

½ cup chopped green onions (8 medium)

1 can (2.5 oz.) sliced ripe olives, drained

1 bag (12 oz.) gold tortilla chips (extra thick)

Sour cream if desired

1) Heat oven to 350°F. Spray 13x9-inch (3-quart) glass baking dish with cooking spray. In 12-inch nonstick skillet, cook ground beef over medium-high heat, stirring frequently, until thoroughly cooked; drain.

2) Stir in water and taco seasoning mix. Bring to a boil; cook 2 to 4 minutes, stirring occasionally, until thickened. Stir in chiles.

3) Spread refried beans in baking dish. Top with ground beef mixture. Cover tightly with foil.

4) Bake 30 to 40 minutes or until bubbly around edges.

5) Remove from oven. Uncover; sprinkle with cheese, tomato, onions and olives. Arrange 18 to 20 tortilla chips around outside edges of baking dish. Return to oven; bake uncovered about 10 minutes longer or until cheese is melted. If desired, top with sour cream. Serve with remaining tortilla chips for scooping.

HIGH ALTITUDE (3500-6000 FT.): Heat oven to 375°F. Continue as directed above.

Nutrition Information Per Serving:
Serving Size: 1/10 of Recipe

Calories:	470	From Fat:	200
Total Fat			22g
Saturated			6g
Cholesterol			65mg
Sodium			1300mg
Total Carbohydrate			44g
Dietary Fiber			9g
Sugars			8g
Protein			32g

Sweet-and-Sour Shrimp over Rice

PREP TIME: 35 MINUTES
SERVINGS: 4

🄴 EASY 🅕 LOW FAT

1 cup uncooked regular long-grain white rice

2 cups water

¼ teaspoon salt

2 medium green bell peppers, cut into 16 (1½-inch) pieces

12 or 16 shelled deveined uncooked large shrimp (about ½ lb.), tails removed

1 (8-oz.) can pineapple chunks in light syrup, drained

1 cup purchased sweet-and-sour sauce

1) Cook rice in water with salt as directed on package.

2) Meanwhile, heat gas or charcoal grill. Thread bell pepper, shrimp and pineapple onto four 8 to 10-inch metal skewers.

3) When grill is heated, place kabobs on gas grill over medium heat or on charcoal grill 4 to 6 inches from medium coals. Cover grill; cook 6 to 8 minutes or until shrimp turn pink, brushing frequently with sweet-and-sour sauce.

4) To serve, place any remaining sauce in small microwave-safe bowl. Microwave on High for about 1 minute or until thoroughly heated. Remove bell pepper, shrimp and pineapple from skewers; serve over rice with warm sauce.

HIGH ALTITUDE (ABOVE 3500 FT.): Cook rice following High Altitude directions on package. Continue as directed above.

Nutrition Information Per Serving:
Serving Size: 1/4 of Recipe

Calories:	345	From Fat:	25
Total Fat		3g	
Saturated		1g	
Cholesterol		80mg	
Sodium		1020mg	
Total Carbohydrate		65g	
Dietary Fiber		2g	
Sugars		18g	
Protein		14g	

Chili-Cheese-Potato Casserole

PREP TIME: 10 MINUTES (READY IN 1 HOUR 10 MINUTES)
SERVINGS: 6 (1-1/4 CUPS EACH)

 LOW FAT

1 bag (1 lb. 4 oz.) refrigerated sliced potatoes

2 cans (15 oz. each) 99% fat-free turkey chili

1/3 cup 100% fat-free chicken broth with 33% less sodium (from 14-oz. can)

1 cup cubed (1/4 to 1/2-inch) Mexican pasteurized prepared cheese product with jalapeño peppers (3 oz.)

1/2 cup sliced green onions (8 medium)

1 medium tomato, seeded, chopped

1/2 cup light sour cream, if desired

Nutrition Information Per Serving:
Serving Size: 1-1/4 Cups

Calories:	320	From Fat:	65
Total Fat			7g
Saturated			3g
Cholesterol			70mg
Sodium			1250mg
Total Carbohydrate			41g
Dietary Fiber			4g
Sugars			7g
Protein			23g

1) Heat oven to 350°F. Spray 13x9-inch (3-quart) glass baking dish with cooking spray. Arrange potato slices in baking dish.

2) In medium bowl, mix chili and broth; pour evenly over potatoes. Cover tightly with foil.

3) Bake 40 to 50 minutes or until potatoes are tender and mixture is hot and bubbly.

4) Remove from oven. Uncover; sprinkle with cheese, onions and tomato. Return to oven; bake uncovered about 10 minutes longer or until cheese is melted. Serve with sour cream.

HIGH ALTITUDE (3500-6000 FT.): No change.

tip

To seed a tomato, first core it, then slice it in half horizontally. Gently squeeze each half to shake out the seeds and membranes. Or, scoop them out with a small spoon.

Taco Nachos

PREP TIME: 15 MINUTES
SERVINGS: 4

EASY

1 (20-oz.) tub Old El Paso® Refrigerated Taco Sauce with Seasoned Ground Beef

8 cups hint-of-lime white corn tortilla chips (from 13.5-oz. pkg.)

3 oz. (3/4 cup) shredded taco-flavored cheese blend

2 cups shredded lettuce

1/4 cup sour cream

Nutrition Information Per Serving:
Serving Size: 1/4 of Recipe

Calories:	605	From Fat:	315
Total Fat			35g
Saturated			13g
Cholesterol			70mg
Sodium			1380mg
Total Carbohydrate			47g
Dietary Fiber			3g
Sugars			10g
Protein			25g

1) Heat taco sauce with ground beef as directed on tub.

2) For each serving, place 2 cups chips on individual serving plate. Top with 1/2 cup warm taco sauce with ground beef, 3 tablespoons cheese, 1/2 cup lettuce and 1 tablespoon sour cream.

HIGH ALTITUDE (ABOVE 3500 FT.): Heat taco sauce with ground beef following High Altitude directions on tub.

Chicken Pizza Primavera

JANET BURNS | VIRGINIA BEACH, VIRGINIA

PREP TIME: 15 MINUTES (READY IN 40 MINUTES)
SERVINGS: 4

1 (13.8-oz.) can Pillsbury® Refrigerated Pizza Crust

Olive oil cooking spray

2 tablespoons shredded Asiago cheese

¼ to ½ teaspoon garlic salt

2 tablespoons light ranch dressing

1 (6-oz.) pkg. refrigerated cooked Italian-style chicken breast strips, chopped

⅓ cup finely chopped red bell pepper

⅓ cup thinly sliced red onion

½ cup torn baby spinach

6 oz. (1½ cups) shredded Italian cheese blend

1 teaspoon dried pizza seasoning

1) Heat oven to 400°F. Lightly grease 12-inch pizza pan or pizza stone with shortening or spray with cooking spray. Unroll dough; place on greased pan. Starting at center, press out dough to edge of pan.

2) Lightly spray dough with olive oil cooking spray. Sprinkle Asiago cheese and garlic salt over dough. Bake at 400°F. for 8 to 10 minutes or until lightly browned.

3) Remove partially baked crust from oven. Spread ranch dressing over crust. Top with chicken, bell pepper, onion and spinach. Sprinkle Italian cheese blend and pizza seasoning over top.

4) Return to oven; bake an additional 9 to 12 minutes or until cheese is melted and pizza is thoroughly heated. Cut into wedges.

HIGH ALTITUDE (ABOVE 3500 FT.): No change.

Nutrition Information Per Serving:
Serving Size: 1/4 of Recipe

Calories:	500	From Fat:	170
Total Fat			19g
Saturated			9g
Cholesterol			70mg
Sodium			1450mg
Total Carbohydrate			50g
Dietary Fiber			2g
Sugars			9g
Protein			33g

Easy Chicken Manicotti Carbonara

PREP TIME: 25 MINUTES (READY IN 2 HOURS 10 MINUTES)
SERVINGS: 7 (2 SHELLS EACH)

4 cups refrigerated Alfredo sauce

1 cup milk

1½ lb. chicken breast tenders

1 teaspoon garlic salt

14 uncooked manicotti (8 oz.)

1 cup shredded fresh Parmesan cheese (4 oz.)

1 cup Green Giant Select® LeSueur® frozen baby sweet peas (from 1-lb. bag), thawed

½ cup cooked ham strips (2x¼x¼-inch)

1) Heat oven to 350°F. Spray 13x9-inch (3-quart) glass baking dish with cooking spray. In medium bowl, mix Alfredo sauce and milk; spread 1 cup mixture in baking dish.

2) Sprinkle chicken tenders with garlic salt. Fill each uncooked manicotti with chicken, stuffing into each end; place stuffed manicotti in baking dish. Reserve ½ cup sauce mixture for topping; pour remaining 3½ cups sauce mixture over manicotti. Cover tightly with foil.

3) Bake 1¼ hours. Meanwhile, in medium bowl, mix reserved ½ cup sauce mixture, the Parmesan cheese, peas and ham.

4) Remove from oven. Uncover; pour sauce mixture over manicotti. Return to oven; bake uncovered 15 to 20 minutes longer or until cheese is melted. Let stand 10 minutes before serving.

HIGH ALTITUDE (3500-6000 FT.): Increase milk to 1½ cups. Continue as directed above.

Nutrition Information Per Serving:
Serving Size: 2 Shells

Calories:	573	From Fat:	219
Total Fat			25g
Saturated			14g
Cholesterol			125mg
Sodium			1270mg
Total Carbohydrate			42g
Dietary Fiber			2g
Sugars			8g
Protein			45g

Chicken tenders are the narrow strips of white meat lying alongside the breast. They're sold in large, resealable plastic bags, making it easy to pop out what you need and keep the rest in the freezer.

Orange Pork and Sweet Potatoes

APRIL CARTY-SIPP | COLLINGSWOOD, NEW JERSEY

PREP TIME: 15 MINUTES (READY IN 1 HOUR 5 MINUTES)
SERVINGS: 4

3 tablespoons butter or margarine

4 boneless pork loin chops (about 1 lb.)

1 teaspoon salt

½ to 1 teaspoon pepper

2 medium dark-orange sweet potatoes, peeled, cut into ½-inch-thick slices (about 1 lb.)

¼ cup orange juice

3 tablespoons packed brown sugar

1 (6-oz.) container Yoplait® Original 99% Fat Free Orange Crème Yogurt

1) Heat oven to 375°F. In 10-inch skillet, melt butter over medium-high heat. Add pork chops; sprinkle with salt and pepper. Cook 2 to 4 minutes, turning once, until browned on both sides.

2) In ungreased 8-inch square (2-quart) glass baking dish, layer sweet potato slices. Place pork chops over potatoes.

3) In same skillet, cook orange juice and brown sugar over medium heat until brown sugar is melted; pour over pork and potatoes. Cover dish tightly with foil.

4) Bake at 375°F. for 35 to 50 minutes or until pork is no longer pink and meat thermometer inserted into center of pork chop reads 160°F.

5) Remove pork chops and potatoes from dish; place on serving platter. Pour remaining liquid from dish into small saucepan; stir in yogurt. Cook over medium heat, stirring occasionally, until sauce is thoroughly heated. Pour sauce over pork chops and sweet potatoes.

HIGH ALTITUDE (ABOVE 3500 FT.): No change.

Nutrition Information Per Serving: Serving Size: 1/4 of Recipe		
Calories: 410	From Fat:	160
Total Fat		18g
Saturated		9g
Cholesterol		95mg
Sodium		720mg
Total Carbohydrate		37g
Dietary Fiber		2g
Sugars		29g
Protein		27g

Sour Cream-Chicken Enchiladas

PREP TIME:	25 MINUTES (READY IN 1 HOUR 5 MINUTES)	EASY
SERVINGS:	6 (2 ENCHILADAS EACH)	

1 can (10 3/4 oz.) condensed cream of chicken soup

1 container (8 oz.) sour cream

1 can (4.5 oz.) Old El Paso® chopped green chiles

1 package (10.5 oz.) Old El Paso® flour tortillas for soft tacos & fajitas (twelve 6-inch tortillas)

3 cups shredded Cheddar cheese (12 oz.)

3 cups chopped cooked chicken or 2 boxes (9 oz. each) frozen diced cooked chicken, thawed

1) Heat oven to 350°F. Spray 13x9-inch (3-quart) glass baking dish with cooking spray. In medium bowl, mix soup, sour cream and green chiles.

2) Spoon 2 tablespoons soup mixture down center of each tortilla; set remaining mixture aside. Reserve 1/2 cup cheese for garnish. Top each tortilla with about 1/4 cup chicken and scant 1/4 cup cheese. Fold sides of tortillas over filling; place seam side down in baking dish. Spoon remaining soup mixture over filled tortillas. Cover tightly with foil.

3) Bake 30 to 35 minutes or until hot and bubbly.

4) Remove from oven. Uncover; sprinkle with reserved 1/2 cup cheese. Return to oven; bake uncovered about 5 minutes longer or until cheese is melted. If desired, serve with chopped tomato and shredded lettuce.

HIGH ALTITUDE (3500-6000 FT.): Bake at 350°F. 45 to 50 minutes. Continue as directed above.

Nutrition Information Per Serving:
Serving Size: 2 Enchiladas

Calories:	640	From Fat:	340
Total Fat			38g
Saturated			20g
Cholesterol			150mg
Sodium			1110mg
Total Carbohydrate			35g
Dietary Fiber			2g
Sugars			4g
Protein			40g

Sloppy Joe Biscuit Pot Pies

PREP TIME: 15 MINUTES (READY IN 40 MINUTES)
SERVINGS: 2

½ lb. lean (at least 80%) ground beef

¼ cup chopped onion (½ medium)

¾ cup Green Giant® frozen mixed vegetables (from 1-lb. bag)

1 teaspoon packed brown sugar

¼ teaspoon dry ground mustard

½ cup chili sauce

1 tablespoon Worcestershire sauce

2 Pillsbury® Oven Baked frozen buttermilk biscuits (from 25-oz. bag)

1 egg, beaten, if desired

½ teaspoon sesame seed, if desired

1) Heat oven to 400ºF. In 8-inch nonstick skillet, cook ground beef and onion over medium-high heat, stirring frequently, until beef is thoroughly cooked. Drain.

2) Stir in frozen mixed vegetables, brown sugar, mustard, chili sauce and Worcestershire sauce. Cook 2 to 3 minutes, stirring occasionally, until vegetables are crisp-tender.

3) Spoon beef mixture into 2 (1½-cup) ungreased ovenproof bowls or ramekins. Top each with frozen biscuit. Brush each biscuit with beaten egg; sprinkle with sesame seed.

4) Bake 22 to 25 minutes or until biscuits are deep golden brown.

HIGH ALTITUDE (3500-6500 FT.): No change.

Nutrition Information Per Serving:
Serving Size: 1 Pot Pie

Calories:	550	From Fat:	230
Total Fat			26g
Saturated			9g
Cholesterol			65mg
Sodium			1540mg
Total Carbohydrate			55g
Dietary Fiber			5g
Sugars			27g
Protein			28g

tip

Look for ramekins in the supermarket baking aisle or at kitchen specialty shops. They're great for individual casseroles.

Caesar Chicken Salad Squares

LISA HUFF | BIRMINGHAM, ALABAMA

PREP TIME: 15 MINUTES (READY IN 40 MINUTES)
SERVINGS: 4

FILLING

2 cups cubed (⅛ to ¼ inch) cooked chicken breast or 1 (12.5-oz.) can chunk chicken breast in water, drained

2 oz. (½ cup) shredded mozzarella cheese or Italian cheese blend

1 tablespoon grated Parmesan cheese

1 tablespoon bacon flavor bits

2 tablespoons regular or reduced-fat Caesar dressing

1 tablespoon regular or light mayonnaise

1 teaspoon minced garlic

1 teaspoon lemon juice

CRUST

1 (8-oz.) can Pillsbury® Refrigerated Regular or Reduced Fat Crescent Dinner Rolls

GARNISH, (IF DESIRED)

¼ cup Caesar dressing

1 cup shredded romaine lettuce

1) Heat oven to 375°F. In medium bowl, mix all filling ingredients until well combined.

2) Unroll dough; separate into 4 rectangles. Place on ungreased cookie sheet; press each into 6x4-inch rectangle, firmly pressing perforations to seal. Spoon about ½ cup chicken mixture onto center of each dough rectangle. With knife, cut each corner of each rectangle from edge to within ½ inch of filling. Bring the 8 points of each rectangle up over filling; firmly pinch to seal, forming a square.

3) Bake at 375°F. for 16 to 21 minutes or until deep golden brown. Remove from cookie sheet. Garnish each with 1 tablespoon Caesar dressing and ¼ cup shredded lettuce.

HIGH ALTITUDE (ABOVE 3500 FT.): No change.

Nutrition Information Per Serving:
Serving Size: 1 Salad Square

Calories:	410	From Fat:	180
Total Fat			20g
Saturated			6g
Cholesterol			70mg
Sodium			950mg
Total Carbohydrate			28g
Dietary Fiber			1g
Sugars			8g
Protein			30g

Sloppy Joe Tater Nugget Hot Dish

PREP TIME: 20 MINUTES (READY IN 1 HOUR 10 MINUTES)
SERVINGS: 5 (1-1/3 CUPS EACH)

1 lb. lean (at least 80%) ground beef

¾ cup chopped onions (1½ medium)

½ cup chopped celery (1 medium stalk)

1 can (15.5 oz.) sloppy Joe sandwich sauce

1 can (10¾ oz.) condensed cream of chicken soup

1 cup Green Giant® Niblets® frozen corn (from 1-lb. bag), thawed

1 bag (16 oz.) frozen potato nuggets (4 cups)

1) Heat oven to 375°F. In 10-inch nonstick skillet, cook ground beef, onions and celery over medium heat, stirring frequently, until beef is thoroughly cooked; drain.

2) Stir in sandwich sauce, soup and corn; spoon into ungreased 11x7-inch (2-quart) glass baking dish. Top with potato nuggets.

3) Bake 40 to 50 minutes or until mixture is bubbly and potato nuggets are golden brown.

HIGH ALTITUDE (3500-6000 FT.): After stirring in sandwich sauce, soup and corn, cook until thoroughly heated before spooning into baking dish.

Nutrition Information Per Serving:
Serving Size: 1-1/3 Cups

Calories:	495	From Fat:	215
Total Fat			24g
Saturated			10g
Cholesterol			60mg
Sodium			1690mg
Total Carbohydrate			50g
Dietary Fiber			5g
Sugars			9g
Protein			25g

Honey-Maple Pork Chops

PREP TIME:	20 MINUTES	EASY	LOW FAT
SERVINGS:	4		

2 tablespoons honey

2 tablespoons maple-flavored syrup

⅛ teaspoon allspice or ginger

4 (6-oz.) pork loin chops (¾ inch thick)

¼ teaspoon salt

⅛ teaspoon pepper

Nutrition Information Per Serving:
Serving Size: 1 Pork Chop

Calories:	255	From Fat:	80
Total Fat			9g
Saturated			3g
Cholesterol			75mg
Sodium			210mg
Total Carbohydrate			16g
Dietary Fiber			0g
Sugars			12g
Protein			27g

1) Heat gas or charcoal grill. In small bowl, combine honey, syrup and allspice; mix well. Sprinkle pork chops with salt and pepper.

2) When grill is heated, brush pork with honey mixture; place on gas grill over medium heat or on charcoal grill 4 to 6 inches from medium coals. Cover grill; cook 10 to 12 minutes or until pork is no longer pink in center, turning once and brushing occasionally with honey mixture.

HIGH ALTITUDE (ABOVE 3500 FT.): Cook pork chops in covered gas grill over medium-low heat or in covered charcoal grill over medium-low coals using times above as a guide, turning once and brushing occasionally with honey mixture.

Easy Alfredo Tortellini

PREP TIME:	25 MINUTES (READY IN 25 MINUTES)	EASY
SERVINGS:	2 (1-1/2 CUPS EACH)	

1 package (9 oz.) refrigerated chicken-filled tortellini

½ cup Green Giant® frozen sweet peas (from 1-lb. bag)

¾ cup half-and-half

4 tablespoons grated Parmesan cheese

2 tablespoons cream cheese spread (from 8-oz. container)

Freshly ground black pepper

Nutrition Information Per Serving:
Serving Size: 1-1/2 Cups

Calories:	500	From Fat:	240
Total Fat			26g
Saturated			14g
Cholesterol			170mg
Sodium			960mg
Total Carbohydrate			38g
Dietary Fiber			3g
Sugars			6g
Protein			28g

1) In 3-quart saucepan, cook tortellini and peas as directed on tortellini package. Drain in colander; cover to keep warm.

2) In same saucepan, mix half-and-half, 2 tablespoons of the Parmesan cheese and the cream cheese spread with wire whisk. Cook over low heat, stirring constantly, until smooth.

3) Stir in cooked tortellini and peas. Cook 1 to 3 minutes, stirring occasionally, until thoroughly heated. Sprinkle individual servings with remaining 2 tablespoons Parmesan cheese and the pepper.

Spicy Mango Chicken

PREP TIME: 25 MINUTES
SERVINGS: 5 (1-3/4 CUPS EACH)

 EASY LOW FAT

8 oz. uncooked vermicelli

2 tablespoons oil

1 lb. chicken breast strips for stir-frying

1 small onion, cut into thin wedges (about ½ cup)

1 (1-lb.) pkg. Green Giant Select® Frozen Broccoli, Carrots & Cauliflower

1 (8-oz.) can sliced water chestnuts, drained

2 tablespoons water

1 cup cubed (½-inch) mango (from 24-oz. jar)

¾ cup purchased spicy stir-fry sauce

1) Cook vermicelli as directed on package. Drain.

2) Meanwhile, heat 1 tablespoon of the oil in wok or 12-inch skillet over medium-high heat until hot. Add chicken; cook and stir 5 to 6 minutes or until no longer pink in center. Remove chicken from wok; place on plate and cover to keep warm.

3) Add remaining tablespoon oil to wok. Add onion, frozen vegetables and water chestnuts; cook and stir 2 minutes. Add 2 tablespoons water; cover and cook 2 to 3 minutes or until vegetables are crisp-tender.

4) Add mango, stir-fry sauce and return chicken to wok; cook and stir an additional 2 to 3 minutes or until sauce has thickened. Serve over vermicelli.

HIGH ALTITUDE (ABOVE 3500 FT.): After adding mango, stir-fry sauce and returning chicken to wok, increase cook time to 4 minutes.

Nutrition Information Per Serving:
Serving Size: 1-3/4 Cups

Calories:	425	From Fat:	80
Total Fat			9g
Saturated			2g
Cholesterol			55mg
Sodium			1920mg
Total Carbohydrate			61g
Dietary Fiber			6g
Sugars			13g
Protein			31g

Turkey Fried Rice

PREP TIME: 30 MINUTES   EASY
SERVINGS: 4 (1-1/4 CUPS EACH)

2 cups uncooked instant brown rice

Water

2 eggs, beaten

½ lb. lean ground turkey

½ cup sliced green onions
(8 medium)

2 teaspoons minced garlic in water
(from a jar) or 2 garlic cloves,
minced

2 cups Green Giant® Frozen Mixed
Vegetables (from 1-lb. pkg.)

¼ cup soy sauce

2 teaspoons light sesame or
vegetable oil

¼ teaspoon ground red pepper
(cayenne)

1) Cook rice in water as directed on
package.

2) Meanwhile, spray wok or 12-inch
nonstick skillet with nonstick cooking
spray; heat over medium heat until hot.
Add eggs to wok; cook 1 minute or until
firm but still moist, stirring occasionally.
Remove eggs from wok; place on plate.
Cut egg into pieces; cover to keep warm.

3) In same wok, cook ground turkey, onions
and garlic over medium heat for 6 to 8
minutes or until turkey is no longer pink,
stirring frequently. Add frozen vegetables;
cook and stir an additional 4 to 5
minutes or until vegetables are thawed.

4) In 1-cup glass measuring cup, combine
soy sauce, oil and ground red pepper;
mix well. Stir into turkey mixture. Add
cooked rice and return eggs to wok; cook
and stir an additional 2 to 3 minutes or
until thoroughly heated.

HIGH ALTITUDE (ABOVE 3500 FT.): No change.

Nutrition Information Per Serving:
Serving Size: 1-1/4 Cups

Calories:	510	From Fat:	100
Total Fat			11g
Saturated			3g
Cholesterol			145mg
Sodium			1890mg
Total Carbohydrate			86g
Dietary Fiber			10g
Sugars			5g
Protein			27g

tip

If you have leftover meat or
vegetables from last night's
dinner, they make easy
substitutions in this recipe.

Chicken and Shrimp Stir-Fry

PREP TIME:	20 MINUTES	 EASY	LOW FAT
SERVINGS:	4 (2-1/4 CUPS EACH)		

2 cups uncooked instant white rice

2⅓ cups water

3 tablespoons soy sauce

2 tablespoons dry sherry

2 teaspoons cornstarch

1 garlic clove, minced

1 tablespoon oil

½ lb. chicken breast strips for stir-frying

1 (1-lb.) pkg. Green Giant Select® Frozen Broccoli, Carrots & Cauliflower

1 (8-oz.) can sliced water chestnuts, drained

½ lb. shelled deveined uncooked medium shrimp (about 16 shrimp), tails removed

1) Cook rice in 2 cups of the water as directed on package.

2) Meanwhile, in small bowl, combine remaining ⅓ cup water, soy sauce, sherry, cornstarch and garlic; mix well. Set aside.

3) Heat oil in wok or 12-inch skillet over medium-high heat until hot. Add chicken; cook and stir 4 minutes or until chicken begins to brown.

4) Stir in frozen vegetables and water chestnuts. Cover; cook 2 to 3 minutes or until vegetables are thawed, stirring once. Add shrimp; cover and cook 3 to 4 minutes or until chicken is no longer pink in center and shrimp turn pink, stirring once.

5) Stir cornstarch mixture until smooth. Add to wok; cook and stir until sauce is bubbly and thickened. Serve over rice.

HIGH ALTITUDE (ABOVE 3500 FT.): Cook rice using high altitude directions on package. Increase water in cornstarch mixture to ½ cup. After adding frozen vegetables and water chestnuts, increase cooking time to 4 to 5 minutes. After adding shrimp, cover and cook 5 to 6 minutes.

Nutrition Information Per Serving:
Serving Size: 2-1/4 Cups

Calories:	400	From Fat:	55
Total Fat		6g	
Saturated		1g	
Cholesterol		115mg	
Sodium		1480mg	
Total Carbohydrate		63g	
Dietary Fiber		5g	
Sugars		2g	
Protein		29g	

Easy Italian Pasta

PREP TIME: 20 MINUTES
SERVINGS: 4 (1-1/2 CUPS EACH)

 EASY

8 oz. (2^1/$_2$ cups) uncooked cavatappi (short ridged spiral macaroni)

^{1}/$_2$ lb. bulk spicy Italian pork sausage

6 to 7 medium Italian plum tomatoes, seeded, chopped (about 1^1/$_2$ cups)

1 cup whipping cream

2 oz. (^{1}/$_2$ cup) shredded fresh Parmesan cheese

Nutrition Information Per Serving:		
Serving Size: 1-1/2 Cups		
Calories: 600	From Fat:	305
Total Fat		34g
Saturated		18g
Cholesterol		110mg
Sodium		860mg
Total Carbohydrate		51g
Dietary Fiber		2g
Sugars		6g
Protein		23g

1) Cook cavatappi as directed on package. Drain.

2) Meanwhile, brown sausage in large skillet over medium heat, stirring frequently. Drain; return to skillet.

3) Add tomatoes, cream and cooked cavatappi to sausage; stir gently to mix. Cook over medium heat until thoroughly heated, stirring frequently. (Do not boil.) Sprinkle with cheese.

HIGH ALTITUDE (ABOVE 3500 FT.): No change.

One-Dish Macaroni and Cheese with Sausage

PREP TIME: 20 MINUTES (READY IN 20 MINUTES)
SERVINGS: 4 (1-1/4 CUPS EACH)

 EASY

1 box (9 oz.) Green Giant® frozen cut broccoli

1 lb. purchased macaroni and cheese (from deli)

^{1}/$_2$ lb. fully cooked Polish sausage, cut into ^{1}/$_2$-inch pieces

1 tablespoon butter or margarine

^{1}/$_4$ cup crushed round buttery crackers

Nutrition Information Per Serving:		
Serving Size: 1-1/4 Cups		
Calories: 335	From Fat:	190
Total Fat		21g
Saturated		9g
Cholesterol		45mg
Sodium		1120mg
Total Carbohydrate		25g
Dietary Fiber		2g
Sugars		4g
Protein		12g

1) In 1^1/$_2$-quart microwavable casserole, cook broccoli as directed on package; drain.

2) Stir in macaroni and cheese, and sausage. Microwave on High 6 to 8 minutes or until thoroughly heated, stirring once or twice.

3) In small microwavable bowl, microwave butter on High 25 to 30 seconds or until melted. Stir in crushed crackers; sprinkle over top of macaroni mixture.

4) Microwave casserole on High 1 to 3 minutes or until crumbs are hot.

HIGH ALTITUDE (3500-6000 FT.): No change.

tip
Your favorite sausage, such as kielbasa or wieners, can be used in place of the Polish sausage in this recipe.

Gingered Beef and Noodles

PREP TIME: 40 MINUTES
SERVINGS: 4 (2 CUPS EACH)

 LOW FAT

8 oz. (5 cups) uncooked extra-wide egg noodles

1 tablespoon soy sauce

2 garlic cloves, minced

1 lb. boneless beef top sirloin steak, cut into thin bite-sized strips

1 tablespoon oil

1 cup beef broth

1 tablespoon cornstarch

3 tablespoons oyster sauce

1 teaspoon grated gingerroot

1 (6-oz.) pkg. prewashed fresh baby spinach (about 7 cups)

1) Cook noodles as directed on package. Drain.

2) Meanwhile, in medium bowl, combine soy sauce, garlic and beef strips; toss to coat. Heat oil in wok or 12-inch skillet over medium-high heat until hot. Add beef mixture; cook and stir 5 to 6 minutes or until beef is no longer pink in center.

3) In medium bowl, mix broth, cornstarch, oyster sauce and gingerroot until smooth. Add to wok; cook and stir 2 to 3 minutes or until sauce has thickened. Gently fold spinach into beef mixture; cook and stir 2 to 3 minutes or until spinach is slightly wilted.

4) In large serving bowl, combine cooked noodles and beef mixture; toss gently to coat.

HIGH ALTITUDE (ABOVE 3500 FT.): No change.

Nutrition Information Per Serving:
Serving Size: 2 Cups

Calories: 375	From Fat: 80
Total Fat	9g
Saturated	2g
Cholesterol	110mg
Sodium	1140mg
Total Carbohydrate	42g
Dietary Fiber	2g
Sugars	2g
Protein	32g

tip

Don't have gingerroot on hand? Substitute ¼ teaspoon ground ginger instead.

Teriyaki Meat Loaf and Vegetable Packets

PREP TIME: 15 MINUTES (READY IN 50 MINUTES)
SERVINGS: 4

(f) LOW FAT

1 egg

½ cup purchased teriyaki baste and glaze

¼ cup Progresso® Plain Bread Crumbs

½ teaspoon garlic-pepper blend

1 lb. extra-lean (at least 90%) ground beef

2 cups ready-to-eat baby-cut carrots

1 (15-oz.) can baby corn nuggets, drained

1) Heat gas or charcoal grill. Cut four 18x12-inch sheets of heavy-duty foil; spray foil with nonstick cooking spray.

2) In medium bowl, beat egg. Stir in 2 tablespoons of the baste and glaze, the bread crumbs, garlic-pepper blend and ground beef. Shape mixture into four 4x2-inch oblong loaves, about 1 inch thick.

3) Place 1 loaf on sprayed side of each foil sheet; place ½ cup of the carrots and ¼ of the corn around each loaf. Drizzle with remaining baste and glaze. Wrap each packet securely using double-fold seals, allowing room for heat expansion.

4) When grill is heated, place packets on gas grill over medium heat or on charcoal grill 4 to 6 inches from medium coals. Cover grill; cook 25 to 35 minutes or until loaves are thoroughly cooked and carrots are tender, turning packets over once halfway through cooking. Carefully open packets to allow steam to escape; meat thermometer inserted into center of loaves should read 160°F.

*NOTE: To bake packets, place on cookie sheet; bake at 400°F. using times above as a guide, turning packets over once halfway through baking.

HIGH ALTITUDE (ABOVE 3500 FT.): Cook on grill over medium-low heat.

Nutrition Information Per Serving:
Serving Size: 1/4 of Recipe

Calories:	365	From Fat:	80
Total Fat		9g	
Saturated		3g	
Cholesterol		120mg	
Sodium		1760mg	
Total Carbohydrate		37g	
Dietary Fiber		4g	
Sugars		11g	
Protein		34g	

Italian Meatball and Potato Bake

PREP TIME: 10 MINUTES (READY IN 1 HOUR 5 MINUTES)
SERVINGS: 6 (1 CUP EACH)

1 (24-oz.) pkg. frozen shredded potatoes O'Brien with onions and peppers, thawed, drained

8 oz. (2 cups) finely shredded Cheddar cheese

1 cup sour cream with chives and onion

1/2 teaspoon dried Italian seasoning

1/2 teaspoon peppered seasoned salt

1 (10 3/4-oz.) can condensed cream of celery soup

12 frozen cooked Italian meatballs (about 12 oz.), thawed

1) Heat oven to 350°F. Spray 11x7-inch (2-quart) glass baking dish with nonstick cooking spray.

2) In medium bowl, combine potatoes, 1 1/2 cups of the cheese, the sour cream, Italian seasoning, peppered seasoned salt and soup; mix well. Spread in sprayed baking dish. Cover tightly with foil. Bake at 350°F. for 30 minutes.

3) Remove from oven. Uncover; arrange meatballs in rows over potatoes, pressing in slightly. Sprinkle with remaining 1/2 cup cheese.

4) Return to oven; bake uncovered an additional 20 to 25 minutes or until golden brown and hot in center.

HIGH ALTITUDE (ABOVE 3500 FT.): Heat oven to 375°F. Spray 13x9-inch (3-quart) glass baking dish with non-stick cooking spray. After covering with foil, bake at 375°F. for 35 minutes. After adding meatballs and cheese, bake uncovered an additional 15 to 20 minutes.

Nutrition Information Per Serving:
Serving Size: 1 Cup

Calories:	575	From Fat:	295
Total Fat			33g
Saturated			17g
Cholesterol			130mg
Sodium			1100mg
Total Carbohydrate			44g
Dietary Fiber			3g
Sugars			6g
Protein			25g

Hunter's-Style Oven Beef Stew

PREP TIME: 15 MINUTES (READY IN 1 HOUR)
SERVINGS: 4 (1-1/2 CUPS EACH)

e EASY   **f** LOW FAT

- 2 cups Green Giant® frozen cut green beans (from 1-lb. bag)
- 1 cup frozen sliced carrots
- 1 box (9 oz.) frozen seasoned beef strips
- 1 can (14.5 oz.) diced tomatoes, drained
- 1 can (10 3/4 oz.) condensed golden mushroom soup
- 1 jar (6 oz.) Green Giant® sliced mushrooms, drained

Nutrition Information Per Serving:
Serving Size: 1-1/2 Cups

Calories:	245	From Fat:	90
Total Fat			10g
Saturated			3g
Cholesterol			45mg
Sodium			1200mg
Total Carbohydrate			20g
Dietary Fiber			4g
Sugars			8g
Protein			19g

1) Heat oven to 375°F. In colander or large strainer, rinse frozen green beans and carrots with cold water until thawed; drain well.

2) In large microwavable bowl, microwave beef strips on High 1 to 2 minutes or until thawed. Cut into bite-sized pieces; return to bowl. Stir in tomatoes, soup, mushrooms, green beans and carrots; pour into ungreased 2-quart casserole.

3) Bake 35 to 45 minutes or until hot and bubbly.

HIGH ALTITUDE (3500-6000 FT.): No change.

Ravioli with Tomatoes and Olives

PREP TIME: 25 MINUTES (READY IN 25 MINUTES)
SERVINGS: 2 (1-3/4 CUPS EACH)

e EASY

- 1 package (9 oz) refrigerated cheese-filled ravioli
- 1 small onion, cut into thin wedges
- 1 can (14.5 oz) diced tomatoes with basil, garlic and oregano, undrained
- 1/4 cup sliced ripe olives
- 2 tablespoons shredded Parmesan cheese
- 1 tablespoon chopped fresh basil

Nutrition Information Per Serving:
Serving Size: 1-3/4 Cups

Calories:	340	From Fat:	130
Total Fat			15g
Saturated			6g
Cholesterol			135mg
Sodium			1610mg
Total Carbohydrate			34g
Dietary Fiber			4g
Sugars			8g
Protein			19g

1) Cook ravioli as directed on package; drain.

2) Meanwhile, in 8-inch nonstick skillet, cover and cook onion over medium heat 3 to 5 minutes, stirring occasionally, until crisp-tender. Uncover; stir in tomatoes and olives. Cook uncovered 3 to 5 minutes, stirring frequently, until thoroughly heated.

3) Gently stir in cooked ravioli. Cook 3 to 5 minutes, stirring occasionally, until sauce is desired consistency. Sprinkle individual servings with cheese and basil.

Lemon and Herb-Roasted Turkey Breast

PREP TIME: 15 MINUTES (READY IN 3 HOURS)
SERVINGS: 8

1 medium lemon

2 cloves garlic, minced

2 tablespoons finely chopped fresh parsley

½ teaspoon salt

½ teaspoon dried sage leaves

½ teaspoon dried marjoram leaves

¼ teaspoon pepper

1 tablespoon olive oil

1 fresh or frozen bone-in whole turkey breast (5 to 5½ lb.), thawed

1) Heat oven to 325°F. Spray 13x9-inch pan and 16x12-inch sheet of foil with cooking spray. Grate peel from lemon. Cut lemon into quarters; set aside. In small bowl, mix lemon peel, garlic, parsley, salt, sage, marjoram, pepper and oil.

2) Loosen skin covering turkey breast and pull away, leaving attached at neck. If necessary, use sharp knife to loosen. Rub herb mixture evenly over turkey breast meat. Replace skin over breast, tucking under bottom of breast. Rub any remaining mixture over skin.

3) Place lemon quarters in neck opening. Place turkey, skin side up, in pan; cover tightly with foil, sprayed side down.

4) Bake 1 hour. Uncover pan; insert meat thermometer into turkey so bulb reaches center of thickest part of breast meat, but does not rest on bone.

5) Bake uncovered 1¼ to 1¾ hours longer or until turkey is fork-tender, its juices run clear and meat thermometer reads 170°F. Let stand 5 minutes before serving. Remove and discard lemon from neck opening before cutting turkey into slices.

HIGH ALTITUDE (3500-6000 FT.): Bake covered at 350°F. 2 hours. Uncover; bake 15 to 45 minutes longer.

Nutrition Information Per Serving:
Serving Size: 1/8 of Recipe

Calories:	360	From Fat:	145
Total Fat			16g
Saturated			4g
Cholesterol			145mg
Sodium			270mg
Total Carbohydrate			0g
Dietary Fiber			0g
Sugars			0g
Protein			54g

Chicken à la King Pasta Bake

PREP TIME: 25 MINUTES (READY IN 1 HOUR 45 MINUTES)
SERVINGS: 6 (1-1/4 CUPS EACH)

 LOW FAT

2 cans (10 3/4 oz. each) condensed 98% fat-free cream of chicken soup with 30% less sodium

1 can (12 oz.) evaporated fat-free milk

1/2 cup dry sherry or chicken broth

3/4 teaspoon salt

2 cups coarsely chopped cooked chicken breast

2 cups uncooked wide egg noodles (4 oz.)

1 cup chopped onions (2 medium)

1 cup chopped green bell pepper (1 medium)

2 jars (6 oz. each) Green Giant® whole mushrooms, drained

2 jars (2 oz. each) diced pimientos, drained

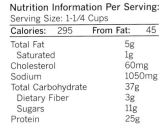

Nutrition Information Per Serving:
Serving Size: 1-1/4 Cups

Calories:	295	From Fat:	45
Total Fat		5g	
Saturated		1g	
Cholesterol		60mg	
Sodium		1050mg	
Total Carbohydrate		37g	
Dietary Fiber		3g	
Sugars		11g	
Protein		25g	

1) Heat oven to 350°F. Spray 13x9-inch (3-quart) glass baking dish with cooking spray. In large bowl, mix soup, milk, sherry and salt. Stir in all remaining ingredients; pour into baking dish. Cover tightly with foil.

2) Bake 60 to 70 minutes or until noodles are tender and mixture is hot and bubbly. Let stand 10 minutes before serving.

HIGH ALTITUDE (3500-6000 FT.): No change.

Orange-Glazed Ham And Pineapple Kabobs

PREP TIME: 30 MINUTES (READY IN 30 MINUTES)
SERVINGS: 4 (2 KABOBS EACH)

 EASY

1 lb. cooked ham, cut into 32 (1-inch) cubes

2 cans (8 oz. each) pineapple chunks, drained

2 medium green bell peppers, cut into 32 (1-inch) pieces

1/2 cup barbecue sauce

1/4 cup orange marmalade

Nutrition Information Per Serving:
Serving Size: 2 Kabobs

Calories:	380	From Fat:	90
Total Fat		11g	
Saturated		3.5g	
Cholesterol		65mg	
Sodium		2020mg	
Total Carbohydrate		46g	
Dietary Fiber		3g	
Sugars		36g	
Protein		27g	

1) Onto 8 (10-inch) wooden skewers, alternately thread ham, pineapple and bell pepper.

2) Heat closed contact grill 5 minutes. Meanwhile, in small bowl, stir together barbecue sauce and marmalade. Reserve half of mixture.

3) When grill is heated, place kabobs on bottom grill surface. Brush with half of remaining barbecue sauce mixture; close grill. Cook 2 minutes. Rotate kabobs 1/4 turn; brush with remaining sauce mixture. Close grill; cook 2 to 3 minutes longer or until thoroughly heated. Serve with reserved sauce.

HIGH ALTITUDE (3500-6500 FT.): No change.

Lemon-Garlic Roasted Pork and Vegetables

PREP TIME: 10 MINUTES (READY IN 50 MINUTES)
SERVINGS: 6

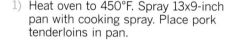 EASY   LOW FAT

PORK

2 to 3 pork tenderloins (about 1½ lb.)

1 clove garlic, minced

1 teaspoon lemon-pepper seasoning

VEGETABLES

1 bag (19 oz.) Green Giant® frozen roasted potatoes with garlic & herbs, thawed*

3 cups Green Giant Select® frozen broccoli, carrots and cauliflower (from 1-lb. bag), thawed*

2 teaspoons lemon juice

Did you know that frozen vegetables are just as nutritious as fresh vegetables? Freezing vegetables at the peak of ripeness helps preserve their nutrients.

1) Heat oven to 450°F. Spray 13x9-inch pan with cooking spray. Place pork tenderloins in pan.

2) In small bowl, mix garlic and lemon-pepper seasoning; rub over pork.

3) In ungreased 2-quart casserole, mix all vegetable ingredients except lemon juice; cover.

4) Bake pork and vegetables 30 to 40 minutes or until pork has slight blush of pink in center, meat thermometer inserted in center of pork reads 160°F. and vegetables are tender. (If vegetables are tender before pork is done, remove casserole from oven.) Stir lemon juice into vegetables before serving.

*NOTE: To thaw box of frozen potatoes and bag of frozen vegetables, refrigerate at least 8 hours or overnight.

HIGH ALTITUDE (ABOVE 3500 FT.): No change.

Nutrition Information Per Serving:
Serving Size: 1/6 of Recipe

Calories:	250	From Fat:	80
Total Fat			9g
Saturated			2g
Cholesterol			70mg
Sodium			320mg
Total Carbohydrate			14g
Dietary Fiber			2g
Sugars			1g
Protein			28g

Philly Cheesy Beef Pizza

PREP TIME: 15 MINUTES (READY IN 35 MINUTES)
SERVINGS: 4

1 (13.8-oz.) can Pillsbury® Refrigerated Pizza Crust

½ lb. lean (at least 80%) ground beef

1 cup coarsely chopped green bell pepper (1 medium)

1 cup coarsely chopped onions (2 medium)

¼ teaspoon salt

⅛ teaspoon pepper

2 tablespoons purchased Italian salad dressing

1 large tomato, seeded, chopped (1 cup)

1 (6-oz.) pkg. thinly sliced provolone cheese

1) Heat oven to 400°F. Lightly grease 12-inch pizza pan. Unroll dough; place in greased pan. Starting at center, press out dough to edge of pan. Bake at 400°F. for 6 to 8 minutes or until crust begins to brown.

2) Meanwhile, in 12-inch nonstick skillet, break up ground beef. Add bell pepper and onion; sprinkle with salt and pepper. Cook over medium-high heat until beef is thoroughly cooked, stirring frequently. Drain. Stir in salad dressing.

3) Remove partially baked crust from oven. Spoon and spread ground beef mixture evenly over crust. Sprinkle with tomato; arrange cheese slices over top.

4) Return to oven; bake an additional 15 to 20 minutes or until cheese is melted and crust is golden brown. To serve, cut into wedges.

HIGH ALTITUDE (ABOVE 3500 FT.): No change.

Nutrition Information Per Serving:
Serving Size: 1/4 of Recipe

Calories:	565	From Fat:	215
Total Fat			24g
Saturated			11g
Cholesterol			65mg
Sodium			1320mg
Total Carbohydrate			56g
Dietary Fiber			3g
Sugars			12g
Protein			31g

Italian Pasta and Beef Bake

PREP TIME: 25 MINUTES (READY IN 50 MINUTES)
SERVINGS: 4 (1-3/4 CUPS EACH)

e EASY   **lf** LOW FAT

6 oz. (1½ cups) uncooked mostaccioli or penne (tube-shaped pasta)

½ lb. lean (at least 80%) ground beef

1 (15-oz.) can Italian-style tomato sauce

1 (14.5-oz.) can diced tomatoes with basil, garlic and oregano, undrained

1 (4.5-oz.) jar Green Giant® Sliced Mushrooms, drained

2 oz. (½ cup) shredded mozzarella cheese

1) Heat oven to 350°F. Spray 8-inch square (2-quart) glass baking dish with nonstick cooking spray. Cook mostaccioli as directed on package. Drain.

2) Meanwhile, in 12-inch nonstick skillet, brown ground beef over medium-high heat until thoroughly cooked, stirring frequently. Drain. Stir in tomato sauce, tomatoes and mushrooms. Bring to a boil. Remove from heat; pour into sprayed baking dish.

3) Add cooked mostaccioli; stir gently to mix. Spray sheet of foil with cooking spray; place sprayed side down on baking dish and seal tightly.

4) Bake at 350°F. for 15 minutes. Uncover; sprinkle with cheese. Bake uncovered an additional 5 to 10 minutes or until casserole is bubbly and cheese is melted.

HIGH ALTITUDE (ABOVE 3500 FT.): No change.

Nutrition Information Per Serving:
Serving Size: 1-3/4 Cups

Calories:	375	From Fat:	90
Total Fat			10g
Saturated			4g
Cholesterol			40mg
Sodium			1200mg
Total Carbohydrate			47g
Dietary Fiber			4g
Sugars			8g
Protein			24g

Garlic-Stroganoff Shepherd's Pie

PREP TIME: 20 MINUTES (READY IN 1 HOUR)
SERVINGS: 6 (1-1/3 CUPS EACH)

FILLING

6 slices bacon, cut into ½-inch pieces

1 lb. lean (at least 80%) ground beef

1½ cups ready-to-eat baby-cut carrots, cut in half crosswise

¼ cup chili sauce

1 (12-oz.) jar beef gravy

1½ cups Green Giant Select® LeSueur® Frozen Baby Sweet Peas (from 1-lb. pkg.)

½ cup sour cream

POTATOES

1 pouch roasted garlic mashed potatoes (from 7.2-oz. pkg.)

1¼ cups hot water

⅔ cup milk

2 tablespoons butter or margarine

1 tablespoon chopped fresh chives

1) Heat oven to 375°F. In 12-inch nonstick skillet, cook bacon over medium heat until crisp. Drain bacon on paper towels; set aside. Discard drippings in skillet.

2) In same skillet, brown ground beef over medium-high heat until thoroughly cooked, stirring frequently. Drain.

3) Stir in half of the bacon, the carrots, chili sauce and gravy. Reserve remaining bacon for topping. Reduce heat to medium-low; cook 5 minutes, stirring occasionally. Stir in peas and sour cream; cook 2 minutes. Spoon into ungreased 8-inch square (2-quart) glass baking dish.

4) Prepare mashed potatoes as directed on package using hot water, milk and butter. Spoon or pipe around edge of hot beef mixture. Sprinkle with reserved bacon.

5) Bake at 375°F. for 30 to 40 minutes or until carrots are tender. Sprinkle with chives.

HIGH ALTITUDE (ABOVE 3500 FT.): Before adding carrots to ground beef, microwave halved carrots on High 1 to 2 minutes or until partially cooked. Use an ungreased 11x7-inch (2-quart) glass baking dish. Bake at 375°F. for 35 to 40 minutes.

Nutrition Information Per Serving:
Serving Size: 1-1/3 Cups

Calories:	400	From Fat:	190
Total Fat			21g
Saturated			10g
Cholesterol			80mg
Sodium			690mg
Total Carbohydrate			29g
Dietary Fiber			4g
Sugars			9g
Protein			24g

tip

Instead of the baby carrots and frozen peas, substitute about 2 cups Green Giant® frozen mixed vegetables.

Easy Grilled Nacho Pizzas

PREP TIME: 20 MINUTES
SERVINGS: 4 PIZZAS   EASY

½ cup spicy bean dip

4 (6-inch) prebaked Italian pizza crusts (two 10-oz. pkg.)

1 cup Old El Paso® Refrigerated Taco Sauce with Seasoned Ground Beef (from 18-oz. tub)

1 (4.5-oz.) can Old El Paso® Chopped Green Chiles

1 medium tomato, chopped (½ cup)

½ cup sliced green onions (8 medium)

8 oz. (2 cups) finely shredded Cheddar cheese

1) Heat gas or charcoal grill. Spread 2 tablespoons of the bean dip evenly on each pizza crust. Spoon and spread ground beef mixture evenly over dip. Sprinkle each with green chiles, tomato, onions and cheese.

2) When grill is heated, place pizzas on gas grill over medium heat or on charcoal grill 4 to 6 inches from medium coals. Cover grill; cook 8 to 10 minutes or until crusts are crisp and toppings are thoroughly heated. If crust browns too quickly, place sheet of foil between crust and grill rack.

*NOTE: To bake pizzas, place on large cookie sheet; bake at 450°F. using times above as a guide.

HIGH ALTITUDE (ABOVE 3500 FT.): Place pizzas on sheet of foil; place foil and pizzas on grill rack. Cook on grill over medium-low heat.

Nutrition Information Per Serving:
Serving Size: 1 Pizza

Calories:	775	From Fat:	325
Total Fat			36g
Saturated			20g
Cholesterol			100mg
Sodium			1780mg
Total Carbohydrate			75g
Dietary Fiber			4g
Sugars			7g
Protein			38g

Salisbury Steak Dinner

PREP TIME: 40 MINUTES
SERVINGS: 4

1 egg

¼ cup chili sauce

1 medium onion, finely chopped
(½ cup)

¼ cup crushed butter-flavor crackers

½ teaspoon peppered seasoned salt

1 lb. lean (at least 80%) ground beef

2 cups cubed (½-inch) unpeeled
russet potatoes

1 (14.5-oz.) can diced tomatoes,
undrained

1 (12-oz.) jar beef gravy

1) In medium bowl, beat egg. Stir in chili sauce, onion, crushed crackers, peppered seasoned salt and ground beef. Shape mixture into 4 patties, ½ inch thick.

2) Spray 12-inch nonstick skillet with nonstick cooking spray; heat over medium-high heat until hot. Add patties; cook 4 to 6 minutes or until browned on both sides. Drain if necessary.

3) In medium bowl, combine potatoes, tomatoes and gravy; mix well. Pour over patties. Bring to a boil. Reduce heat to medium-low; cover and simmer 15 to 20 minutes or until potatoes are tender and beef is thoroughly cooked, turning patties and stirring once.

HIGH ALTITUDE (ABOVE 3500 FT.): No change.

Nutrition Information Per Serving:
Serving Size: 1/4 of Recipe

Calories:	410	From Fat:	160
Total Fat			18g
Saturated			7g
Cholesterol			125mg
Sodium			1120mg
Total Carbohydrate			31g
Dietary Fiber			3g
Sugars			9g
Protein			31g

To reduce the fat in each serving of this recipe by about 8 grams, use lean ground turkey in place of the ground beef, and fat-free egg product in place of the egg.

Gingered Rice and Beef

PREP TIME: 30 MINUTES
SERVINGS: 4 (1-1/3 CUPS EACH)

e EASY   **lf** LOW FAT

- 1 lb. extra-lean (at least 90%) ground beef
- 1 tablespoon grated gingerroot
- 1 (6.2-oz.) pkg. fried rice-flavor rice and vermicelli mix
- 2 cups water
- 1 medium red bell pepper, coarsely chopped (1 cup)
- 2 cups Green Giant Select® Frozen Sugar Snap Peas (from 1-lb. pkg.)

1) In 12-inch nonstick skillet, cook ground beef and gingerroot over medium-high heat until beef is thoroughly cooked, stirring frequently. Drain.

2) Add rice and vermicelli mix with contents of seasoning packet; cook and stir 2 minutes. Add water; bring to a boil. Reduce heat to low; cover and simmer 15 minutes, stirring occasionally.

3) Stir in bell pepper and sugar snap peas; cover and cook 5 to 10 minutes or until vegetables are tender, stirring occasionally.

HIGH ALTITUDE (ABOVE 3500 FT.): Increase water to 2¼ cups.

Nutrition Information Per Serving:
Serving Size: 1-1/3 Cups

Calories:	335	From Fat:	65
Total Fat			7g
Saturated			3g
Cholesterol			70mg
Sodium			510mg
Total Carbohydrate			36g
Dietary Fiber			3g
Sugars			5g
Protein			32g

Pick up some frozen egg rolls to heat and serve with this dish.

Asian Turkey Patties

PREP TIME: 20 MINUTES (READY IN 20 MINUTES)
SERVINGS: 6

 EASY  LOW FAT

1 lb. lean ground turkey breast

½ cup chopped fresh mushrooms

¼ cup chopped green onions (4 medium)

¼ cup finely chopped red bell pepper (¼ medium)

2 tablespoons reduced-sodium soy sauce

1 teaspoon chopped garlic in water (from 4.5-oz. jar)

1 tablespoon teriyaki baste and glaze (from 12-oz. bottle)

Nutrition Information Per Serving:
Serving Size: 1 Patty plus Glaze

Calories:	110	From Fat:	40
Total Fat			4g
Saturated			1g
Cholesterol			50mg
Sodium			340mg
Total Carbohydrate			2g
Dietary Fiber			0g
Sugars			1g
Protein			17g

1) Heat closed contact grill for 5 minutes.

2) Meanwhile, in large bowl, mix all ingredients except teriyaki baste and glaze. Shape mixture into 6 patties, ½ inch thick.

3) When grill is heated, place patties on bottom grill surface. Close grill; cook 8 to 10 minutes or until patties are no longer pink in center.

4) Spread ½ teaspoon teriyaki baste and glaze on each patty.

HIGH ALTITUDE (ABOVE 3500 FT.): No change.

Easy Chicken with Rice Casserole

PREP TIME: 15 MINUTES (READY IN 2 HOURS 15 MINUTES)
SERVINGS: 5

 EASY

1 cup uncooked regular long-grain white rice

1 can (10¾ oz.) condensed cream of celery soup

1 can (10¾ oz.) condensed cream of chicken with herbs soup

1½ cups water

5 bone-in chicken breast halves with skin

2 tablespoons butter or margarine, melted

1 teaspoon paprika

Nutrition Information Per Serving:
Serving Size: 1/5 of Recipe

Calories:	475	From Fat:	180
Total Fat			20g
Saturated			7g
Cholesterol			90mg
Sodium			970mg
Total Carbohydrate			42g
Dietary Fiber			1g
Sugars			1g
Protein			32g

1) Heat oven to 325°F. Spray 13x9-inch (3-quart) glass baking dish with cooking spray. In large bowl, mix uncooked rice, both soups and water; pour into baking dish.

2) Arrange chicken, skin side up, over rice mixture. Brush chicken with melted butter; drizzle with any remaining butter. Sprinkle with paprika. Cover tightly with foil.

3) Bake 1½ hours. Uncover; bake 20 to 30 minutes longer or until chicken is fork-tender, its juices run clear and skin is slightly crisp.

HIGH ALTITUDE (3500-6000 FT.): No change.

Creamy Seafood Pasta

ANGELA BUCHANAN | BOULDER, COLORADO

Bake-Off

PREP TIME:	30 MINUTES (READY IN 30 MINUTES)
SERVINGS:	8 (1-1/4 CUPS EACH)

e EASY

16 oz. uncooked linguine

1 (18.5-oz.) can Progresso® Traditional New England Clam Chowder

1 cup milk

2 oz. (½ cup) shredded Parmesan cheese

2 cloves garlic, minced

2 tablespoons olive oil

1½ lb. uncooked deveined shelled large shrimp, tail shells removed

1 (8-oz.) pkg. (3 cups) sliced fresh mushrooms

4 medium green onions, chopped (¼ cup)

¼ to ½ teaspoon crushed red pepper flakes

½ cup chopped fresh parsley

Salt and pepper to taste, if desired

2 oz. (½ cup) shredded Parmesan cheese, if desired

1) In 5- to 6-quart Dutch oven, cook linguine as directed on package. Drain well; return to Dutch oven and cover to keep warm.

2) Meanwhile, in blender, place clam chowder, milk, ½ cup Parmesan cheese and the garlic; blend on medium speed until mixture is smooth. Set aside.

3) In 12-inch nonstick skillet or wok, heat oil over medium-high heat until hot. Add shrimp, mushrooms and onions; cook about 5 minutes, stirring frequently, until shrimp turn pink.

4) Stir in pepper flakes and soup mixture; cook until thoroughly heated. Stir in parsley. Salt and pepper to taste.

5) Pour over cooked linguine in Dutch oven; toss gently to coat. Top individual servings with shredded Parmesan cheese.

HIGH ALTITUDE (ABOVE 3500 FT.): No change.

Nutrition Information Per Serving:
Serving Size: 1-1/4 Cups

Calories:	430	From Fat:	110
Total Fat			12g
Saturated			3g
Cholesterol			130mg
Sodium			780mg
Total Carbohydrate			55g
Dietary Fiber			3g
Sugars			5g
Protein			27g

Chicken Cordon Bleu Lasagna

PREP TIME: 25 MINUTES (READY IN 1 HOUR 40 MINUTES)
SERVINGS: 9

2 eggs

1 container (15 oz.) ricotta cheese

1 cup cottage cheese

½ cup grated Parmesan cheese

¼ cup chopped fresh parsley

2 cups diced (¼- to ½-inch) cooked chicken

2 cups diced (¼- to ½-inch) cooked ham

¼ teaspoon garlic powder

1 jar (16 oz.) creamy garlic Alfredo sauce

6 uncooked lasagna noodles

2 cups shredded mozzarella cheese (8 oz.)

1 cup shredded Swiss cheese (4 oz.)

2 tablespoons chopped fresh parsley

1) Heat oven to 350°F. In medium bowl, beat eggs. Stir in ricotta, cottage and Parmesan cheeses and ¼ cup parsley; set aside.

2) In another medium bowl, mix chicken, ham, garlic powder and Alfredo sauce. In ungreased 13x9-inch (3-quart) glass baking dish, spread about ½ cup chicken mixture.

3) Top chicken mixture with 3 uncooked noodles, half of the cheese mixture, half of the remaining chicken mixture and half each of the mozzarella and Swiss cheeses. Repeat layers starting with noodles, ending with Swiss cheese. Cover tightly with foil.

4) Bake 1 hour or until very hot and bubbly. Let stand covered 15 minutes before serving. Sprinkle with 2 tablespoons parsley.

HIGH ALTITUDE (3500-6000 FT.): Add ⅓ cup water to chicken mixture. Continue as directed above.

Nutrition Information Per Serving:
Serving Size: 1/9 of Recipe

Calories:	585	From Fat:	335
Total Fat			37g
Saturated			21g
Cholesterol			190mg
Sodium			1130mg
Total Carbohydrate			19g
Dietary Fiber			0g
Sugars			3g
Protein			44g

tip

Cordon Bleu is a French dish combining chicken or veal with ham or prosciutto and Swiss or Gruyère cheese. In this recipe, those flavors are simplified to produce a luscious lasagna.

Italian Classic Lasagna

PREP TIME: 45 MINUTES (READY IN 2 HOURS 10 MINUTES)
SERVINGS: 9

6 uncooked lasagna noodles

1 lb. lean (at least 80%) ground beef

½ lb. bulk Italian pork sausage

¾ cup chopped onions (1½ medium)

1 can (28 oz.) Italian-style peeled tomatoes, undrained, cut up

1 can (6 oz.) tomato paste

1 teaspoon dried basil leaves

½ teaspoon sugar

½ teaspoon dried oregano leaves

¼ teaspoon salt

¼ teaspoon garlic powder

2 eggs

1 container (15 oz.) ricotta cheese

1 cup cottage cheese

½ cup grated Parmesan cheese

¼ cup chopped fresh parsley

4 cups shredded mozzarella cheese (16 oz.)

1) Cook lasagna noodles as directed on package; drain and place in cold water to cool.

2) Meanwhile, in 4-quart saucepan or Dutch oven, cook ground beef, sausage and onions over medium-high heat 5 to 7 minutes, stirring frequently, until beef and sausage are thoroughly cooked; drain. Stir in tomatoes, tomato paste, basil, sugar, oregano, salt and garlic powder. Bring to a boil. Reduce heat to low; simmer 30 to 45 minutes, stirring occasionally, until very thick.

3) In medium bowl, beat eggs. Stir in ricotta, cottage and Parmesan cheeses and parsley; set aside.

4) Heat oven to 350°F. In ungreased 13x9-inch (3-quart) glass baking dish, spread about ½ cup beef mixture. Drain noodles. Top beef mixture with 3 noodles, half of the cheese mixture, half of the remaining beef mixture and half of the mozzarella cheese. Repeat layers, starting with noodles and ending with mozzarella cheese.

5) Bake 35 to 45 minutes or until lasagna is bubbly and top is golden brown. Cover with foil; let stand 10 to 15 minutes before serving.

HIGH ALTITUDE (3500-6000 FT.): When making beef mixture, simmer covered over medium-low heat 30 to 45 minutes. After making lasagna, spray sheet of foil with cooking spray; cover lasagna with foil, sprayed side down. Bake at 350°F. 30 minutes. Remove foil; bake 20 minutes longer. Continue as directed above.

Nutrition Information Per Serving:
Serving Size: 1/9 of Recipe

Calories:	515	From Fat:	245
Total Fat			27g
Saturated			14g
Cholesterol			140mg
Sodium			1130mg
Total Carbohydrate			25g
Dietary Fiber			2g
Sugars			6g
Protein			43g

Lamb Chops with Orange Butter

PREP TIME: 20 MINUTES (READY IN 20 MINUTES)
SERVINGS: 2 (1 LAMB CHOP AND 1-1/2 TABLESPOONS BUTTER EACH)

 EASY

2 tablespoons butter, softened

1 tablespoon orange marmalade

¼ teaspoon dried marjoram leaves

2 lamb shoulder chops
   (½ to ¾ inch thick)

¼ teaspoon seasoned salt

¼ teaspoon paprika

¼ teaspoon black and red pepper blend

Nutrition Information Per Serving:
Serving Size: 1/2 of Recipe

Calories: 310	From Fat: 180
Total Fat	20g
Saturated	10g
Cholesterol	115mg
Sodium	320mg
Total Carbohydrate	7g
Dietary Fiber	0g
Sugars	5g
Protein	26g

1) Heat closed contact grill 5 minutes. In small bowl, mix butter, marmalade and marjoram; set aside.

2) When grill is heated, sprinkle lamb chops with seasoned salt, paprika and pepper blend; place on bottom grill surface. Close grill; cook 8 to 12 minutes, turning once, until desired doneness. Top lamb chops with butter mixture.

Cheesy Tuna Bake

PREP TIME: 20 MINUTES (READY IN 55 MINUTES)
SERVINGS: 6 (1-2/3 CUPS EACH)

4 cups uncooked wide egg noodles
   (8 oz.)

1½ cups Green Giant® frozen sweet peas (from 1-lb. bag)

1 can (10¾ oz.) condensed Cheddar cheese soup

1 can (12 oz.) evaporated milk

1 cup shredded Cheddar and American cheese blend (4 oz.)

¼ cup finely chopped onion
   (½ medium)

2 cans (6 oz. each) tuna in water, drained, flaked

1 cup cheese-flavored fish-shaped crackers (about 3 oz.)

1) Cook noodles as directed on package, adding peas during last minute of cooking time; drain.

2) Meanwhile, heat oven to 350°F. In ungreased 2-quart casserole, mix soup, milk, cheese and onion.

3) Stir cooked noodles and tuna into soup mixture; cover. Bake 30 minutes.

4) Remove from oven. Uncover; stir mixture well. Sprinkle with crackers. Return to oven; bake uncovered about 5 minutes longer or until crackers are light golden brown.

HIGH ALTITUDE (3500-6000 FT.): Bake at 350°F. 35 minutes. Continue as directed above.

Nutrition Information Per Serving:
Serving Size: 1-2/3 Cups

Calories: 500	From Fat: 180
Total Fat	20g
Saturated	10g
Cholesterol	95mg
Sodium	1220mg
Total Carbohydrate	47g
Dietary Fiber	3g
Sugars	10g
Protein	33g

Chipotle-Honey Pork

PREP TIME:	35 MINUTES (READY IN 35 MINUTES)
SERVINGS:	6

 EASY LOW FAT

⅓ cup honey

⅓ cup fresh lime juice

2 chipotle chiles in adobo sauce (from 7-oz. can), drained, finely chopped

1 teaspoon adobo sauce (from can of chipotle chiles)

2 pork tenderloins (¾ lb. each)

¼ teaspoon salt

⅛ teaspoon pepper

Cooking spray

1) Heat gas or charcoal grill. In ½ - to 1-quart saucepan, mix honey, lime juice, chiles and adobo sauce.

2) When grill is heated, sprinkle pork tenderloins with salt and pepper; lightly spray with cooking spray. Place pork on gas grill over medium heat or on charcoal grill over medium coals; cover grill. Cook 15 to 20 minutes, turning occasionally and brushing with honey mixture during last 10 minutes of cooking time, until pork has slight blush of pink in center and meat thermometer inserted in center reads 160°F.

3) Heat any remaining honey mixture to rolling boil; boil 1 minute. Cut pork into slices; serve with honey mixture.

HIGH ALTITUDE (3500-6500 FT.): Place pork on gas grill over medium-low heat or on charcoal grill over medium-low coals; cover grill. Cook using times above as a guide, turning occasionally and brushing with honey mixture during last 10 minutes of cooking time.

Nutrition Information Per Serving:
Serving Size: 1/6 of Recipe

Calories:	210	From Fat:	40
Total Fat			4.5g
Saturated			1.5g
Cholesterol			70mg
Sodium			210mg
Total Carbohydrate			17g
Dietary Fiber			0g
Sugars			16g
Protein			26g

Pecan-Crusted Salmon

PREP TIME: 25 MINUTES (READY IN 25 MINUTES)   ➔ EASY
SERVINGS: 4

1 salmon fillet (1 lb.)

1 teaspoon olive oil

2 tablespoons mayonnaise

1 teaspoon Dijon mustard

¼ cup croutons, crushed

¼ cup chopped pecans

1) Heat closed contact grill 5 minutes. Meanwhile, brush both sides of salmon fillet with oil.

2) When grill is heated, place salmon, skin-side down, on bottom grill surface; close grill. Cook 5 minutes.

3) Meanwhile, in small bowl, mix mayonnaise and mustard. In another small bowl, stir together crushed croutons and pecans.

4) With back of spoon, spread mayonnaise mixture over salmon and sprinkle with crumb mixture; close grill. Cook 1 to 2 minutes longer or until salmon flakes easily with fork. Cut salmon into serving pieces to serve.

HIGH ALTITUDE (3500-6500 FT.): No change.

Nutrition Information Per Serving:
Serving Size: 1/4 of Recipe

Calories:	270	From Fat:	170
Total Fat			18g
Saturated			3.5g
Cholesterol			80mg
Sodium			180mg
Total Carbohydrate			3g
Dietary Fiber			0g
Sugars			0g
Protein			25g

tip

Make easy work of crushing salad croutons by placing them in a small resealable plastic bag. Close the bag and crush with a rolling pin. Then add the chopped pecans to the bag and shake lightly to mix.

Turkey-Sweet Potato Pot Pies

DOLLY CRAIG | DENVER, COLORADO

PREP TIME: 15 MINUTES (READY IN 55 MINUTES)
SERVINGS: 4

1 (15-oz.) can sweet potatoes, drained, cut into bite-size pieces (2 cups)

1½ cups cubed cooked turkey or chicken

1 cup Green Giant® Frozen Sweet Peas (from 1-lb. bag), thawed, drained*

3 tablespoons chopped sweet yellow onion

3 teaspoons curry powder

Salt and pepper to taste, if desired

1 (18.6-oz.) can Progresso® Rich & Hearty Chicken Pot Pie Style Soup

1 Pillsbury® Refrigerated Pie Crust (from 15-oz. box), softened as directed on box

1) Heat oven to 400°F. In large bowl, mix all ingredients except pie crust. Divide mixture evenly into 4 (1¼- to 2-cup) ungreased individual ramekins.**

2) Remove pie crust from pouch; place crust flat on cutting board. Cut crust into 4 quarters. Top each filled ramekin with 1 quarter crust. With kitchen scissors or knife, trim crust edges. Pinch and flute edge, filling in areas with trimmed pie crust pieces where needed. With knife, cut several small slits in crusts for steam to escape. If using ramekins, place on cookie sheet.

3) Bake at 400°F. for 25 to 33 minutes or until filling is bubbly and crust is deep golden brown, covering crust edge with foil during last 10 to 15 minutes of baking to prevent excessive browning. Cool 5 minutes before serving.

*NOTE: *To quickly thaw frozen peas, place in colander or strainer; rinse with warm water until thawed. Drain well. **A 1¼- to 1½-quart casserole can be substituted for ramekins. Place whole crust over filled casserole.

HIGH ALTITUDE (ABOVE 3500 FT.): No change.

Nutrition Information Per Serving:
Serving Size: 1 Pot Pie

Calories:	475	From Fat:	160
Total Fat			18g
Saturated			5g
Cholesterol			55mg
Sodium			890mg
Total Carbohydrate			57g
Dietary Fiber			5g
Sugars			16g
Protein			27g

Italian Sunday Supper

PREP TIME: 30 MINUTES (READY IN 2 HOURS)
SERVINGS: 6 (1-1/2 CUPS EACH)

1 lb. lean (at least 80%) ground beef

½ lb. bulk Italian pork sausage

1 can (19 oz.) Progresso® Vegetable Classics creamy tomato soup

1 can (14.5 oz.) diced tomatoes with Italian-style herbs, undrained

1 bag (1 lb. 4 oz.) refrigerated sliced potatoes

1 medium onion, halved, thinly sliced

1 cup shredded mozzarella cheese (4 oz.)

1½ cups shredded Gruyère cheese (6 oz.)

3 tablespoons chopped fresh flat-leaf parsley

1) Heat oven to 350°F. Spray 13x9-inch (3-quart) glass baking dish or 3-quart oval casserole with cooking spray. Heat 12-inch nonstick skillet over medium-high heat. Add ground beef and sausage; cook, stirring frequently, until beef is thoroughly cooked and sausage is no longer pink. Drain; stir in soup and tomatoes.

2) Layer half each of the potatoes and onion in baking dish; repeat layers. Sprinkle evenly with mozzarella cheese. Pour meat mixture over cheese; stir gently to mix. Cover tightly with foil.

3) Bake 60 to 70 minutes or until potatoes are tender and mixture is hot and bubbly. Uncover; sprinkle evenly with Gruyère cheese. Bake uncovered about 10 minutes longer or until cheese is melted. Let stand 10 minutes before serving. Sprinkle with parsley.

HIGH ALTITUDE (3500-6000 FT.): No change.

Nutrition Information Per Serving:
Serving Size: 1-1/2 Cups

Calories:	570	From Fat:	260
Total Fat			29g
Saturated			13g
Cholesterol			110mg
Sodium			990mg
Total Carbohydrate			39g
Dietary Fiber			3g
Sugars			7g
Protein			38g

Mexican Bubble Pizza

KAREN HAMILTON | TITONKA, IOWA

PREP TIME: 15 MINUTES (READY IN 50 MINUTES)
SERVINGS: 8

1½ lb. lean (at least 80%) ground beef

1 package (1.25 oz.) Old El Paso® taco seasoning mix

¾ cup water

1 can (10¾ oz.) condensed tomato soup

1 can (16.3 oz.) Pillsbury® Grands!® Homestyle refrigerated buttermilk biscuits or 1 can (17.3 oz.) Pillsbury® Grands!® refrigerated golden corn biscuits

2 cups shredded Cheddar cheese (8 oz.)

2 cups shredded lettuce

2 medium tomatoes, chopped (about 1½ cups)

1 cup Old El Paso® Thick 'n Chunky salsa

1 can (2¼ oz.) sliced ripe olives, drained

1 container (8 oz.) sour cream

3 medium green onions, sliced, if desired

1) Heat oven to 375°F. In 10-inch skillet, cook ground beef over medium-high heat, stirring frequently, until thoroughly cooked; drain. Stir in taco seasoning mix, water and soup; heat to boiling. Reduce heat to low; simmer uncovered 3 minutes.

2) Separate dough into 8 biscuits; cut each into 8 pieces. Gently stir biscuit pieces into ground beef mixture. Spoon mixture into ungreased 13x9-inch pan.

3) Bake 18 to 23 minutes or until sauce is bubbly and biscuits are golden brown. Sprinkle cheese over top. Bake 8 to 10 minutes longer or until cheese is bubbly. Cut pizza into 8 squares; top each with lettuce, tomatoes, salsa, olives, sour cream and onions.

HIGH ALTITUDE (3500-6500 FT.): No change.

Nutrition Information Per Serving:
Serving Size: 1/8 of Recipe

Calories:	580	From Fat:	320
Total Fat			35g
Saturated			16g
Cholesterol			100mg
Sodium			1550mg
Total Carbohydrate			39g
Dietary Fiber			2g
Sugars			12g
Protein			28g

Sweet Plum-Pork Stir-Fry

PREP TIME: 35 MINUTES
SERVINGS: 4 (1-1/2 CUPS EACH)

1 cup uncooked instant white rice

1¼ cups water

¾ lb. pork tenderloin

2 tablespoons oil

1 medium sweet onion (such as Walla Walla or Maui), cut into thin wedges (¾ cup)

1 medium carrot, diagonally sliced (½ cup)

1 medium red bell pepper, cut into thin bite-sized strips

1 cup fresh snow pea pods, trimmed

⅓ cup plum jelly or jam

1 tablespoon soy sauce

1 tablespoon cornstarch

½ teaspoon ginger

¼ teaspoon salt

1) Cook rice in 1 cup of the water as directed on package.

2) Cut tenderloin into ¼-inch thick slices; cut slices into thin bite-sized strips. Meanwhile, heat 1 tablespoon of the oil in wok or 12-inch skillet over medium-high heat until hot. Add pork; cook and stir 4 to 5 minutes or until pork is no longer pink in center. Remove pork from wok; place on plate and cover to keep warm.

3) Add remaining tablespoon oil to wok. Add onion and carrot; cook and stir 3 minutes. Add bell pepper and pea pods; cook and stir an additional 2 to 3 minutes or until vegetables are crisp-tender.

4) In small bowl, mix jelly, soy sauce, cornstarch, ginger, salt and remaining ¼ cup water until smooth. Add jelly mixture and return pork to wok; cook and stir an additional 2 minutes or until sauce has thickened. Serve over rice.

HIGH ALTITUDE (ABOVE 3500 FT.): Cook rice using high altitude directions on package. Increase water in jelly mixture to ½ cup.

Nutrition Information Per Serving:
Serving Size: 1-1/2 Cups

Calories:	390	From Fat:	100
Total Fat		11g	
Saturated		2g	
Cholesterol		55mg	
Sodium		750mg	
Total Carbohydrate		50g	
Dietary Fiber		2g	
Sugars		17g	
Protein		23g	

tip Maui onions, from the Hawaiian Islands, are sweet, mild and white to pale yellow, and are in season from April to July. Walla Walla onions, from Walla Walla, Washington, are also yellow and sweet and are available from June through September.

Grilled Asian Tuna Steaks

PREP TIME: 20 MINUTES
SERVINGS: 2

⊖ EASY

¼ cup lite soy sauce

¼ cup water

1 teaspoon sugar

2 garlic cloves, minced

1 green onion, finely chopped

2 (8-oz.) tuna steaks
(about 1-inch thick)

1) In 8-inch square (2-quart) glass baking dish, combine all ingredients except tuna steaks; mix well. Add tuna; turn to coat. Let stand while grill is heating.

2) Heat gas or charcoal grill. When grill is heated, remove tuna from soy sauce mixture; reserve mixture. Place tuna on gas grill over medium heat or on charcoal grill 4 to 6 inches from medium coals. Cover grill; cook 10 to 12 minutes or until fish flakes easily with fork and is opaque in center, turning once and brushing frequently with soy sauce mixture.

3) Bring any remaining soy sauce mixture to a boil in small saucepan. Serve tuna with warm soy sauce mixture.

HIGH ALTITUDE (ABOVE 3500 FT.): Cook tuna in covered gas grill over medium-low heat or in covered charcoal grill 4 to 6 inches from medium-low coals using times above as a guide, turning once and brushing frequently with soy sauce mixture.

Nutrition Information Per Serving:
Serving Size: 1/2 of Recipe

Calories:	310	From Fat:	110
Total Fat		12g	
Saturated		3g	
Cholesterol		135mg	
Sodium		1190mg	
Total Carbohydrate		6g	
Dietary Fiber		0g	
Sugars		3g	
Protein		45g	

Mini Roast Beef Pizza

PREP TIME: 15 MINUTES (READY IN 25 MINUTES)
SERVINGS: 2

 EASY

1 tablespoon olive or vegetable oil

1 cup thin bite-size green bell pepper strips

½ cup sliced onion

2 oz. thinly sliced cooked seasoned roast beef (from deli), cut into strips

1 package (10 oz.) prebaked personal-size Italian pizza crusts (2 crusts)

²/3 cup shredded Swiss cheese (2²/3 oz.)

Nutrition Information Per Serving:
Serving Size: 1 Mini Pizza

Calories:	640	From Fat:	240
Total Fat			27g
Saturated			12g
Cholesterol			65mg
Sodium			1170mg
Total Carbohydrate			69g
Dietary Fiber			4g
Sugars			5g
Protein			32g

1) Heat oven to 400°F. In 8-inch skillet, heat oil over medium-high heat. Add bell pepper and onion; cook 3 to 4 minutes, stirring frequently, until crisp-tender. Remove from heat. Stir in roast beef.

2) Place pizza crusts on ungreased cookie sheet. Divide roast beef mixture evenly onto crusts. Sprinkle with cheese.

3) Bake 8 to 10 minutes or until cheese is melted and crust is hot.

Pepper-Herb Beef Stroganoff

PREP TIME: 20 MINUTES (READY IN 20 MINUTES)
SERVINGS: 2 (1 CUP EACH)

 EASY

1 tablespoon butter or margarine

½ lb. boneless beef sirloin steak, cut into thin bite-size strips

¼ teaspoon garlic salt

¼ teaspoon coarse ground black pepper

1½ cups sliced fresh mushrooms (4 oz.)

¼ cup beef broth

1 tablespoon chili sauce

¼ teaspoon dried thyme leaves

¼ cup chive-and-onion sour cream

2 tablespoons chopped fresh parsley

Hot cooked noodles, if desired

Nutrition Information Per Serving:
Serving Size: 1 Cup

Calories:	260	From Fat:	140
Total Fat			15g
Saturated			8g
Cholesterol			95mg
Sodium			460mg
Total Carbohydrate			6g
Dietary Fiber			1g
Sugars			4g
Protein			26g

1) In 8-inch nonstick skillet, melt butter over medium-high heat. Add beef strips; sprinkle with garlic salt and pepper. Cook 2 to 3 minutes, stirring frequently, until browned.

2) Add mushrooms; cook 2 minutes, stirring frequently. Stir in broth, chili sauce and thyme. Cook 3 to 5 minutes, stirring occasionally, until flavors are blended.

3) Reduce heat to medium-low; stir in sour cream until well blended. Sprinkle with parsley. Serve over hot cooked noodles.

Italian Vegetarian Lasagna

PREP TIME: 40 MINUTES (READY IN 1 HOUR 20 MINUTES)
SERVINGS: 8

LOW FAT

12 uncooked lasagna noodles

½ cup dry sherry or unsweetened apple juice

1 medium onion, finely chopped (½ cup)

1 package (8 oz.) sliced fresh mushrooms (3 cups)

2 large zucchini, shredded (about 4 cups)

2 medium red or green bell peppers, chopped (1 cup)

½ teaspoon salt

2 cups chopped fresh spinach

1 teaspoon dried basil leaves

½ teaspoon dried oregano leaves

1 container (15 oz.) light ricotta cheese

1 cup fat-free or low-fat cottage cheese

¼ cup grated Parmesan cheese

1 can (8 oz.) tomato sauce

1 cup shredded mozzarella cheese (4 oz.)

1) Heat oven to 425°F. Spray 13x9-inch (3-quart) glass baking dish and sheet of foil (large enough to cover dish) with cooking spray. Cook lasagna noodles as directed on package; drain.

2) Meanwhile, in 12-inch nonstick skillet or Dutch oven, heat sherry to boiling over medium-high heat. Add onion; cook 3 minutes, stirring frequently. Stir in mushrooms, zucchini, bell peppers and salt. Cook 5 minutes, stirring occasionally. Stir in spinach, basil and oregano. Cook 2 minutes. Remove from heat; drain well.

3) In medium bowl, mix ricotta cheese, cottage cheese and Parmesan cheese.

4) Place 3 cooked noodles in bottom of baking dish. Top with ⅓ of ricotta mixture and ⅓ of vegetable mixture. Repeat layers 2 more times. Top with remaining 3 lasagna noodles, tomato sauce and mozzarella cheese. Cover tightly with foil, sprayed side down.

5) Bake 25 to 30 minutes or until bubbly around edges. Uncover baking dish; bake 5 minutes longer or until top is light golden brown. Let stand 5 minutes before serving. Cut into squares.

HIGH ALTITUDE (3500-6000 FT.): Bake at 425°F. 30 to 35 minutes. Uncover; bake 5 to 10 minutes longer or until top is light golden brown.

Nutrition Information Per Serving:
Serving Size: 1/8 of Recipe

Calories:	300	From Fat:	70
Total Fat			8g
Saturated			5g
Cholesterol			30mg
Sodium			720mg
Total Carbohydrate			36g
Dietary Fiber			3g
Sugars			8g
Protein			21g

If you don't have a pasta pot with a removable inner basket, use a metal colander inside a pot of boiling water to cook the pasta. Simply lift the colander and shake it to drain off excess water.

Squash with Vegetarian Sausage and Rice Stuffing

PREP TIME: 25 MINUTES (READY IN 25 MINUTES)
SERVINGS: 2

 EASY  LOW FAT

1 medium acorn squash

½ cup Green Giant® frozen sweet peas

½ cup water

¼ teaspoon dried thyme leaves

⅛ teaspoon salt

½ cup uncooked instant brown rice

3 frozen meatless breakfast sausage patties (from 8-oz. box)

2 tablespoons shredded fresh Parmesan cheese

1) Cut squash in half lengthwise; remove seeds. In 8-inch square (2-quart) glass baking dish, place squash halves, cut side down. Cover with microwavable plastic wrap. Microwave on High 9 to 11 minutes or until squash is fork-tender.

2) Meanwhile, in 2-quart saucepan, heat peas, water, thyme and salt to boiling over high heat. Stir in rice; return to boiling. Reduce heat to low; cover and simmer 5 minutes. Remove from heat; stir. Let stand covered 5 minutes or until liquid is absorbed.

3) Heat 8-inch nonstick skillet over medium heat. Add sausage patties; cook 5 to 6 minutes or until lightly browned and thoroughly heated, breaking up patties into ½-inch pieces as they thaw.

4) Fluff rice mixture with fork; stir in sausage and cheese. Spoon rice mixture into squash halves.

HIGH ALTITUDE (ABOVE 3500 FT.): No change.

Nutrition Information Per Serving:
Serving Size: 1 Squash Half

Calories:	450	From Fat:	80
Total Fat			9g
Saturated			2g
Cholesterol			5mg
Sodium			590mg
Total Carbohydrate			75g
Dietary Fiber			8g
Sugars			7g
Protein			23g

Night-Before Taco Bake

PREP TIME: 20 MINUTES (READY IN 4 HOURS 50 MINUTES)
SERVINGS: 8

1 lb. lean (at least 80%) ground beef

2 cups frozen bell pepper and onion stir-fry (from 16-oz. bag)

1 can (11 oz.) Green Giant® super sweet yellow and white corn

1 can (4.5 oz.) Old El Paso® chopped green chiles

1 package (1.25 oz.) Old El Paso® 40% less-sodium taco seasoning mix

1 jar (8 oz.) taco sauce

3 cups coarsely broken white corn chips (about 5 oz.)

2 cups shredded Mexican cheese blend (8 oz.)

1) Spray 12x8-inch (2-quart) glass baking dish and sheet of foil (large enough to cover dish) with cooking spray. In 12-inch nonstick skillet, cook ground beef over medium-high heat 5 to 7 minutes, stirring frequently, until beef is thoroughly cooked; drain.

2) Stir in bell pepper and onion stir-fry, corn, green chiles and taco seasoning mix. Cook 5 minutes, stirring frequently, until bell peppers and onions are tender. Stir in taco sauce. Remove from heat.

3) Spoon half of beef mixture evenly in bottom of baking dish. Cover with 2 cups of the chips. Sprinkle $3/4$ cup of the cheese over chips. Spoon remaining half of beef mixture evenly over cheese. Sprinkle with 1 cup cheese. Top evenly with remaining 1 cup chips. Cover baking dish tightly with foil, sprayed side down. Refrigerate at least 4 hours or overnight.

4) When ready to bake, heat oven to 375°F. Bake casserole, covered, 20 minutes. Uncover; sprinkle with remaining $1/4$ cup cheese. Bake uncovered 5 to 10 minutes longer or until casserole is thoroughly heated and cheese is melted. Cut into squares.

HIGH ALTITUDE (3500-6000 FT.): Bake covered at 375°F. 35 minutes. Uncover; add cheese. Bake 5 to 10 minutes longer.

Nutrition Information Per Serving:
Serving Size: 1/8 of Recipe

Calories:	370	From Fat:	210
Total Fat			23g
Saturated			10g
Cholesterol			60mg
Sodium			890mg
Total Carbohydrate			22g
Dietary Fiber			2g
Sugars			4g
Protein			18g

Potato-Topped Oven Swiss Steak

PREP TIME: 20 MINUTES (READY IN 2 HOURS 35 MINUTES)
SERVINGS: 8

SWISS STEAK

1½ lb. boneless beef round steak
(½ inch thick), cut into pieces

3 medium carrots, sliced (1½ cups)

1 large onion, cut into thin wedges
(2 cups)

1 can (14.5 oz.) diced tomatoes with
Italian herbs, undrained

1 jar (12 oz.) beef gravy

TOPPING

1 box (7.2 oz.) mashed potatoes
seasoned with butter and herb
(2 pouches)

2½ cups water

1⅓ cups milk

¼ cup butter or margarine

1 egg, beaten

1) Heat oven to 325°F. In ungreased 13x9-
inch (3-quart) glass baking dish, arrange
beef in single layer. Top with carrots and
onion.

2) In medium bowl, mix tomatoes and
gravy; spoon over beef and vegetables.
Cover with foil; bake 2 hours.

3) In 3-quart saucepan, make both pouches
of potatoes as directed on box using
water, milk and butter. Stir in egg until
well blended.

4) Remove baking dish from oven. Uncover;
spoon or pipe potato mixture over hot
mixture. Return to oven; bake uncovered
15 to 20 minutes longer or until potatoes
are set and light golden brown.

Enjoy this casserole
with a crisp salad.
Toss purchased salad
greens, sliced fresh
strawberries and
slivered almonds
with a balsamic
vinaigrette.

Nutrition Information Per Serving:
Serving Size: 1/8 of Recipe

Calories:	350	From Fat:	120
Total Fat			13g
Saturated			4g
Cholesterol			80mg
Sodium			710mg
Total Carbohydrate			34g
Dietary Fiber			4g
Sugars			6g
Protein			23g

Beef Stroganoff

PREP TIME: 15 MINUTES (READY IN 35 MINUTES)
SERVINGS: 8 (1-1/4 CUPS EACH)

LOW FAT

6 cups uncooked egg noodles

$^1/_3$ cup all-purpose flour

$^1/_2$ teaspoon salt

$^1/_8$ teaspoon pepper

2$^1/_2$ lb. boneless beef sirloin steak, cut into 3x$^1/_2$x$^1/_4$-inch strips

1 package (8 oz.) sliced fresh mushrooms (about 3 cups)

1 can (10$^1/_2$ oz.) condensed beef broth

$^1/_2$ cup water

3 tablespoons tomato paste

1 tablespoon Worcestershire sauce

1$^1/_2$ cups nonfat sour cream

Chopped fresh parsley, if desired

1) Cook noodles as directed on package; drain.

2) Meanwhile, in food storage plastic bag, mix flour, salt and pepper. Add beef strips; shake to coat.

3) Heat 12-inch nonstick skillet or Dutch oven over medium-high heat. Add beef; cook about 6 minutes, stirring occasionally, until browned. Add mushrooms; cook and stir 1 minute.

4) Stir in broth, water, tomato paste and Worcestershire sauce. Reduce heat to medium-low; simmer uncovered 15 to 20 minutes or until beef is tender.

5) Stir in sour cream; cook about 2 minutes or until thoroughly heated (do not boil). Serve over noodles. Sprinkle with parsley.

HIGH ALTITUDE (ABOVE 3500 FT.): Increase water to $^3/_4$ cup.

Nutrition Information Per Serving:
Serving Size: 1-1/4 Cups

Calories:	330	From Fat:	50
Total Fat			6g
Saturated			2g
Cholesterol			105mg
Sodium			660mg
Total Carbohydrate			32g
Dietary Fiber			2g
Sugars			5g
Protein			39g

Sloppy Joe Loaf

HELENA CRUTCHER | HAZEL GREEN, ALABAMA

PREP TIME: 20 MINUTES (READY IN 50 MINUTES)
SERVINGS: 6

1 lb. extra-lean (at least 90%) ground beef

1 small onion, chopped (about 1/3 cup)

1 can (8 oz.) tomato sauce

1 tablespoon Pillsbury® BEST® all-purpose flour

1/4 teaspoon dried basil leaves

1/4 teaspoon dried oregano leaves

1/4 teaspoon fennel seed

1 can (11 oz.) Pillsbury® refrigerated crusty French loaf

1 cup shredded mozzarella cheese (4 oz.)

1) Heat oven to 350°F. Spray cookie sheet and 10-inch skillet with cooking spray. In skillet, cook ground beef and onion over medium heat, stirring frequently, until beef is thoroughly cooked; drain. Stir in tomato sauce, flour, basil, oregano and fennel seed. Reduce heat to medium-low; simmer uncovered 5 minutes.

2) Meanwhile, remove dough from can; place on lightly floured surface. Cut loaf in half lengthwise; with rolling pin, roll each half into 16x4-inch rectangle. Place 1 dough rectangle on cookie sheet (be careful not to change shape).

3) Stir 1/2 cup of the cheese into ground beef mixture; spoon and spread mixture over dough rectangle on cookie sheet. Sprinkle with remaining 1/2 cup cheese; top with remaining dough rectangle.

4) Bake 25 to 30 minutes or until golden brown. Cut into slices.

HIGH ALTITUDE (3500-6500 FT.): No change.

Nutrition Information Per Serving:
Serving Size: 1/6 of Recipe

Calories:	310	From Fat:	100
Total Fat			12g
Saturated			5g
Cholesterol			55mg
Sodium			670mg
Total Carbohydrate			28g
Dietary Fiber			2g
Sugars			5g
Protein			24g

Sesame Asian Grilled Cornish Hen Halves

PREP TIME: 1 HOUR (READY IN 5 HOURS)
SERVINGS: 4

 EASY

2 Cornish game hens (24 oz. each), thawed if frozen

⅓ cup soy sauce

2 tablespoons packed brown sugar

2 cloves garlic, minced

1 tablespoon sesame seed

Nutrition Information Per Serving:		
Serving Size: 1/2 Game Hen		
Calories: 260	From Fat: 160	
Total Fat		18g
Saturated		5g
Cholesterol		120mg
Sodium		350mg
Total Carbohydrate		3g
Dietary Fiber		0g
Sugars		2g
Protein		21g

1) With kitchen scissors, cut game hens in half lengthwise; rinse well. In large nonmetal dish or resealable food-storage bag, place hen halves. In 1-cup glass measuring cup, mix soy sauce, brown sugar and garlic; pour over hen halves. Stir or turn bag to coat. Cover dish or seal bag; refrigerate at least 4 hours, stirring or turning occasionally, to marinate.

2) Heat gas or charcoal grill. Remove hen halves from marinade; discard marinade. Sprinkle skin side of hen halves with sesame seed.

3) When grill is heated, place hen halves, skin side up, on gas grill over medium heat or on charcoal grill over medium coals; cover grill. Cook 30 to 40 minutes, turning hen halves twice, until fork-tender and juices run clear.

HIGH ALTITUDE (3500-6500 FT.): Place hen halves, skin side up, on gas grill over low heat or on charcoal grill over low coals; cover grill. Cook using times above as a guide, turning hen halves twice.

Southwestern Pork and Black Bean Stir-Fry

PREP TIME: 30 MINUTES (READY IN 30 MINUTES)
SERVINGS: 4 (1-1/2 CUPS EACH)

 EASY   LOW FAT

1 tablespoon olive or vegetable oil

¾ lb. pork tenderloin, cut into 2x½x¼-inch strips

1 medium onion, cut into thin wedges

1 small red bell pepper, cut into thin bite-size strips

2 cloves garlic, minced

2 cups Green Giant® Niblets® frozen corn, thawed*

1 can (15 oz.) black beans, drained, rinsed

1 small zucchini, chopped (about 1 cup)

½ cup Old El Paso® Thick 'n Chunky salsa

Nutrition Information Per Serving:		
Serving Size: 1-1/2 Cups		
Calories: 370	From Fat: 70	
Total Fat		8g
Saturated		2g
Cholesterol		55mg
Sodium		590mg
Total Carbohydrate		50g
Dietary Fiber		10g
Sugars		8g
Protein		32g

1) In 10-inch nonstick skillet, heat oil over medium-high heat. Add pork, onion, bell pepper and garlic; cook 6 to 8 minutes, stirring frequently, until pork is no longer pink in center and vegetables are crisp-tender.

2) Stir in all remaining ingredients. Reduce heat to medium; cover and simmer 5 to 7 minutes, stirring occasionally, until zucchini is crisp-tender and flavors are blended. If desired, season to taste with salt and pepper.

*NOTE: To quickly thaw corn, place in colander or strainer; rinse with warm water until thawed. Drain well.

HIGH ALTITUDE (ABOVE 3500 FT.): No change.

Cheesy Chicken Tortilla Lasagna

PREP TIME: 25 MINUTES (READY IN 1 HOUR 10 MINUTES)
SERVINGS: 6

1 can (10 oz.) Old El Paso® enchilada sauce

2 package (9 oz.) frozen southwestern-seasoned cooked chicken breast strips, thawed, diced

1 container (8 oz.) sour cream

½ cup sliced green onions (8 medium)

1 tablespoon Old El Paso® taco seasoning mix (from 1.25-oz. envelope)

8 corn tortillas (6 inch), halved

2 cups shredded Colby-Monterey Jack cheese (8 oz.)

1 cup tortilla chips

1 cup chopped tomatoes (2 medium)

2 tablespoons ripe olives

1) Heat oven to 375°F. Spray 13x9–inch (3–quart) glass baking dish with cooking spray. Reserve ¼ cup enchilada sauce. In large bowl, mix remaining enchilada sauce, chicken, sour cream, ¼ cup of the onions and taco seasoning mix.

2) Spoon ¼ cup enchilada sauce in bottom of baking dish. Arrange 8 tortilla pieces over sauce, overlapping as necessary. Spoon half of chicken mixture over tortillas; sprinkle with ⅔ cup of the cheese. Repeat layers. Cover with foil.

3) Bake 30 to 35 minutes or until thoroughly heated. Uncover; layer tortilla chips, tomatoes, olives, remaining ¼ cup onions and remaining ⅔ cup cheese over top of casserole. Bake uncovered about 5 minutes longer. Let stand 10 minutes before serving.

Nutrition Information Per Serving:
Serving Size: 1/6 of Recipe

Calories:	500	From Fat:	235
Total Fat			26g
Saturated			13g
Cholesterol			135mg
Sodium			970mg
Total Carbohydrate			27g
Dietary Fiber			3g
Sugars			6g
Protein			40g

tip

For an easy garnish, top with tomato wedges and green onion.

Pineapple-Glazed Chicken Breasts with Couscous Pilaf

PREP TIME: 25 MINUTES (READY IN 25 MINUTES)
SERVINGS: 2

EASY   **LOW FAT**

PILAF

2 tablespoons finely chopped red bell pepper

¼ teaspoon chicken-flavor instant bouillon

¾ cup water

½ cup uncooked couscous

2 tablespoons sliced green onions (2 medium)

CHICKEN

¼ cup pineapple preserves

2 teaspoons sweet hot mustard

2 boneless skinless chicken breast halves (about ½ lb.)

2 teaspoons water

1) In 1-quart saucepan, heat bell pepper, bouillon and water to boiling over high heat. Remove from heat; stir in couscous. Cover; let stand 5 minutes. Stir in onions; set aside; transfer half of mixture to a small microwavable bowl.

2) Meanwhile, line broiler pan with foil; spray with cooking spray. Place chicken breast halves on pan. Broil 4 to 6 inches from heat 5 minutes. In small bowl, mix preserves and mustard; transfer half of mixture to a small microwavable bowl.

3) Turn chicken. Brush chicken with half of preserves mixture; discard any remaining. Broil 3 to 5 minutes longer or until chicken is fork-tender and juices run clear.

4) Stir couscous mixture lightly with fork; divide evenly onto 2 individual serving plates. Top each with chicken. Stir water into remaining preserves mixture. Microwave on High 20 to 40 seconds or until warm; spoon over chicken. If desired, garnish with additional sliced green onions.

HIGH ALTITUDE (ABOVE 3500 FT.): No change.

Nutrition Information Per Serving:		
Serving Size: 1/2 of Recipe		
Calories: 410	From Fat:	40
Total Fat		4g
Saturated		1g
Cholesterol		70mg
Sodium		360mg
Total Carbohydrate		63g
Dietary Fiber		3g
Sugars		21g
Protein		31g

Chicken and Noodles Alfredo

PREP TIME: 15 MINUTES (READY IN 6 HOURS 35 MINUTES)
SERVINGS: 5 (1-1/3 CUPS EACH)

 EASY

1 lb. boneless skinless chicken thighs, cut into $3/4$-inch pieces

1 can (14 oz.) quartered artichokes, drained

1 jar (16 oz.) Alfredo pasta sauce

1 cup water

$1/2$ cup chopped sun-dried tomatoes (not in oil)

3 cups uncooked medium egg noodles (5 oz.)

2 tablespoons shredded Parmesan cheese

Nutrition Information Per Serving:
Serving Size: 1-1/3 Cups

Calories:	620	From Fat:	340
Total Fat			38g
Saturated			21g
Cholesterol			170mg
Sodium			830mg
Total Carbohydrate			36g
Dietary Fiber			6g
Sugars			4g
Protein			34g

1) In 3- to 4-quart slow cooker, mix chicken, artichokes, pasta sauce and water.

2) Cover; cook on Low setting 5 to 6 hours.

3) About 25 minutes before serving, stir tomatoes and uncooked noodles into chicken mixture.

4) Increase heat setting to High; cover and cook 15 to 20 minutes longer or until noodles are tender. Sprinkle cheese over individual servings.

HIGH ALTITUDE (ABOVE 3500 FT.): Use $1^1/4$ cups water.

Pepper-Rubbed Steaks with Caramelized Onions

PREP TIME: 20 MINUTES (READY IN 20 MINUTES)
SERVINGS: 4

 EASY   LOW FAT

1 large sweet onion (Maui, Texas Sweet or Walla Walla), thinly sliced, separated into rings

1 tablespoon sugar

2 tablespoons water

1 tablespoon balsamic vinegar

$1/2$ to 1 teaspoon seasoned pepper blend

4 boneless beef strip steaks, $1/2$ to $3/4$-inch thick (4 oz. each), trimmed of fat

Nutrition Information Per Serving:
Serving Size: 1/4 of Recipe

Calories:	150	From Fat:	30
Total Fat			4g
Saturated			1g
Cholesterol			60mg
Sodium			45mg
Total Carbohydrate			7g
Dietary Fiber			0g
Sugars			5g
Protein			23g

1) Heat 12-inch nonstick skillet over medium heat. Add onion; cook 3 to 4 minutes, stirring frequently, just until it begins to brown. Stir in sugar and water. Reduce heat to medium-low; cover and cook 6 to 8 minutes, stirring frequently, until onion is tender and golden. Remove from heat; stir in vinegar.

2) Meanwhile, heat closed contact grill for 5 minutes. Rub pepper blend on both sides of each steak.

3) When grill is heated, place steaks on bottom grill surface. Close grill; cook 3 to 5 minutes or until desired doneness. Serve steaks with onions.

HIGH ALTITUDE (ABOVE 3500 FT.): No change.

Beef Stew

PREP TIME:	30 MINUTES (READY IN 30 MINUTES)
SERVINGS:	5 (1-1/2 CUPS EACH)

 EASY   LOW FAT

¾ lb. boneless beef top sirloin steak, cut into ½-inch pieces

1 small onion, chopped (⅓ cup)

3 cups frozen southern-style hash-brown potatoes (from 32-oz. bag)

1½ cups thinly sliced carrots (1½ medium)

1 cup thinly sliced celery (1¾ medium stalks)

1 jar (4.5 oz.) Green Giant® sliced mushrooms, drained

1 envelope (1.5 oz.) beef-mushroom soup mix (dry)

¼ teaspoon dried thyme leaves, crushed

¼ teaspoon salt

⅛ teaspoon pepper

3 cups water

1) Heat nonstick Dutch oven or 4-quart saucepan over medium-high heat. Add beef and onion; cook 5 minutes, stirring occasionally, until beef is browned.

2) Stir in potatoes, carrots, celery and mushrooms. Cook 2 minutes, stirring frequently. Stir in all remaining ingredients. Heat to boiling. Reduce heat to low; simmer uncovered 15 minutes or until vegetables are tender. If desired, sprinkle individual servings with chopped fresh parsley.

HIGH ALTITUDE (ABOVE 3500 FT.): After stirring in all remaining ingredients, heat to boiling. Reduce heat to low; cover and simmer 15 minutes.

Nutrition Information Per Serving:
Serving Size: 1-1/2 Cups

Calories:	235	From Fat:	20
Total Fat			2g
Saturated			1g
Cholesterol			35mg
Sodium			1050mg
Total Carbohydrate			37g
Dietary Fiber			5g
Sugars			7g
Protein			17g

This hearty stew is an excellent source of vitamin A, and also contributes to your daily vitamin C and iron needs.

Pork Medallions with Dijon-Mushroom Sauce

FRANK HOLLANDS | MOORHEAD, MINNESOTA

PREP TIME: 30 MINUTES (READY IN 30 MINUTES)
SERVINGS: 2

⊖ EASY

5 teaspoons butter

1 shallot, finely chopped
  (2 tablespoons)

1 jar (4.5 oz.) Green Giant®
  sliced mushrooms, drained

1 teaspoon vegetable oil

1 pork tenderloin (½ to ¾ lb.),
  cut into 8 (¾-inch-thick) slices

⅛ teaspoon salt

⅛ teaspoon pepper

1 tablespoon cognac or apple juice

1 tablespoon Dijon mustard

½ cup whipping cream

  Fresh thyme sprigs or basil leaves,
  if desired

1) In 8-inch skillet, melt 2 teaspoons of the butter over medium heat. Add shallot and mushrooms; cook and stir 1 minute or until tender. Remove from skillet.

2) To same skillet, add remaining 3 teaspoons butter and the oil. Add pork; cook 8 to 10 minutes, turning slices halfway through cooking, until browned and no longer pink in center. Sprinkle with salt and pepper. Remove from skillet; cover to keep warm.

3) Gradually add cognac to same skillet; stir in mustard and cream. Heat to boiling; boil 1 to 2 minutes, stirring constantly, until slightly thickened. Add mushroom mixture; cook 1 minute or until thoroughly heated. Serve sauce over pork slices; garnish with thyme.

HIGH ALTITUDE (3500-6500 FT.): No change.

Nutrition Information Per Serving:
Serving Size: 1/2 of Recipe

Calories:	480	From Fat:	350
Total Fat			39g
Saturated			20g
Cholesterol			180mg
Sodium			740mg
Total Carbohydrate			6g
Dietary Fiber			2g
Sugars			3g
Protein			29g

Beef 'n Vegetable Stir-Fry for Two

PREP TIME: 15 MINUTES (READY IN 15 MINUTES)
SERVINGS: 2 (2 CUPS EACH)

  EASY   LOW FAT

1 cup uncooked instant white rice

1 cup water

¼ lb. extra-lean (at least 90%) ground beef

1 small onion, sliced

1½ cups Green Giant Select® frozen broccoli florets (from 14-oz. bag), thawed*

½ medium red bell pepper, cut into thin bite-size strips

¼ cup stir-fry sauce

2 tablespoons water, if desired

Nutrition Information Per Serving: Serving Size: 2 Cups		
Calories: 360	From Fat: 40	
Total Fat	5g	
Saturated	2g	
Cholesterol	30mg	
Sodium	2060mg	
Total Carbohydrate	61g	
Dietary Fiber	4g	
Sugars	9g	
Protein	22g	

1) Cook rice in 1 cup water as directed on package.

2) Meanwhile, in 8-inch nonstick skillet, cook ground beef and onion over medium heat, stirring frequently, until beef is thoroughly cooked; drain.

3) Stir in all remaining ingredients except rice. Cover; cook 4 to 6 minutes, stirring occasionally, until vegetables are crisp-tender. Serve over rice.

*NOTE: To quickly thaw frozen broccoli, place in colander or strainer; rinse with warm water until thawed. Drain well.

Fantastic Pot Roast

PREP TIME: 10 MINUTES (READY IN 10 HOURS 10 MINUTES)
SERVINGS: 8

EASY   LOW FAT

1 package Slow Cooker Helper® pot roast

1½ to 2 lb. boneless beef roast, thawed if frozen

4½ cups hot water

¾ cup chili sauce (from 12-oz. bottle)

1 can (12 oz.) cola

2 cloves garlic, if desired

Nutrition Information Per Serving: Serving Size: 1/8 of Recipe		
Calories: 315	From Fat: 90	
Total Fat	10g	
Saturated	4g	
Cholesterol	50mg	
Sodium	970mg	
Total Carbohydrate	36g	
Dietary Fiber	3g	
Sugars	16g	
Protein	20g	

1) In 3- to 4½-quart slow cooker, stir uncooked Vegetables and Sauce Mix, uncooked Potatoes and remaining ingredients until sauce mix is dissolved.

2) Cover; cook on Low setting 8 to 10 hours (or High heat setting 4 to 5 hours) or until beef is tender.

3) Turn slow cooker off. Remove beef. Stir vegetable mixture; let stand uncovered 5 minutes. Slice beef; serve with vegetables and sauce.

HIGH ALTITUDE (ABOVE 3500 FT.): No change.

Mustard-Glazed Meat Loaf

PREP TIME: 10 MINUTES (READY IN 1 HOUR 25 MINUTES)
SERVINGS: 6

MEAT LOAF
- 2 eggs
- 2 tablespoons Dijon mustard
- ½ cup Progresso® Garlic Herb Bread Crumbs
- ½ teaspoon dried thyme leaves
- 1½ lb. lean (at least 80%) ground beef

GLAZE
- 2 tablespoons apple jelly
- 2 tablespoons Dijon mustard
- 2 tablespoons chopped green onions

1) Heat oven to 350°F. In large bowl, beat eggs. Stir in all remaining meat loaf ingredients. Press mixture in ungreased 8x4-inch loaf pan. Bake at 350°F. for 40 minutes.

2) Meanwhile, in small microwave-safe measuring cup, combine all glaze ingredients. Microwave on High for 1 to 2 minutes or until jelly is melted, stirring every 30 seconds.

3) Remove pan from oven. Using pancake turner to hold meat loaf in pan, drain off fat. Spoon glaze over meat loaf.

4) Return to oven; bake an additional 20 to 25 minutes or until meat thermometer inserted in center reads 160°F. Let stand 5 to 10 minutes before serving.

HIGH ALTITUDE (ABOVE 3500 FT.): No change.

Nutrition Information Per Serving:
Serving Size: 1/6 of Recipe

Calories:	295	From Fat:	145
Total Fat			16g
Saturated			5g
Cholesterol			140mg
Sodium			400mg
Total Carbohydrate			12g
Dietary Fiber			0g
Sugars			4g
Protein			26g

Tex-Mex Pasta

KAREN WETCH | SANTA ROSA, CALIFORNIA

PREP TIME: 25 MINUTES (READY IN 25 MINUTES)
SERVINGS: 6

EASY

8 oz. uncooked penne (tube-shaped) pasta

1 lb. bulk Italian turkey sausage

1 medium onion, chopped (½ cup)

1 medium red bell pepper, chopped (1 cup)

1 small zucchini, chopped (about 1 cup)

2 cups Green Giant® Niblets® frozen corn (from 1-lb. bag)

1 cup Old El Paso® Thick 'n Chunky salsa

1 can (14.5 oz.) diced tomatoes, undrained

¾ teaspoon dried oregano leaves

1½ cups reduced-fat shredded Cheddar cheese (6 oz.)

½ cup fresh cilantro, chopped

1) Cook pasta as directed on package; drain and cover to keep warm.

2) Meanwhile, heat nonstick wok or 10-inch nonstick skillet over medium-high heat. Add sausage; cook about 5 minutes, stirring frequently, until no longer pink and thoroughly cooked. Drain. Stir in onion, bell pepper, zucchini, corn, salsa, tomatoes and oregano. Heat to boiling; cook 5 minutes, stirring occasionally.

3) Reserve ½ cup of the cheese and 2 tablespoons of the cilantro. Stir remaining 1 cup cheese and remaining cilantro into sausage mixture. Toss in cooked pasta. Spoon mixture onto serving platter; garnish with reserved cheese and cilantro.

HIGH ALTITUDE (3500-6500 FT.): No change.

Nutrition Information Per Serving:		
Serving Size: 1/6 of Recipe		
Calories: 400	From Fat:	120
Total Fat		13g
Saturated		4g
Cholesterol		80mg
Sodium		1320mg
Total Carbohydrate		48g
Dietary Fiber		4g
Sugars		8g
Protein		27g

Santa Fe Country Ribs

PREP TIME: 15 MINUTES (READY IN 9 HOURS 15 MINUTES)
SERVINGS: 6

 EASY

2 lb. boneless country-style pork ribs

½ teaspoon salt

¾ cup Old El Paso® Thick 'n Chunky salsa

¾ cup chili sauce

1 teaspoon ground cumin

¼ teaspoon ground red pepper (cayenne)

2 tablespoons tomato paste (from 6-oz. can)

Nutrition Information Per Serving:
Serving Size: 1/6 of Recipe

Calories:	340	From Fat:	160
Total Fat			18g
Saturated			6g
Cholesterol			95mg
Sodium			840mg
Total Carbohydrate			13g
Dietary Fiber			1g
Sugars			10g
Protein			32g

1) Spray 3- to 4-quart slow cooker with cooking spray. Place pork ribs in slow cooker; sprinkle with salt. In small bowl, mix salsa, chili sauce, cumin and ground red pepper; spoon over ribs.

2) Cover; cook on Low setting 8 to 9 hours.

3) Remove ribs from slow cooker; place on serving platter. Into 2-cup measuring cup or bowl, pour 1 cup cooking juices from slow cooker. Stir in tomato paste; spoon over ribs.

HIGH ALTITUDE (ABOVE 3500 FT.): No change.

Easy Beef and Noodle Dinner

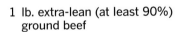

PREP TIME: 15 MINUTES
SERVINGS: 4 (1-1/3 CUPS EACH)

e EASY

1 lb. extra-lean (at least 90%) ground beef

½ cup chopped onion (1 medium)

1 (14.5-oz.) can diced tomatoes with basil, garlic and oregano, undrained

1 cup water

1 teaspoon dried Italian seasoning

1 (3-oz.) pkg. beef-flavor ramen noodle soup mix

1½ cups Green Giant® Frozen Cut Green Beans (from 1-lb. pkg.)

Nutrition Information Per Serving:
Serving Size: 1-1/3 Cups

Calories:	305	From Fat:	100
Total Fat			11g
Saturated			4g
Cholesterol			70mg
Sodium			570mg
Total Carbohydrate			22g
Dietary Fiber			3g
Sugars			5g
Protein			30g

1) In 12-inch nonstick skillet, cook ground beef and onion over medium-high heat until beef is thoroughly cooked, stirring frequently. Drain.

2) Add tomatoes, water, Italian seasoning and contents of seasoning packet from soup mix; mix well. Bring to a boil. Break up noodles; stir in noodles and beans.

3) Return to a boil. Reduce heat to low; cover and simmer 5 minutes or until noodles and beans are tender, stirring occasionally.

HIGH ALTITUDE (ABOVE 3500 FT.): Thaw frozen green beans before use.

Golden Layers Biscuit Taco Casserole

LOUISE V. DAVIS | OAKLEY, MICHIGAN

PREP TIME: 30 MINUTES (READY IN 40 MINUTES)
SERVINGS: 8

1 jar (16 oz.) taco sauce

1 can (12 oz.) Pillsbury® Golden Layers®
refrigerated buttermilk biscuits

1 cup shredded sharp
Cheddar cheese (4 oz.)

1 cup shredded mozzarella cheese
(4 oz.)

1 can (2 1/4 oz.) sliced ripe olives,
drained

1/2 lb. lean (at least 80%) ground beef

1/4 cup chopped red bell pepper,
if desired

1/4 cup chopped green bell pepper,
if desired

1 can (4 oz.) Green Giant® mushroom
pieces and stems, drained, if desired

1) Heat oven to 400°F. Lightly spray
13x9-inch (3-quart) glass baking dish
with cooking spray. Spread taco sauce
evenly in bottom of dish.

2) Separate dough into 10 biscuits;
cut each into quarters. Place biscuit
pieces in taco sauce; turn to coat.
Sprinkle 1/2 cup of the Cheddar
cheese, 1/2 cup of the mozzarella
cheese and the olives over top; stir
gently to mix.

3) Bake 15 to 18 minutes or until bubbly. Meanwhile, in 8-inch skillet, cook
ground beef, bell peppers and mushrooms over medium-high heat,
stirring frequently, until beef is thoroughly cooked; drain.

4) Remove baking dish from oven. Sprinkle remaining 1/2 cup Cheddar cheese
and 1/2 cup mozzarella cheese over mixture. Top evenly with ground beef
mixture.

5) Return to oven; bake 5 to 7 minutes longer or until mixture bubbles
vigorously around edges.

HIGH ALTITUDE (3500-6500 FT.): Bake biscuit pieces mixed with taco sauce and topped with cheese
and olives at 400°F. 18 to 21 minutes. Continue as directed above.

Nutrition Information Per Serving:
Serving Size: 1/8 of Recipe

Calories:	320	From Fat:	170
Total Fat			19g
Saturated			8g
Cholesterol			40mg
Sodium			930mg
Total Carbohydrate			22g
Dietary Fiber			2g
Sugars			6g
Protein			15g

Reuben in the Round Crescents

MRS. IRENE DUNN | CUYAHOGA FALLS, OHIO

PREP TIME: 25 MINUTES (READY IN 50 MINUTES)
SERVINGS: 8

2 cans (8 oz. each) Pillsbury® refrigerated crescent dinner rolls

1 package (8 oz.) thinly sliced pastrami or corned beef

1 package (6 oz.) Swiss or mozzarella cheese (4 slices)

1 can (8 oz.) sauerkraut (1 cup), drained

½ teaspoon caraway seed

½ teaspoon sesame seed

Nutrition Information Per Serving:
Serving Size: 1/8 of Recipe

Calories:	340	From Fat:	180
Total Fat			20g
Saturated			9g
Cholesterol			35mg
Sodium			1040mg
Total Carbohydrate			24g
Dietary Fiber			1g
Sugars			5g
Protein			16g

1) Heat oven to 400°F. Separate 1 can of dough into 4 rectangles; place in ungreased 12-inch pizza pan or 13x9-inch pan. Press over bottom and ½ inch up sides to form crust, firmly pressing perforations to seal.

2) Layer pastrami, cheese and sauerkraut over dough; sprinkle with caraway seed. Separate second can of dough into 8 triangles; with points toward center, arrange spoke-fashion over filling (do not seal outer edges of triangles to bottom crust). Sprinkle with sesame seed.

3) Bake 15 to 25 minutes or until golden brown. Cut into wedges or squares.

HIGH ALTITUDE (3500-6500 FT.): No change.

Fennel–Garlic Pork Roast

PREP TIME: 10 MINUTES (READY IN 1 HOUR 15 MINUTES)
SERVINGS: 8

1 rolled boneless pork loin roast (2½ lb.)

1 tablespoon fennel seed

1 tablespoon chopped fresh thyme or 1 teaspoon dried thyme leaves

½ teaspoon salt

½ teaspoon coarse ground black pepper

2 tablespoons olive oil

3 cloves garlic, minced

Nutrition Information Per Serving:
Serving Size: 1/8 of Recipe

Calories:	265	From Fat:	135
Total Fat			15g
Saturated			4g
Cholesterol			90mg
Sodium			200mg
Total Carbohydrate			0g
Dietary Fiber			0g
Sugars			0g
Protein			32g

1) Heat oven to 375°F. In shallow baking pan, place pork roast. In small bowl, mix all remaining ingredients; spread over roast.

2) Bake 40 to 50 minutes or until pork has blush of pink in center and meat thermometer inserted in center reads 160°F.

3) Remove roast from pan. Cover with tent of foil; let stand 10 to 15 minutes. Remove string from roast; cut into slices.

HIGH ALTITUDE (3500-6000 FT.): No change.

Chipotle Beef–Stuffed Peppers

PREP TIME: 20 MINUTES (READY IN 1 HOUR 10 MINUTES)
SERVINGS: 4

1 cup uncooked instant white rice

1 cup water

1 lb. lean (at least 80%) ground beef

1 (11-oz.) can Green Giant® Mexicorn® Whole Kernel Corn, Red and Green Peppers, drained

2 chipotle chiles in adobo sauce, chopped (2 tablespoons)

1 egg, beaten

6 oz. (1 1/2 cups) shredded Monterey Jack cheese

4 medium red and/or green bell peppers

1 cup Old El Paso® Thick 'n Chunky salsa

1/4 cup chopped green onions

1) Heat oven to 375°F. Cook rice in water as directed on package.

2) Meanwhile, in 12-inch nonstick skillet, brown ground beef over medium-high heat until thoroughly cooked, stirring frequently. Drain. Add corn, chiles and egg; mix well.

3) Stir in cooked rice and 1 cup of the cheese. Cut bell peppers in half lengthwise; remove seeds and membrane. Place cut side up in ungreased 13x9-inch (3-quart) glass baking dish. Spoon about 3/4 cup beef mixture into each pepper half, mounding as necessary. Top each with 2 tablespoons salsa. Cover tightly with foil.

4) Bake at 375°F. for 35 to 40 minutes or until peppers are crisp-tender. Uncover; sprinkle with remaining 1/2 cup cheese and the onions. Bake uncovered an additional 5 to 10 minutes or until cheese is melted.

HIGH ALTITUDE (ABOVE 3500 FT.): Bake at 375°F. for 50 to 55 minutes. Uncover; sprinkle with remaining 1/2 cup cheese and the onions. Bake uncovered an additional 5 to 10 minutes.

Nutrition Information Per Serving:
Serving Size: 1/4 of Recipe

Calories:	595	From Fat:	250
Total Fat			28g
Saturated			13g
Cholesterol			160mg
Sodium			950mg
Total Carbohydrate			50g
Dietary Fiber			5g
Sugars			9g
Protein			41g

Spicy Apricot-Glazed Chicken

PREP TIME: 50 MINUTES (READY IN 50 MINUTES)
SERVINGS: 6

e EASY   **f** LOW FAT

1 cup apricot or peach preserves

1 tablespoon cider vinegar

½ teaspoon garlic salt

½ teaspoon ground ginger

¼ cup Old El Paso® chopped green chiles (from 4.5-oz. can)

3 to 3½ lb. cut-up whole chicken, skin removed if desired

Nutrition Information Per Serving:	
Serving Size: 1/6 of Recipe	
Calories: 290	From Fat: 50
Total Fat	6g
Saturated	1.5g
Cholesterol	70mg
Sodium	200mg
Total Carbohydrate	37g
Dietary Fiber	0g
Sugars	26g
Protein	23g

1) Heat gas or charcoal grill. In small bowl, mix all ingredients except chicken, breaking up large pieces of fruit. Reserve ⅓ cup preserves mixture.

2) When grill is heated, place chicken on gas grill over medium heat or on charcoal grill over medium coals; cover grill. Cook 15 minutes.

3) Turn chicken; brush with preserves mixture. Cover grill; cook 20 to 30 minutes longer, turning frequently and brushing with preserves mixture, until chicken is fork-tender and juices run clear. Serve chicken with reserved preserves mixture.

HIGH ALTITUDE (3500-6500 FT.): Set grill to medium-low heat. Grill as directed, but brush with preserves during the last 10 minutes of grilling.

Jamaican Pork with Mango Salsa

PREP TIME: 30 MINUTES (READY IN 30 MINUTES)
SERVINGS: 4

e EASY   **f** LOW FAT

1 cup cubed peeled mango (about 1 medium)

1 jalapeño chile, seeded, finely chopped

2 tablespoons chopped fresh cilantro

1 tablespoon lime juice

2 teaspoons honey

1 pork tenderloin (1 lb.), cut into ½-inch-thick slices

1½ teaspoons Jamaican or Caribbean jerk seasoning

Nutrition Information Per Serving:	
Serving Size: 1/4 of Recipe	
Calories: 180	From Fat: 40
Total Fat	4.5g
Saturated	1.5g
Cholesterol	70mg
Sodium	160mg
Total Carbohydrate	10g
Dietary Fiber	0g
Sugars	8g
Protein	26g

1) In small bowl, mix mango, chile, cilantro, lime juice and honey. Cover; refrigerate until serving time.

2) Heat closed contact grill 5 minutes. Meanwhile, sprinkle both sides of each pork slice with jerk seasoning.

3) When grill is heated, place pork on bottom grill surface; close grill. Cook 5 to 6 minutes or until pork is no longer pink in center. Serve with mango salsa.

HIGH ALTITUDE (3500-6500 FT.): No change.

Herb-Stuffed Flank Steak

PREP TIME: 50 MINUTES (READY IN 4 HOURS 50 MINUTES)
SERVINGS: 6

MARINADE

    3 tablespoons dry red wine

    3 tablespoons olive oil

    1 tablespoon fresh lemon juice

    1 teaspoon beef-flavor instant bouillon

    1 large clove garlic, minced

STEAK

    1 beef flank steak (2 lb.)

STUFFING

    3 tablespoons olive oil

    ¼ cup finely chopped onion
      (½ medium)

    3 cloves garlic, thinly sliced

    2 tablespoons chopped fresh parsley

    2 tablespoons Progresso® plain bread
      crumbs

    1 teaspoon grated lemon peel

1) In large, shallow nonmetal dish or resealable plastic bag, mix all marinade ingredients. Make pocket in side of flank steak by cutting lengthwise almost but not completely through opposite side. Add steak to marinade; turn to coat. Cover dish or seal bag; refrigerate at least 4 hours or overnight to marinate.

2) In 8-inch skillet, heat oil over medium heat. Add onion; cook 2 minutes, stirring occasionally, until tender. Stir in garlic and parsley; cook and stir 1 minute. Add bread crumbs and lemon peel; cook and stir 1 minute. Remove from heat.

3) Heat grill. Remove steak from marinade; discard marinade. Fill pocket in steak with stuffing. Secure opening with toothpicks.

4) Place steak on gas grill over medium heat; cover grill. Cook 12 to 20 minutes, turning once, until steak is desired doneness. Cut steak across grain into ½-inch-thick slices.

HIGH ALTITUDE (3500-6500 FT.): Place steak on gas grill over medium-low heat or on charcoal grill over medium-low coals; cover grill. Cook using times above as a guide, turning once.

Nutrition Information Per Serving:
Serving Size: 1/6 of Recipe

Calories:	320	From Fat:	170
Total Fat			19g
Saturated			5g
Cholesterol			85mg
Sodium			135mg
Total Carbohydrate			3g
Dietary Fiber			0g
Sugars			0g
Protein			33g

Breaded Veal Cutlets

PREP TIME: 10 MINUTES (READY IN 25 MINUTES)
SERVINGS: 2

 EASY

1 egg

⅓ cup Progresso® plain bread crumbs

2 veal cutlets (3 oz. each)

1 tablespoon vegetable oil

1 can (8 oz.) tomato sauce

½ teaspoon Italian seasoning

½ cup shredded mozzarella cheese
(2 oz.)

Nutrition Information Per Serving:
Serving Size: 1 Cutlet

Calories:	360	From Fat:	170
Total Fat			18g
Saturated			6g
Cholesterol			175mg
Sodium			1070mg
Total Carbohydrate			23g
Dietary Fiber			2g
Sugars			6g
Protein			28g

1) In shallow bowl, beat egg with fork. In shallow dish, place bread crumbs. Dip each veal cutlet into egg; coat with bread crumbs.

2) In 8-inch nonstick skillet, heat oil over medium-high heat. Add veal; cook on both sides until browned.

3) Reduce heat to low; stir in tomato sauce and Italian seasoning. Cover; simmer 12 to 15 minutes or until veal is tender. Sprinkle with cheese; cover and cook 1 to 2 minutes longer or until cheese is melted.

Mint Marinated Lamb Chops

PREP TIME: 35 MINUTES (READY IN 1 HOUR 5 MINUTES)
SERVINGS: 4

EASY   LOW FAT

8 loin lamb chops (1 inch thick)

½ cup orange juice

4 tablespoons chopped fresh mint

2 cloves garlic, minced

3 tablespoons orange marmalade

Nutrition Information Per Serving:
Serving Size: 2 Lamb Chops

Calories:	180	From Fat:	60
Total Fat			6g
Saturated			2g
Cholesterol			60mg
Sodium			55mg
Total Carbohydrate			12g
Dietary Fiber			0g
Sugars			8g
Protein			19g

1) Heat gas or charcoal grill. In large nonmetal dish or resealable plastic bag set in shallow dish, arrange lamb chops in single layer. Add orange juice, 3 tablespoons of the mint and the garlic; stir or turn bag to coat. Cover dish or seal bag; let stand at room temperature 15 to 30 minutes to marinate.

2) Meanwhile, in small bowl, mix marmalade and remaining 1 tablespoon mint; set aside.

3) When grill is heated, remove chops from marinade; discard marinade. Place chops on gas grill over medium heat or on charcoal grill over medium coals; cover grill. Cook 10 minutes, turning once.

4) Brush chops with half of marmalade mixture; cover grill. Cook 2 to 4 minutes longer, turning once and brushing with remaining marmalade mixture, until chops are browned and desired doneness.

HIGH ALTITUDE (3500-6500 FT.): Place chops on gas grill over medium-low heat or on charcoal grill over medium-low coals; cover grill. Cook using times above as a guide, turning once.

Sage and Rosemary Pork Chops

PREP TIME: 15 MINUTES (READY IN 15 MINUTES)
SERVINGS: 2

⊖ EASY

2 boneless pork loin chops
  (³⁄₄ inch thick)

2 teaspoons olive or vegetable oil

¹⁄₂ teaspoon dried sage leaves

¹⁄₂ teaspoon garlic-pepper blend

¹⁄₄ teaspoon dried rosemary leaves,
  crushed

¹⁄₄ teaspoon salt

Nutrition Information Per Serving:	
Serving Size: 1 Pork Chop	
Calories: 300	From Fat: 160
Total Fat	17g
Saturated	5g
Cholesterol	105mg
Sodium	360mg
Total Carbohydrate	1g
Dietary Fiber	0g
Sugars	0g
Protein	36g

1) Heat closed contact grill 5 minutes. Brush both sides of pork chops with oil; sprinkle with sage, garlic-pepper blend, rosemary and salt.

2) When grill is heated, place pork chops on bottom grill surface. Close grill; cook 5 to 7 minutes or until pork is no longer pink and meat thermometer inserted in center reads 160°F.

Stroganoff in Biscuits

PREP TIME: 15 MINUTES (READY IN 40 MINUTES)
SERVINGS: 2

¹⁄₄ cup frozen diced onion
  (from 10-oz. bag), thawed

1 tablespoon dry brown gravy mix
  (from 1.2-oz. envelope)

¹⁄₈ teaspoon coarsely ground black
  pepper

³⁄₄ cup half-and-half

1 tablespoon Dijon mustard

6 oz. thinly sliced cooked roast beef
  (from deli), cut into bite-sized strips
  (1 cup)

1 jar (4.5 oz.) Green Giant® sliced
  mushrooms, undrained

2 Pillsbury® Home Baked Classics® Extra
  Large Easy Split™ frozen biscuits

Nutrition Information Per Serving:	
Serving Size: 1/2 of Recipe	
Calories: 475	From Fat: 260
Total Fat	29g
Saturated	13g
Cholesterol	120mg
Sodium	1550mg
Total Carbohydrate	31g
Dietary Fiber	2g
Sugars	8g
Protein	23g

1) Heat oven to 400°F. In ungreased 1¹⁄₂-quart casserole, mix onion, gravy mix, pepper, half-and-half and mustard. Gently stir in beef and mushrooms.

2) Place casserole on ungreased large cookie sheet. Place biscuits 1 inch apart on cookie sheet next to casserole.

3) Bake 17 to 23 minutes or until mixture is bubbly and thickened, and biscuits are golden brown.

4) To serve, split biscuits in half; place bottom halves on individual serving plates. Top with beef mixture and top halves of biscuits.

HIGH ALTITUDE (3500-6000 FT.): No change.

Spicy Chicken Enchiladas

PREP TIME: 15 MINUTES (READY IN 1 HOUR)
SERVINGS: 2

2 boneless skinless chicken breasts, cut into bite-size pieces

½ cup chopped onion (1 medium)

¼ teaspoon salt

¼ teaspoon dried oregano leaves

⅛ teaspoon pepper

½ cup Old El Paso® enchilada sauce (from 10-oz. can)

1 cup shredded Cheddar cheese (4 oz.)

½ cup sour cream

2 tablespoons Old El Paso® chopped green chiles (from 4.5-oz. can)

4 Old El Paso® flour tortillas for burritos (8 inch) (from 11.5-oz. package)

½ cup chopped lettuce

½ cup chopped tomato (1 small)

1) Heat oven to 350°F. Spray 8-inch square (2-quart) glass baking dish with cooking spray. Heat 8-inch nonstick skillet over medium-high heat. Add chicken; cook 2 to 3 minutes, stirring frequently, until lightly browned.

2) Stir in onion, salt, oregano and pepper. Cook 3 to 5 minutes, stirring frequently, until chicken is no longer pink in center. Cool 5 minutes.

3) Meanwhile, spread ¼ cup of the enchilada sauce in baking dish.

4) Stir ½ cup of the cheese, the sour cream and chiles into chicken mixture. Spoon mixture evenly down center of each tortilla; roll up and place seam side down over sauce in dish. Spoon remaining ¼ cup enchilada sauce over tortillas. Cover with foil.

5) Bake 30 to 40 minutes or until thoroughly heated. Uncover; sprinkle remaining ½ cup cheese over top. Bake uncovered 4 to 5 minutes longer or until cheese is melted. Sprinkle individual servings with lettuce and tomato.

HIGH ALTITUDE (3500-6000 FT.): Bake 40 to 45 minutes. Continue as directed above.

Nutrition Information Per Serving:
Serving Size: 1/2 of Recipe

Calories:	800	From Fat:	360
Total Fat			40g
Saturated			22g
Cholesterol			170mg
Sodium			1470mg
Total Carbohydrate			61g
Dietary Fiber			5g
Sugars			9g
Protein			52g

Salisbury-Style Meatball and Potato Bake

PREP TIME: 25 MINUTES (READY IN 1 HOUR 10 MINUTES)
SERVINGS: 6 (1 CUP EACH)

¹/₄ cup butter

2 cups frozen pearl onions
(from 16-oz. bag)

1 tablespoon brown sugar

¹/₂ box (7.2 oz. size) roasted garlic
mashed potato mix (1 pouch
Potatoes and Seasoning)

1¹/₄ cups hot water

²/₃ cup milk

16 oz. frozen Swedish-style cooked
meatballs (about 32 meatballs),
thawed

1 jar (12 oz.) mushroom-beef gravy

1) Heat oven to 375°F. In 10-inch
nonstick skillet, melt 2 tablespoons of
the butter over medium-low heat. Add
onions and brown sugar; cover and
cook 5 minutes, stirring occasionally.
Uncover and increase heat to
medium-high; cook 6 to 8 minutes
longer, stirring occasionally, until
onions begin to turn golden brown.

2) Meanwhile, in 1¹/₂-quart microwavable
bowl, stir potato mix, hot water, milk and remaining 2 tablespoons butter
until moistened. Cover with microwavable plastic wrap, folding over one
corner to vent. Microwave on High 2 to 6 minutes or until hot. Stir gently
until blended; whip until smooth.

3) Gently stir meatballs and gravy into onion mixture in skillet; spoon into
ungreased 2¹/₂-quart casserole. Spoon or pipe potatoes around outside
edge of mixture.

4) Bake 35 to 45 minutes or until potatoes are golden brown and set, and
mixture is hot and bubbly.

HIGH ALTITUDE (3500-6000 FT.): No change.

Nutrition Information Per Serving:
Serving Size: 1 Cup

Calories:	415	From Fat:	205
Total Fat			23g
Saturated			11g
Cholesterol			105mg
Sodium			840mg
Total Carbohydrate			32g
Dietary Fiber			2g
Sugars			7g
Protein			20g

Honey-Glazed Cashew-Chicken Stir-Fry

PREP TIME: 30 MINUTES (READY IN 30 MINUTES)
SERVINGS: 2 (2-1/2 CUPS EACH)

 EASY

1 cup uncooked instant white rice

1 cup water

¾ cup orange juice

¼ cup honey

1 tablespoon cornstarch

½ teaspoon salt

1 tablespoon vegetable oil

2 large boneless skinless chicken breasts (about 6 oz. each), cut into thin bite-size strips

1 cup ready-to-eat baby-cut carrots, cut in half lengthwise

1 small onion, thinly sliced

1 clove garlic, minced

1 cup Green Giant® frozen sugar snap peas (from 1-lb. bag)

⅓ cup whole cashews

1) Cook rice in water as directed on package.

2) Meanwhile, in small bowl, mix orange juice, honey, cornstarch and salt until well blended; set aside.

3) In 10-inch nonstick skillet or wok, heat oil over medium-high heat. Add chicken, carrots, onion and garlic; cook and stir 4 to 5 minutes or until chicken is no longer pink in center. Stir in sugar snap peas. Cover; cook 3 to 4 minutes, stirring occasionally, until vegetables are crisp-tender.

4) Stir orange juice mixture; add to skillet. Cook and stir 1 to 2 minutes or until mixture thickens. Stir in cashews. Serve over rice.

Nutrition Information Per Serving:
Serving Size: 2-1/2 Cups

Calories:	860	From Fat:	210
Total Fat			23g
Saturated			5g
Cholesterol			105mg
Sodium			1410mg
Total Carbohydrate			116g
Dietary Fiber			6g
Sugars			52g
Protein			49g

tip Chopped garlic in jars, found in the produce department, is perfect to keep on hand for recipes that call for just a small amount of garlic. Use about ½ teaspoon for 1 clove minced garlic.

5-Way Cincinnati Pizza

MELODY LEVAULT | MULKEYTOWN, ILLINIOS

PREP TIME: 15 MINUTES (READY IN 30 MINUTES)
SERVINGS: 6

EASY

1 can (13.8 oz.) Pillsbury® refrigerated pizza crust

½ lb. lean (at least 80%) ground beef

½ cup chopped onion (1 medium)

½ cup barbecue sauce

1 to 2 teaspoons chili powder

½ teaspoon salt

½ teaspoon ground cumin

½ teaspoon apple pie spice

1 can (15.5 oz.) Green Giant® red kidney beans, drained, rinsed

2 cups shredded Cheddar cheese (8 oz.)

1) Heat oven to 425°F. Spray 12-inch pizza pan or 13x9-inch pan with cooking spray. Unroll dough; place in pan. Starting at center, press out dough to edge of pan to form crust. Bake 7 to 10 minutes or until light golden brown.

2) Meanwhile, in 10-inch skillet, cook ground beef and onion over medium-high heat, stirring frequently, until ground beef is thoroughly cooked; drain. Stir in barbecue sauce, chili powder, salt, cumin and apple pie spice. Cook 1 minute, stirring constantly.

3) Remove partially baked crust from oven. Spread ground beef mixture over crust; top with beans and cheese.

4) Return to oven; bake 11 to 14 minutes longer or until crust is deep golden brown. Cut into wedges or squares to serve.

HIGH ALTITUDE (3500-6500 FT.): Bake crust at 425°F. 10 to 13 minutes. Continue as directed above.

Nutrition Information Per Serving:
Serving Size: 1/6 of Recipe

Calories:	490	From Fat:	170
Total Fat			19g
Saturated			10g
Cholesterol			65mg
Sodium			1290mg
Total Carbohydrate			56g
Dietary Fiber			6g
Sugars			11g
Protein			27g

tip If you don't have apple pie spice on hand, make your own by combining ½ teaspoon ground cinnamon, ¼ teaspoon ground nutmeg, ⅛ teaspoon ground allspice and ⅛ teaspoon ground cardamom. Measure ½ teaspoon for recipe. Discard the rest or store in an air-tight container for another use.

Chicken Enchilada Tortilla Cups

PREP TIME:	25 MINUTES	
SERVINGS:	2	ⓔ EASY

2 Old El Paso® flour tortillas
for burritos (8 inch)
(from 11.5-oz. package)

2 teaspoons vegetable oil

½ cup Old El Paso® refrigerated taco
sauce with seasoned shredded
chicken (from 18-oz. container)

1 can (7 oz.) Green Giant® Mexicorn®
whole kernel corn, red and green
peppers, drained (1 cup)

½ cup chopped Italian plum tomatoes
(1½ medium)

¼ cup Old El Paso® enchilada sauce or
Thick 'n Chunky salsa

½ cup finely shredded Colby-Monterey
Jack cheese (2 oz.)

2 tablespoons chopped green onions
(green tops only)

1) Heat oven to 375°F. Line 15x10-inch
pan with sides with foil. Place 2
(10-oz.) custard cups upside down
in pan. Brush outsides of cups with
1 teaspoon of the oil.

2) Brush one side of tortillas with
remaining 1 teaspoon oil; place tortillas
over cups, oil side up. Bake 8 to 10
minutes or until light golden (tortillas
will soften and drape over cups as they
bake). Carefully remove tortillas from
custard cups; turn tortilla cups over.
Cool 2 minutes.

3) In medium microwavable bowl, place taco sauce with shredded chicken.
Cover and microwave on High 2 to 4 minutes stirring halfway through, until
hot. Stir in corn, tomatoes and enchilada sauce. Microwave on High 1 to 2
minutes or until warm. Spoon warm mixture evenly into baked tortilla cups.
Top each with cheese and onions.

HIGH ALTITUDE (3500-6000 FT.): If using Old El Paso® tortillas, bake 10 to 12 minutes.

Nutrition Information Per Serving:
Serving Size: 1/2 of Recipe

Calories:	440	From Fat:	170
Total Fat			19g
Saturated			8g
Cholesterol			50mg
Sodium			950mg
Total Carbohydrate			50g
Dietary Fiber			6g
Sugars			6g
Protein			19g

Honey-Mustard Turkey Tenderloins

PREP TIME: 30 MINUTES (READY IN 30 MINUTES)
SERVINGS: 6

 EASY

2 fresh turkey breast tenderloins (³/4 lb. each)

1 tablespoon olive oil

¹/2 teaspoon salt

¹/4 teaspoon pepper

1 cup honey-mustard dressing

¹/4 cup chopped fresh basil

1) Heat gas or charcoal grill. Brush turkey tenderloins with oil; sprinkle with salt and pepper. In ¹/2 - to 1-quart saucepan, mix dressing and basil.

2) When grill is heated, place turkey on gas grill over medium heat or on charcoal grill over medium coals; cover grill. Cook 15 to 20 minutes, turning and brushing with dressing mixture 2 or 3 times, until turkey is fork-tender and juices run clear.

3) Heat any remaining dressing mixture to rolling boil; boil 1 minute. Serve with turkey.

HIGH ALTITUDE (3500-6500 FT.): Place turkey on gas grill over medium-low heat or on charcoal grill over medium-low coals; cover grill. Cook 25 to 30 minutes, turning and brushing with dressing mixture 2 or 3 times, until meat thermometer inserted in center of turkey reads 170°F.

Nutrition Information Per Serving:
Serving Size: 1/6 of Recipe

Calories:	270	From Fat:	150
Total Fat			17g
Saturated			2.5g
Cholesterol			75mg
Sodium			500mg
Total Carbohydrate			4g
Dietary Fiber			0g
Sugars			4g
Protein			26g

Marinated Family Steak

PREP TIME: 20 MINUTES (READY IN 4 HOURS 20 MINUTES)
SERVINGS: 4

 EASY   LOW FAT

1 tablespoon sugar

½ teaspoon dried marjoram leaves

½ teaspoon pepper

½ cup dry red wine

2 tablespoons olive oil

2 tablespoons soy sauce

2 tablespoons Dijon mustard

2 cloves garlic, minced

1 lb. boneless beef top round or family steak (1 to 1½ inches thick)

1) In large nonmetal dish or resealable plastic bag, mix all ingredients except steak. Add steak; turn to coat. Cover dish or seal bag; refrigerate at least 4 hours or overnight to marinate.

2) When ready to grill, heat gas or charcoal grill. When grill is heated, remove steak from marinade; reserve marinade. Place steak on gas grill over medium heat or on charcoal grill over medium coals; cover grill. Cook 10 to 15 minutes, turning and brushing with reserved marinade once or twice, until desired doneness. Discard any remaining marinade. Cut steak across grain into slices to serve.

HIGH ALTITUDE (3500-6500 FT.): Place steak on gas grill over medium-low heat or on charcoal grill over medium-low coals; cover grill. Cook using times above as a guide, turning and brushing with reserved marinade once or twice.

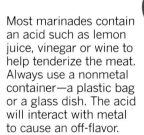

Most marinades contain an acid such as lemon juice, vinegar or wine to help tenderize the meat. Always use a nonmetal container—a plastic bag or a glass dish. The acid will interact with metal to cause an off-flavor.

Nutrition Information Per Serving:
Serving Size: 1/4 of Recipe

Calories:	140	From Fat:	50
Total Fat			5g
Saturated			1.5g
Cholesterol			60mg
Sodium			200mg
Total Carbohydrate			1g
Dietary Fiber			0g
Sugars			0g
Protein			23g

Side
Dishes

A little something on the side
adds excitement to entrees.

TANGY BEANS AND BACON
PG. 225

PARMESAN-ASPARAGUS
AND BELL PEPPER
PG. 229

TERIYAKI SUMMER VEGETABLE
PACKETS
PG. 238

Creamy Vegetable Divan Casserole

PREP TIME: 10 MINUTES (READY IN 40 MINUTES)
SERVINGS: 16 (1/2 CUP EACH)

6 tablespoons butter or margarine

1/3 cup all-purpose flour

1/2 teaspoon pepper

1 cup chicken broth

1 cup milk

2 cups shredded American cheese (8 oz.)

1 bag (1 lb.) Green Giant® frozen mixed vegetables, thawed

2 boxes (9 oz. each) Green Giant® frozen cut broccoli, thawed

1 cup soft bread crumbs

1) Heat oven to 350°F. In 3-quart saucepan, melt 4 tablespoons of the butter over medium heat. Stir in flour and pepper; cook, stirring constantly, until mixture is smooth and bubbly. Gradually add broth and milk, cooking and stirring about 4 minutes or until mixture is bubbly and thickened.

2) Stir in cheese, mixed vegetables and broccoli; pour into ungreased 2 1/2- to 3-quart casserole.

3) In medium microwavable bowl, microwave remaining 2 tablespoons butter on High 20 to 30 seconds or until melted. Stir in bread crumbs until coated; sprinkle over vegetable mixture.

4) Bake 25 to 30 minutes or until edges are bubbly.

HIGH ALTITUDE (3500-6000 FT.): Heat oven to 375°F. Bake casserole without topping, covered with foil, 25 minutes. Remove foil; stir and add topping. Return to oven; bake 25 to 30 minutes longer.

Nutrition Information Per Serving:
Serving Size: 1/2 Cup

Calories:	140	From Fat:	80
Total Fat			9g
Saturated			6g
Cholesterol			25mg
Sodium			330mg
Total Carbohydrate			9g
Dietary Fiber			2g
Sugars			3g
Protein			6g

tip

For variety, use two cups of your favorite vegetable, such as green beans or carrot coins, in place of the mixed vegetables.

Easy Cheesy Salsa Potatoes

SHANNON FOUNTAIN | WINOOSKI, VERMONT

PREP TIME: 10 MINUTES (READY IN 1 HOUR 10 MINUTES)
SERVINGS: 8 (1 CUP EACH)

2 cups shredded Cheddar cheese
  (8 oz.)

1 cup Old El Paso® Thick 'n Chunky
  salsa

½ cup finely chopped onion
  (1 medium)

½ cup sour cream

1 can (10¾ oz.) condensed Cheddar
  cheese soup

½ teaspoon pepper

1 bag (24 oz.) frozen hash-brown
  potatoes (about 8 cups), thawed

½ cup Progresso® plain bread crumbs

¼ cup butter or margarine, melted

Nutrition Information Per Serving:
Serving Size: 1 Cup

Calories:	380	From Fat:	190
Total Fat			22g
Saturated			12g
Cholesterol			60mg
Sodium			880mg
Total Carbohydrate			37g
Dietary Fiber			3g
Sugars			4g
Protein			12g

1) Heat oven to 350°F. Grease 13x9-inch (3-quart) glass baking dish or pan with shortening. In large bowl, mix cheese, salsa, onion, sour cream, soup and pepper. Stir in thawed potatoes. Spread in dish.

2) In small bowl, mix bread crumbs and butter; sprinkle over potatoes.

3) Bake 45 to 60 minutes or until cheese is melted and potatoes are tender.

HIGH ALTITUDE (3500-6500 FT.): No change.

Two-Potato Grill

PREP TIME: 25 MINUTES (READY IN 25 MINUTES)
SERVINGS: 2 (3/4 CUP EACH)

🄔 EASY

1 small dark-orange sweet potato,
  peeled, cut into ⅛- to ¼-inch-thick
  slices (about 1¼ cups)

1 small russet potato, unpeeled, cut
  into ⅛- to ¼-inch-thick slices
  (about 1 cup)

2 tablespoons ranch dressing

⅛ teaspoon coarse ground black
  pepper

⅛ teaspoon dried thyme leaves

Nutrition Information Per Serving:
Serving Size: 3/4 Cup

Calories:	190	From Fat:	60
Total Fat			7g
Saturated			1g
Cholesterol			5mg
Sodium			160mg
Total Carbohydrate			30g
Dietary Fiber			3g
Sugars			11g
Protein			3g

1) Heat closed contact grill 5 minutes. In medium bowl, mix all ingredients to coat well.

2) When grill is heated, place potatoes evenly on bottom grill surface. Close grill; cook 15 to 20 minutes, stirring and turning 2 or 3 times, until potatoes are fork-tender.

Grilled Vegetables with Red Lentils and Herbs

PREP TIME: 25 MINUTES)
SERVINGS: 5 (1/2 CUP EACH) EASY

½ cup dried red lentils, rinsed, sorted

4 cups water

1 medium red bell pepper, cut into ½-inch pieces (about 1 cup)

1 medium zucchini, quartered lengthwise, sliced (about 1 cup)

1 cup sliced fresh mushrooms

2 tablespoons olive oil

1 garlic clove, minced

½ teaspoon coriander

¼ teaspoon salt

¼ teaspoon curry powder

2 tablespoons chopped fresh parsley

1) Heat gas or charcoal grill. In 2-quart saucepan, bring lentils and water to a boil. Reduce heat to low; cover and simmer 7 to 9 minutes or until lentils are tender. Drain.

2) Meanwhile, in medium bowl, combine bell pepper, zucchini, mushrooms and 1 tablespoon of the oil; toss to coat. Place vegetables in grill basket (grill "wok").

3) When grill is heated, place grill basket on gas grill over medium heat or on charcoal grill 4 to 6 inches from medium coals. Cook 8 to 12 minutes or until vegetables are tender, stirring occasionally.

4) In same medium bowl, combine cooked vegetables, lentils, garlic, coriander, salt, curry powder and remaining tablespoon oil; toss to coat. Sprinkle with parsley.

HIGH ALTITUDE (ABOVE 3500 FT.): No change.

Nutrition Information Per Serving:
Serving Size: 1/2 Cup

Calories: 115	From Fat: 55
Total Fat	6g
Saturated	1g
Cholesterol	0mg
Sodium	120mg
Total Carbohydrate	14g
Dietary Fiber	5g
Sugars	2g
Protein	6g

Tangy Beans and Bacon

PREP TIME: 25 MINUTES
SERVINGS: 8 (1/2 CUP EACH)

 EASY

1 tablespoon oil

1 medium onion, sliced (¾ cup)

1 (1-lb.) pkg. Green Giant® Frozen Cut Green Beans

2 tablespoons water

½ cup purchased sweet-and-sour sauce

2 tablespoons cider vinegar

1 (15.5-oz.) can great northern beans, drained, rinsed

6 slices precooked bacon, cut into bite-sized pieces

Nutrition Information Per Serving:
Serving Size: 1/2 Cup

Calories:	150	From Fat:	45
Total Fat			5g
Saturated			1g
Cholesterol			5mg
Sodium			140mg
Total Carbohydrate			23g
Dietary Fiber			5g
Sugars			6g
Protein			8g

1) Heat oil in wok or 12-inch nonstick skillet over medium-high heat until hot. Add onion; cook and stir 3 to 4 minutes or until onion is tender and lightly browned.

2) Add frozen green beans; cook and stir 3 minutes. Add water; cover and cook 5 to 6 minutes or until beans are tender, stirring occasionally. Meanwhile, in 1-cup glass measuring cup, mix sweet-and-sour sauce and vinegar.

3) Add sauce mixture, great northern beans and bacon to wok; cook and stir 1 to 2 minutes or until thoroughly heated.

HIGH ALTITUDE (ABOVE 3500 FT.): No change.

Orange-Glazed Carrots and Sugar Snap Peas

PREP TIME: 15 MINUTES (READY IN 15 MINUTES)
SERVINGS: 6 (1/2 CUP EACH)

 EASY LOW FAT

2 cups ready-to-eat baby-cut carrots

1 cup Green Giant Select® frozen sugar snap peas (from 1-lb. bag)

2 tablespoons orange marmalade

¼ teaspoon salt

Dash pepper

Nutrition Information Per Serving:
Serving Size: 1/2 Cup

Calories:	45	From Fat:	0
Total Fat			0g
Saturated			0g
Cholesterol			0mg
Sodium			115mg
Total Carbohydrate			10g
Dietary Fiber			2g
Sugars			6g
Protein			1g

1) In 2-quart saucepan, heat 1 cup water to boiling. Add carrots; return to boiling. Reduce heat to low; cover and simmer 8 to 10 minutes or until carrots are tender, adding sugar snap peas during last 5 minutes of cooking time. Drain; return to saucepan.

2) Stir in marmalade, salt and pepper. Cook and stir over medium heat until marmalade is melted and vegetables are glazed.

HIGH ALTITUDE (ABOVE 3500 FT.): No change.

Grilled Veggie Stir-Fry

PREP TIME: 35 MINUTES (READY IN 1 HOUR 5 MINUTES)
SERVINGS: 6 (1 CUP EACH)

 EASY

1	lb. small new potatoes, quartered
2	tablespoons water
2	cups fresh broccoli florets
1/2	medium red onion, cut into thin wedges
1/2	cup medium pitted ripe olives, if desired
1/2	cup Italian dressing
3/4	teaspoon seasoned salt
	Freshly ground black pepper

Nutrition Information Per Serving:
Serving Size: 1 Cup

Calories:	160	From Fat:	80
Total Fat			8g
Saturated			0.5g
Cholesterol			0mg
Sodium			360mg
Total Carbohydrate			19g
Dietary Fiber			3g
Sugars			4g
Protein			3g

1) In 1½-quart microwavable casserole, place potatoes and water; cover tightly. Microwave on High 5 to 6 minutes, stirring once, just until potatoes are almost tender.

2) Add broccoli and onion; cover. Microwave on High 1½ to 2 minutes or until broccoli is bright green; drain. Add olives, dressing, seasoned salt and pepper; toss gently to coat. Let stand 10 to 30 minutes, stirring occasionally, to marinate.

3) Heat gas or charcoal grill. When grill is heated, with slotted spoon, place vegetables in grill basket (grill "wok"). Place basket on gas grill over medium heat or on charcoal grill over medium coals; cover grill. Cook 10 to 15 minutes, stirring 2 or 3 times, until potatoes are lightly browned.

HIGH ALTITUDE (3500-6500 FT.): Set grill heat to medium-low.

Cheesy Green Beans

PREP TIME: 15 MINUTES
SERVINGS: 2 (1/2 CUP EACH)

 EASY  LOW FAT

1/2	teaspoon margarine or butter
1	tablespoon finely chopped onion
1	small clove garlic, minced
1	cup Green Giant® frozen cut green beans
1	tablespoon shredded Cheddar cheese

Nutrition Information Per Serving:
Serving Size: 1/2 Cup

Calories:	40	From Fat:	20
Total Fat			2g
Saturated			1g
Cholesterol			4mg
Sodium			35mg
Total Carbohydrate			4g
Dietary Fiber			2g
Sugars			2g
Protein			2g

1) Melt margarine in small nonstick saucepan or skillet over medium heat. Add onion and garlic; cook, stirring frequently, until onion begins to brown. Remove from saucepan; cover to keep warm.

2) In same saucepan, cook beans as directed on package; drain. Add onion mixture; cook until thoroughly heated. Add cheese; toss gently to mix.

Crispy Potato Barbeque Stacks

JUDI MILLER | LAKELAND, FLORIDA

PREP TIME: 10 MINUTES (READY IN 45 MINUTES)
SERVINGS: 4

½ cup Progresso® Plain Bread Crumbs

1 teaspoon seasoned salt

1 egg

1 tablespoon water

8 frozen hash-brown patties
(from 33-oz. pkg.)

1 cup Lloyd's® Refrigerated Original
Barbeque Sauce with Shredded
Chicken or Pork (from 18-oz.
container)

4 (½-oz.) slices Swiss cheese

1) Heat oven to 425°F. Line large cookie sheet with parchment paper; spray paper with cooking spray. In shallow pie pan, mix bread crumbs and seasoned salt; set aside. In another shallow pan, beat egg and water with wire whisk until well blended; set aside.

2) On each of 4 of the frozen hash-brown patties, place ¼ cup barbeque sauce with shredded chicken. Top each with 1 slice cheese, folded to fit. Cover each with remaining potato patty.

3) Carefully dip both sides of each stack into egg mixture; coat each with bread crumb mixture. Place on sprayed paper-lined cookie sheet.

4) Bake at 425°F. for 15 minutes. Remove from oven. Carefully turn stacks over.

5) Return to oven; bake an additional 11 to 16 minutes or until centers are thoroughly heated and cheese is melted.

HIGH ALTITUDE (ABOVE 3500 FT.): After turning stacks over, bake at 425°F. for an additional 13 to 16 minutes.

Nutrition Information Per Serving:
Serving Size: 1/4 of Recipe

Calories:	370	From Fat:	70
Total Fat			8g
Saturated			4g
Cholesterol			65mg
Sodium			1000mg
Total Carbohydrate			59g
Dietary Fiber			4g
Sugars			12g
Protein			16g

Grilled Potato Strips

PREP TIME: 30 MINUTES
SERVINGS: 5 (1/2 CUP EACH)

 EASY

1 large dark-orange sweet potato
   (8 oz.), cut into 2x^1/$_4$x^1/$_4$-inch strips

1 large russet potato (8 oz.), cut into
   2x^1/$_4$x^1/$_4$-inch strips

2 tablespoons oil

1 to 2 teaspoons finely chopped
   chipotle chiles in adobo sauce

^{1}/$_2$ teaspoon salt

^{1}/$_4$ teaspoon cumin

1) Heat gas or charcoal grill. In medium
   bowl, combine potatoes and 1 tablespoon
   of the oil; toss gently to coat. Place
   vegetables in grill basket (grill "wok").

2) In small bowl, combine remaining
   tablespoon oil, the chiles, salt and
   cumin; mix well. Set aside.

3) When grill is heated, place grill basket on
   gas grill over medium-high heat or on
   charcoal grill 4 to 6 inches from medium-
   high coals. Cook 10 to 15 minutes until
   potatoes are lightly browned and tender,
   stirring occasionally.

4) Place potatoes in serving bowl. Pour
   reserved oil mixture over top; toss gently
   to coat.

HIGH ALTITUDE (ABOVE 3500 FT.): Cook potatoes
in grill basket on grill over medium heat.

Nutrition Information Per Serving:
Serving Size: 1/2 Cup

Calories:	120	From Fat:	55
Total Fat			6g
Saturated			1g
Cholesterol			0mg
Sodium			250mg
Total Carbohydrate			15g
Dietary Fiber			1g
Sugars			4g
Protein			1g

Parmesan-Asparagus and Bell Pepper

PREP TIME: 20 MINUTES (READY IN 20 MINUTES)
SERVINGS: 2

 EASY

8 oz. fresh asparagus spears, trimmed

½ medium red or yellow bell pepper, cut into ¼-inch-wide strips

2 tablespoons balsamic vinaigrette dressing

1 tablespoon shredded Parmesan cheese

Nutrition Information Per Serving:
Serving Size: 1/2 of Recipe

Calories:	110	From Fat:	70
Total Fat			8g
Saturated			2g
Cholesterol			5mg
Sodium			210mg
Total Carbohydrate			5g
Dietary Fiber			2g
Sugars			3g
Protein			3g

1) Heat closed contact grill 5 minutes. In large resealable food-storage plastic bag, mix asparagus, bell pepper and vinaigrette dressing to coat well.

2) When grill is heated, place half of vegetables crosswise on bottom grill surface. Close grill; cook 4 to 6 minutes or until vegetables are crisp-tender. Place vegetables in serving bowl. Repeat with remaining vegetables. Sprinkle with cheese.

Tomato and Cheese-Stuffed Baked Potatoes

PREP TIME: 45 MINUTES (READY IN 45 MINUTES)
SERVINGS: 6

EASY

3 baking potatoes (8 to 10 oz. each)

1 cup shredded Cheddar cheese (4 oz.)

¼ cup sliced green onions (4 medium)

½ cup sour cream

½ teaspoon salt

¾ cup chopped tomatoes

Freshly ground black pepper

Nutrition Information Per Serving:
Serving Size: 1 Stuffed Potato Half

Calories:	200	From Fat:	90
Total Fat			10g
Saturated			6g
Cholesterol			30mg
Sodium			330mg
Total Carbohydrate			21g
Dietary Fiber			2g
Sugars			2g
Protein			8g

1) Prick potatoes several times with fork; place on paper towels in microwave. Microwave on High 10 to 15 minutes, turning potatoes over several times, just until potatoes are almost tender. Let stand 10 minutes.

2) Heat gas or charcoal grill. Cut potatoes in half lengthwise. With spoon, scoop out pulp from each potato, leaving a ¼-inch layer in each half. Chop potato pulp; place in large bowl. Add cheese, onions, sour cream and salt; mix lightly to coat potatoes evenly. Gently stir in tomatoes. Spoon mixture into potato shells; sprinkle with pepper.

3) When grill is heated, place potatoes on gas grill over medium heat or on charcoal grill over medium coals; close grill or cover with tent of foil. Cook 10 to 12 minutes or until cheese is melted.

HIGH ALTITUDE (3500-6500 FT.): Place potatoes on gas grill over low heat or on charcoal grill over low coals; cover grill. Cook using times above as a guide.

Ratatouille Toss

PREP TIME: 20 MINUTES
SERVINGS: 6 (1/2 CUP EACH)

 EASY

1 tablespoon olive oil

3 small zucchini, cut in half lengthwise, cut into ¼-inch-thick slices (1¾ cups)

2 small Japanese eggplant, cut in half lengthwise, cut into ¼-inch slices (2 cups)

1 small sweet onion (such as Walla Walla or Maui), cut into thin wedges (1 cup)

2 garlic cloves, minced

1 medium tomato, cut into thin wedges

¼ cup purchased balsamic vinaigrette dressing

2 tablespoons chopped fresh basil

½ teaspoon salt

1 oz. (¼ cup) shredded fresh Parmesan cheese

Nutrition Information Per Serving:
Serving Size: 1/2 Cup

Calories: 110	From Fat: 70
Total Fat	8g
Saturated	2g
Cholesterol	5mg
Sodium	380mg
Total Carbohydrate	6g
Dietary Fiber	1g
Sugars	3g
Protein	3g

1) Heat oil in wok or 12-inch skillet over medium-high heat until hot. Add zucchini, eggplant, onion and garlic; cook and stir 5 to 6 minutes or until vegetables are almost tender. Add tomato; cook and stir an additional 2 minutes or until vegetables are tender.

2) In medium serving bowl, combine cooked vegetables, dressing, basil and salt; toss gently to coat. Sprinkle with cheese.

HIGH ALTITUDE (ABOVE 3500 FT.): No change.

Orange and Ginger Stuffed Sweet Potatoes

PREP TIME: 35 MINUTES (READY IN 35 MINUTES)
SERVINGS: 4

 EASY

2 large dark-orange sweet potatoes (about 12 oz. each)

2 tablespoons butter or margarine, melted

2 tablespoons orange marmalade

½ teaspoon salt

Butter, if desired

Nutrition Information Per Serving:
Serving Size: 1 Stuffed Potato Half

Calories: 170	From Fat: 50
Total Fat	6g
Saturated	3g
Cholesterol	15mg
Sodium	350mg
Total Carbohydrate	29g
Dietary Fiber	3g
Sugars	18g
Protein	2g

1) Prick sweet potatoes several times with fork; place on paper towel in microwave. Microwave on High 8 to 10 minutes, turning potatoes over once halfway through cooking, just until potatoes are almost tender. Let stand 10 minutes.

2) Heat gas or charcoal grill. Cut potatoes in half lengthwise. Scoop pulp into medium bowl, leaving a ¼-inch layer in each half. Mash pulp well. Stir in 2 tablespoons butter, the marmalade and salt. Spoon mixture into potato shells.

3) When grill is heated, place potatoes on gas grill over medium heat or on charcoal grill over medium coals; close grill or cover with tent of foil. Cook 8 to 10 minutes or until thoroughly heated. Top with butter before serving.

HIGH ALTITUDE (3500-6500 FT.): Place potatoes on gas grill over medium-low heat or on charcoal grill over medium-low coals; close grill or cover with tent of foil. Cook using times above as a guide.

Corn and Cheese-Stuffed Peppers

GLORIA RENDON | MURRAY, UTAH

Pillsbury Bake-Off

PREP TIME: 15 MINUTES (READY IN 1 HOUR 10 MINUTES)
SERVINGS: 4

4 large red, green and/or yellow bell peppers, tops cut off, seeds and membranes removed

12 oz. polenta (from 18-oz. roll), cut into ¼-inch pieces (2 cups)

1 (11-oz.) can Green Giant® Mexicorn® Whole Kernel Corn, Red and Green Peppers, drained

3 oz. (¾ cup) shredded Monterey Jack cheese

3 oz. (¾ cup) shredded provolone cheese

Salt and pepper to taste, if desired

1 cup light sour cream, if desired

1) Heat oven to 350°F. If necessary, cut thin slice off bottom of each bell pepper so peppers stand upright.

2) In medium bowl, mix polenta pieces, corn, and half of each of the cheeses. Salt and pepper to taste. Spoon polenta mixture into bell peppers; sprinkle with remaining cheese. Place filled peppers in ungreased 8-inch square (2-quart) glass baking dish. Fill dish halfway with water. Spray 12-inch square piece of foil with cooking spray; cover dish tightly.

3) Carefully place dish in oven. Bake at 350°F. for 30 minutes.

4) Remove foil; bake an additional 15 to 20 minutes or until bell peppers are crisp-tender and filling is thoroughly heated. Cool 5 minutes. Carefully remove bell peppers from dish. Garnish each with sour cream.

HIGH ALTITUDE (ABOVE 3500 FT.): No change.

Nutrition Information Per Serving:
Serving Size: 1 Stuffed Pepper

Calories:	530	From Fat:	130
Total Fat			14g
Saturated			8g
Cholesterol			35mg
Sodium			330mg
Total Carbohydrate			88g
Dietary Fiber			10g
Sugars			14g
Protein			21g

Honey-Mustard Sweet Onion Blossoms

PREP TIME: 55 MINUTES (READY IN 55 MINUTES)
SERVINGS: 4

 EASY

2 large sweet onions

½ cup honey-mustard dressing

½ teaspoon dried thyme leaves

½ cup garlic croutons, crushed

Use a sharp knife to cut onions. Carefully cut to within 1/2 inch of bottom of onion.

1) Heat gas or charcoal grill. Cut 4 (18 x 12-inch) sheets of heavy-duty foil.

2) Cut off ¼-inch-thick slice from both ends of each onion so they will sit flat; peel onions. Cut each onion in half crosswise. With cut side up, make 4 cuts in each onion half, cutting to within ½ inch of bottom, to make 8 wedges.

3) Place onion half in center of each sheet of foil. Gently separate wedges slightly without breaking apart at base. Spread 1 tablespoon of the dressing over each onion half, letting dressing drip between layers. Sprinkle each with thyme. Wrap each packet securely using double-fold seals, allowing room for heat expansion.

4) When grill is heated, place packets on gas grill over medium heat or on charcoal grill over medium coals; cover grill. Cook 15 to 20 minutes or just until onions are almost tender.

5) Remove packets from grill. Open packets carefully to allow steam to escape. Sprinkle each with crushed croutons. Return to grill, leaving packets open; cover grill. Cook 8 to 10 minutes longer or until onions are tender and lightly browned. Serve with remaining honey-mustard dressing.

HIGH ALTITUDE (3500-6500 FT.): Place packets on gas grill over medium-low heat or on charcoal grill over medium-low coals; cover grill. Cook 20 to 25 minutes, removing packets from grill, opening packets, sprinkling with croutons and cooking as directed above.

Nutrition Information Per Serving:
Serving Size: 1 Onion Blossom

Calories:	150	From Fat:	100
Total Fat			11g
Saturated			1.5g
Cholesterol			0mg
Sodium			250mg
Total Carbohydrate			13g
Dietary Fiber			2g
Sugars			7g
Protein			1g

Taco Taters

PATRICIA HARMON | BADEN, PENNSYLVANIA

PREP TIME: 15 MINUTES (READY IN 25 MINUTES)
SERVINGS: 4

⊖ EASY

4 medium russet potatoes
(about 1⅓ lb.)

1 package (1.25 oz.) Old El Paso®
taco seasoning mix

3 tablespoons cornmeal

¼ cup olive or vegetable oil

Nutrition Information Per Serving:		
Serving Size: 1/4 of Recipe		
Calories: 280	From Fat: 130	
Total Fat		14g
Saturated		2g
Cholesterol		0mg
Sodium		370mg
Total Carbohydrate		37g
Dietary Fiber		4g
Sugars		6g
Protein		4g

1) Heat oven to 450°F. Pierce potatoes with fork; place on microwavable paper towel or roasting rack in microwave. Microwave on High 6 to 8 minutes, turning once halfway through cooking, until almost tender.

2) Meanwhile, in large resealable food-storage plastic bag, mix taco seasoning mix and cornmeal.

3) Cut cooked potatoes lengthwise into quarters; place in large shallow dish. Drizzle with oil; toss to coat. With large slotted spoon, place potatoes in plastic bag with seasoning mixture; shake to coat. Arrange potatoes on ungreased cookie sheet.

4) Bake 8 minutes or until golden brown and tender. Serve with salsa, if desired.

HIGH ALTITUDE (3500-6500 FT.): No change.

Light Creamed Corn

PREP TIME: 10 MINUTES (READY IN 4 HOURS 10 MINUTES)
SERVINGS: 10 (1/2 CUP EACH)

⊖ EASY

2 bags (1 lb. each) Green Giant® Niblets® frozen corn

2 packages (3 oz. each) reduced-fat cream cheese (Neufchâtel), cut into cubes

¾ cup fat-free (skim) milk

2 tablespoons butter or margarine, melted

1 teaspoon sugar

1 teaspoon salt

¼ teaspoon pepper

2 tablespoons bacon flavor bits

Nutrition Information Per Serving:		
Serving Size: 1/2 Cup		
Calories: 150	From Fat: 60	
Total Fat		7g
Saturated		4g
Cholesterol		20mg
Sodium		350mg
Total Carbohydrate		19g
Dietary Fiber		2g
Sugars		3g
Protein		5g

1) In 3- to 4-quart slow cooker, spread corn to cover bottom. Top with cream cheese cubes. In small bowl, mix milk, butter, sugar, salt and pepper; pour over corn and cream cheese.

2) Cover; cook on High setting 3 to 4 hours.

3) Cream cheese may look curdled. Sprinkle bacon bits over top; stir until cream cheese is smooth and creamy. If necessary, add additional milk until desired creamy consistency.

HIGH ALTITUDE (ABOVE 3500 FT.): No change.

Broccoli and Red Pepper with Lemon–Horseradish Sauce

PREP TIME: 10 MINUTES (READY IN 10 MINUTES)
SERVINGS: 6 (3/4 CUP EACH)

⊖ EASY   ⊞ LOW FAT

BROCCOLI

1 bag (1 lb.) Green Giant Select® frozen broccoli spears

1 medium red bell pepper, cut into thin bite-size strips

SAUCE

⅓ cup nonfat sour cream

½ to 1 teaspoon prepared horseradish

¼ teaspoon salt

2 teaspoons lemon juice

2 teaspoons Dijon mustard

1) Cook broccoli as directed on bag, adding bell pepper with broccoli. Drain; place in serving bowl.

2) Meanwhile, in small bowl, mix all sauce ingredients until smooth.

3) Pour sauce over vegetables.

HIGH ALTITUDE (ABOVE 3500 FT.): No change.

Nutrition Information Per Serving:
Serving Size: 3/4 Cup

Calories:	35	From Fat:	0
Total Fat			0g
Saturated			0g
Cholesterol			0mg
Sodium			170mg
Total Carbohydrate			6g
Dietary Fiber			2g
Sugars			3g
Protein			3g

Au Gratin Potatoes and Onion

PREP TIME: 20 MINUTES (READY IN 8 HOURS 20 MINUTES)
SERVINGS: 12 (1/2 CUP EACH)

⊖ EASY

1 cup shredded Cheddar-American cheese blend (4 oz.)

½ cup coarsely chopped onion (1 medium)

½ teaspoon dried thyme leaves

½ cup milk

1 can (10 ¾ oz.) condensed cream of mushroom soup

6 cups sliced peeled red potatoes (6 medium)

Nutrition Information Per Serving:
Serving Size: 1/2 Cup

Calories:	130	From Fat:	45
Total Fat			5g
Saturated			2.5g
Cholesterol			10mg
Sodium			280mg
Total Carbohydrate			17g
Dietary Fiber			1g
Sugars			2g
Protein			4g

1) In small bowl, mix cheese, onion, thyme, milk and soup.

2) In 3- to 4-quart slow cooker, layer half each of the potatoes and cheese mixture; repeat layers.

3) Cover; cook on Low setting 7 to 8 hours.

HIGH ALTITUDE (ABOVE 3500 FT.): No change.

Roasted-Vegetable Stew

PREP TIME: 20 MINUTES (READY IN 1 HOUR 35 MINUTES)
SERVINGS: 8 (1-1/3 CUPS EACH)

LOW FAT

1 medium eggplant, cut into 1-inch-thick slices

1 large red bell pepper, quartered

1 large green bell pepper, quartered

1 large sweet onion (Bermuda, Maui, Spanish or Walla Walla), quartered

2 medium zucchini, cut into 1-inch-thick slices

2 tablespoons olive oil

3 cloves garlic, minced

2 cans (28 oz. each) diced tomatoes, undrained

3 teaspoons chili powder

1 teaspoon ground cumin

¼ teaspoon garlic salt

1) Heat oven to 450°F. Spray 15x10x1-inch pan with cooking spray. Spread cut-up fresh vegetables evenly in pan (pan will be full). In small bowl, mix oil and garlic; drizzle evenly over vegetables.

2) Bake 20 to 25 minutes, turning vegetables occasionally, until tender and beginning to brown. Cool 5 minutes.

3) In 3-quart Dutch oven or casserole, mix tomatoes, chili powder, cumin and garlic salt. Coarsely chop all roasted vegetables; stir into tomato mixture.

4) Reduce oven temperature to 375°F. Bake 40 to 50 minutes or until mixture is hot and bubbly.

HIGH ALTITUDE (3500-6000 FT.): No change.

Nutrition Information Per Serving:
Serving Size: 1-1/3 Cups

Calories:	110	From Fat:	35
Total Fat			4g
Saturated			1g
Cholesterol			0mg
Sodium			340mg
Total Carbohydrate			20g
Dietary Fiber			5g
Sugars			10g
Protein			4g

Orzo–Barley Pilaf

PREP TIME: 5 MINUTES (READY IN 25 MINUTES)
SERVINGS: 4 (3/4 CUP EACH)

e EASY **f** LOW FAT

1 can (14 oz.) fat-free chicken
broth with 33% less sodium

¼ cup water

½ teaspoon dried thyme leaves

¼ teaspoon salt

1 cup sliced fresh mushrooms
(about 3 oz.)

½ cup uncooked orzo or rosamarina
(rice-shaped pasta) (3 oz.)

½ cup uncooked quick-cooking barley

2 tablespoons sliced green onions
(2 medium)

½ teaspoon grated lemon peel

1) In 2-quart nonstick saucepan, heat broth,
water, thyme and salt to boiling. Stir
in mushrooms, orzo and barley. Return
to boiling.

2) Reduce heat to low; cover and simmer
15 to 18 minutes or until orzo and barley
are tender and liquid is absorbed.

3) Stir in onions and lemon peel. If desired,
season to taste with pepper.

HIGH ALTITUDE (ABOVE 3500 FT.): Increase water
to 1/3 cup.

Nutrition Information Per Serving:
Serving Size: 3/4 Cup

Calories:	160	From Fat:	10
Total Fat			1g
Saturated			0g
Cholesterol			0mg
Sodium			360mg
Total Carbohydrate			33g
Dietary Fiber			5g
Sugars			1g
Protein			7g

Quick cooking barley provides
a convenient way to get more
whole grains in your diet.

Summer Squash with Red Onion

PREP TIME: 25 MINUTES (READY IN 25 MINUTES)
SERVINGS: 4 (1/2 CUP EACH)

 EASY

2 tablespoons olive oil

½ teaspoon peppered seasoned salt

¼ teaspoon ground cumin

½ medium red onion, quartered

2 medium yellow summer squash, halved, cut into ½-inch-thick slices

Nutrition Information Per Serving:
Serving Size: 1/2 Cup

Calories:	90	From Fat:	60
Total Fat			7g
Saturated			1g
Cholesterol			0mg
Sodium			170mg
Total Carbohydrate			6g
Dietary Fiber			2g
Sugars			2g
Protein			1g

1) Heat gas or charcoal grill. In large bowl, mix oil, peppered seasoned salt and cumin. Add onion; toss to coat.

2) When grill is heated, with slotted spoon, place onion in grill basket (grill "wok"); reserve oil mixture in bowl to coat squash. Place basket on gas grill over medium heat or on charcoal grill over medium coals. Cook 10 minutes, turning basket occasionally.

3) Meanwhile, add summer squash to reserved oil mixture in bowl; toss to coat.

4) Place squash in basket with onion; cook 5 to 7 minutes longer, turning basket occasionally, until vegetables are tender.

HIGH ALTITUDE (3500-6500 FT.): Place basket on gas grill over medium-low heat or on charcoal grill over from medium-low coals. Cook using times above as a guide, turning basket occasionally, adding squash and cooking as directed above.

Alfredo-Green Bean Casserole

PREP TIME: 10 MINUTES (READY IN 4 HOURS 10 MINUTES)
SERVINGS: 25 (1/2 CUP EACH)

1 bag (1 lb. 12 oz.) Green Giant® frozen cut green beans

1 can (8 oz.) sliced water chestnuts, drained

½ cup roasted red bell pepper strips (from a jar)

¼ teaspoon salt

1 container (10 oz.) refrigerated Alfredo pasta sauce

1 can (2.8 oz.) french fried onions

Nutrition Information Per Serving:
Serving Size: 1/2 Cup

Calories:	180	From Fat:	125
Total Fat			14g
Saturated			7g
Cholesterol			30mg
Sodium			260mg
Total Carbohydrate			13g
Dietary Fiber			3g
Sugars			3g
Protein			4g

1) In 4- to 6-quart slow cooker, mix all ingredients except onions. Stir in half of the onions.

2) Cover; cook on High setting 3 to 4 hours, stirring after 1 to 1½ hours.

3) About 5 minutes before serving, in 8-inch skillet, heat remaining half of onions over medium-high heat 2 to 3 minutes, stirring frequently, until hot. Stir bean mixture; sprinkle with warm onions.

HIGH ALTITUDE (3500-6000 FT.): No change.

Oven-Roasted Potatoes and Vegetables

PREP TIME: 10 MINUTES (READY IN 30 MINUTES)
SERVINGS: 6 (2/3 CUP EACH)

EASY   **LOW FAT**

2½ cups refrigerated new potato wedges (from 1 lb. 4-oz. bag)

1 medium red bell pepper, cut into 1-inch pieces

1 small zucchini, cut into ½-inch pieces

4 oz. fresh whole mushrooms, quartered (about 1 cup)

2 teaspoons olive oil

½ teaspoon dried Italian seasoning

¼ teaspoon garlic salt

Nutrition Information Per Serving: Serving Size: 2/3 Cup		
Calories: 70	From Fat:	15
Total Fat		2g
Saturated		0g
Cholesterol		0mg
Sodium		200mg
Total Carbohydrate		14g
Dietary Fiber		2g
Sugars		2g
Protein		2g

1) Heat oven to 450°F. Spray 15x10x1-inch pan with cooking spray. In large bowl, toss all ingredients to coat. Spread evenly in pan.

2) Bake 15 to 20 minutes, stirring once halfway through baking time, until vegetables are tender and lightly browned.

HIGH ALTITUDE (ABOVE 3500 FT.): No change.

Teriyaki Summer Vegetable Packets

PREP TIME: 15 MINUTES (READY IN 35 MINUTES)
SERVINGS: 4 (3/4 CUP EACH)

EASY   **LOW FAT**

2 cups ready-to-eat baby-cut carrots

2 cups Green Giant Select® frozen sugar snap peas (from 1-lb. bag)

1 medium red bell pepper, cut lengthwise into 8 wedges

¼ cup teriyaki baste and glaze

⅛ teaspoon ground ginger

¼ cup chopped fresh cilantro

Nutrition Information Per Serving: Serving Size: 3/4 Cup		
Calories: 70	From Fat:	0
Total Fat		0g
Saturated		0g
Cholesterol		0mg
Sodium		710mg
Total Carbohydrate		16g
Dietary Fiber		4g
Sugars		9g
Protein		4g

1) Heat gas or charcoal grill. Cut 4 (18x12-inch) sheets of heavy-duty foil. Place one-fourth each of carrots, frozen sugar snap peas and bell pepper in center of each sheet.

2) In small bowl, mix teriyaki baste and glaze and ginger; drizzle over vegetables. Wrap each packet securely using double-fold seals, allowing room for heat expansion.

3) When grill is heated, place packets, seam side up, on gas grill over medium heat or on charcoal grill over medium coals; cover grill. Cook 15 to 20 minutes or until vegetables are crisp-tender.

4) Open packets carefully to allow steam to escape. Sprinkle each with cilantro.

HIGH ALTITUDE (3500-6500 FT.): Place packets, seam side up, on gas grill over low heat or on charcoal grill over low coals; cover grill. Cook using times above as a guide, turning packets every 5 minutes.

Spicy Asian Green Beans

PREP TIME: 20 MINUTES (READY IN 20 MINUTES)
SERVINGS: 4 (3/4 CUP EACH)

EASY **LOW FAT**

BEANS

1 bag (14 oz.) Green Giant Select® frozen whole green beans

SAUCE

¼ cup orange juice

1 teaspoon cornstarch

3 tablespoons reduced-sodium soy sauce

⅛ to ¼ teaspoon crushed red pepper flakes

1 small clove garlic, minced

1) Cook green beans as directed on bag. Drain; place in serving bowl.

2) Meanwhile, in 1-quart saucepan, mix all sauce ingredients until well blended. Heat to boiling. Reduce heat to low; simmer 1 to 2 minutes, stirring constantly, until thickened and clear.

3) Stir sauce into cooked green beans to coat.

HIGH ALTITUDE (ABOVE 3500 FT.): No change.

Nutrition Information Per Serving:
Serving Size: 3/4 Cup

Calories:	40	From Fat:	0
Total Fat			0g
Saturated			0g
Cholesterol			0mg
Sodium			410mg
Total Carbohydrate			9g
Dietary Fiber			3g
Sugars			4g
Protein			2g

Green beans provide fiber and vitamin A. These two nutrients are important for good health.

Basil-Sugar Snap Peas with Mushrooms

PREP TIME: 20 MINUTES (READY IN 20 MINUTES)
SERVINGS: 5 (1/2 CUP EACH)

 EASY LOW FAT

1 tablespoon olive oil

1 cup sliced fresh mushrooms (about 3 oz.)

1 clove garlic, minced

3 cups Green Giant Select® frozen sugar snap peas (from 1-lb. bag)

½ cup halved cherry tomatoes

2 teaspoons chopped fresh or ½ teaspoon dried basil leaves

1 tablespoon grated Parmesan cheese

1) In 2-quart saucepan, heat oil over medium heat. Add mushrooms and garlic; cook 3 to 5 minutes, stirring frequently, until tender. Remove from saucepan; place on plate and cover to keep warm.

2) In same saucepan, heat ⅓ cup water to boiling. Add sugar snap peas; return to boiling. Stir; reduce heat to low. Cover; simmer 3 to 5 minutes or until peas are crisp-tender. Drain; return peas to saucepan.

3) Return mushrooms with garlic to saucepan; stir in tomatoes and basil. Spoon into serving bowl; sprinkle with cheese.

HIGH ALTITUDE (ABOVE 3500 FT.): No change.

Nutrition Information Per Serving:
Serving Size: 1/2 Cup

Calories: 70	From Fat: 30
Total Fat	3g
Saturated	1g
Cholesterol	0mg
Sodium	30mg
Total Carbohydrate	7g
Dietary Fiber	3g
Sugars	3g
Protein	4g

Rice Pilaf with Green Beans and Carrots

PREP TIME: 10 MINUTES (READY IN 2 HOURS 40 MINUTES)
SERVINGS: 12 (1/2 CUP EACH)

 LOW FAT

2 tablespoons olive oil

1½ cups uncooked converted long-grain white rice

½ cup sliced carrot (1 medium)

½ teaspoon salt

½ teaspoon lemon-pepper seasoning

1 cup water

1 can (14 oz.) chicken broth with roasted garlic

1¼ cups Green Giant® frozen cut green beans (from 1-lb. bag), thawed*

2 medium green onions, sliced (2 tablespoons)

1) In 12-inch skillet, heat oil over medium-high heat. Add rice, carrot, salt and lemon-pepper seasoning; cook 8 to 10 minutes, stirring frequently, until rice is golden brown. Add water and broth; heat to boiling. Remove from heat.

2) Meanwhile, spray 3- to 4-quart slow cooker with cooking spray.

3) Pour rice mixture into slow cooker. Stir in thawed green beans and onions (make sure all rice is under liquid and not sticking to side of slow cooker).

4) Cover; cook on Low setting 2 to 2½ hours. If desired, keep rice mixture warm on Low setting up to 2 hours, stirring occasionally.

*NOTE: To thaw frozen green beans, place in colander or strainer; rinse with warm water until thawed. Drain well.

HIGH ALTITUDE (ABOVE 3500 FT.): Use 1-1/4 cups water.

Nutrition Information Per Serving:
Serving Size: 1/2 Cup

Calories:	130	From Fat:	25
Total Fat			3g
Saturated			0g
Cholesterol			0mg
Sodium			270mg
Total Carbohydrate			25g
Dietary Fiber			0g
Sugars			1g
Protein			3g

Couscous-Stuffed Tomatoes

PREP TIME: 10 MINUTES
SERVINGS: 2

⊜ EASY

2 large ripe tomatoes

6 oz. (1 cup) couscous salad (from deli)

2 tablespoons chopped salted cashews

Nutrition Information Per Serving:
Not possible to calculate because couscous salad may vary from deli to deli.

1) Cut each tomato into 4 wedges, cutting to but not through bottom of tomato. Place on individual serving plates.

2) Spoon ½ cup couscous salad into center of each tomato. Sprinkle with chopped cashews.

HIGH ALTITUDE (ABOVE 3500 FT.): No change.

Slow-Cooker Dishes

A perfect way to solve the dinner dilemma when you're gone all day.

BEEF AND BACON STEW
PG. 247

PORK CHOPS WITH CORN STUFFING
PG. 264

EASY BURRITO ROLL-UPS
PG. 256

Chicken Delicious

PREP TIME: 10 MINUTES (READY IN 10 HOURS 10 MINUTES)
SERVINGS: 8

EASY · **LOW FAT**

1 package Slow Cooker Helper® chicken and dumplings

1 lb. boneless skinless chicken breasts, thawed if frozen

4 cups hot water

1 can (10 3/4 oz.) condensed cream of mushroom soup

1/3 cup dry sherry, dry white wine or apple juice

1/4 cup water

1/2 cup grated Parmesan cheese

1) In 3- to 4 1/2-quart slow cooker, stir uncooked Vegetables and Sauce Mix, chicken, 4 cups hot water, the soup and sherry until sauce mix is dissolved.

2) Cover; cook on Low setting 8 to 10 hours (or High heat setting 4 to 5 hours) or until chicken is tender.

3) In small bowl, stir Bisquick Mix and 1/4 cup water until dough forms; set aside.

4) Stir chicken mixture to break up chicken. Drop dumpling mixture by 8 to 10 spoonfuls onto chicken mixture. Sprinkle cheese over dumplings. Cover; cook on High setting about 20 minutes, without stirring, until dumplings look dry and spring back when touched.

HIGH ALTITUDE (ABOVE 3500 FT.): Use 4 1/2 cups hot water. Cover and cook dumplings on High heat setting about 25 minutes.

Nutrition Information Per Serving:
Serving Size: 1/8 of Recipe

Calories:	275	From Fat:	90
Total Fat			10g
Saturated			4g
Cholesterol			40mg
Sodium			1150mg
Total Carbohydrate			27g
Dietary Fiber			2g
Sugars			3g
Protein			19g

Onion-Topped Ham and au Gratins

PREP TIME: 10 MINUTES (READY IN 6 HOURS 15 MINUTES)
SERVINGS: 2 (1-1/2 CUPS EACH)

1½ cups frozen potatoes O'Brien with
onions and peppers
(from 28-oz. bag), thawed

1 cup finely chopped cooked ham

1 cup shredded Cheddar cheese
(4 oz.)

1 cup Green Giant® frozen cut green
beans (from 1-lb. bag), thawed

1 can (10¾ oz.) condensed cream
of potato soup

¼ cup chive-and-onion sour cream

½ cup french-fried onions, if desired

Nutrition Information Per Serving: Serving Size: 1-1/2 Cups		
Calories: 660	From Fat:	300
Total Fat		33g
Saturated		19g
Cholesterol		125mg
Sodium		2510mg
Total Carbohydrate		56g
Dietary Fiber		6g
Sugars		8g
Protein		36g

1) Spray 1½-quart slow cooker with cooking spray. In slow cooker, mix all
ingredients except sour cream and onions.

2) Cover; cook 5 to 6 hours (if slow cooker has heat settings, cook on Low).

3) Stir sour cream into potato mixture; sprinkle onions over top. Cover; cook
5 minutes longer or until onions are thoroughly heated.

Teriyaki Pork Ribs

PREP TIME: 5 MINUTES (READY IN 8 HOURS 5 MINUTES)
SERVINGS: 2

e EASY

¾ to 1 lb. boneless country-style
pork ribs

½ teaspoon garlic-pepper blend

¼ teaspoon ground ginger

¼ cup teriyaki baste and glaze

2 tablespoons chili sauce or ketchup

2 tablespoons pineapple preserves

Nutrition Information Per Serving: Serving Size: 1/2 of Recipe		
Calories: 420	From Fat:	180
Total Fat		20g
Saturated		7g
Cholesterol		105mg
Sodium		1650mg
Total Carbohydrate		25g
Dietary Fiber		0g
Sugars		18g
Protein		37g

1) Spray 1½-quart slow cooker with cooking spray. Trim fat from ribs and cut
in half to fit slow cooker. Sprinkle ribs with garlic-pepper blend and ginger;
place in slow cooker.

2) In small bowl, mix all remaining ingredients; pour over ribs.

3) Cover; cook 7 to 8 hours (if slow cooker has heat settings, cook on Low).

4) Remove ribs from slow cooker. Skim off and discard fat from surface of
liquid in slow cooker. Stir mixture well; serve with ribs.

Slow-Cooked Chili

PREP TIME: 20 MINUTES (READY IN 8 HOURS 20 MINUTES)
SERVINGS: 6 (1-1/2 CUPS EACH)

- 1 lb. lean (at least 80%) ground beef
- ½ lb. bulk Italian pork sausage
- 1 medium onion, chopped (about ½ cup)
- 1 can (28 oz.) whole tomatoes, undrained, cut up
- 1 can (15 oz.) tomato sauce
- 1 teaspoon sugar
- 1 to 1½ teaspoons ground cumin
- 2 teaspoons chili powder
- 1 teaspoon dried oregano leaves
- 1 can (15 oz.) spicy chili beans, undrained
- 1 can (15 oz.) garbanzo beans or chickpeas, drained, rinsed

  Sour cream, if desired

  Sliced green onions, if desired

1) In 10-inch skillet, cook ground beef, sausage and onion over medium-high heat 5 to 7 minutes, stirring frequently, until beef is thoroughly cooked; drain.

2) In 3½- to 4-quart slow cooker, mix beef mixture with all remaining ingredients except sour cream and green onions.

3) Cover; cook on Low setting 7 to 8 hours. Top individual servings with sour cream and green onions.

   HIGH ALTITUDE (3500-6000 FT.): No change.

Nutrition Information Per Serving:
Serving Size: 1-1/2 Cups

Calories:	450	From Fat:	190
Total Fat			21g
Saturated			7g
Cholesterol			65mg
Sodium			1540mg
Total Carbohydrate			44g
Dietary Fiber			11g
Sugars			10g
Protein			32g

Beef and Bacon Stew

PREP TIME: 10 MINUTES (READY IN 8 HOURS 10 MINUTES)
SERVINGS: 2 (1-1/4 CUPS EACH)

2   slices bacon, cut into ½-inch pieces

¾   lb. beef stew meat

1   small onion, thinly sliced

1   cup ready-to-eat baby-cut carrots, halved lengthwise

1   tablespoon all-purpose flour

2   teaspoons packed brown sugar

¼   teaspoon salt

¼   teaspoon dried thyme leaves

½   cup apple juice or beer

Nutrition Information Per Serving:
Serving Size: 1-1/4 Cups

Calories:	450	From Fat:	210
Total Fat			23g
Saturated			9g
Cholesterol			110mg
Sodium			500mg
Total Carbohydrate			24g
Dietary Fiber			3g
Sugars			16g
Protein			38g

1) In 10-inch skillet, cook bacon over medium heat until brown but not crisp. Add beef stew meat and onion; cook 3 to 5 minutes, stirring occasionally, until beef is browned.

2) Into 1½-quart slow cooker, spoon mixture; stir in carrots. In small bowl, mix all remaining ingredients; gently stir into mixture in slow cooker.

3) Cover; cook 7 to 8 hours (if slow cooker has heat settings, cook on Low).

Bavarian Beef Roast with Gravy

PREP TIME: 15 MINUTES (READY IN 10 HOURS 15 MINUTES)
SERVINGS: 8

1   boneless beef rump or tip roast (3 lb.), trimmed of fat

3   tablespoons stone-ground mustard

1   tablespoon creamy horseradish sauce

1   envelope (0.87 oz.) brown gravy mix

½   cup beer or apple juice

½   cup water

3   tablespoons all-purpose flour

1   tablespoon chopped chives

Nutrition Information Per Serving:
Serving Size: 1/8 of Recipe

Calories:	210	From Fat:	50
Total Fat			6g
Saturated			2g
Cholesterol			90mg
Sodium			310mg
Total Carbohydrate			5g
Dietary Fiber			0g
Sugars			0g
Protein			35g

1) In 3½- to 4-quart slow cooker, place beef roast. In small bowl, mix mustard, horseradish sauce and gravy mix. Spread mixture over roast. Pour beer around edge of roast, not on top of roast.

2) Cover; cook on Low setting 9 to 10 hours.

3) Remove roast from slow cooker; place on serving platter and cover to keep warm. In 2-quart saucepan, blend water and flour until smooth. Pour cooking juices from slow cooker into saucepan. Heat to boiling over medium-high heat, stirring constantly. Stir in chives. Cut roast into slices; serve with gravy.

HIGH ALTITUDE (ABOVE 3500 FT.): No change.

Pork Roast and Sauerkraut Dinner

PREP TIME: 15 MINUTES (READY IN 8 HOURS 15 MINUTES)
SERVINGS: 6

1 package (32 oz.) refrigerated sauerkraut, drained

2 medium apples, peeled, sliced

1 teaspoon caraway seed

¼ cup apple juice or water

1 boneless pork roast (2½ to 3 lb.), string removed, trimmed of fat

6 small red potatoes (about 18 oz.), cut in half

1 tablespoon Dijon mustard

MUSTARD SAUCE

3 tablespoons Dijon mustard

2 tablespoons packed brown sugar

Nutrition Information Per Serving:
Serving Size: 1/6 of Recipe

Calories:	450	From Fat:	140
Total Fat			16g
Saturated Fat			5g
Cholesterol			120mg
Sodium			1330mg
Total Carbohydrate			34g
Dietary Fiber			6g
Sugars			12g
Protein			46g

1) In 5- to 6-quart slow cooker, lightly mix sauerkraut, apples, caraway seed and apple juice. With spoon, make indention in center of mixture; place pork roast in center.

2) Arrange potato halves around roast on sauerkraut mixture. Spread 1 tablespoon mustard over roast.

3) Cover; cook on Low setting 7 to 8 hours.

4) In small bowl, mix sauce ingredients. Remove roast from slow cooker; place on serving platter. Cut roast into slices. Arrange potatoes around slices. With slotted spoon, remove sauerkraut mixture from slow cooker; place in serving bowl. Serve roast slices and potatoes with sauerkraut mixture and mustard sauce.

HIGH ALTITUDE (ABOVE 3500 FT.): No change.

Twenty-Garlic Chicken Dinner

PREP TIME: 15 MINUTES (READY IN 8 HOURS 15 MINUTES)
SERVINGS: 6

 EASY

1 teaspoon salt

1 teaspoon paprika

½ teaspoon pepper

1 teaspoon olive oil

3 to 3½ lb. cut-up frying chicken

1 large onion, sliced

1 medium bulb garlic (about 20 cloves)

Nutrition Information Per Serving:
Serving Size: 1/6 of Recipe

Calories:	260	From Fat:	130
Total Fat			14g
Saturated			4g
Cholesterol			85mg
Sodium			480mg
Total Carbohydrate			6g
Dietary Fiber			0g
Sugars			1g
Protein			28g

1) In small bowl, mix salt, paprika, pepper and oil to form paste; spread evenly over each piece of chicken.

2) In 5- to 6-quart slow cooker, place onion slices. Arrange chicken over onion. Separate garlic into cloves; do not peel cloves. Place garlic cloves around chicken.

3) Cover; cook on Low setting 7 to 8 hours.

4) With slotted spoon, remove chicken, onion and garlic from slow cooker; place on serving platter. Squeeze garlic cloves to use cooked garlic on mashed potatoes, vegetables or bread.

HIGH ALTITUDE (ABOVE 3500 FT.): No change.

Green Chile Swiss Steak

PREP TIME: 15 MINUTES (READY IN 9 HOURS 15 MINUTES)
SERVINGS: 2

 LOW FAT

2 teaspoons vegetable oil

8 oz. boneless beef round steak, well trimmed, cut into 2 serving-size pieces

2 tablespoons Old El Paso® taco seasoning mix (from 1.25-oz. package)

1 small onion, sliced

¼ cup Old El Paso® chopped green chiles (from 4.5-oz. can)

½ cup Old El Paso® Thick 'n Chunky salsa

2 tablespoons chili sauce

1) Spray 1½-quart slow cooker with cooking spray. In 10-inch skillet, heat oil over medium-high heat. Add beef; cook 4 to 5 minutes or until browned on both sides. Sprinkle both sides of browned steak with 1 tablespoon of the taco seasoning mix.

2) In a small bowl, mix remaining 1 tablespoon taco seasoning mix with all remaining ingredients. Place 1 steak in bottom of slow cooker. Cover with half of the salsa mixture. Repeat with remaining steak and salsa mixture.

3) Cover; cook 8 to 9 hours (if slow cooker has heat settings, cook on Low).

Nutrition Information Per Serving:
Serving Size: 1/2 of Recipe

Calories:	250	From Fat:	80
Total Fat		9g	
Saturated		2g	
Cholesterol		60mg	
Sodium		1060mg	
Total Carbohydrate		20g	
Dietary Fiber		3g	
Sugars		14g	
Protein		25g	

Slow-Simmered Meat Sauce for Spaghetti

PREP TIME: 45 MINUTES (READY IN 10 HOURS 45 MINUTES)
SERVINGS: 8

1 lb. lean (at least 80%) ground beef

½ lb. bulk Italian pork sausage

1 medium onion, chopped (½ cup)

1 medium green bell pepper, chopped (1 cup)

2 cloves garlic, minced

1 cup finely chopped carrot

1 can (28 oz.) Progresso® crushed tomatoes, undrained

1 can (8 oz.) tomato sauce

1 can (6 oz.) tomato paste

1 tablespoon packed brown sugar

3 teaspoons dried Italian seasoning

½ teaspoon salt

¼ teaspoon pepper

16 oz. uncooked spaghetti

Shredded Parmesan cheese, if desired

1) In 12-inch skillet, cook ground beef and sausage over medium heat 8 to 10 minutes, stirring frequently, until beef is thoroughly cooked and sausage is no longer pink; drain.

2) In 3½- to 4-quart slow cooker, mix beef mixture and all remaining ingredients except spaghetti and Parmesan cheese.

3) Cover; cook on Low setting 8 to 10 hours.

4) About 20 minutes before serving, cook spaghetti as directed on package; drain. Serve sauce over cooked spaghetti. Sprinkle with Parmesan cheese.

HIGH ALTITUDE (3500-6000 FT.): No change.

Nutrition Information Per Serving:
Serving Size: 1/8 of Recipe

Calories:	480	From Fat:	145
Total Fat			16g
Saturated			6g
Cholesterol			50mg
Sodium			1160mg
Total Carbohydrate			62g
Dietary Fiber			5g
Sugars			10g
Protein			27g

tip

Not serving eight for dinner tonight? Cook only as much spaghetti as you need, and serve it with a proportionate amount of sauce. Refrigerate or freeze the remaining sauce for another time.

Slow-Cooked Corned Beef Dinner

PREP TIME: 20 MINUTES (READY IN 12 HOURS 20 MINUTES)
SERVINGS: 6

6 medium carrots, cut into 1-inch-thick slices (3 cups)

4 medium potatoes, unpeeled, cut into 1-inch pieces (4 cups)

1 large onion, cut into thin wedges

1 corned beef brisket (2 to 2½ lb.)

5 to 6 cups water

¼ teaspoon coarse ground black pepper

6 whole cloves

1 dried bay leaf

Nutrition Information Per Serving:	
Serving Size: 1/6 of Recipe	
Calories: 370 From Fat: 180	
Total Fat	20g
Saturated	7g
Cholesterol	105mg
Sodium	1240mg
Total Carbohydrate	26g
Dietary Fiber	4g
Sugars	6g
Protein	22g

1) In 5- to 6-quart slow cooker, mix carrots, potatoes and onion.

2) If necessary, cut corned beef brisket to fit into slow cooker; place over vegetables. Add enough of the water to cover. If brisket is packaged with spice packet, add contents of spice packet and omit pepper, cloves and bay leaf. If not, add pepper, cloves and bay leaf.

3) Cover; cook on Low setting 10 to 12 hours.

4) Remove and discard bay leaf. Remove brisket from slow cooker; place on serving platter. Cut brisket into thin slices. With slotted spoon, place vegetables in serving bowl.

HIGH ALTITUDE (ABOVE 3500 FT.): No change.

Harvest Sausage and Vegetable Casserole

PREP TIME: 10 MINUTES (READY IN 10 HOURS 10 MINUTES)
SERVINGS: 8

 EASY   LOW FAT

1 package Slow Cooker Helper® beef stew

1 ring (1 lb.) fully cooked smoked sausage, thawed if frozen, cut into 1-inch pieces

5 cups hot water

2 cups chopped green cabbage

1 can (14.5 oz.) stewed tomatoes with green pepper, celery and onion, undrained

3 tablespoons zesty Italian dressing

1 tablespoon Dijon mustard

Nutrition Information Per Serving:	
Serving Size: 1/8 of Recipe	
Calories: 235 From Fat: 70	
Total Fat	8g
Saturated	2g
Cholesterol	30mg
Sodium	1660mg
Total Carbohydrate	30g
Dietary Fiber	4g
Sugars	9g
Protein	12g

1) In 3- to 4½-quart slow cooker, stir uncooked Vegetables and Sauce Mix, uncooked Potatoes and remaining ingredients until sauce mix is dissolved.

2) Cover; cook on Low setting 8 to 10 hours (or High heat setting 4 to 5 hours) or until sausage is tender.

HIGH ALTITUDE (ABOVE 3500 FT.): No change.

Texas Two-Meat Slow-Cooked Chili

PREP TIME: 25 MINUTES (READY IN 9 HOURS 25 MINUTES)
SERVINGS: 6 (1-1/2 CUPS EACH)

1 lb. boneless beef chuck steak, cut into 1-inch pieces

1 lb. pork tenderloin, cut into 1-inch pieces

1/4 cup all-purpose flour

1 tablespoon vegetable oil

2 cans (10 oz. each) tomatoes with green chiles, undrained

1 can (15 to 16 oz.) pinto beans, undrained

1 can (12 oz.) beer (1 1/2 cups)

1/2 cup chopped red onion

2 tablespoons chili powder

1 teaspoon ground cumin

1/2 teaspoon salt

1/2 teaspoon garlic powder

1/8 teaspoon ground cinnamon

Sliced green onion, if desired

1) In large bowl, mix beef, pork and flour until evenly coated. In 12-inch skillet, heat oil over medium-high heat. Add beef and pork; cook 8 to 10 minutes, stirring frequently, until browned on all sides (if necessary, cook meat in batches).

2) In 4- to 5-quart slow cooker, mix browned beef and pork and all remaining ingredients except green onion.

3) Cover; cook on Low setting 7 to 9 hours. Before serving, skim off fat. Sprinkle with green onion.

HIGH ALTITUDE (ABOVE 3500 FT.): No change.

Nutrition Information Per Serving:
Serving Size: 1-1/2 Cups

Calories:	410	From Fat:	130
Total Fat			15g
Saturated			5g
Cholesterol			95mg
Sodium			670mg
Total Carbohydrate			34g
Dietary Fiber			9g
Sugars			7g
Protein			40g

Tex-Mex Chicken and Rice

PREP TIME: 10 MINUTES (READY IN 7 HOURS 15 MINUTES)
SERVINGS: 5 (1-1/3 CUPS EACH)

1 lb. boneless skinless chicken thighs, cut into ³⁄₄-inch pieces

1¹⁄₂ cups uncooked converted long-grain white rice

1 cup Old El Paso® Thick 'n Chunky salsa

1 can (14 oz.) chicken broth

1 can (4.5 oz.) Old El Paso® chopped green chiles

1 cup sour cream

1 cup shredded Colby-Monterey Jack cheese blend (4 oz.)

Nutrition Information Per Serving: Serving Size: 1-1/3 Cups		
Calories: 600	From Fat:	220
Total Fat		24g
Saturated		13g
Cholesterol		110mg
Sodium		880mg
Total Carbohydrate		63g
Dietary Fiber		2g
Sugars		5g
Protein		34g

1) In 3- to 4-quart slow cooker, mix chicken, rice, salsa, broth and chiles.

2) Cover; cook on Low setting 6 to 7 hours.

3) About 5 minutes before serving, turn off heat on slow cooker. Stir in sour cream and half of the cheese; sprinkle remaining cheese over top. Cover; let stand 5 minutes or until cheese is melted. Serve with additional salsa, if desired.

HIGH ALTITUDE (ABOVE 3500 FT.): Not recommended.

Slow-Cooked Turkey-Wild Rice Casserole

PREP TIME: 25 MINUTES (READY IN 7 HOURS 25 MINUTES)
SERVINGS: 5 (1-1/2 CUPS EACH)

(f) LOW FAT

4 slices bacon, cut into ¹⁄₂-inch pieces

1 lb. turkey breast tenderloins, cut into ¹⁄₂-to 1-inch pieces

1 cup coarsely chopped carrots (3 to 4 medium)

¹⁄₂ cup coarsely chopped onion (1 medium)

¹⁄₂ cup sliced celery (1 medium stalk)

1 cup uncooked wild rice

1 can (10³⁄₄ oz.) condensed cream of chicken soup

2 cups water

2 tablespoons soy sauce

¹⁄₄ to ¹⁄₂ teaspoon dried marjoram leaves

¹⁄₈ teaspoon pepper

Nutrition Information Per Serving: Serving Size: 1-1/2 Cups		
Calories: 345	From Fat:	70
Total Fat		8g
Saturated		2g
Cholesterol		70mg
Sodium		950mg
Total Carbohydrate		38g
Dietary Fiber		3g
Sugars		3g
Protein		30g

1) In 10-inch nonstick skillet, cook bacon over medium heat until crisp, stirring frequently.

2) Stir in turkey, carrots, onion and celery. Cook 2 minutes, stirring frequently, until turkey is browned. Spoon into 3- to 4-quart slow cooker. Stir in all remaining ingredients.

3) Cover; cook on Low setting for 6 to 7 hours.

HIGH ALTITUDE (3500-6000 FT.): No change.

Maple-Mustard Country-Style Ribs

PREP TIME: 15 MINUTES (READY IN 8 HOURS 15 MINUTES)
SERVINGS: 4

⊖ EASY

1 large onion, cut into ¼-inch-thick slices, separated into rings

⅓ cup maple-flavored syrup

¼ cup spicy brown mustard or country-style Dijon mustard

2½ to 3 lb. country-style pork ribs, trimmed of fat

Nutrition Information Per Serving:	
Serving Size: 1/4 of Recipe	
Calories: 410	From Fat: 170
Total Fat	19g
Saturated	7g
Cholesterol	100mg
Sodium	460mg
Total Carbohydrate	25g
Dietary Fiber	0g
Sugars	12g
Protein	34g

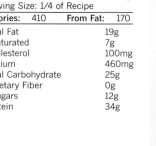

1) In 3- to 4-quart slow cooker, place onion rings.

2) In small bowl, mix syrup and mustard; spread evenly over ribs. Place coated ribs over onion.

3) Cover; cook on Low setting 7 to 8 hours. If desired, serve with additional mustard.

HIGH ALTITUDE (ABOVE 3500 FT.): No change.

Stroganoff Round Steak Strips

PREP TIME: 15 MINUTES (READY IN 8 HOURS 40 MINUTES)
SERVINGS: 6 (1-3/4 CUPS EACH)

1½ lb. boneless beef round steak, trimmed of fat, cut into bite-size strips

2 tablespoons onion soup mix (from 1-oz. envelope)

1 jar (4.5 oz.) Green Giant® sliced mushrooms, drained

1 can (10¾ oz.) condensed cream of mushroom soup

1½ cups uncooked regular long-grain white rice

3 cups water

½ cup sour cream

2 tablespoons chopped chives

Nutrition Information Per Serving:	
Serving Size: 1-3/4 Cups	
Calories: 390	From Fat: 100
Total Fat	11g
Saturated	4g
Cholesterol	75mg
Sodium	700mg
Total Carbohydrate	47g
Dietary Fiber	1g
Sugars	3g
Protein	28g

For a smaller family, freeze half of the meat mixture for another meal. Thaw and heat it in the microwave oven. If desired, serve over pasta or split baked potatoes.

1) In 2- to 3-quart slow cooker, mix beef strips and soup mix until evenly coated. Top with mushrooms and soup.

2) Cover; cook on Low setting 7 to 8 hours.

3) About 30 minutes before serving, cook rice in water as directed on package. Just before serving, stir sour cream into beef mixture. Sprinkle with chopped chives. Serve over rice.

HIGH ALTITUDE (ABOVE 3500 FT.): No change.

Burgundy Beef and Mushrooms

PREP TIME: 10 MINUTES (READY IN 10 HOURS 35 MINUTES)
SERVINGS: 8

1 package Slow Cooker Helper® beef stroganoff

1 to 1½ lb. beef stew meat, thawed if frozen

3½ cups hot water

4 slices bacon, cooked and crumbled

3 large carrots, cut into 1-inch chunks

1 medium onion, sliced

½ cup condensed beef broth (from 10½-oz. can)

½ cup dry red wine or nonalcoholic red wine

1 tablespoon Worcestershire sauce

1) In 3- to 4½-quart slow cooker, stir uncooked Vegetables and Sauce Mix, Mushrooms and remaining ingredients except Pasta until sauce mix is dissolved.

2) Cover; cook on Low setting 8 to 10 hours (or High heat setting 4 to 5 hours) or until beef is tender.

3) About 25 minutes before serving, stir in uncooked Pasta. Cover; cook on High setting about 20 minutes or until pasta is tender.

4) Stir beef mixture. Turn slow cooker off. Let stand uncovered 5 minutes (sauce will thicken as it stands).

HIGH ALTITUDE (ABOVE 3500 FT.): After adding Pasta, cover and cook on High heat setting 25 to 30 minutes.

Nutrition Information Per Serving:
Serving Size: 1/8 of Recipe

Calories:	290	From Fat:	100
Total Fat			11g
Saturated			4g
Cholesterol			40mg
Sodium			710mg
Total Carbohydrate			29g
Dietary Fiber			3g
Sugars			5g
Protein			18g

Easy Burrito Roll-Ups

PREP TIME: 20 MINUTES (READY IN 8 HOURS 20 MINUTES)
SERVINGS: 12

BURRITOS

- 1 can (15 oz.) black beans, drained, rinsed
- 2½ lb. boneless skinless chicken thighs
- 2 cloves garlic, minced
- 2 tablespoons chopped chipotle chiles in adobo sauce (from 7- to 11-oz. can)
- 1 teaspoon ground cumin
- 1 cup Old El Paso® Thick 'n Chunky salsa
- 12 flour tortillas (10 inch)

TOPPINGS

- 1 cup sour cream
- 1½ cups shredded Colby-Monterey Jack cheese blend (6 oz.)
- ½ cup sliced ripe olives
- ½ cup chopped fresh cilantro

1) In 3- to 4-quart slow cooker, layer beans, chicken thighs, garlic, chiles, cumin and salsa.

2) Cover; cook on Low setting 7 to 8 hours.

3) About 15 minutes before serving, heat oven to 350°F. Wrap tortillas in foil; heat in oven about 15 minutes or until warm. Meanwhile, place all topping ingredients in individual serving dishes.

4) Remove chicken from slow cooker; place on large plate. With fork or potato masher, mash beans slightly to thicken sauce. Shred chicken with 2 forks; return to slow cooker and mix with bean mixture to moisten.

5) Place warm tortillas on serving plates. Spoon about ½ cup chicken mixture onto each tortilla; top with desired toppings. Fold sides of tortilla over filling; secure with toothpick.

HIGH ALTITUDE (ABOVE 3500 FT.): No change.

Nutrition Information Per Serving:
Serving Size: 1/12 of Recipe

Calories:	510	From Fat:	190
Total Fat			21g
Saturated			9g
Cholesterol			85mg
Sodium			760mg
Total Carbohydrate			49g
Dietary Fiber			5g
Sugars			3g
Protein			33g

Southwestern Chicken Chili

PREP TIME: 20 MINUTES (READY IN 8 HOURS 20 MINUTES)
SERVINGS: 6 (1-1/3 CUPS EACH)

 LOW FAT

1 cup chopped onions (2 medium)

1 medium green bell pepper, chopped (1 cup)

3 cloves garlic, minced

3 tablespoons cornmeal

2 tablespoons chili powder

3 teaspoons dried oregano leaves

1 teaspoon ground cumin

½ teaspoon salt

1¼ lb. boneless skinless chicken thighs, cut into 1-inch pieces

1 jar (16 oz.) medium picante sauce

1 can (15 to 16 oz.) pinto beans, undrained

1 can (14.5 oz.) diced tomatoes, undrained

Sliced green onion, if desired

Nutrition Information Per Serving:
Serving Size: 1-1/3 Cups

Calories:	310	From Fat:	80
Total Fat			9g
Saturated			3g
Cholesterol			60mg
Sodium			820mg
Total Carbohydrate			35g
Dietary Fiber			10g
Sugars			7g
Protein			29g

1) In 3- to 4-quart slow cooker, mix onions, bell pepper and garlic.

2) In large bowl, mix cornmeal, chili powder, oregano, cumin and salt. Add chicken; toss to coat. Add chicken and any remaining seasoning mixture to vegetables in slow cooker. Gently stir in picante sauce, beans and tomatoes.

3) Cover; cook on Low setting 6 to 8 hours. Sprinkle with green onion.

HIGH ALTITUDE (ABOVE 3500 FT.): No change.

Three-Cheese Creamy Lasagna

PREP TIME: 10 MINUTES (READY IN 5 HOURS 10 MINUTES)
SERVINGS: 6 (1 CUP EACH)

8 no-boil lasagna noodles (from 16-oz. package)

½ cup chive-and-onion cream cheese spread (from 8-oz. container)

1 can (18 oz.) Progresso® Vegetable Classics creamy mushroom soup

2 cups shredded Cheddar cheese (8 oz.)

1 cup milk

¼ cup shredded Parmesan cheese (1 oz.)

Paprika

Nutrition Information Per Serving:
Serving Size: 1 Cup

Calories:	400	From Fat:	220
Total Fat			25g
Saturated			14g
Cholesterol			70mg
Sodium			690mg
Total Carbohydrate			27g
Dietary Fiber			1g
Sugars			5g
Protein			18g

1) Spray 3- to 4-quart slow cooker with cooking spray. Layer half of the noodles in slow cooker, breaking noodles and overlapping as necessary.

2) In small microwavable bowl, microwave cream cheese spread on High 20 to 30 seconds until soft. Stir in soup until well blended. Pour half of soup mixture over noodles. Sprinkle with half of the Cheddar cheese.

3) Repeat layering with remaining noodles, soup mixture and Cheddar cheese. Carefully pour milk over all. Sprinkle Parmesan cheese and paprika over top.

4) Cover; cook on Low setting 4 to 5 hours.

HIGH ALTITUDE (ABOVE 3500 FT.): No change.

Tender Turkey and Wild Rice

PREP TIME: 10 MINUTES (READY IN 6 HOURS 10 MINUTES)
SERVINGS: 2 (4 OUNCES TURKEY AND 1-1/2 CUPS RICE EACH)

 LOW FAT

½ cup uncooked wild rice, rinsed

½ cup chopped carrot

¼ cup chopped onion (½ medium)

¼ cup thinly sliced celery

½ teaspoon seasoned salt

½ teaspoon garlic-pepper blend

½ teaspoon dried marjoram leaves

1 cup chicken broth

2 tablespoons dry sherry or dry white wine

1 turkey tenderloin (½ to ¾ lb.), cut into ½-inch-thick slices

Nutrition Information Per Serving:	
Serving Size: 1/2 of Recipe	
Calories: 320	**From Fat:** 20
Total Fat	2g
Saturated	1g
Cholesterol	75mg
Sodium	930mg
Total Carbohydrate	41g
Dietary Fiber	5g
Sugars	5g
Protein	36g

1) In 1½-quart slow cooker, mix rice, carrot, onion, celery, ¼ teaspoon each of the seasoned salt, garlic-pepper blend and marjoram, the broth and sherry.

2) Arrange turkey slices over rice mixture. Sprinkle with remaining ¼ teaspoon each seasoned salt, garlic-pepper blend and marjoram.

3) Cover; cook 5 to 6 hours (if slow cooker has heat settings, cook on Low).

Old-Fashioned Beef Stew

PREP TIME: 20 MINUTES (READY IN 10 HOURS 20 MINUTES)
SERVINGS: 6 (1-2/3 CUPS EACH)

1 tablespoon vegetable oil

1½ lb. cubed beef stew meat

4 medium carrots, cut into ½-inch-thick slices (2 cups)

3 medium red potatoes, unpeeled, cut into ½-inch cubes (3 cups)

1 large onion, cut into 1-inch pieces (1½ cups)

1 medium stalk celery, cut into 1-inch pieces (1 cup)

3 cups vegetable juice

3 tablespoons quick-cooking tapioca

1 tablespoon beef-flavor instant bouillon

2 teaspoons Worcestershire sauce

¼ teaspoon pepper

Nutrition Information Per Serving:	
Serving Size: 1-2/3 Cups	
Calories: 360	**From Fat:** 140
Total Fat	16g
Saturated	5g
Cholesterol	70mg
Sodium	1060mg
Total Carbohydrate	30g
Dietary Fiber	4g
Sugars	9g
Protein	27g

1) In 12-inch skillet or Dutch oven, heat oil over medium-high heat. Add beef stew meat; cook 4 to 6 minutes, stirring frequently, until browned on all sides.

2) In 4- to 5-quart slow cooker, mix browned beef and all remaining ingredients.

3) Cover; cook on Low setting 9 to 10 hours.

HIGH ALTITUDE (ABOVE 3500 FT.): No change.

Slow-Cooked Paella

PREP TIME: 15 MINUTES (READY IN 6 HOURS 45 MINUTES)
SERVINGS: 6

1½ cups uncooked converted long-grain
    white rice

1   tablespoon olive oil

1   can (14.5 oz.) diced tomatoes,
    undrained

1   can (14 oz.) chicken broth

½   cup quartered sliced pepperoni
    (about 3 oz.)

½   cup water

½   teaspoon salt

¼   teaspoon crushed saffron or
    ⅛ teaspoon turmeric

1   clove garlic, minced

6   boneless skinless chicken thighs
    (about 1¼ lb.)

¼   teaspoon paprika

1   cup Green Giant® frozen sweet peas
    (from 1-lb. bag), thawed*

6   oz. deveined shelled cooked medium
    shrimp, tail shells removed

1) In 4- to 5-quart slow cooker, mix rice and
   oil. Stir in tomatoes, broth, pepperoni,
   water, salt, saffron and garlic. Arrange
   chicken thighs in single layer over rice
   mixture. Sprinkle paprika over top.

2) Cover; cook on Low setting 5 to 6 hours.

3) About 35 minutes before serving,
   sprinkle thawed peas over chicken
   mixture. Arrange shrimp over top.

4) Increase heat setting to High; cover and
   cook 20 to 30 minutes longer or until
   shrimp are thoroughly heated.

*NOTE: To quickly thaw frozen peas, place in colander
       or strainer; rinse with warm water until thawed.
       Drain well.

HIGH ALTITUDE (ABOVE 3500 FT.): No change.

Nutrition Information Per Serving:
Serving Size: 1/6 of Recipe

Calories:	510	From Fat:	160
Total Fat		17g	
Saturated		5g	
Cholesterol		125mg	
Sodium		1020mg	
Total Carbohydrate		53g	
Dietary Fiber		3g	
Sugars		3g	
Protein		36g	

tip

Be sure to purchase
converted rice, not
long-grain white rice, for
this recipe. Converted
rice holds up better in
the slow cooker than
other varieties of rice.

Winter Vegetable Soup

PREP TIME: 40 MINUTES (READY IN 10 HOURS 50 MINUTES)
SERVINGS: 8 (1-1/2 CUPS EACH)

 LOW FAT

1 lb. portobello mushroom caps

3 tablespoons butter or margarine

2 large onions, halved, sliced (3 cups)

2 large dark-orange sweet potatoes, peeled, cut into quarters then into $^1/_2$-inch-thick slices (3 cups)

1 cup chopped celery (2$^1/_2$ medium stalks)

2 cloves garlic, minced

1$^1/_2$ cups Green Giant® Niblets® frozen corn (from 1-lb. bag)

1 can (28 oz.) diced tomatoes, undrained

1 can (15 or 15.5 oz.) kidney beans, drained, rinsed

2 cans (14 oz. each) vegetable broth

4 oz. fresh spinach, chopped (about 4 cups lightly packed)

1 teaspoon dried basil leaves

$^1/_2$ teaspoon salt

$^1/_4$ teaspoon pepper

1) With small spoon, scrape and discard gills from under side of mushroom caps. Cut caps into $^1/_2$-inch-thick slices; set aside.

2) In 10-inch skillet, melt butter over medium heat. Add onions; cook 10 to 15 minutes, stirring occasionally, until onions are tender and have begun to caramelize.

3) Meanwhile, in 6-quart slow cooker, place mushroom slices, sweet potatoes, celery, garlic, corn, tomatoes and beans. Gently stir in broth and caramelized onions.

4) Cover; cook on Low setting 9 to 10 hours.

5) About 10 minutes before serving, turn off heat on slow cooker. Stir in spinach, basil, salt and pepper. Cover; let stand 10 minutes or until spinach is limp.

HIGH ALTITUDE (ABOVE 3500 FT.): No change.

Nutrition Information Per Serving:
Serving Size: 1-1/2 Cups

Calories:	220	From Fat:	45
Total Fat			5g
Saturated			3g
Cholesterol			10mg
Sodium			920mg
Total Carbohydrate			42g
Dietary Fiber			8g
Sugars			13g
Protein			10g

Italian Steak Roll for Two

PREP TIME: 10 MINUTES (READY IN 6 HOURS 10 MINUTES)
SERVINGS: 2

 LOW FAT

¾ lb. beef round steak (½ inch thick), trimmed of fat

½ teaspoon dried Italian seasoning

¼ teaspoon salt

¼ teaspoon pepper

1 thin slice onion, halved

1 clove garlic, minced

½ cup sliced fresh mushrooms

1 medium Italian plum tomato, cut into quarters, sliced

¾ cup savory beef gravy (from 12-oz. jar)

Nutrition Information Per Serving:
Serving Size: 1/2 of Recipe

Calories:	230	From Fat:	60
Total Fat			7g
Saturated			3g
Cholesterol			85mg
Sodium			850mg
Total Carbohydrate			7g
Dietary Fiber			1g
Sugars			1g
Protein			35g

1) Place steak on work surface; sprinkle with Italian seasoning, salt and pepper. Top with onion slice halves. Roll up beef, jelly-roll fashion, with onion inside; tie with string.

2) In 2- to 3-quart slow cooker, place beef roll, seam side down. Sprinkle garlic, mushrooms and tomato around roll. Spoon gravy over roll.

3) Cover; cook on Low setting 5 to 6 hours.

4) Remove beef roll from slow cooker; place on serving platter. Remove string; cut roll into slices. Stir gravy mixture in slow cooker until blended; pour into serving bowl. Serve beef roll slices with gravy.

HIGH ALTITUDE (ABOVE 3500 FT.): No change.

Slow-Cooked Meatball Stew

PREP TIME: 15 MINUTES (READY IN 10 HOURS 15 MINUTES)
SERVINGS: 6 (1-1/2 CUPS EACH)

1 bag (1 lb.) ready-to-eat baby-cut carrots

1 lb. small red potatoes (2½ to 3 inch), cut into quarters

1 jar (4.5 oz.) Green Giant® sliced mushrooms, drained

1 small onion, cut into thin wedges

1 bag (16 oz.) frozen cooked meatballs (about 32)

1 jar (12 oz.) beef gravy

1 can (14.5 oz.) diced tomatoes, undrained

Freshly ground black pepper, if desired

Nutrition Information Per Serving:
Serving Size: 1-1/2 Cups

Calories:	350	From Fat:	140
Total Fat			15g
Saturated			6g
Cholesterol			85mg
Sodium			980mg
Total Carbohydrate			37g
Dietary Fiber			6g
Sugars			9g
Protein			21g

1) In 4- to 5-quart slow cooker, layer all ingredients in order listed.

2) Cover; cook on Low setting 8 to 10 hours. Before serving, gently stir stew.

HIGH ALTITUDE (ABOVE 3500 FT.): No change.

Turkey Breast with Cranberry-Onion Gravy

PREP TIME: 25 MINUTES (READY IN 7 HOURS 25 MINUTES)
SERVINGS: 8

🄴 EASY 🄵 LOW FAT

1 fresh or frozen (thawed) whole turkey breast (4 lb.)

1 can (15 oz.) jellied cranberry sauce

1 envelope (1 oz.) onion soup mix

1 tablespoon prepared yellow mustard

½ teaspoon salt

¼ cup water

3 tablespoons cornstarch

1) Remove and discard skin from turkey breast; place turkey in 5- to 6-quart slow cooker.

2) In small bowl, mix cranberry sauce, soup mix, mustard and salt until well blended; pour over turkey.

3) Cover; cook on Low setting 6 to 7 hours or until meat thermometer inserted into thickest portion of turkey breast reads 170°F.

4) About 15 minutes before serving, remove turkey from slow cooker; place on cutting board and cover to keep warm. Place fine strainer over 3-quart saucepan. Carefully pour cooking juices from slow cooker through strainer into saucepan.

5) In small bowl, blend water and cornstarch until smooth; stir into strained liquid in saucepan. Heat to boiling over medium-high heat, stirring constantly; boil 1 minute.

6) Cut turkey into slices; arrange on serving platter. Spoon about ½ cup gravy over turkey. Serve with remaining gravy.

HIGH ALTITUDE (ABOVE 3500 FT.): No change.

Nutrition Information Per Serving:		
Serving Size: 1/8 of Recipe		
Calories: 290	From Fat:	15
Total Fat		2g
Saturated		1g
Cholesterol		120mg
Sodium		570mg
Total Carbohydrate		26g
Dietary Fiber		0g
Sugars		20g
Protein		43g

Slow-Cooked Beef Burgundy

PREP TIME: 25 MINUTES (READY IN 12 HOURS 55 MINUTES)
SERVINGS: 5 (1-2/3 CUPS EACH)

1½ cups ready-to-eat baby-cut carrots,
     cut in half crosswise

2   lb. cubed beef stew meat

1   cup frozen small whole onions
    (from 16-oz. bag)

1   package (8 oz.) fresh small whole
    mushrooms

1   clove garlic, minced

1   teaspoon salt

¼   teaspoon pepper

1   dried bay leaf

½   cup red Burgundy wine

1   can (10½ oz.) condensed beef
    consommé

2   tablespoons all-purpose flour

2   tablespoons water

1) In 4- to 5-quart slow cooker, layer
   all ingredients except flour and
   water in order listed.

2) Cover; cook on Low setting 10 to
   12 hours.

3) About 35 minutes before serving,
   remove and discard bay leaf. In
   small bowl, blend flour and water
   until smooth. Gradually stir flour
   mixture into beef mixture.

4) Cover; cook on High setting 15 to
   30 minutes longer or until slightly
   thickened.

HIGH ALTITUDE (ABOVE 3500 FT.): No change.

Nutrition Information Per Serving:
Serving Size: 1-2/3 Cups

Calories:	400	From Fat:	190
Total Fat		21g	
Saturated		8g	
Cholesterol		110mg	
Sodium		890mg	
Total Carbohydrate		11g	
Dietary Fiber		2g	
Sugars		4g	
Protein		42g	

Pork Chops with Corn Stuffing

PREP TIME: 20 MINUTES (READY IN 7 HOURS 20 MINUTES)
SERVINGS: 6

1 tablespoon vegetable oil

6 boneless pork loin chops
(about 1 inch thick)

1 teaspoon seasoned salt

4 cups cornbread stuffing mix

½ cup chopped celery
(2 medium stalks)

¼ cup chopped onion (½ medium)

¼ teaspoon dried sage leaves, crushed

1 can (14 oz.) chicken broth

1 can (11 oz.) Green Giant® Mexicorn®
whole kernel corn, red and green
peppers, drained

1) In 12-inch nonstick skillet, heat oil
over medium heat. Add pork chops;
cook 6 to 8 minutes, turning once,
until browned on both sides. Drain;
sprinkle pork with seasoned salt.

2) In large bowl, mix all remaining
ingredients.

3) Spray 3- to 4-quart slow cooker with
cooking spray. Spoon stuffing mixture
into slow cooker. Arrange browned
pork chops over stuffing, in 2 layers
if necessary to fit.

4) Cover; cook on Low setting 6 to 7 hours.

HIGH ALTITUDE (ABOVE 3500 FT.): Brown pork chops over high heat.

Nutrition Information Per Serving:
Serving Size: 1/6 of Recipe

Calories: 410	From Fat: 110
Total Fat	12g
Saturated	4g
Cholesterol	65mg
Sodium	1290mg
Total Carbohydrate	45g
Dietary Fiber	3g
Sugars	3g
Protein	31g

Winter Pork Roast Dinner

PREP TIME: 20 MINUTES (READY IN 8 HOURS 20 MINUTES)
SERVINGS: 6

 EASY

1 rolled boneless pork loin roast
(1¾ to 2 lb.)

1 teaspoon salt

¼ teaspoon pepper

3 large dark-orange sweet potatoes,
peeled, thinly sliced

1 medium onion, sliced, separated
into rings

1½ teaspoons dried thyme leaves

1 quart (4 cups) apple juice

Nutrition Information Per Serving:
Serving Size: 1/6 of Recipe

Calories:	380	From Fat:	100
Total Fat			11g
Saturated			4g
Cholesterol			85mg
Sodium			460mg
Total Carbohydrate			43g
Dietary Fiber			3g
Sugars			30g
Protein			31g

1) Sprinkle pork roast with ½ teaspoon of the salt and the pepper; place in
4- to 5-quart slow cooker. Place sweet potatoes around and on top of roast.
Top with onion; sprinkle with thyme and remaining ½ teaspoon salt. Pour
apple juice over onion.

2) Cover; cook on Low setting 6 to 8 hours.

3) With slotted spoon, remove vegetables from slow cooker; place on serving
platter. Remove roast from slow cooker; place on cutting board. Cut roast
into slices; place on platter. If desired, drizzle some of cooking liquid from
slow cooker over vegetables and roast.

HIGH ALTITUDE (ABOVE 3500 FT.): No change.

Slow-Cooker Cheese Fondue

PREP TIME: 20 MINUTES (READY IN 3 HOURS 20 MINUTES)
SERVINGS: 10 (1/4 CUP FONDUE AND 8 BREAD CUBES EACH)

 EASY

1 can (10¾ oz.) condensed cheese
soup

¼ cup white wine or apple juice

2 packages (8 oz. each) process
Swiss cheese slices, chopped

¼ teaspoon garlic powder

⅛ teaspoon ground nutmeg

1 loaf (16 oz.) French bread,
cut into 1-inch cubes

Nutrition Information Per Serving:
Serving Size: 1/10 of Recipe

Calories:	330	From Fat:	150
Total Fat			17g
Saturated			10g
Cholesterol			45mg
Sodium			660mg
Total Carbohydrate			27g
Dietary Fiber			1g
Sugars			1g
Protein			18g

1) In 1- to 2-quart slow cooker, mix all ingredients except bread.

2) Cover; cook on Low setting 3 hours.

3) Stir fondue until smooth. Serve bread with fondue, spearing bread and
dipping into fondue. If necessary, cover fondue and hold in slow cooker on
Low setting up to 2 hours.

HIGH ALTITUDE (ABOVE 3500 FT.): No change.

Pork and Pineapple on a Stick

1½ lb. boneless pork loin, trimmed of
    fat, cut into about ¾-inch pieces

¼ cup hoisin sauce

1 clove garlic, minced

1 can (8 oz.) pineapple chunks in juice,
   drained, 2 tablespoons juice reserved

¼ cup barbecue sauce

¼ cup Chinese plum sauce

1 large green bell pepper, seeded, cut
   into about ¾-inch pieces

Nutrition Information Per Serving:	
Serving Size: 1/15 of Recipe	
Calories: 110	From Fat: 35
Total Fat	4g
Saturated	1g
Cholesterol	30mg
Sodium	140mg
Total Carbohydrate	7g
Dietary Fiber	0g
Sugars	5g
Protein	11g

1) Spray 1 ½- to 2-quart slow cooker with cooking spray. In slow cooker, mix pork, hoisin sauce, garlic and reserved 2 tablespoons pineapple juice to coat pork evenly. (Refrigerate remaining pineapple.)

2) Cover; cook on Low setting 4 to 5 hours.

3) About 40 minutes before serving, drain cooking juices in slow cooker. In small bowl, mix barbecue sauce and plum sauce. Spoon sauce over pork; stir gently to coat. Add pineapple chunks to pork mixture. Sprinkle with bell pepper.

4) Increase heat setting to High; cover and cook 25 to 30 minutes longer or until pork is glazed.

5) Gently stir pork mixture. Serve with long wooden picks or skewers for spearing pork, pineapple and bell pepper pieces. If necessary, cover and hold in slow cooker on Low setting up to 2 hours.

HIGH ALTITUDE (ABOVE 3500 FT.): No change.

Pork Chops with Salsa Beans

 EASY  LOW FAT

2 bone-in center-cut pork loin chops
   (½ inch thick)

½ teaspoon peppered seasoned salt

½ cup Green Giant® Niblets® frozen corn
   (from 1-lb. bag)

¼ cup Old El Paso® Thick 'n Chunky salsa

1 can (8 oz.) baked beans, undrained

Nutrition Information Per Serving:	
Serving Size: 1/2 of Recipe	
Calories: 320	From Fat: 80
Total Fat	9g
Saturated	3g
Cholesterol	75mg
Sodium	1020mg
Total Carbohydrate	32g
Dietary Fiber	7g
Sugars	8g
Protein	30g

1) Heat 8-inch skillet over medium-high heat. Sprinkle pork chops with peppered seasoned salt; place in skillet. Cook 2 to 4 minutes or until browned on both sides.

2) In 1½-quart slow cooker, mix corn, salsa and beans. Top with pork chops, overlapping as necessary, and pressing gently into bean mixture.

3) Cover; cook 4 to 5 hours (if slow cooker has heat settings, cook on Low).

Jambalaya Red Beans and Rice

PREP TIME: 30 MINUTES (READY IN 9 HOURS)
SERVINGS: 8 (2 CUPS EACH)

1 bag (12 oz.) frozen deveined shelled cooked small shrimp

1 medium onion, chopped (½ cup)

¾ lb. boneless skinless chicken thighs, cut into quarters

1 clove garlic, finely chopped

1 medium green bell pepper, chopped (1 cup)

2 dried bay leaves

1 can (15.5 oz.) red beans, drained, rinsed

1 can (6 oz.) tomato paste

1 can (14.5 oz.) garlic-seasoned diced tomatoes, undrained

1 teaspoon sugar

3 teaspoons dried Creole seasoning

½ lb. precooked kielbasa or Polish sausage, halved lengthwise, cut into 1-inch-thick slices

4 cups uncooked instant white rice

Water

1) Place bag of frozen shrimp in refrigerator to thaw. In 3- to 4-quart slow cooker, layer onion, chicken, garlic, bell pepper, bay leaves, beans, tomato paste, tomatoes, sugar and Creole seasoning.

2) Cover; cook on Low setting 6 to 8 hours.

3) About 35 minutes before serving, remove and discard bay leaves. If necessary, remove tail shells from thawed shrimp; gently stir shrimp and sausage into chicken mixture.

4) Increase heat setting to High; cover and cook 20 to 30 minutes longer or until shrimp and sausage are thoroughly heated. Meanwhile, cook rice in water as directed on package. Serve meat mixture over rice. If desired, serve with red pepper sauce.

HIGH ALTITUDE (ABOVE 3500 FT.): No change.

Nutrition Information Per Serving:
Serving Size: 2 Cups

Calories:	510	From Fat:	110
Total Fat			13g
Saturated			4g
Cholesterol			125mg
Sodium			760mg
Total Carbohydrate			70g
Dietary Fiber			6g
Sugars			5g
Protein			32g

Potluck Pleasers

Cooking for a crowd? Each of these dishes serves 10 or more.

PIZZA JOES
PG. 290

LIME AND MANGO COLESLAW
PG. 289

FIVE-SPICE SHRIMP PUFFS
PG. 278

Salsa Reuben Dip

MARTHA DAVIS | INMAN, SOUTH CAROLINA

Pillsbury Bake-Off

| PREP TIME: | 15 MINUTES (READY IN 45 MINUTES) |
| SERVINGS: | 32 (2 SLICES BREAD AND 2 TABLESPOONS DIP EACH) |

1 package (8 oz.) cream cheese, softened

1 container (8 oz.) sour cream

1 cup Old El Paso® Thick 'n Chunky salsa

4 oz. finely chopped cooked corned beef

¾ cup shredded Swiss cheese (3 oz.)

½ cup sauerkraut, rinsed, drained and chopped

1 to 2 cloves garlic, minced

Dash salt, if desired

Dash pepper, if desired

Chopped fresh cilantro

Cocktail rye bread slices, tortilla chips or cut-up fresh vegetables

1) Heat oven to 350°F. In large bowl with electric mixer, beat cream cheese, sour cream and salsa on medium speed until well blended. Add all remaining ingredients except cilantro and bread; beat on low speed until thoroughly mixed. Spoon mixture into ungreased 9- or 10-inch pie pan or quiche dish.

2) Bake 20 to 30 minutes or until thoroughly heated. Sprinkle with cilantro. Serve warm with bread slices for dipping. Store in refrigerator.

HIGH ALTITUDE (3500-6500 FT.): No change.

Nutrition Information Per Serving:
Serving Size: 2 Slices Bread & 2 Tablespoons Dip

Calories:	100	From Fat:	50
Total Fat			6g
Saturated			3g
Cholesterol			20mg
Sodium			250mg
Total Carbohydrate			8g
Dietary Fiber			0g
Sugars			1g
Protein			3g

Salami Veggie Roll-Ups

PREP TIME: 20 MINUTES (READY IN 1 HOUR 20 MINUTES)
SERVINGS: 32 APPETIZERS

 EASY

½ cup light garden vegetable cream cheese spread (from 8-oz. container)

4 flour or tomato tortillas (10 inch)

3 oz. very thinly sliced salami (about 24 slices)

¾ cup creamy coleslaw (from deli), drained

¼ medium red bell pepper, cut into very thin strips

4 large leaves leaf lettuce

Nutrition Information Per Serving: Serving Size: 1 Appetizer	
Calories: 50	From Fat: 20
Total Fat	2g
Saturated	1g
Cholesterol	5mg
Sodium	110mg
Total Carbohydrate	6g
Dietary Fiber	0g
Sugars	1g
Protein	2g

1) Spread cream cheese spread evenly over tortillas, covering completely.

2) Arrange salami over cheese spread, covering bottom half of each tortilla. Top salami with coleslaw, bell pepper and lettuce.

3) Roll up each tightly; wrap individually in plastic wrap. Refrigerate until completely chilled, at least 1 hour.

4) To serve, trim off ends of each roll; cut each into 8 slices.

HIGH ALTITUDE (3500-6000 FT.): No change.

Southwest Cornbread Salad

PREP TIME: 30 MINUTES
SERVINGS: 15 (1/2 CUP EACH)

 EASY

¾ cup purchased ranch salad dressing

¾ teaspoon curry powder

15 slices purchased precooked bacon

8 cups cubed (¾-inch) cornbread

1 medium tomato, diced (¾ cup)

¼ cup chopped red onion

¼ cup chopped fresh cilantro

1 (11-oz.) can Green Giant® Mexicorn® Whole Kernel Corn, Red and Green Peppers, drained

Nutrition Information Per Serving: Serving Size: 1/2 Cup	
Calories: 260	From Fat: 125
Total Fat	14g
Saturated	3g
Cholesterol	40mg
Sodium	590mg
Total Carbohydrate	28g
Dietary Fiber	2g
Sugars	9g
Protein	6g

1) In 1-cup glass measuring cup, combine salad dressing and curry powder; mix well. Let stand 5 to 10 minutes to blend flavors.

2) Meanwhile, heat bacon as directed on package until crisp. Drain on paper towel; crumble.

3) In large bowl, combine cornbread, tomato, onion, cilantro and corn. Add bacon and dressing mixture; toss gently to coat.

HIGH ALTITUDE (ABOVE 3500 FT.): No change.

Cabbage Salad Vinaigrette
With Crunchy Noodles

BIRDIE CASEMENT | DENVER, COLORADO

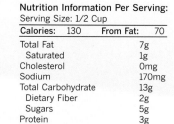

PREP TIME: 25 MINUTES (READY IN 2 HOURS 25 MINUTES)
SERVINGS: 16 (1/2 CUP EACH)

SALAD

- 1½ cups Green Giant Select® LeSueur® frozen baby sweet peas (from 1-lb. bag)
- 4½ cups shredded red or green cabbage (1 medium head)
- 5 medium green onions, thinly sliced including tops (about ⅓ cup)
- 1 can (11 oz.) Green Giant® Niblets® whole kernel sweet corn, drained
- 1 jar (4.5 oz.) Green Giant® sliced mushrooms, undrained

DRESSING

- 1 package (3 oz.) instant Oriental noodles with chicken-flavor seasoning packet
- ¼ cup tarragon vinegar
- ¼ cup vegetable oil
- 3 tablespoons sugar
- ½ teaspoon pepper
- ½ cup slivered almonds, toasted*
- 2 tablespoons sesame seed, toasted**

1) Cook peas as directed on bag. Drain; cool 10 minutes. In large bowl, mix cooled peas and remaining salad ingredients.

2) In small bowl, mix contents of seasoning packet from noodles, vinegar, oil, sugar and pepper until well blended. Pour dressing over salad; toss to coat. Refrigerate until chilled, at least 2 hours.

3) Break noodles into ¾-inch pieces. Before serving, stir noodles, almonds and sesame seed into salad.

*NOTE: To toast almonds, spread on cookie sheet; bake at 375°F. 5 to 6 minutes, stirring occasionally, until light golden brown. Or, spread in thin layer in microwavable pie pan; microwave on High 6 to 7 minutes, stirring frequently, until light golden brown.

**NOTE: To toast sesame seed, spread in baking pan; bake at 375°F. 5 to 7 minutes, stirring occasionally, until light golden brown. Or, spread in 8-inch skillet; cook over medium heat 8 to 10 minutes, stirring frequently, until light golden brown.

HIGH ALTITUDE (3500-6500 FT.): No change.

Nutrition Information Per Serving:
Serving Size: 1/2 Cup

Calories:	130	From Fat:	70
Total Fat			7g
Saturated			1g
Cholesterol			0mg
Sodium			170mg
Total Carbohydrate			13g
Dietary Fiber			2g
Sugars			5g
Protein			3g

Garlic Smashed Red Potatoes

PREP TIME: 15 MINUTES (READY IN 4 HOURS 45 MINUTES)
SERVINGS: 14 (1/2 CUP EACH)

 EASY

3 lb. small red potatoes (2 to 3 inch)

4 cloves garlic, minced

1 teaspoon salt

½ cup water

2 tablespoons olive oil

½ cup chive-and-onion cream cheese spread (from 8-oz. container)

½ to ¾ cup milk

Nutrition Information Per Serving:
Serving Size: 1/2 Cup

Calories:	130	From Fat:	45
Total Fat			5g
Saturated			2g
Cholesterol			10mg
Sodium			210mg
Total Carbohydrate			18g
Dietary Fiber			2g
Sugars			2g
Protein			3g

1) Cut potatoes into halves or quarters as necessary to make similar-size pieces; place in 4- to 6-quart slow cooker. Stir in garlic, salt, water and oil until potato pieces are coated.

2) Cover; cook on High setting 3½ to 4½ hours or until potatoes are tender.

3) With fork or potato masher, mash potatoes and garlic. Stir in cream cheese spread until well blended. Stir in enough milk for soft serving consistency. Serve immediately, or cover and hold in slow cooker on Low setting up to 2 hours.

HIGH ALTITUDE (ABOVE 3500 FT.): No change.

Mini Chicken Caesar Cups

PREP TIME: 20 MINUTES (READY IN 35 MINUTES)
SERVINGS: 20 APPETIZERS

EASY

1 cup finely chopped cooked chicken

3 tablespoons Caesar salad dressing

1 can (12 oz.) Pillsbury® Golden Layers® refrigerated flaky or buttermilk flaky biscuits

¼ cup finely sliced romaine lettuce

1 oz. shaved Parmesan cheese

Nutrition Information Per Serving:
Serving Size: 1 Appetizer

Calories:	80	From Fat:	40
Total Fat			4g
Saturated			1g
Cholesterol			10mg
Sodium			250mg
Total Carbohydrate			8g
Dietary Fiber			0g
Sugars			2g
Protein			4g

1) Heat oven to 400°F. In small bowl, mix chicken and salad dressing.

2) Separate dough into 10 biscuits; divide each into 2 rounds. Press dough rounds in bottom and up sides of 20 ungreased mini muffin cups, extending dough ¼ inch above edge of cups. Fill each cup with about 2 teaspoons chicken mixture.

3) Bake 8 to 11 minutes or until crust is deep golden brown. Remove from cups. Top each with lettuce and Parmesan cheese. Serve warm.

HIGH ALTITUDE (3500-6000 FT.): Bake at 400°F. 10 to 13 minutes.

Minestrone-Stuffed Shells

PREP TIME: 35 MINUTES
SERVINGS: 16

48 uncooked jumbo pasta shells
   (from two 12-oz. pkg.)

2 lb. lean (at least 80%) ground beef

2 cups chopped any color bell peppers
   (4 medium)

1 cup chopped onions (2 medium)

1 teaspoon salt

3/4 cup refrigerated basil pesto
   (from 7-oz. container)

8 oz. (2 cups) shredded mozzarella
   cheese

2 (15-oz.) cans dark red kidney beans,
   drained, rinsed

2 (26-oz.) jars thick and hearty tomato
   pasta sauce

4 oz. (1 cup) shredded fresh
   Parmesan cheese

1) Cook pasta shells as directed on package. Drain. Rinse with cold water to cool; drain well.

2) Meanwhile, in 5 to 6-quart Dutch oven, break up ground beef. Add bell peppers and onions; sprinkle with salt. Cook over medium-high heat until beef is thoroughly cooked, stirring frequently. Drain. Stir in pesto, mozzarella cheese and beans.

3) Fill each cooked pasta shell with scant 1/4 cup beef mixture. Place 12 filled shells in each of 4 large (9 1/2-cup) rectangular freezer/microwave-safe containers. Spoon 1/2 jar (about 1 1/2 cups) of the pasta sauce over each to cover. Sprinkle each with 1/4 cup Parmesan cheese. Cover; refrigerate up to 3 days or freeze up to 2 months.

4) Thaw stuffed shells in refrigerator for 24 hours, or uncover and thaw each container in microwave on Defrost for 15 to 20 minutes.

5) To reheat refrigerated or thawed stuffed shells, cover loosely and microwave on High for 6 to 8 minutes or until thoroughly heated.

HIGH ALTITUDE (ABOVE 3500 FT.): No change.

Nutrition Information Per Serving:		
Serving Size: 1/16 of Recipe		
Calories: 485	From Fat:	190
Total Fat		21g
Saturated		7g
Cholesterol		50mg
Sodium		1150mg
Total Carbohydrate		52g
Dietary Fiber		6g
Sugars		9g
Protein		28g

Quick 'n Chewy Crescent Bars

ISABELLE COLLINS | RAMONA, CALIFORNIA

PREP TIME: 30 MINUTES (READY IN 1 HOUR 30 MINUTES)
SERVINGS: 48 BARS

1 cup flaked or shredded coconut

3/4 cup packed brown sugar

1/2 cup Pillsbury BEST® all-purpose flour

1/2 cup chopped pecans

1/4 cup butter or margarine

1 can (8 oz.) Pillsbury® refrigerated crescent dinner rolls

1 can (14 oz.) sweetened condensed milk (not evaporated)

1) Heat oven to 400°F. In medium bowl, mix coconut, brown sugar, flour and pecans. With pastry blender or fork, cut in butter until mixture resembles coarse crumbs; set aside.

2) Unroll dough into 2 long rectangles. Place in ungreased 15x10x1-inch pan; press in bottom of pan, firmly pressing perforations to seal.

3) Pour condensed milk evenly over dough; spread to within 1/2 inch of edges. Sprinkle coconut mixture over condensed milk; press in lightly.

4) Bake 12 to 15 minutes or until deep golden brown. Cool completely, about 1 hour. Cut into bars.

HIGH ALTITUDE (3500-6500 FT.): After pressing dough in bottom of pan and sealing perforations, bake at 400°F. 3 minutes. Continue as directed above.

Nutrition Information Per Serving:
Serving Size: 1 Bar

Calories:	90	From Fat:	35
Total Fat			4g
Saturated			2g
Cholesterol			5mg
Sodium			65mg
Total Carbohydrate			12g
Dietary Fiber			0g
Sugars			9g
Protein			1g

Celebration Tortellini Salad

PREP TIME: 30 MINUTES (READY IN 1 HOUR 30 MINUTES)
SERVINGS: 16 (1 CUP EACH)

SALAD

4 packages (9 oz. each) refrigerated cheese-filled tortellini

3 jars (6 oz. each) marinated artichoke hearts, drained, liquid reserved

1 can (15 oz.) small pitted ripe olives, drained

1 jar (7.25 oz.) roasted red bell peppers, drained, cut into thin strips

12 oz. salami, cut into ½-inch cubes

2 medium zucchini, quartered lengthwise, sliced (2 cups)

DRESSING

Reserved artichoke liquid

¼ cup balsamic or red wine vinegar

¼ cup chopped fresh basil or 3 teaspoons dried basil leaves

1 teaspoon salt

¼ teaspoon coarse ground black pepper

2 cloves garlic, minced

1) In Dutch oven or 8-quart saucepot, cook tortellini as directed on package; drain. Rinse with cold water to cool; drain well.

2) Meanwhile, coarsely chop artichoke hearts. In large bowl, gently mix artichoke hearts and all remaining salad ingredients. In medium bowl, mix ¾ cup of the reserved artichoke liquid and all dressing ingredients until well blended.

3) Stir cooked tortellini into salad. Pour dressing over salad; toss gently to coat. Cover; refrigerate at least 1 hour to blend flavors. If desired, garnish with shredded Parmesan cheese.

HIGH ALTITUDE (3500-6000 FT.): Cook tortellini following High Altitude package directions.

Nutrition Information Per Serving: Serving Size: 1 Cup		
Calories: 410	From Fat:	210
Total Fat		23g
Saturated		6g
Cholesterol		50mg
Sodium		1030mg
Total Carbohydrate		37g
Dietary Fiber		3g
Sugars		3g
Protein		14g

Ready-and-Waiting Asian Snack Mix

PREP TIME: 10 MINUTES (READY IN 4 HOURS 10 MINUTES)
SERVINGS: 20 (1/2 CUP EACH)

4 cups Corn Chex® cereal

1 package (3.2 to 3.5 oz.) sesame rice crunch crackers, broken in half (about 3 cups)

2 cups tiny pretzel twists

1 package (8 oz.) slivered almonds (1½ cups)

¼ cup butter or margarine, melted

1 tablespoon packed brown sugar

2 tablespoons soy sauce

1 teaspoon curry powder

½ teaspoon garlic powder

Nutrition Information Per Serving: Serving Size: 1/2 Cup		
Calories: 150	From Fat:	70
Total Fat		8g
Saturated		2g
Cholesterol		5mg
Sodium		260mg
Total Carbohydrate		15g
Dietary Fiber		2g
Sugars		2g
Protein		4g

1) In 5- to 6-quart slow cooker, lightly mix cereal, crackers, pretzels and almonds.

2) In small microwavable bowl, microwave butter on High 30 to 45 seconds until melted. Stir in brown sugar, soy sauce, curry powder and garlic powder. Pour over cereal mixture, stirring gently until evenly coated.

3) Cook uncovered on Low setting 3 to 4 hours (or on High setting 2 to 2½ hours), stirring every 30 minutes. If desired, keep snack mix warm on Low setting during serving.

HIGH ALTITUDE (ABOVE 3500 FT.): No change.

Chocolate-Caramel-Pecan Crunch

PREP TIME: 40 MINUTES (READY IN 50 MINUTES)
SERVINGS: 22 (1/2 CUP EACH)

⊖ EASY

1 cup butter or margarine, melted

1 cup packed brown sugar

8 cups corn puffs snacks

2 cups pecan halves

¾ cup semisweet chocolate chips

Nutrition Information Per Serving: Serving Size: 1/2 Cup		
Calories: 250	From Fat:	180
Total Fat		20g
Saturated		7g
Cholesterol		25mg
Sodium		130mg
Total Carbohydrate		17g
Dietary Fiber		1g
Sugars		13g
Protein		1g

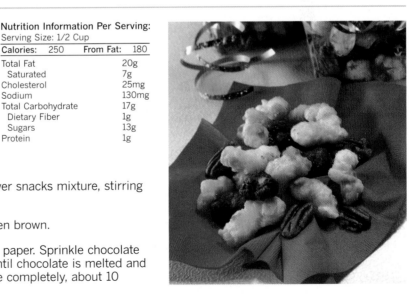

1) Heat oven to 300°F. In medium bowl, mix melted butter and brown sugar. In ungreased 15x10x1-inch pan, place corn puffs snacks and pecans. Pour butter mixture over snacks mixture, stirring to coat evenly.

2) Bake 20 to 25 minutes, stirring twice, until golden brown.

3) Remove 6 cups snacks mixture; place on waxed paper. Sprinkle chocolate chips over remaining hot mixture in pan; toss until chocolate is melted and pieces are completely coated. Cool each mixture completely, about 10 minutes.

4) When mixtures are completely cooled, toss together in large bowl or container.

HIGH ALTITUDE (3500-6000 FT.): Decrease butter to ¾ cup. Bake at 325°F. 30 to 35 minutes.

Five-Spice Shrimp Puffs

MAUREEN MALOY | SANDWICH, MASSACHUSETTS

PREP TIME: 35 MINUTES (READY IN 55 MINUTES)
SERVINGS: 20 APPETIZERS

1 (12-oz.) can Pillsbury® Golden Layers® Refrigerated Buttermilk Biscuits

20 uncooked deveined shelled medium shrimp, tail shells removed

1 teaspoon Chinese five-spice powder

2 tablespoons hot chili sesame oil*

2 tablespoons dry sherry

6 oz. (1½ cups) finely shredded Swiss cheese

3 tablespoons finely chopped green onions (3 medium)

1 tablespoon grated gingerroot

1 tablespoon finely chopped red bell pepper

¼ teaspoon salt

1 clove garlic, minced

¼ cup mayonnaise

1 teaspoon hot or regular chili sauce with garlic

1) Heat oven to 400°F. Separate dough into 10 biscuits; separate each evenly into 2 layers, making 20 dough rounds. Press each round in bottom and up side of ungreased nonstick miniature muffin cup, forming ¼-inch rim above top of cup, using floured fingers if necessary.

2) In medium bowl, toss shrimp and five-spice powder until coated. In 10-inch nonstick skillet, heat oil over high heat until hot. Add shrimp; cook and stir 1 minute. Add sherry; cook and stir an additional minute. Remove from heat.

3) In small bowl, mix all remaining ingredients. Spoon scant 1 tablespoon mixture into each dough-lined muffin cup; press in lightly. Top each with 1 shrimp.

4) Bake at 400°F. for 10 to 15 minutes or until crust is golden brown. Cool 5 minutes. Remove from muffin cups. Serve warm.

*NOTE: To substitute for hot chili sesame oil, use 2 tablespoons vegetable oil mixed with ½ teaspoon hot pepper sauce.

HIGH ALTITUDE (ABOVE 3500 FT.): Bake at 400°F. for 13 to 18 minutes.

Nutrition Information Per Serving:	
Serving Size: 1 Appetizer	
Calories: 130	From Fat: 80
Total Fat	8g
Saturated	3g
Cholesterol	20mg
Sodium	290mg
Total Carbohydrate	9g
Dietary Fiber	0g
Sugars	3g
Protein	5g

Spanish Rice Salad

ANN EVERETT | CORNELIUS, NORTH CAROLINA

| PREP TIME: | 20 MINUTES (READY IN 20 MINUTES) |
| SERVINGS: | 10 (1/2 CUP EACH) |

e EASY

SALAD

- ⅔ cup uncooked regular long-grain white rice

- 1⅓ cups water

- 2 cans (11 oz.) Green Giant® Mexicorn® whole kernel corn with red and green peppers, drained

- ½ cup chopped red onion

- ½ cup chopped green bell pepper (½ medium)

- 1 cup shredded reduced-fat Cheddar cheese (4 oz.)

DRESSING

- ¾ cup Old El Paso® Thick 'n Chunky salsa

- ½ cup light sour cream

- ½ to ¾ teaspoon salt

- ½ teaspoon ground cumin

- ½ teaspoon chili powder

GARNISH

- 1 ripe avocado, pitted, peeled and cut into 10 wedges

- 10 fresh cilantro sprigs

1) Cook rice in water as directed on package. Meanwhile, in large bowl, mix remaining salad ingredients. In medium bowl, mix dressing ingredients until well blended.

2) Stir cooked rice into salad. Add dressing; toss to coat. Spoon salad onto individual plates; garnish each with avocado wedge and cilantro sprig.

HIGH ALTITUDE (3500-6500 FT.): No change.

Nutrition Information Per Serving:
Serving Size: 1/2 Cup

Calories:	180	From Fat:	50
Total Fat			5g
Saturated			2g
Cholesterol			5mg
Sodium			720mg
Total Carbohydrate			27g
Dietary Fiber			3g
Sugars			5g
Protein			6g

Hot Roast Beef Sandwiches Au Jus

PREP TIME: 20 MINUTES (READY IN 8 HOURS 20 MINUTES)
SERVINGS: 10 SANDWICHES

 LOW FAT

1 beef eye of round roast (2½ lb.), trimmed of fat

6 cloves garlic, peeled

2 teaspoons coarsely ground black pepper

1 large onion, thinly sliced

½ cup condensed beef broth (from 10½-oz. can)

10 kaiser rolls, split, toasted

2 large tomatoes, each cut into 5 slices

1) With sharp knife, make 6 evenly spaced slits deep into beef roast. Insert garlic into slits. Sprinkle pepper evenly over entire roast; rub pepper into roast.

2) Spray 3- to 4-quart slow cooker with cooking spray. Place onion slices in slow cooker; pour broth over onion. Place roast over onion and broth.

3) Cover; cook on Low setting 6 to 8 hours.

4) Remove roast from slow cooker; place on cutting board. Cut roast across grain into thin slices; return slices to slow cooker to moisten. Fill each toasted roll with beef, onion and 1 tomato slice. If desired, spoon small amount of broth from slow cooker over beef.

HIGH ALTITUDE (ABOVE 3500 FT.): No change.

Nutrition Information Per Serving:
Serving Size: 1 Sandwich

Calories:	270	From Fat:	50
Total Fat			6g
Saturated			1g
Cholesterol			55mg
Sodium			380mg
Total Carbohydrate			30g
Dietary Fiber			2g
Sugars			2g
Protein			27g

Chex® and Candy Squares

PREP TIME: 10 MINUTES (READY IN 1 HOUR 35 MINUTES)
SERVINGS: 36 BARS

1 (18-oz.) roll Pillsbury® Refrigerated
   Sugar Cookies

1 cup salted cashew halves, chopped

1 cup semisweet chocolate chips

1 cup caramel ice cream topping

2 tablespoons all-purpose flour

4 cups Corn Chex® Cereal

1 cup miniature candy-coated
   semisweet chocolate baking bits

Nutrition Information Per Serving: Serving Size: 1 Bar		
Calories: 170	From Fat: 55	
Total Fat		6g
Saturated		2g
Cholesterol		0mg
Sodium		125mg
Total Carbohydrate		27g
Dietary Fiber		0g
Sugars		17g
Protein		2g

1) Heat oven to 350°F. Spray 13x9-inch pan with nonstick cooking spray.
In medium bowl, break up cookie dough; stir in cashews. Press dough
in sprayed pan to form crust.

2) Bake at 350°F. for 18 to 23 minutes or until golden brown.

3) Remove baked crust from oven. In medium saucepan, combine chocolate
chips, caramel topping and flour; cook and stir over low heat until smooth.

4) Remove from heat; stir in cereal and 1/2 cup of the baking bits. Spread
evenly over crust. Sprinkle with remaining 1/2 cup baking bits; press in
lightly. Cool about 1 hour or until completely cooled. Cut into bars.

HIGH ALTITUDE (ABOVE 3500 FT.): No change.

Slow-Cooked Baked Beans

PREP TIME: 10 MINUTES (READY IN 14 HOURS 10 MINUTES)   🍴 LOW FAT
SERVINGS: 10 (1/2 CUP EACH)

1 bag (16 oz.) dried navy beans,
   sorted, rinsed

1 cup water

1 medium onion, chopped (about 1/2 cup)

1/2 cup molasses

1/3 cup packed brown sugar

1 teaspoon salt

3 teaspoons dry ground mustard

1/2 teaspoon liquid smoke

Nutrition Information Per Serving: Serving Size: 1/2 Cup		
Calories: 240	From Fat: 10	
Total Fat		1g
Saturated		0g
Cholesterol		0mg
Sodium		230mg
Total Carbohydrate		47g
Dietary Fiber		11g
Sugars		17g
Protein		10g

1) In Dutch oven, mix beans and 10 cups water. Heat to boiling. Reduce heat;
cover and simmer 2 hours. Drain and discard liquid.

2) In 3 1/2- to 4-quart slow cooker, mix drained beans, 1 cup water and all
remaining ingredients.

3) Cover; cook on Low setting 10 to 12 hours.

HIGH ALTITUDE (3500-6000 FT.): Add up to an additional 1/2 cup water if mixture gets too thick.

Maple-Apple Cake

PREP TIME: 30 MINUTES (READY IN 2 HOURS 50 MINUTES)
SERVINGS: 16

CAKE

1 cup granulated sugar

½ cup packed brown sugar

¾ cup butter or margarine, softened

¾ cup maple-flavored syrup

4 eggs

3 cups all-purpose flour

2 teaspoons baking powder

1 teaspoon ground cinnamon

½ teaspoon salt

½ teaspoon ground nutmeg

¼ teaspoon ground allspice

3 cups chopped peeled apples (3 medium)

½ cup chopped walnuts

GLAZE

½ cup powdered sugar

3 tablespoons maple-flavored syrup

1 tablespoon butter or margarine, softened

GARNISH

1 tablespoon chopped walnuts

1) Heat oven to 350°F. Grease and flour 12-cup fluted tube pan. In large bowl, beat granulated sugar, brown sugar and ¾ cup butter until smooth. Beat in ¾ cup syrup and eggs until blended.

2) Beat in flour, baking powder, cinnamon, salt, nutmeg and allspice until combined. Stir in apples and ½ cup walnuts. Spread batter evenly in pan.

3) Bake 55 to 65 minutes or until toothpick inserted in center comes out clean. Cool 15 minutes. Remove from pan. Cool completely, about 1 hour.

4) In small bowl, mix glaze ingredients until smooth. Spoon over top of cake. Sprinkle with 1 tablespoon walnuts.

HIGH ALTITUDE (3500-6000 FT.): Decrease granulated sugar to ¾ cup; increase flour to 3½ cups. Bake at 375°F. 50 to 60 minutes.

Nutrition Information Per Serving:		
Serving Size: 1/16 of Recipe		
Calories: 380	From Fat:	130
Total Fat		14g
Saturated		7g
Cholesterol		80mg
Sodium		230mg
Total Carbohydrate		58g
Dietary Fiber		1g
Sugars		33g
Protein		5g

Southwestern Chicken Biscuits

ELIZABETH BARCLAY | ANNAPOLIS, MARYLAND

PREP TIME: 15 MINUTES (READY IN 35 MINUTES)
SERVINGS: 20 SNACKS

2 cans (12 oz. each) Pillsbury® Golden Layers® refrigerated buttermilk biscuits

1 package (9 oz.) frozen cooked southwestern-seasoned chicken breast strips (2 cups), thawed, diced

1 can (4.5 oz.) Old El Paso® chopped green chiles

1 cup shredded Monterey Jack cheese (4 oz.)

1 tablespoon dried minced onion

1 cup Old El Paso® Thick 'n Chunky salsa

Fresh cilantro sprigs

1) Heat oven to 400°F. Spray 20 muffin cups with cooking spray. Separate dough into 20 biscuits. Place 1 biscuit in each muffin cup; press to cover bottom and sides of cup.

2) In medium bowl, mix chicken, chiles, cheese, onion and salsa. Spoon 2 tablespoons mixture into each dough-lined cup; gently press mixture with back of spoon.

3) Bake 13 to 18 minutes or until edges are golden brown. Remove from muffin cups; serve warm garnished with cilantro sprigs.

HIGH ALTITUDE (3500-6500 FT.): Bake at 400°F. 15 to 20 minutes.

Nutrition Information Per Serving:	
Serving Size: 1 Snack	
Calories: 160	From Fat: 80
Total Fat	9g
Saturated	3g
Cholesterol	15mg
Sodium	630mg
Total Carbohydrate	16g
Dietary Fiber	0g
Sugars	4g
Protein	6g

Winter Fruit Salad with Lemon-Poppy Seed Dressing

PREP TIME: 25 MINUTES (READY IN 25 MINUTES)
SERVINGS: 12 (1 CUP EACH)

 EASY

DRESSING
- ½ cup sugar
- 2 teaspoons finely chopped onion
- ½ teaspoon salt
- ⅓ cup lemon juice
- 1 teaspoon Dijon mustard
- ⅔ cup vegetable oil
- 1 tablespoon poppy seed

SALAD
- 1 large head romaine lettuce, torn into bite-size pieces (about 10 cups)
- 1 cup shredded Swiss cheese (4 oz.)
- 1 cup cashews
- ¼ cup sweetened dried cranberries
- 1 medium apple, cubed (1 cup)
- 1 medium pear, cubed (1 cup)

1) In blender or food processor, place sugar, onion, salt, lemon juice and mustard; cover and process until blended.

2) With machine running, add oil in slow steady stream, processing until thick and smooth. Add poppy seed; process a few seconds to mix.

3) In large serving bowl, mix all salad ingredients. Pour dressing over salad; toss to coat.

HIGH ALTITUDE (3500-6000 FT.): No change.

Nutrition Information Per Serving: Serving Size: 1 Cup		
Calories: 280	From Fat:	180
Total Fat		20g
Saturated		4g
Cholesterol		10mg
Sodium		200mg
Total Carbohydrate		20g
Dietary Fiber		2g
Sugars		15g
Protein		5g

Swiss-Potato Casserole

PREP TIME: 20 MINUTES (READY IN 1 HOUR 25 MINUTES)
SERVINGS: 12 (2/3 CUP EACH)

1 bag (2 lb.) frozen southern-style diced hash-brown potatoes

2 cups shredded Swiss cheese (8 oz.)

¼ cup butter or margarine

3 tablespoons all-purpose flour

3 cups milk

1 teaspoon salt

1 teaspoon onion powder

½ teaspoon white pepper

½ teaspoon ground nutmeg, if desired

Nutrition Information Per Serving:
Serving Size: 2/3 Cup

Calories:	230	From Fat:	90
Total Fat			10g
Saturated			7g
Cholesterol			30mg
Sodium			330mg
Total Carbohydrate			27g
Dietary Fiber			2g
Sugars			4g
Protein			10g

1) Heat oven to 350°F. Spray 13x9-inch (3-quart) glass baking dish with cooking spray. In baking dish, toss potatoes and cheese to mix.

2) In 1½-quart saucepan, melt butter over medium heat. Stir in flour; cook, stirring constantly, until bubbly. Gradually add milk, stirring constantly. Stir in salt, onion powder, pepper and nutmeg. Cook, stirring constantly, until mixture boils. Remove from heat; pour over potato mixture.

3) Bake 55 to 65 minutes or until mixture is set and top is lightly browned.

HIGH ALTITUDE (3500-6000 FT.): In Step 2, cook over medium-high heat.

Gulf Shrimp Crostini

PREP TIME: 20 MINUTES (READY IN 20 MINUTES)
SERVINGS: 12 APPETIZERS

e EASY   f LOW FAT

½ cup frozen deveined shelled salad shrimp (3 oz.), thawed, drained

¼ cup sliced green onions (4 medium)

1 Italian plum tomato, seeded, chopped

¼ teaspoon grated lime peel

1 tablespoon fresh lime juice

⅛ teaspoon hot pepper sauce

1 clove garlic, minced

1 whole wheat pita (pocket) bread (6.5-inch)

Nutrition Information Per Serving:
Serving Size: 1 Appetizer

Calories:	20	From Fat:	0
Total Fat			0g
Saturated			0g
Cholesterol			10mg
Sodium			45mg
Total Carbohydrate			3g
Dietary Fiber			0g
Sugars			1g
Protein			2g

1) Coarsely chop shrimp. In medium bowl, gently mix all ingredients except pita bread; set aside.

2) Split each pita bread into 2 rounds; cut each round into 6 wedges and place on ungreased cookie sheet. Broil 4 to 6 inches from heat 2 to 4 minutes, turning once, until lightly toasted on both sides.

3) Spoon shrimp mixture onto toasted pita wedges. If desired, top with additional sliced green onions.

HIGH ALTITUDE (ABOVE 3500 FT.): No change.

Southwest Lasagna

PREP TIME: 40 MINUTES (READY IN 1 HOUR 40 MINUTES)
SERVINGS: 12

9 uncooked lasagna noodles

1 lb. extra-lean (at least 90%) ground beef

1 package (1.25-oz.) Old El Paso® 40% less-sodium taco seasoning mix

¾ cup water

1 container (15 oz.) ricotta cheese

1 can (4.5 oz.) Old El Paso® chopped green chiles

2 eggs

1 jar (26 to 28 oz.) tomato pasta sauce

1 can (15 oz.) black beans, drained, rinsed

1 box (9 oz.) Green Giant® Niblets® frozen corn, thawed

2 teaspoons ground cumin

3 cups shredded Monterey Jack cheese (12 oz.)

1) Place cookie sheet or foil in oven on rack below middle oven rack; heat oven to 375°F. Spray 13x9-inch (3-quart) glass baking dish with cooking spray.

2) Cook lasagna noodles as directed on package; drain. Rinse with cold water to cool; drain well.

3) Meanwhile, in 10-inch skillet, cook ground beef over medium-high heat 5 to 7 minutes, stirring frequently, until thoroughly cooked; drain. Stir in taco seasoning mix and water. Reduce heat; simmer 5 minutes or until thickened.

4) In small bowl, mix ricotta cheese, chiles and eggs.

5) Stir pasta sauce, beans, corn and cumin into beef mixture. Cook about 5 minutes, stirring occasionally, until thoroughly heated.

6) To assemble lasagna, arrange 3 cooked noodles in bottom of baking dish. Spoon and spread ⅓ of ricotta mixture over noodles; top with ⅓ each of beef mixture and cheese. Repeat layers 2 more times, reserving last ⅓ of cheese.

7) Place baking dish on middle oven rack; bake 25 minutes. Sprinkle with reserved cheese; bake 15 to 25 minutes longer or until lasagna is bubbly and cheese is melted. Let stand 10 minutes before serving. Cut into squares.

HIGH ALTITUDE (3500-6000 FT.): In Step 7, bake at 375°F. 35 minutes. Add cheese; bake 10 to 15 minutes longer or until lasagna is bubbly and cheese is melted.

Nutrition Information Per Serving:
Serving Size: 1/2 of Recipe

Calories:	390	From Fat:	170
Total Fat			19g
Saturated			9g
Cholesterol			95mg
Sodium			840mg
Total Carbohydrate			30g
Dietary Fiber			4g
Sugars			3g
Protein			25g

Cheesy Potatoes

PREP TIME: 20 MINUTES (READY IN 1 HOUR 5 MINUTES)
SERVINGS: 18 (1/2 CUP EACH)

POTATOES

1 bag (32 oz.) frozen southern-style diced hash-brown potatoes

2 cups shredded Colby, Cheddar or Monterey Jack cheese (8 oz.)

1 container (16 oz.) sour cream

1 can (10 $\frac{3}{4}$ oz.) condensed cream of mushroom soup

$\frac{1}{4}$ cup chopped onion ($\frac{1}{2}$ medium)

$\frac{1}{4}$ cup butter or margarine, melted

1 teaspoon salt

$\frac{1}{4}$ teaspoon pepper

TOPPING

$\frac{1}{4}$ cup butter or margarine

2 cups crushed corn flakes cereal

1) Heat oven to 350°F. Spray 13x9-inch (3-quart) glass baking dish with cooking spray. In large microwavable bowl, microwave potatoes on Defrost 12 to 15 minutes or until thawed, stirring once or twice. Stir in all remaining potato ingredients; spread in baking dish.

2) In small microwavable bowl, microwave $\frac{1}{4}$ cup butter on High 30 to 60 seconds or until melted. Stir in crushed cereal; sprinkle evenly over potato mixture.

3) Bake 30 to 45 minutes or until browned and bubbly around edges.

HIGH ALTITUDE (3500-6000 FT.): Heat oven to 375°F. Continue as directed above.

Nutrition Information Per Serving:
Serving Size: 1/2 Cup

Calories:	235	From Fat:	135
Total Fat			15g
Saturated			9g
Cholesterol			45mg
Sodium			410mg
Total Carbohydrate			19g
Dietary Fiber			1g
Sugars			2g
Protein			6g

For an even creamier texture, substitute cheese product, cubed, (the foil-wrapped cheese in a box), for some of the shredded cheese in this recipe.

Three-Grain Salad

PREP TIME: 20 MINUTES (READY IN 1 HOUR 10 MINUTES)
SERVINGS: 12 (1/2 CUP EACH)

SALAD

5 cups water

4 teaspoons vegetable-flavor instant bouillon

1/2 teaspoon salt

1 cup (about 7 oz.) uncooked wheat berries, rinsed

1/3 cup uncooked medium pearl barley

1/3 cup uncooked regular long-grain brown rice

1 1/2 cups coarsely chopped unpeeled red apple (1 to 2 medium)

1/2 cup chopped red onion

1/2 cup raisins

1/2 cup pecan halves, toasted, chopped

DRESSING

1/4 cup oil

1/4 cup cider vinegar

2 tablespoons honey

3/4 teaspoon grated gingerroot

1) In 3-quart saucepan, bring water, bouillon and salt to a boil over medium-high heat. Add wheat berries; return to a boil. Reduce heat to low; cover and simmer 10 minutes.

2) Add barley and rice; cook an additional 50 minutes or until all grains are tender. Drain.

3) In large serving bowl, combine wheat berry mixture, apple, onion and raisins; mix well.

4) In small bowl, combine all dressing ingredients; mix well. Pour dressing over salad; toss to coat. Serve immediately, or cover and refrigerate 2 to 6 hours before serving. Just before serving, fold in pecans.

HIGH ALTITUDE (ABOVE 3500 FT.): After adding wheat berries to boiling water; return to a boil. Reduce heat to medium-low; cover and simmer 10 minutes. Add barley and rice; simmer over medium-low heat 50 minutes. Continue as directed above.

Nutrition Information Per Serving:
Serving Size: 1/2 Cup

Calories:	185	From Fat:	55
Total Fat			9g
Saturated			1g
Cholesterol			0mg
Sodium			540mg
Total Carbohydrate			29g
Dietary Fiber			3g
Sugars			10g
Protein			4g

Lime and Mango Coleslaw

PREP TIME: 10 MINUTES (READY IN 10 MINUTES)
SERVINGS: 12 (1/2 CUP EACH)

 EASY   LOW FAT

2 containers (6 oz. each)
  Yoplait® Original 99%
  Fat Free Key lime pie yogurt

1 tablespoon sugar

2 tablespoons vinegar

1/2 teaspoon ground cumin

5 cups coleslaw blend
  (from 16-oz. bag)

1 large mango, seed removed, peeled
  and chopped (about 1 1/2 cups)

Nutrition Information Per Serving:
Serving Size: 1/2 Cup

Calories:	60	From Fat:	0
Total Fat			0g
Saturated			0g
Cholesterol			0mg
Sodium			20mg
Total Carbohydrate			12g
Dietary Fiber			1g
Sugars			9g
Protein			2g

1) In small bowl, mix yogurt, sugar, vinegar and cumin.

2) In 2-quart serving bowl, place coleslaw blend. Top with mango; spoon yogurt mixture over mango. Serve immediately, or cover tightly and refrigerate up to 8 hours. Before serving, toss salad lightly to mix.

HIGH ALTITUDE (ABOVE 3500 FT.): No change.

Turkey Barbecue Sandwiches

PREP TIME: 25 MINUTES (READY IN 9 HOURS 25 MINUTES)
SERVINGS: 16 SANDWICHES

 LOW FAT

3 lb. turkey breast tenderloins, cut
  crosswise into 1/4-inch-thick slices*

2 cups chopped onions (4 medium)

2 cups chopped green bell peppers
  (2 medium)

1/3 cup packed brown sugar

2 tablespoons all-purpose flour

1 teaspoon salt

1 1/2 teaspoons dry ground mustard

4 teaspoons chili powder

1/4 cup vinegar

1 tablespoon Worcestershire sauce

1 can (6 oz.) tomato paste

16 sandwich buns, split

Nutrition Information Per Serving:
Serving Size: 1 Sandwich

Calories:	250	From Fat:	30
Total Fat			3g
Saturated			1g
Cholesterol			55mg
Sodium			530mg
Total Carbohydrate			33g
Dietary Fiber			3g
Sugars			11g
Protein			24g

1) In 4- to 5-quart slow cooker, mix all ingredients except buns.

2) Cover; cook on Low setting 7 to 9 hours.

3) Break turkey into pieces with spoon; serve in buns.

*NOTE: For easier slicing, freeze turkey slightly.

HIGH ALTITUDE (ABOVE 3500 FT.): No change.

Pizza Joes

PREP TIME: 25 MINUTES (READY IN 6 HOURS 25 MINUTES)
SERVINGS: 18 SANDWICHES

2 lb. lean (at least 80%) ground beef

2 medium onions, chopped (about 1 cup)

½ cup chopped green bell pepper (½ medium)

2 jars (14 oz. each) pizza sauce

1 package (3.5 oz.) sliced pepperoni, chopped (about ¾ cup)

1 teaspoon dried basil leaves

½ teaspoon dried oregano leaves

18 sandwich buns, split

2 cups shredded mozzarella cheese (2 oz.)

1) In 12-inch skillet, cook ground beef and onions over medium-high heat 5 to 7 minutes, stirring frequently, until beef is thoroughly cooked; drain.

2) Spray 3½- to 4-quart slow cooker with cooking spray. Spoon beef mixture into slow cooker. Stir in bell pepper, pizza sauce, pepperoni, basil and oregano.

3) Cover; cook on Low setting 4 to 6 hours.

4) To assemble sandwiches, spoon about ⅓ cup beef mixture onto bottom halves of buns. Top each with scant 2 tablespoons cheese. Cover with top halves of buns.

HIGH ALTITUDE (3500-6000 FT.): No change.

Nutrition Information Per Serving:
Serving Size: 1 Sandwich

Calories:	320	From Fat:	145
Total Fat			16g
Saturated			6g
Cholesterol			40mg
Sodium			630mg
Total Carbohydrate			26g
Dietary Fiber			2g
Sugars			7g
Protein			18g

Fudgy S'more Bars

PREP TIME: 25 MINUTES (READY IN 1 HOUR 35 MINUTES)
SERVINGS: 32 BARS

CRUST

½ cup all-purpose flour

1 cup graham cracker crumbs (12 squares)

¾ cup packed brown sugar

½ teaspoon baking soda

½ cup butter or margarine, softened

TOPPING

4 cups miniature marshmallows

¾ cup candy-coated chocolate pieces

¼ cup hot fudge ice cream topping, heated

1) Heat oven to 350°F. Grease 13x9-inch pan with shortening. In large bowl, beat all crust ingredients with electric mixer on low speed until coarse crumbs form. Press mixture in bottom of pan. Bake 10 to 12 minutes or until golden brown.

2) Remove partially baked crust from oven. Sprinkle marshmallows over crust. Return to oven; bake 1 to 2 minutes longer or until marshmallows begin to puff.

3) Remove pan from oven. Sprinkle chocolate pieces evenly over marshmallows. Drizzle warm ice cream topping over top. Cool completely, about 1 hour. Cut into bars.

HIGH ALTITUDE (3500-6000 FT.): No change.

Nutrition Information Per Serving:
Serving Size: 1 Bar

Calories:	120	From Fat:	40
Total Fat			4g
Saturated			3g
Cholesterol			10mg
Sodium			70mg
Total Carbohydrate			19g
Dietary Fiber			0g
Sugars			14g
Protein			1g

tip
To keep marshmallows from drying out, store them in an airtight plastic bag in the freezer. To soften hard marshmallows, place them in an airtight plastic bag with 2 or 3 slices of soft fresh white bread for three days.

Cookies Bars & Candies

Simple solutions for when you're craving something sweet.

FUDGY BONBONS
PG. 313

HOLIDAY PINWHEELS
PG. 300

NUTTY CHOCOLATE CHIP BISCOTTI
PG. 302

Peanut Butter Brownie Cookies

DEB MCGOWAN | LOUISVILLE, OHIO

Bake·Off
Pillsbury

PREP TIME: 1 HOUR (READY IN 1 HOUR 30 MINUTES)
SERVINGS: 24 COOKIES

1 (19.5-oz.) box Pillsbury®
Brownie Classics Traditional
Fudge Brownie Mix

¼ cup butter or margarine, melted

4 oz. cream cheese (from 8-oz. pkg.),
softened

1 egg

1 cup powdered sugar

1 cup creamy peanut butter

½ (16-oz.) can chocolate fudge ready-
to-spread frosting

1) Heat oven to 350°F. In medium bowl, beat brownie mix, melted butter, cream cheese and egg 50 strokes with spoon until well blended (dough will be sticky).

2) Drop dough by rounded tablespoonfuls 2 inches apart onto ungreased cookie sheets to make 24 cookies; smooth edge of each to form round cookie.

3) In small bowl, mix powdered sugar and peanut butter with spoon until mixture forms a ball. With hands, roll rounded teaspoonfuls peanut butter mixture into 24 balls. Lightly press 1 ball into center of each ball of dough.

4) Bake at 350°F. for 10 to 14 minutes or until edges are set. Cool 1 minute; remove from cookie sheets. Cool at least 30 minutes.

5) Spread thin layer of frosting over peanut butter portion of each cooled cookie.

HIGH ALTITUDE (ABOVE 3500 FT.): Before baking, flatten cookies slightly. Bake at 350°F. for 11 to 15 minutes.

Nutrition Information Per Serving:
Serving Size: 1 Cookie

Calories:	260	From Fat:	110
Total Fat			13g
Saturated			6g
Cholesterol			20mg
Sodium			160mg
Total Carbohydrate			32g
Dietary Fiber			0g
Sugars			25g
Protein			4g

Chocolate Chip-Popcorn Bars

FRAN NEAVOLL | SALEM , OREGON

PREP TIME: 20 MINUTES (READY IN 2 HOURS 10 MINUTES)
SERVINGS: 36 BARS

CRUST

1 (18-oz.) roll Pillsbury® Refrigerated Chocolate Chip Cookies

4 Nature Valley® Oats 'n Honey Crunchy Granola Bars (2 pouches from 8.9-oz. box), crushed*

TOPPING

3½ cups miniature marshmallows

⅔ cup light corn syrup

¼ cup butter or margarine

1 (10-oz.) bag peanut butter chips

4 cups popped Pop•Secret® Toffee Butter Microwave Popcorn (from 3.5-oz. bag in 10.5-oz. box)

1 cup semisweet chocolate chips

1) Heat oven to 350°F. In large bowl, break up cookie dough. Stir in crushed granola bars. Press mixture in bottom of ungreased 13x9-inch pan. Bake at 350°F. for 10 to 15 minutes or until puffed and edges are golden brown.

2) Remove from oven. Immediately sprinkle with marshmallows. Return to oven; bake an additional 1 to 2 minutes or until marshmallows begin to puff.

3) Remove from oven; place on wire rack. In 3-quart saucepan, heat corn syrup, butter and peanut butter chips over medium heat for 3 to 4 minutes, stirring frequently, until chips are melted and mixture is smooth. Stir in popcorn (mixture will be thick). Spoon mixture over marshmallows; spread evenly to just barely cover marshmallows. Cool 30 minutes.

4) In small microwavable bowl, microwave chocolate chips on High for 1 to 1½ minutes or until melted, stirring once halfway through microwaving. Pour melted chocolate into quart-size resealable food-storage plastic bag. Cut off tiny bottom corner of bag; drizzle chocolate over bars. Refrigerate at least 1 hour before serving. Cut into bars.

*NOTE: To easily crush granola bars, do not unwrap. Use rolling pin to crush bars.

Nutrition Information Per Serving:
Serving Size: 1 Bar

Calories:	200	From Fat:	80
Total Fat			9g
Saturated			3g
Cholesterol			5mg
Sodium			115mg
Total Carbohydrate			27g
Dietary Fiber			1g
Sugars			16g
Protein			3g

Holiday Cookie Packages

PREP TIME: 25 MINUTES (READY IN 1 HOUR 40 MINUTES)
SERVINGS: 64 COOKIES

COOKIES

1 cup butter, softened

½ cup packed brown sugar

¼ teaspoon ground cinnamon

1 teaspoon vanilla

2¼ cups all-purpose flour

FROSTING

2 cups powdered sugar

⅓ cup butter, softened

½ teaspoon vanilla

1 to 2 tablespoons half-and-half or milk

Food color

1) Line 8-inch square pan with plastic wrap. In large bowl with electric mixer, beat all cookie ingredients except flour at medium speed, scraping bowl occasionally, until creamy. Reduce speed to low; beat in flour, scraping bowl occasionally, until mixture forms a dough. Press dough firmly and evenly in pan. Refrigerate 30 minutes.

2) Heat oven to 350°F. Using edges of plastic wrap, lift dough from pan. With sharp knife, cut into 8 rows in each direction to make 64 squares; carefully place squares 1 inch apart on ungreased cookie sheets.

3) Bake 13 to 17 minutes or until edges are lightly browned. Cool 5 minutes; remove from cookie sheets. Cool completely, about 10 minutes.

4) In medium bowl, mix all frosting ingredients except food color until smooth, adding enough half-and-half for desired spreading consistency. In small bowl, mix ⅓ cup of the frosting and enough food color until desired color and well blended; place in small resealable food storage plastic bag and partially seal.

5) Spread uncolored frosting over cooled cookies. Cut small hole in bottom corner of bag of colored frosting. Squeeze bag to pipe frosting onto each cookie to resemble bows.

HIGH ALTITUDE (3500-6000 FT.): No change.

Nutrition Information Per Serving:
Serving Size: 1 Cookie

Calories:	75	From Fat:	35
Total Fat			4g
Saturated			2g
Cholesterol			10mg
Sodium			25mg
Total Carbohydrate			9g
Dietary Fiber			0g
Sugars			5g
Protein			1g

White Chocolate-Ginger Cookies

ROBIN WILSON | ALTAMONTE SPRINGS, FLORIDA

Bake-Off

PREP TIME:	1 HOUR 20 MINUTES (READY IN 1 HOUR 20 MINUTES)
SERVINGS:	12 LARGE COOKIES

COOKIES

- 1 (18-oz.) roll Pillsbury® Refrigerated Sugar Cookies
- 1/4 cup packed dark brown sugar
- 1 1/4 teaspoons ground cinnamon
- 1/4 teaspoon ground ginger
- 1/4 teaspoon ground nutmeg
- 2 teaspoons grated orange peel
- 1 (6-oz.) pkg. white chocolate baking bars, coarsely chopped
- 3/4 cup chopped pecans
- 1/3 cup finely chopped crystallized ginger*

GLAZE

- 1/2 cup powdered sugar
- 1/8 teaspoon ground cinnamon
- 3 to 3 1/2 teaspoons orange juice

1) Heat oven to 350°F. In large bowl, break up cookie dough. Stir in brown sugar, 1 1/4 teaspoons cinnamon, the ginger, nutmeg and orange peel until well combined. Stir in white chocolate, pecans and crystallized ginger.

2) Drop dough by 1/4 cupfuls 3 inches apart onto ungreased cookie sheets.

3) Bake at 350°F. for 13 to 17 minutes or until edges are golden brown. Cool 2 minutes. Remove from cookie sheets; place on wire racks. Cool completely, about 15 minutes.

4) In small bowl, blend powdered sugar, 1/8 teaspoon cinnamon and enough orange juice for desired drizzling consistency until smooth. Drizzle glaze over cooled cookies; let stand until glaze is set before storing.

*NOTE: To easily chop crystallized ginger, cut with kitchen scissors into small pieces.

HIGH ALTITUDE (ABOVE 3500 FT.): No change.

Nutrition Information Per Serving:
Serving Size: 1 Large Cookie

Calories:	350	From Fat:	140
Total Fat			16g
Saturated			5g
Cholesterol			5mg
Sodium			190mg
Total Carbohydrate			49g
Dietary Fiber			1g
Sugars			37g
Protein			3g

Quick Peanut Butter Cup Cookies

| PREP TIME: | 5 MINUTES (READY IN 25 MINUTES) | EASY |
| SERVINGS: | 2 COOKIES | |

2 Pillsbury® Ready to Bake!™ refrigerated chocolate candy and chocolate chip cookies (from 18 oz. package)

1 package (1.5 oz.) milk chocolate-covered peanut butter cups, unwrapped

1) Heat oven to 350°F. On ungreased cookie sheet, place cookie dough rounds about 2 inches apart.

2) Bake 10 to 14 minutes or until edges are light golden brown. Remove cookie sheet from oven. Immediately top each cookie with 1 peanut butter cup; press lightly into dough. Cool 5 minutes; remove from cookie sheet.

Nutrition Information Per Serving: Serving Size: 1 Cookie		
Calories: 480	From Fat: 230	
Total Fat		28g
Saturated		10g
Cholesterol		70mg
Sodium		180mg
Total Carbohydrate		51g
Dietary Fiber		2g
Sugars		27g
Protein		6g

Hazelnut Marble Bark

| PREP TIME: | 20 MINUTES (READY IN 1 HOUR 20 MINUTES) | EASY |
| SERVINGS: | 24 PIECES | |

1 box (6 oz.) white chocolate baking bars

6 oz. semisweet baking chocolate

3 oz. hazelnuts (filberts), toasted,* finely chopped (½ cup)

Nutrition Information Per Serving: Serving Size: 1 Piece		
Calories: 105	From Fat: 65	
Total Fat		7g
Saturated		3g
Cholesterol		0mg
Sodium		5mg
Total Carbohydrate		9g
Dietary Fiber		0g
Sugars		8g
Protein		1g

1) Line cookie sheet with foil or waxed paper. In medium microwavable bowl, microwave white chocolate on High 1 minute, stirring once halfway through microwaving, until melted. If necessary, continue to microwave on High in 15-second increments, stirring until smooth.

2) In another medium microwavable bowl, microwave semisweet chocolate on High 1 minute, stirring once halfway through microwaving, until melted. If necessary, continue to microwave on High in 15-second increments, stirring until smooth.

3) Stir ¼ cup of the hazelnuts into each bowl of chocolate. Alternately spoon white mixture and brown mixture in rows, side by side, onto cookie sheet; spread evenly to about ¼-inch thickness. With knife or small metal spatula, cut through both mixtures to swirl for marbled design. Refrigerate until firm, about 1 hour. Break into pieces.

*NOTE: To toast hazelnuts, spread whole nuts on cookie sheet; bake at 350°F. 8 to 10 minutes, stirring occasionally, until skins begin to crack open and flake. If desired, to remove skins, place warm nuts on cloth towel and fold towel over nuts; rub vigorously. Finely chop nuts to make ½ cup.

HIGH ALTITUDE (3500-6000 FT.): No change.

tip

This is an easy candy to give as a hostess gift for holiday or other special-occasion parties.

Peanut Butter–Chocolate Chip Cookie Bars

PREP TIME: 15 MINUTES (READY IN 1 HOUR 5 MINUTES)
SERVINGS: 24 BARS

 EASY

1 (18-oz.) roll Pillsbury® Refrigerated Chocolate Chip Cookies

1 cup creamy peanut butter

½ cup vanilla whipped ready-to-spread frosting (from 12-oz. can)

1 teaspoon oil

¼ cup semisweet chocolate chips

¼ cup miniature candy-coated milk chocolate baking bits

1) Heat oven to 350°F. Break up cookie dough into ungreased 13x9-inch pan. Press dough evenly in bottom of pan to form crust.

2) Bake at 350°F. for 14 to 18 minutes or until golden brown. Cool 5 minutes.

3) Meanwhile, in medium bowl, combine peanut butter, frosting and oil; mix well.

4) Spread peanut butter mixture over warm crust. Place chocolate chips in small resealable food storage plastic bag; seal bag. Microwave on High for 1 to 2 minutes or until melted. Snip very small hole in one corner of bag; squeeze bag to drizzle chocolate over peanut butter mixture. Sprinkle baking bits evenly over top. Let stand at least 30 minutes or until chocolate is set. Cut into bars.

HIGH ALTITUDE (ABOVE 3500 FT.): No change.

Nutrition Information Per Serving:
Serving Size: 1 Bar

Calories:	225	From Fat:	110
Total Fat			12g
Saturated			4g
Cholesterol			0mg
Sodium			135mg
Total Carbohydrate			24g
Dietary Fiber			1g
Sugars			14g
Protein			5g

Holiday Pinwheels

PREP TIME: 1 HOUR (READY IN 2 HOURS)
SERVINGS: 32 COOKIES

 EASY

1 roll (18 oz.) Pillsbury® refrigerated sugar cookies

½ cup all-purpose flour

3 tablespoons red sugar

3 tablespoons green sugar

Nutrition Information Per Serving: Serving Size: 1 Cookie		
Calories: 80	From Fat:	25
Total Fat		3g
Saturated		1g
Cholesterol		4mg
Sodium		55mg
Total Carbohydrate		13g
Dietary Fiber		0g
Sugars		7g
Protein		1g

1) Remove cookie dough from wrapper; cut roll in half crosswise. Sprinkle ¼ cup of the flour onto work surface. Roll out half of dough into 12x7-inch rectangle. Repeat with remaining half of dough and ¼ cup flour.

2) Sprinkle 1 rectangle evenly with red sugar; sprinkle green sugar evenly over second rectangle. Starting with one short side of each rectangle, roll up. Wrap rolls in waxed paper; refrigerate at least 1 hour for easier handling.

3) Heat oven to 350°F. Cut each roll into 16 slices; place 1 inch apart on ungreased cookie sheets.

4) Bake 10 to 13 minutes or until edges are light golden brown. Cool 1 minute; remove from cookie sheets.

Rocky Road Fudge

PREP TIME: 35 MINUTES (READY IN 2 HOURS 5 MINUTES)
SERVINGS: 36 CANDIES

2½ cups sugar

½ cup butter or margarine

1 can (5 oz.) evaporated milk (⅔ cup)

1 jar (7 oz.) marshmallow creme (2 cups)

1 bag (12 oz.) semisweet chocolate chips (2 cups)

¾ cup chopped walnuts

1 teaspoon vanilla

2 cups miniature marshmallows

Nutrition Information Per Serving: Serving Size: 1 Candy		
Calories: 175	From Fat:	65
Total Fat		7g
Saturated		4g
Cholesterol		10mg
Sodium		25mg
Total Carbohydrate		27g
Dietary Fiber		0g
Sugars		25g
Protein		1g

1) Line 9-inch square or 13x9-inch pan with foil, extending foil over sides of pan; butter foil. In 3-quart saucepan, cook sugar, butter and milk over medium heat, stirring constantly, until mixture comes to a boil; boil 5 minutes, stirring constantly. Remove from heat.

2) Stir in marshmallow creme and chocolate chips until smooth. Stir in walnuts and vanilla. Stir in marshmallows (marshmallows should not melt completely). Quickly spread in pan. Cool completely, about 30 minutes. Refrigerate until firm, about 1 hour.

3) Using foil, lift fudge from pan; remove foil from fudge. With large knife, cut into squares. Store in refrigerator.

HIGH ALTITUDE (3500-6000 FT.): No change.

Almond-Toffee-Mocha Squares

BEVERLY STARR | NASHVILLE, ARKANSAS

PREP TIME: 20 MINUTES (READY IN 2 HOURS 50 MINUTES)
SERVINGS: 16 BARS

BROWNIES

1 (19.5-oz.) box Pillsbury® Brownie Classics Fudge Toffee or Traditional Fudge Brownie Mix

1 teaspoon instant coffee granules or crystals

½ cup butter or margarine, melted

¼ cup water

2 eggs

½ cup finely chopped toffee candy bars (two 1.4-oz. bars)

½ cup slivered almonds, toasted*

TOPPING

4 oz. cream cheese (from 8-oz. pkg.), softened

⅓ cup packed brown sugar

1 teaspoon instant coffee granules or crystals

1½ cups whipping cream

1 teaspoon vanilla

1 cup chopped toffee candy bar (four 1.4-oz. bars)

½ cup slivered almonds, toasted*

1) Heat oven to 350°F. Grease bottom only of 13x9-inch pan with shortening or spray with cooking spray. In large bowl, beat brownie mix, 1 teaspoon instant coffee, butter, water and eggs with electric mixer on low speed for 1 minute. Gently stir in ½ cup chopped candy bars and ½ cup almonds. Spread batter in greased pan.

2) Bake at 350°F. for 24 to 28 minutes or until edges are firm. DO NOT OVERBAKE. Cool completely in pan on wire rack, about 1 hour.

3) In medium bowl, beat cream cheese, brown sugar and 1 teaspoon instant coffee with electric mixer on medium speed until smooth. Increase speed to high; beat in cream and vanilla until soft peaks form.

4) Spread cream cheese mixture over cooled brownies. Sprinkle 1 cup chopped candy bars and ½ cup almonds over top. Refrigerate at least 1 hour before serving. Cut into bars. Store in refrigerator.

*NOTE: To toast almonds, spread on cookie sheet; bake at 350°F. for 5 to 7 minutes, stirring occasionally, until golden brown. Or spread almonds in thin layer in microwavable pie pan; microwave on High for 4 to 7 minutes, stirring frequently, until golden brown.

HIGH ALTITUDE (ABOVE 3500 FT.): Make brownies following High Altitude directions on box. Bake at 350°F. for 28 to 32 minutes.

Nutrition Information Per Serving:	
Serving Size: 1 Bar	
Calories: 440	From Fat: 240
Total Fat	26g
Saturated	13g
Cholesterol	85mg
Sodium	250mg
Total Carbohydrate	45g
Dietary Fiber	1g
Sugars	35g
Protein	5g

Nutty Chocolate Chip Biscotti

PAULA CONSOLINI | WILLIAMSTOWN, MASSACHUSETTS

PREP TIME: 35 MINUTES (READY IN 2 HOURS 40 MINUTES)
SERVINGS: 40 COOKIES

1 roll (18 oz.) Pillsbury® refrigerated chocolate chip cookies

1½ teaspoons vanilla

½ teaspoon rum extract

1½ cups chopped almonds, hazelnuts (filberts) or pecans, lightly toasted*

1 cup semisweet chocolate chips

1) Heat oven to 350°F. Grease large cookie sheet with shortening; lightly flour. Into large bowl, break up cookie dough. Sprinkle vanilla and rum extract over dough; mix well. Stir in toasted almonds.

2) Divide dough into 4 equal portions; shape each into 8x1-inch log. Place logs 3 inches apart on cookie sheet; flatten each until about 1½ inches wide.

3) Bake 15 to 20 minutes or until golden brown. Cool 15 minutes. Reduce oven temperature to 200°F.

4) With serrated knife, carefully cut each log into 10 (¾-inch) slices; place cut side down on same cookie sheet.

5) Return to oven; bake at 200°F. 1 hour. Remove cookies from cookie sheet; cool completely, about 20 minutes. Meanwhile, in small microwavable bowl, microwave chocolate chips on High 1 minute. Stir; microwave 1 minute longer, stirring every 15 seconds, until smooth.

6) Dip ¼ of each cookie into melted chocolate; place on waxed paper-lined cookie sheet. Refrigerate 10 minutes to set chocolate before storing.

*NOTE: To toast almonds, spread on cookie sheet; bake at 350°F. 5 to 7 minutes, stirring occasionally, until golden brown. Or spread almonds in thin layer in microwavable pie pan; microwave on High 4 to 7 minutes, stirring frequently, until golden brown.

HIGH ALTITUDE (3500-6500 FT.): Add ⅓ cup flour to cookie dough in bowl. Continue as directed above.

Nutrition Information Per Serving:
Serving Size: 1 Cookie

Calories:	110	From Fat:	60
Total Fat			7g
Saturated			2g
Cholesterol			0mg
Sodium			40mg
Total Carbohydrate			11g
Dietary Fiber			1g
Sugars			7g
Protein			2g

Guess-Again Candy Crunch

PAT PARSONS | BAKERSFIELD, CALIFORNIA

PREP TIME: 30 MINUTES (READY IN 30 MINUTES)
SERVINGS: 50 PIECES

Ⓔ EASY

½ cup white chocolate candy melts for candy making*

½ cup creamy or crunchy peanut butter

1 cup Progresso® plain bread crumbs

1 cup light or dark chocolate candy melts for candy making*

¼ cup dry-roasted peanuts, finely chopped

1) Line cookie sheet with waxed paper. In small microwavable bowl, mix white chocolate candy melts and peanut butter; microwave on Medium 2 minutes. Stir until smooth; stir in bread crumbs. Place mixture on cookie sheet. Top with another sheet of waxed paper; pat or roll into ¼-inch-thick rectangle. Remove top waxed paper.

2) In small microwavable bowl, microwave ½ cup of the light chocolate candy melts on Medium 2 minutes. Stir until smooth; spread evenly over peanut butter layer. Sprinkle with 2 tablespoons of the peanuts. Freeze 5 minutes or refrigerate 15 minutes to set chocolate.

3) In same small microwavable bowl, microwave remaining ½ cup light chocolate candy melts on Medium 2 minutes. Stir until smooth.

4) Remove candy from freezer. Turn candy over; remove waxed paper. Spread light chocolate over peanut butter layer. Immediately sprinkle with remaining 2 tablespoons peanuts; press in lightly. Refrigerate until firm, about 10 minutes. Break or cut into small pieces. Store in refrigerator; serve cold.

*NOTE: Chopped vanilla-flavored and chocolate-flavored candy coating, or white vanilla chips and semi-sweet chocolate chips can be substituted for the white and light or dark chocolate candy melts for candy making.

HIGH ALTITUDE (3500-6500 FT.): No change.

Nutrition Information Per Serving:
Serving Size: 1 Piece

Calories:	60	From Fat:	30
Total Fat			3.5g
Saturated			1.5g
Cholesterol			0mg
Sodium			40mg
Total Carbohydrate			5g
Dietary Fiber			0g
Sugars			3g
Protein			1g

Chocolate-Drizzled Walnut Cookies

PREP TIME: 1 HOUR 15 MINUTES (READY IN 1 HOUR 15 MINUTES)
SERVINGS: 3 DOZEN COOKIES

1 cup butter, softened

$\frac{1}{2}$ cup powdered sugar

1 teaspoon vanilla

2$\frac{1}{4}$ cups all-purpose flour

$\frac{1}{4}$ teaspoon salt

$\frac{3}{4}$ cup finely chopped walnuts

2 oz. semisweet baking chocolate, chopped

1) Heat oven to 375°F. In medium bowl, beat butter and powdered sugar with electric mixer on medium speed until creamy. Beat in vanilla. On low speed, beat in flour and salt until mixture is crumbly. Stir in $\frac{1}{2}$ cup of the walnuts.

2) Shape dough into walnut-sized balls; roll each into 3x$\frac{3}{4}$-inch log. Place on ungreased cookie sheets.

3) Bake 9 to 12 minutes or until set and bottoms are golden brown. Immediately remove from cookie sheets; place on wire racks. Cool completely, about 10 minutes.

4) Meanwhile, in small microwavable bowl, microwave chocolate on High 30 seconds; stir until smooth.

5) Place cooled cookies on sheet of waxed paper. Drizzle chocolate over cookies; sprinkle with remaining $\frac{1}{4}$ cup walnuts.

HIGH ALTITUDE (3500-6000 FT.): No change.

Nutrition Information Per Serving:
Serving Size: 1 Cookie

Calories:	100	From Fat:	60
Total Fat			7g
Saturated			4g
Cholesterol			15mg
Sodium			70mg
Total Carbohydrate			9g
Dietary Fiber			0g
Sugars			3g
Protein			1g

Cream Cheese Sugar Cookies

PREP TIME: 1 HOUR (READY IN 2 HOURS)
SERVINGS: 6 DOZEN COOKIES

1 cup sugar

1 cup butter, softened

1 package (3 oz.) cream cheese, softened

½ teaspoon salt

½ teaspoon almond extract

½ teaspoon vanilla

1 egg yolk

2 cups all-purpose flour

Colored sugar or sprinkles, if desired

Nutrition Information Per Serving:
Serving Size: 1 Undecorated Cookie

Calories:	50	From Fat:	25
Total Fat			3g
Saturated			2g
Cholesterol			10mg
Sodium			45mg
Total Carbohydrate			6g
Dietary Fiber			0g
Sugars			3g
Protein			1g

1) In large bowl, beat all ingredients except flour and colored sugar with electric mixer on medium speed until light and fluffy. Beat in flour until well combined.

2) Shape dough into 3 disks. Wrap dough in plastic wrap; refrigerate 1 hour for easier handling.

3) Heat oven to 375°F. On floured surface with rolling pin, roll out 1 disk of dough at a time to ⅛-inch thickness (keep remaining dough refrigerated). Cut dough with lightly floured 2½-inch round or desired shape cookie cutters; place 1 inch apart on ungreased cookie sheets. Decorate with colored sugar or sprinkles.

4) Bake 6 to 10 minutes or until light golden brown. Immediately remove from cookie sheets.

HIGH ALTITUDE (3500-6000 FT.): Increase flour to 2¼ cups. Bake as directed above.

*Note: To toast pecans, spread on cookie sheet; bake at 350°F. 5 to 7 minutes, stirring occasionally, until golden brown. Or spread pecans in thin layer in microwavable pie pan; microwave on High 4 to 7 minutes, stirring frequently, until golden brown.

Turtles in a Pretzel Tree

PREP TIME: 25 MINUTES (READY IN 35 MINUTES)
SERVINGS: 24 CANDIES

€ EASY

24 small pretzel trees

24 vanilla caramels, unwrapped

¾ cup milk chocolate chips, melted

24 pecan halves, toasted*

Nutrition Information Per Serving:
Serving Size: 1 Candy

Calories:	90	From Fat:	35
Total Fat			4g
Saturated			2g
Cholesterol			0mg
Sodium			55mg
Total Carbohydrate			12g
Dietary Fiber			0g
Sugars			8g
Protein			1g

1) Heat oven to 300°F. Line extra-large cookie sheet with foil; spray foil with cooking spray. Arrange pretzels 1 inch apart on cookie sheet. Top each pretzel with 1 caramel.

2) Bake 5 to 8 minutes or just until caramels begin to melt.

3) Remove cookie sheet from oven. Spoon about 1 teaspoon melted chocolate onto each caramel; immediately press 1 pecan half onto each. Place cookie sheet in freezer until candy is set, about 10 minutes. Peel candies from foil.

HIGH ALTITUDE (3500-6000 FT.): No change.

Chocolate Chip-Peanut Butter Squares

BARRY GARCIA | WEST PALM BEACH, FLORIDA

PREP TIME: 15 MINUTES (READY IN 2 HOURS 20 MINUTES)
SERVINGS: 12 BARS

1½ cups powdered sugar

1½ cups creamy peanut butter

1½ teaspoons vanilla

1 roll (18 oz.) Pillsbury® refrigerated chocolate chip cookies

1) Heat oven to 350°F. In medium bowl, mix powdered sugar, peanut butter and vanilla.

2) Cut cookie dough in half crosswise. With floured fingers, press half of dough in bottom of ungreased 8- or 9-inch square pan. Press peanut butter mixture evenly over dough. Crumble remaining half of dough over peanut butter mixture; carefully spread as evenly as possible.

3) Bake 30 to 35 minutes or until golden brown and firm to the touch. Cool 30 minutes. Refrigerate until chilled, about 1 hour. Cut into bars; serve chilled or at room temperature.

HIGH ALTITUDE (3500-6500 FT.): No change.

Nutrition Information Per Serving: Serving Size: 1 Bar		
Calories: 460	From Fat:	240
Total Fat		27g
Saturated		6g
Cholesterol		5mg
Sodium		290mg
Total Carbohydrate		47g
Dietary Fiber		3g
Sugars		32g
Protein		10g

Linzer Bars

PREP TIME: 25 MINUTES (READY IN 1 HOUR 40 MINUTES)
SERVINGS: 16 BARS

⊖ EASY ⓕ LOW FAT

½ (18-oz.) roll Pillsbury® Refrigerated Sugar Cookies

½ cup seedless raspberry preserves

1 teaspoon cornstarch

¼ cup sliced almonds

Nutrition Information Per Serving: Serving Size: 1 Bar		
Calories: 105	From Fat:	25
Total Fat		3g
Saturated		1g
Cholesterol		0mg
Sodium		57mg
Total Carbohydrate		18g
Dietary Fiber		0g
Sugars		12g
Protein		1g

1) Heat oven to 350°F. Break up cookie dough into ungreased 8-inch square pan. With floured fingers, press dough evenly in bottom of pan to form crust.

2) Bake at 350°F. for 12 to 17 minutes or until edges are golden brown.

3) Meanwhile, in small saucepan, combine preserves and cornstarch; mix well. Cook over medium heat just until mixture comes to a boil, stirring constantly.

4) Remove partially baked crust from oven. Pour preserves mixture evenly over crust; spread to within ¼ inch of edges. Sprinkle evenly with almonds.

5) Return to oven; bake an additional 10 minutes. Cool 1 hour or until completely cooled. Cut into bars.

HIGH ALTITUDE (ABOVE 3500 FT.): Heat oven to 375°F.; use ungreased 9-inch square pan. Bake crust at 375°F. for 12 to 17 minutes. After topping crust, bake an additional 12 minutes.

Cranberry-Pistachio Candy Squares

PREP TIME: 20 MINUTES (READY IN 4 HOURS 10 MINUTES)
SERVINGS: 96 CANDIES

1 bag (12 oz.) semisweet chocolate chips

1 cup butter or margarine

1 package (8 oz.) cream cheese, softened

1/2 cup evaporated milk

1 box (3.4 oz.) instant pistachio pudding and pie filling mix

4 cups powdered sugar

1/2 cup chopped shelled pistachios

1 package (20 oz.) vanilla-flavored candy coating or almond bark, chopped

3/4 cup sweetened dried cranberries

1) Line 13x9-inch pan with foil; spray foil with cooking spray. In 1 1/2-quart saucepan, melt chocolate chips and 1/2 cup of the butter over low heat, stirring frequently, until smooth. Remove from heat. With wire whisk, beat in 1/2 package (4 oz.) of the cream cheese until smooth. Spread in pan. Freeze until set, about 30 minutes.

2) In 2-quart saucepan, melt remaining 1/2 cup butter. Remove from heat. Stir in evaporated milk and pudding mix until blended. Stir in powdered sugar until smooth. Stir in pistachios. Carefully spread thick pudding mixture over frozen chocolate layer. Refrigerate 30 minutes.

3) Meanwhile, in another 2-quart saucepan, melt almond bark over low heat, stirring constantly, until smooth. Stir in remaining 1/2 package cream cheese and the cranberries. Pour over chilled pudding layer; spread to cover. Refrigerate until firm, at least 3 hours.

4) Remove candy from pan by lifting foil. Cut into 1-inch squares; remove from foil. Store in refrigerator.

HIGH ALTITUDE (3500-6000 FT.): No change.

Nutrition Information Per Serving: Serving Size: 1 Candy		
Calories: 110	From Fat:	60
Total Fat		6g
Saturated		4g
Cholesterol		10mg
Sodium		45mg
Total Carbohydrate		13g
Dietary Fiber		0g
Sugars		12g
Protein		1g

White Chocolate-Cinnamon Triangles

ROBIN WILSON | ALTAMONTE SPRINGS, FLORIDA

PREP TIME: 10 MINUTES (READY IN 1 HOUR 55 MINUTES)
SERVINGS: 32 BARS

BARS

- 1 roll (18 oz.) Pillsbury® refrigerated sugar cookies
- 1 cup white chocolate chunks or white vanilla chips
- ½ cup honey-roasted cashews, chopped
- ½ cup toffee bits
- 1 teaspoon ground cinnamon

GLAZE

- ½ cup powdered sugar
- ¼ teaspoon ground cinnamon
- 2½ to 3 teaspoons milk

Nutrition Information Per Serving:
Serving Size: 1 Bar

Calories:	130	From Fat:	50
Total Fat			6g
Saturated			2.5g
Cholesterol			0mg
Sodium			65mg
Total Carbohydrate			18g
Dietary Fiber			0g
Sugars			14g
Protein			2g

1) Heat oven to 350°F. Into large bowl, break up cookie dough. Stir in remaining bar ingredients; press in bottom of ungreased 9-inch square pan.

2) Bake 23 to 27 minutes or until golden brown. Cool 30 minutes.

3) In small bowl, mix glaze ingredients until smooth, adding enough milk for desired drizzling consistency; drizzle over bars. Cool completely, about 45 minutes. Cut into 16 bars; cut each bar in half diagonally to make triangles.

HIGH ALTITUDE (3500-6500 FT.): Bake at 350°F. 26 to 30 minutes. Continue as directed above.

Festive Chex Mix® Wreath

PREP TIME: 15 MINUTES (READY IN 1 HOUR)
SERVINGS: 12

⊖ EASY

- 2 tablespoons butter or margarine
- 25 regular marshmallows
- 1 bag (8.75 oz.) Chex Mix® honey nut snack mix
- ¼ cup small green gumdrops, cut in half
- ¼ cup small red gumdrops, cut in half

Nutrition Information Per Serving:
Serving Size: 1/12 of Recipe

Calories:	195	From Fat:	45
Total Fat			5g
Saturated			2g
Cholesterol			5mg
Sodium			185mg
Total Carbohydrate			35g
Dietary Fiber			0g
Sugars			18g
Protein			2g

1) Spray large cookie sheet with cooking spray. In 4-quart saucepan, melt butter over low heat. Add marshmallows; cook, stirring constantly, until completely melted.

2) Stir in snack mix and red and green gumdrops until well mixed; pour onto cookie sheet.

3) Spray sheet of waxed paper with cooking spray. With paper, sprayed side down, and hands, shape mixture into wreath shape with 4-inch hole in center. Cool completely, about 45 minutes. To serve, cut into slices.

HIGH ALTITUDE (3500-6000 FT.): No change.

Lemon Surprise Cookies

SANDI LAMBERTON | SOLVANG, CALIFORNIA

Pillsbury Bake-Off

PREP TIME: 1 HOUR 15 MINUTES (READY IN 2 HOURS 15 MINUTES)
SERVINGS: 6 DOZEN COOKIES

1½ cups butter or margarine, softened

¾ cup sugar

1 tablespoon lemon extract

2¾ cups Pillsbury BEST® all-purpose flour

1½ cups finely chopped almonds

1 bag (13 oz.) KISSES® milk chocolates, unwrapped

Powdered sugar

½ cup semisweet chocolate chips

1 tablespoon shortening

1) In large bowl with electric mixer, beat butter, sugar and lemon extract on medium speed until light and fluffy. Add flour and almonds; beat on low speed until well blended. Cover; refrigerate at least 1 hour for easier handling.

2) Heat oven to 375°F. Shape 1 scant tablespoon dough around each milk chocolate candy, covering completely; roll in hands to form ball. Place on ungreased cookie sheets.

3) Bake 8 to 12 minutes or until set and bottom edges are light golden brown. Cool 1 minute; remove from cookie sheets. Cool completely, about 15 minutes.

4) Lightly sprinkle cooled cookies with powdered sugar. In 1-quart saucepan, melt chocolate chips and shortening over low heat, stirring until smooth; drizzle over each cookie.

HIGH ALTITUDE (3500-6500 FT.): Decrease butter to 1¼ cups. Bake as directed above.

Nutrition Information Per Serving: Serving Size: 1 Cookie		
Calories: 110	From Fat: 70	
Total Fat		7g
Saturated		3g
Cholesterol		10mg
Sodium		30mg
Total Carbohydrate		10g
Dietary Fiber		0g
Sugars		6g
Protein		2g

Split Seconds

ROBERT E. FELLOWS | SILVER SPRING, MARYLAND

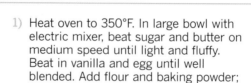

PREP TIME: 1 HOUR 15 MINUTES (READY IN 1 HOUR 15 MINUTES)
SERVINGS: 4 DOZEN COOKIES

²/₃ cup sugar

³/₄ cup butter or margarine, softened

2 teaspoons vanilla

1 egg

2 cups Pillsbury BEST® all-purpose flour

½ teaspoon baking powder

½ cup red jelly or preserves

If your family prefers, substitute apricot or blueberry preserves for the red jelly.

1) Heat oven to 350°F. In large bowl with electric mixer, beat sugar and butter on medium speed until light and fluffy. Beat in vanilla and egg until well blended. Add flour and baking powder; beat on low speed until dough forms.

2) Divide dough into 4 equal portions. On lightly floured surface, shape each portion into 12x³/₄-inch roll; place on ungreased cookie sheets. With handle of wooden spoon or finger, make indentation about ½ inch wide and ¼ inch deep lengthwise down center of each roll. Fill each with 2 tablespoons jelly.

3) Bake 15 to 20 minutes or until light golden brown. Cool slightly, 3 to 5 minutes. Cut each baked roll diagonally into 12 cookies; remove from cookie sheets.

HIGH ALTITUDE (3500-6500 FT.): No change.

Nutrition Information Per Serving:
Serving Size: 1 Cookie

Calories:	70	From Fat:	25
Total Fat			3g
Saturated			1.5g
Cholesterol			10mg
Sodium			25mg
Total Carbohydrate			9g
Dietary Fiber			0g
Sugars			4g
Protein			0g

Peanut Brittle Bars

PREP TIME: 10 MINUTES (READY IN 1 HOUR 45 MINUTES)
SERVINGS: 48 BARS

CRUST
2 cups all-purpose flour

1 cup packed brown sugar

1 teaspoon baking soda

¼ teaspoon salt

1 cup butter or margarine

TOPPING
2 cups salted peanuts

1 cup milk chocolate chips

1 jar (12.5 oz.) caramel topping

3 tablespoons all-purpose flour

Nutrition Information Per Serving:
Serving Size: 1 Bar

Calories:	150	From Fat:	70
Total Fat			8g
Saturated			3g
Cholesterol			10mg
Sodium			120mg
Total Carbohydrate			17g
Dietary Fiber			1g
Sugars			10g
Protein			3g

1) Heat oven to 350°F. Grease 15x10x1-inch pan with shortening. In large bowl, mix all base ingredients except butter. With pastry blender or fork, cut in butter until crumbly. Press mixture evenly in bottom of pan. Bake 8 to 14 minutes or until golden brown.

2) Remove partially baked base from oven. Sprinkle peanuts and chocolate chips over warm base. In small bowl, mix caramel topping and 3 tablespoons flour until well blended. Drizzle evenly over chocolate chips and peanuts.

3) Return to oven; bake 12 to 18 minutes longer or until topping is set and golden brown. Cool completely, about 1 hour. Cut into bars.

HIGH ALTITUDE (3500-6000 FT.): No change.

Caramel Cashew Bars

KATHLEEN KILDSIG | KIEL, WISCONSIN

PREP TIME: 20 MINUTES (READY IN 1 HOUR 25 MINUTES)
SERVINGS: 36 BARS

1 roll (18 oz.) Pillsbury® refrigerated chocolate chip cookies

1 bag (11.5 oz.) milk chocolate chips

1 container (16 oz.) caramel apple dip (1½ cups)

3 cups crisp rice cereal

1¼ cups chopped cashews

Nutrition Information Per Serving:
Serving Size: 1 Bar

Calories:	190	From Fat:	80
Total Fat			9g
Saturated			3g
Cholesterol			0mg
Sodium			150mg
Total Carbohydrate			26g
Dietary Fiber			0g
Sugars			17g
Protein			2g

1) Heat oven to 375°F. Cut cookie dough in half crosswise; cut each section in half lengthwise. Press dough in bottom of ungreased 13x9-inch pan.

2) Bake 10 to 18 minutes or until light golden brown. Cool 15 minutes.

3) In 3-quart saucepan, place 1 cup of the chips and 1 cup of the dip; cook over medium heat, stirring constantly, until melted and smooth. Remove from heat. Stir in cereal and cashews; spread over cooled crust.

4) In 1-quart saucepan, place remaining 1 cup chips and ½ cup dip; cook over medium heat, stirring constantly, until melted and smooth. Spread over cereal mixture. Refrigerate until set, about 30 minutes. Cut into bars.

HIGH ALTITUDE (3500-6500 FT.): Bake at 375°F. 12 to 16 minutes. Continue as directed above.

Honey-Walnut Delights

JOLENE GOEDEN-MASSUCH | OJIBWA , WISCONSIN

PREP TIME: 15 MINUTES (READY IN 55 MINUTES)
SERVINGS: 48 BARS

BARS

1 roll (18 oz.) Pillsbury® refrigerated sugar cookies

1 cup finely chopped walnuts

¼ cup firmly packed brown sugar

1 teaspoon ground cinnamon

¼ cup honey

1 teaspoon lemon juice

GLAZE

½ cup powdered sugar

2 teaspoons water

1 teaspoon honey

1) Heat oven to 350°F. Cut cookie dough into ½-inch slices; arrange in bottom of ungreased 15x10x1- or 17x11x1-inch pan. With floured fingers, press dough evenly in pan.

2) In medium bowl, mix remaining bar ingredients. Drop mixture by ½ teaspoonfuls evenly over cookie dough; spread slightly (dough will not be completely covered).

3) Bake 15 to 20 minutes or until light golden brown. Cool completely, about 20 minutes.

4) In medium bowl, mix glaze ingredients until smooth; drizzle over bars. Cut into bars.

HIGH ALTITUDE (3500-6500 FT.): Bake at 350°F. 17 to 22 minutes. Continue as directed above.

Nutrition Information Per Serving:
Serving Size: 1 Bar

Calories:	80	From Fat:	25
Total Fat			3g
Saturated			0.5g
Cholesterol			0mg
Sodium			35mg
Total Carbohydrate			12g
Dietary Fiber			0g
Sugars			8g
Protein			0g

Fudgy Bonbons

MARY ANNE TYNDALL | WHITEVILLE , NORTH CAROLINA

Pillsbury
Bake-Off

PREP TIME: 1 HOUR 10 MINUTES (READY IN 1 HOUR 10 MINUTES)
SERVINGS: 5 DOZEN COOKIES

1 bag (12 oz.) semisweet chocolate chips (2 cups)

¼ cup butter or margarine

1 can (14 oz.) sweetened condensed milk (not evaporated)

2 cups Pillsbury BEST® all-purpose flour

½ cup finely chopped nuts, if desired

1 teaspoon vanilla

60 KISSES® milk chocolates, unwrapped

2 oz. white chocolate baking bar or vanilla-flavored candy coating (almond bark)

1 teaspoon shortening or oil

1) Heat oven to 350°F. In 2-quart saucepan, cook chocolate chips and butter over very low heat, stirring constantly, until chips are melted and smooth (mixture will be stiff). Stir in condensed milk. In large bowl, mix chocolate mixture, flour, nuts and vanilla until dough forms.

2) Shape 1 tablespoon dough (use measuring spoon) around each milk chocolate candy, covering completely; place 1 inch apart on ungreased cookie sheets.

3) Bake 6 to 8 minutes (do not overbake). Cookies will be soft and appear shiny but will become firm as they cool. Remove from cookie sheets. Cool completely, about 15 minutes.

4) Meanwhile, in 1-quart saucepan, cook baking bar and shortening over low heat, stirring constantly, until melted and smooth. Drizzle over cooled cookies; let stand until set. Store in tightly covered container.

HIGH ALTITUDE (3500-6500 FT.): Increase flour to 2¼ cups. Bake as directed above.

Nutrition Information Per Serving:
Serving Size: 1 Cookie

Calories:	100	From Fat:	45
Total Fat			5g
Saturated Fat			3g
Cholesterol			5mg
Sodium			20mg
Total Carbohydrate			14g
Dietary Fiber			0g
Sugars			10g
Protein			2g

More Scrumptious Desserts

Decadent desserts guaranteed to
dazzle your taste buds!

CHERRY-ALMOND TORTE
PG. 334

IRISH CREAM-TOPPED BROWNIE
DESSERT
PG. 323

GINGERED APPLE-BERRY CRISP
PG. 330

Almond Crumble Cherry Pie

| PREP TIME: | 15 MINUTES (READY IN 55 MINUTES) |
| SERVINGS: | 8 |

CRUST

1 Pillsbury® refrigerated pie crust (from 15-oz. box), softened as directed on box

TOPPING

4 oz. marzipan (about 1/3 cup)

3 tablespoons butter or margarine, softened

1/2 cup old-fashioned oats

2 tablespoons all-purpose flour

FILLING

2 cans (21 oz. each) cherry pie filling

1/4 teaspoon almond extract

1) Heat oven to 375°F. Make pie crust as directed on box for one-crust baked shell using 9-inch glass pie pan. Bake 8 to 10 minutes or just until set but not brown.

2) Meanwhile, in small bowl, place marzipan and butter; with pastry blender or fork, mix until well blended. Stir in oats and flour until crumbly. In large bowl, mix filling ingredients.

3) Remove partially baked shell from oven. Pour filling into shell. Crumble topping over filling.

4) Return to oven; bake 30 to 40 minutes longer or until topping is golden brown and filling is bubbly around edges. If necessary, after 15 minutes of baking, cover edge of crust with strips of foil to prevent excessive browning.

HIGH ALTITUDE (3500-6000 FT.): Use 9-inch deep-dish pie pan. In Step 1, bake crust at 375°F. 10 to 12 minutes. In Step 4, bake 35 to 45 minutes and continue as directed.

Nutrition Information Per Serving:
Serving Size: 1/8 of Recipe

Calories:	430	From Fat:	140
Total Fat			16g
Saturated			6g
Cholesterol			20mg
Sodium			160mg
Total Carbohydrate			68g
Dietary Fiber			2g
Sugars			43g
Protein			4g

Rum-Caramel Tropical Sundaes

PREP TIME: 15 MINUTES (READY IN 15 MINUTES)
SERVINGS: 6

⊖ EASY   ⏹ LOW FAT

½ cup fat-free caramel ice cream
topping

1 tablespoon rum

4 slices (½-inch-thick) cored fresh
pineapple

2 small bananas

3 cups fat-free vanilla ice cream
or frozen yogurt

Nutrition Information Per Serving:
Serving Size: 1/6 of Recipe

Calories:	220	From Fat:	5
Total Fat			1g
Saturated			0g
Cholesterol			0mg
Sodium			140mg
Total Carbohydrate			51g
Dietary Fiber			4g
Sugars			36g
Protein			4g

1) In 10-inch skillet, mix ice cream topping and rum. Cook over medium heat 2 to 3 minutes, stirring occasionally, until topping is melted and mixture is smooth.

2) Cut each pineapple slice into 6 wedges. Peel bananas; cut diagonally into ½-inch-thick slices. Gently stir pineapple and bananas into topping mixture. Cook over medium heat about 2 minutes, stirring gently, until fruit is thoroughly heated.

3) Into each dessert dish, spoon ½ cup ice cream. Top each with fruit mixture.

HIGH ALTITUDE (ABOVE 3500 FT.): No change.

Caribbean Sponge Cake Desserts

PREP TIME: 10 MINUTES
SERVINGS: 4

⊖ EASY

4 individually wrapped cream-filled
sponge cakes (from 15-oz. pkg.)

¼ cup lemon curd (from 10-oz. jar)

½ cup chopped refrigerated mango
(from 24-oz. jar)

1 (7-oz.) aerosol can whipped cream

1 tablespoon coconut, toasted

Nutrition Information Per Serving:
Serving Size: 1/4 of Recipe

Calories:	335	From Fat:	145
Total Fat			16g
Saturated			5g
Cholesterol			20mg
Sodium			240mg
Total Carbohydrate			45g
Dietary Fiber			1g
Sugars			27g
Protein			3g

1) Unwrap sponge cakes. For each dessert, cut 1 sponge cake crosswise into 4 pieces; arrange pieces, cut side down, on individual dessert plate.

2) Spoon 1 tablespoon lemon curd onto each. Top with mango and whipped cream. Sprinkle with toasted coconut.

HIGH ALTITUDE (ABOVE 3500 FT.): No change.

Orange Cappuccino Tart

PREP TIME: 20 MINUTES (READY IN 2 HOURS)
SERVINGS: 12

TART

1 box (1 lb. 3.8 oz.) fudge brownie mix

¼ cup instant orange cappuccino-flavored coffee drink mix

1 teaspoon grated orange peel

½ cup vegetable oil

¼ cup water

2 eggs

TOPPING

¾ cup hot fudge ice cream topping

¼ cup instant orange cappuccino-flavored coffee drink mix

3 cups vanilla ice cream or frozen yogurt

1) Heat oven to 350°F. Wrap foil around outside bottom and side of ungreased 10-inch tart pan with removable bottom; spray pan with cooking spray. In large bowl, mix brownie mix, ¼ cup drink mix, the orange peel, oil, water and eggs with spoon until well blended. Pour and spread batter evenly into pan.

2) Bake 30 to 38 minutes or until edges pull away from side of pan. Cool completely in pan on wire rack, about 1 hour.

3) In 1-quart saucepan, heat fudge topping over low heat, stirring constantly, until thoroughly heated. Stir in ¼ cup drink mix.

4) To serve, cut tart into wedges; place on individual dessert plates. Top each serving with ¼ cup ice cream; drizzle each with 1 tablespoon warm topping mixture.

HIGH ALTITUDE (3500-6000 FT.): Add 3 tablespoons flour to dry brownie mix, decrease oil to ¼ cup and increase water to ⅓ cup. Continue as directed above.

Nutrition Information Per Serving:
Serving Size: 1/12 of Recipe

Calories:	440	From Fat:	160
Total Fat			18g
Saturated			5g
Cholesterol			50mg
Sodium			290mg
Total Carbohydrate			65g
Dietary Fiber			0g
Sugars			48g
Protein			5g

Banana Dessert Wraps

HEATHER SNEDIC | LISLE, ILLINOIS

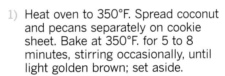

PREP TIME: 20 MINUTES (READY IN 40 MINUTES)
SERVINGS: 4

½ cup coconut

½ cup chopped pecans

1 Pillsbury® Refrigerated Pie Crust (from 15-oz. box), softened as directed on box

¼ cup sugar

½ teaspoon ground cinnamon

¼ teaspoon ground nutmeg

4 (5 to 6 inch) firm, ripe bananas

⅓ cup semisweet chocolate chips

1 (12-oz.) jar hot caramel ice cream topping, heated

Whipped cream, if desired

1 cup vanilla ice cream

tip

If your family prefers, substitute vanilla chips or milk chocolate chips and hot fudge ice cream topping.

1) Heat oven to 350°F. Spread coconut and pecans separately on cookie sheet. Bake at 350°F. for 5 to 8 minutes, stirring occasionally, until light golden brown; set aside.

2) Increase oven temperature to 450°F. Remove pie crust from pouch; place crust flat on work surface. If necessary, press out folds or creases. With rolling pin, roll crust until 12 inches in diameter.

3) In small bowl, mix sugar, cinnamon and nutmeg. Reserve 1 tablespoon sugar mixture; sprinkle remaining sugar mixture evenly over crust. Cut crust into 4 wedge-shaped pieces.

4) Place 1 banana lengthwise on each crust wedge, about ¾ inch from curved edge (if banana is too long, trim ends so it fits within crust, at least ¼ inch from each edge). Push about 1 rounded tablespoon chocolate chips, points first, into top and sides of each banana.

5) Bring curved edge and point of each crust wedge up over banana to meet; pinch seam and ends to seal, shaping crust around banana. Sprinkle tops of wrapped bananas with reserved 1 tablespoon sugar mixture; place on ungreased cookie sheet.

6) Bake at 450°F. for 10 to 14 minutes or until golden brown. Immediately remove from cookie sheet. Cool 5 minutes.

7) To serve, drizzle or spread about 2 tablespoons warm caramel topping on each individual dessert plate. Top each with baked banana, whipped cream and additional caramel topping, if desired. Sprinkle coconut and pecans over top of each. Serve with ice cream.

HIGH ALTITUDE (ABOVE 3500 FT.): After toasting coconut and pecans, increase oven temperature to 425°F. Bake wrapped bananas at 425°F. for 15 to 19 minutes.

Nutrition Information Per Serving: Serving Size: 1/4 of Recipe		
Calories: 675	From Fat:	335
Total Fat		37g
Saturated		15g
Cholesterol		25mg
Sodium		330mg
Total Carbohydrate		85g
Dietary Fiber		5g
Sugars		45g
Protein		6g

Chocolate-Almond Ice Cream Pie

PREP TIME: 30 MINUTES (READY IN 5 HOURS 30 MINUTES)   EASY
SERVINGS: 8

3 tablespoons butter or margarine, melted

³/₄ cup sliced almonds

¹/₃ cup sugar

1 Pillsbury® refrigerated pie crust (from 15-oz. box), softened as directed on box

1 quart (4 cups) chocolate ice cream, slightly softened

1) Heat oven to 400°F. In small bowl, mix melted butter, almonds and sugar. Spoon ¹/₃ of mixture into shallow baking pan; spread evenly. Bake 5 to 7 minutes, stirring once, until toasted. Set aside to cool, stirring once.

2) Meanwhile, place pie crust in ungreased 9-inch glass pie pan; press crust firmly against sides and bottom. Fold excess crust under and press together to form thick crust edge; flute. DO NOT PRICK CRUST. Spoon remaining ²/₃ of almond mixture into bottom and up side of crust; press against crust.

3) Bake crust 12 to 14 minutes or until golden brown. Cool completely, about 1 hour.

4) Spoon ice cream into cooled baked crust. Sprinkle cooled almond mixture over ice cream. Freeze uncovered until firm, about 4 hours. Let pie stand at room temperature 10 minutes before cutting. Pie can be stored in freezer up to 1 week.

HIGH ALTITUDE (3500-6500 FT.): No change.

Nutrition Information Per Serving:
Serving Size: 1/8 of Recipe

Calories:	720	From Fat:	390
Total Fat		43g	
Saturated		18g	
Cholesterol		50mg	
Sodium		490mg	
Total Carbohydrate		79g	
Dietary Fiber		3g	
Sugars		28g	
Protein		7g	

tip

Substitute your favorite flavor ice cream or a different type of nut. Caramel ice cream and cashews are a tasty combo.

Granola–Apple Mini Cheesecakes

NICK DEMATTEO | SUNNYSIDE, NEW YORK

PREP TIME: 25 MINUTES (READY IN 2 HOURS 5 MINUTES)
SERVINGS: 24 MINI CHEESECAKES

1 (8.9-oz.) box Nature Valley® Roasted Almond Crunchy Granola Bars (12 bars)

¼ cup butter or margarine, melted

3 (8-oz.) pkg. cream cheese, softened

¾ cup sugar

1 teaspoon vanilla

3 eggs

1 (21-oz.) can apple pie filling

1) Heat oven to 350°F. Line 24 regular-size muffin cups with foil baking cups. Break 8 granola bars into pieces; place in gallon-size resealable food-storage plastic bag or in food processor; seal bag and crush with rolling pin or meat mallet or process until fine crumbs form.

2) In medium bowl, mix crumbs and melted butter until well combined. Place scant tablespoon crumb mixture in each foil-lined muffin cup; press in bottom of cup to form crust.

3) In large bowl, beat cream cheese and sugar with electric mixer on medium speed until creamy. Beat in vanilla and eggs until well combined. Cut or break remaining 4 granola bars into ½-inch pieces; stir into cream cheese mixture. Spoon scant ¼ cup mixture over crust in each cup.

4) Bake at 350°F. for 20 to 25 minutes or until set. Cool in pans on wire rack 15 minutes. Top each cheesecake with 1 tablespoon apple pie filling. Refrigerate until chilled, about 1 hour.

5) To serve, remove cheesecakes from muffin pans. Store in refrigerator.

HIGH ALTITUDE (ABOVE 3500 FT.): No change.

Nutrition Information Per Serving:
Serving Size: 1 Mini Cheesecake

Calories:	220	From Fat:	125
Total Fat			14g
Saturated			8g
Cholesterol			65mg
Sodium			150mg
Total Carbohydrate			20g
Dietary Fiber			1g
Sugars			15g
Protein			4g

Candy Bar Cheesecake

PREP TIME: 20 MINUTES (READY IN 4 HOURS 35 MINUTES)
SERVINGS: 12

CRUST

2 cups chocolate cookie crumbs (from 15-oz. box)

⅓ cup granulated sugar

¼ cup butter or margarine, melted

FILLING

2 Snickers® candy bars (3.7 oz. each), unwrapped

3 packages (8 oz. each) cream cheese, softened

1 cup packed brown sugar

1 container (8 oz.) sour cream

1 teaspoon vanilla

2 eggs

TOPPING

Milk chocolate ice cream topping, if desired

1) Heat oven to 350°F. In ungreased 9-inch springform pan, mix cookie crumbs and granulated sugar. Drizzle melted butter over mixture; toss with fork until well combined. Firmly press mixture in bottom and 2 inches up side of pan to form crust.

2) Cut each candy bar in half lengthwise; cut each half into 8 pieces. Set aside. In large bowl, beat cream cheese and brown sugar with electric mixer on medium speed until fluffy. Beat in sour cream, vanilla and eggs until smooth, scraping down sides of bowl once. Stir in candy pieces. Pour mixture into crust-lined pan.

3) Bake 1¼ hours or until knife inserted slightly off center comes out clean (center will be slightly jiggly). Cool completely in pan on wire rack, about 1 hour.

4) Carefully remove side of pan. Refrigerate until chilled before serving, at least 2 hours.

5) Cut cheesecake into wedges; place on individual dessert plates. Drizzle each serving with ice cream topping. Store in refrigerator.

HIGH ALTITUDE (3500-6000 FT.): When baking cheesecake, place small pan with 1 inch water in oven on lowest oven rack to help prevent cracking.

Nutrition Information Per Serving:
Serving Size: 1/12 of Recipe

Calories:	580	From Fat:	320
Total Fat			36g
Saturated			20g
Cholesterol			120mg
Sodium			410mg
Total Carbohydrate			54g
Dietary Fiber			1g
Sugars			44g
Protein			9g

Irish Cream-Topped Brownie Dessert

PREP TIME: 15 MINUTES (READY IN 3 HOURS 45 MINUTES)
SERVINGS: 9

BROWNIE BASE

1 box (10.25 oz.) fudge brownie mix

¼ cup vegetable oil

2 tablespoons Irish cream liqueur

2 eggs

IRISH CREAM TOPPING

1 carton (8 oz.) whipping cream (1 cup)

¼ cup milk

¼ cup instant vanilla pudding and pie filling mix (half of 3.4 oz. box)

3 tablespoons Irish cream liqueur

1 bar (1.4 oz.) chocolate-covered toffee candy, crushed

Nutrition Information Per Serving: Serving Size: 1/9 of Recipe	
Calories: 340	From Fat: 170
Total Fat	19g
Saturated	8g
Cholesterol	85mg
Sodium	230mg
Total Carbohydrate	38g
Dietary Fiber	0g
Sugars	29g
Protein	4g

1) Heat oven to 350°F. Grease bottom only of 8-inch square pan with shortening. In large bowl, stir brownie mix, oil, 2 tablespoons liqueur and eggs with spoon about 50 strokes or until blended. Spread batter in pan.

2) Bake 23 to 26 minutes or until toothpick inserted in center comes out clean. Cool completely, about 1 hour.

3) In medium bowl, beat whipping cream, milk, pudding mix and 3 tablespoons liqueur with electric mixer on high speed 4 to 6 minutes or until soft peaks form. Spread mixture over cooled brownies. Sprinkle with crushed candy. Cover; refrigerate at least 2 hours before serving. Cut into squares. Store in refrigerator.

HIGH ALTITUDE (3500-6000 FT.): No change.

Mint Meringue Parfaits

PREP TIME: 15 MINUTES
SERVINGS: 4   EASY

1 cup frozen whipped topping, thawed

⅛ teaspoon mint extract

1 pint (2 cups) chocolate ice cream

½ cup chocolate ice cream topping

8 mint meringue cookies (from 4.25-oz. pkg.), coarsely crushed

Nutrition Information Per Serving: Serving Size: 1/4 of Recipe	
Calories: 335	From Fat: 100
Total Fat	11g
Saturated	5g
Cholesterol	20mg
Sodium	85mg
Total Carbohydrate	55g
Dietary Fiber	1g
Sugars	42g
Protein	4g

1) In medium bowl, combine whipped topping and mint extract; stir gently to blend.

2) In each of four tall glasses, layer ¼ cup ice cream, 1 tablespoon chocolate topping, 1 heaping tablespoon crushed cookies and 2 tablespoons mint-flavored whipped topping. Repeat layers. Sprinkle with remaining crushed cookies. Serve immediately.

HIGH ALTITUDE (ABOVE 3500 FT.): No change.

Oats 'n Honey Granola Pie

SUZANNE CONRAD | FINDLAY, OHIO

Pillsbury Bake-Off

PREP TIME: 15 MINUTES (READY IN 1 HOUR 35 MINUTES)
SERVINGS: 8

CRUST

1 Pillsbury® Refrigerated Pie Crust (from 15-oz. box), softened as directed on box

FILLING

½ cup butter or margarine

½ cup packed light brown sugar

¾ cup corn syrup

⅛ teaspoon salt

1 teaspoon vanilla

3 eggs, lightly beaten

4 Nature Valley® Oats 'n Honey Crunchy Granola Bars (2 pouches from 8.9-oz. box), crushed*

½ cup chopped walnuts

¼ cup quick-cooking or old-fashioned oats

¼ cup chocolate chips

Whipped cream or ice cream, if desired

1) Heat oven to 350°F. Place pie crust in 9-inch glass pie pan as directed on box for one-crust filled pie.

2) In large microwavable bowl, microwave butter on High for 50 to 60 seconds or until melted. Stir in brown sugar and corn syrup until blended. Beat in salt, vanilla and eggs. Stir crushed granola bars and all remaining filling ingredients into brown sugar mixture. Pour into pie crust-lined pan.

3) Bake at 350°F. for 40 to 50 minutes or until filling is set and crust is golden brown, covering crust edge with foil during last 15 to 20 minutes of baking to prevent excessive browning. Cool at least 30 minutes before serving. Serve warm, at room temperature or chilled. Serve with whipped cream or ice cream. Store in refrigerator.

*NOTE: To easily crush granola bars, do not unwrap. Use rolling pin to crush bars.

HIGH ALTITUDE (ABOVE 3500 FT.): No change.

Nutrition Information Per Serving:
Serving Size: 1/8 of Recipe

Calories:	525	From Fat:	250
Total Fat			28g
Saturated			11g
Cholesterol			110mg
Sodium			370mg
Total Carbohydrate			61g
Dietary Fiber			2g
Sugars			32g
Protein			7g

Caramel-Coffee Ice Cream Sandwiches

PREP TIME: 45 MINUTES (READY IN 2 HOURS 45 MINUTES EASY
SERVINGS: 6 SANDWICHES

1 (1 lb. 2-oz.) pkg. Pillsbury® Ready To Bake!™ Big Deluxe Classics® Chocolate Chip Cookies

¼ cup hot caramel ice cream topping (do not heat)

1 pint (2 cups) coffee ice cream, slightly softened

¼ cup chocolate and/or colored sprinkles

1) Heat oven to 350°F. Place cookie dough about 2 inches apart on ungreased cookie sheet. Bake at 350°F. for 12 to 16 minutes or until light golden brown. Cool 1 minute. Remove from cookie sheets; place on wire racks. Cool 15 minutes or until completely cooled.

2) Cut six 12x9-inch sheets of foil. Place 2 baked cookies, bottom side up, on each foil sheet. Spread 1 teaspoon caramel topping on each cookie.

3) For each sandwich, place about ⅓ cup ice cream in center of 1 caramel-topped cookie; flatten slightly. Place second cookie, caramel side down, on ice cream. Gently press cookies together in center to form ice cream sandwich; ice cream should spread to edge of cookies. Gently roll ice cream edge of sandwich in chocolate sprinkles. Quickly wrap sandwich in foil; immediately place in freezer. Freeze at least 2 hours or until firm. Let stand 5 to 10 minutes before serving.

HIGH ALTITUDE (ABOVE 3500 FT.): Bake cookies at 350°F. for 13 to 17 minutes.

Nutrition Information Per Serving:
Serving Size: 1 Sandwich

Calories:	595	From Fat:	225
Total Fat			25g
Saturated			9g
Cholesterol			15mg
Sodium			420mg
Total Carbohydrate			83g
Dietary Fiber			3g
Sugars			47g
Protein			10g

tip

If your kids are not coffee lovers, use other favorite ice cream varieties and toppings to make this super simple dessert.

Raspberry-Amaretto Tarts

PREP TIME: 20 MINUTES
SERVINGS: 6

 EASY

1 (8-oz.) container whipped cream cheese spread

¼ cup powdered sugar

1 to 2 tablespoons amaretto

6 single-serve baked sweet tart shells (from 8.5-oz. pkg.) or graham cracker crusts (from 4-oz. pkg.)

36 fresh raspberries (about ¾ cup)

1) In medium bowl, combine cream cheese spread, powdered sugar and amaretto; beat until smooth.

2) Divide cream cheese mixture evenly into tart shells. Top each with 6 raspberries.

HIGH ALTITUDE (ABOVE 3500 FT.): No change.

Nutrition Information Per Serving:
Serving Size: 1 Tart

Calories:	255	From Fat:	155
Total Fat			17g
Saturated			10g
Cholesterol			55mg
Sodium			260mg
Total Carbohydrate			20g
Dietary Fiber			1g
Sugars			11g
Protein			5g

Pumpkin Pie Squares

PREP TIME: 15 MINUTES (READY IN 2 HOURS)
SERVINGS: 12

CRUST

¾ cup all-purpose flour

¾ cup quick-cooking or old-fashioned oats

½ to 1 cup chopped nuts

½ cup butter or margarine, softened

1 box (3.5 oz.) butterscotch pudding and pie filling mix (not instant)

FILLING

2 eggs

1 cup flaked or shredded coconut, if desired

1½ teaspoons pumpkin pie spice

1 can (15 oz.) pumpkin (2 cups)

1 can (14 oz.) sweetened condensed milk (not evaporated)

1) Heat oven to 350°F. In large bowl, mix all crust ingredients until well combined. Press mixture in bottom of ungreased 13x9-inch pan.

2) In same bowl, beat eggs. Stir in all remaining filling ingredients until blended. Pour over crust.

3) Bake 35 to 45 minutes or until knife inserted in center comes out clean. Cool completely, about 1 hour. Cut into squares. If desired, serve topped with whipped cream or ice cream and sprinkle with pumpkin pie spice. Store in refrigerator.

HIGH ALTITUDE (3500-6000 FT.): Bake crust at 375°F. about 8 minutes. Add filling; bake 38 to 48 minutes.

Nutrition Information Per Serving:
Serving Size: 1/12 of Recipe

Calories: 315	From Fat: 135
Total Fat	15g
Saturated	7g
Cholesterol	65mg
Sodium	150mg
Total Carbohydrate	38g
Dietary Fiber	2g
Sugars	25g
Protein	7g

tip

Pecans are a good choice for the chopped nuts in this recipe, but you can use walnuts or almonds.

White Chocolate-Cranberry-Pecan Tart

PREP TIME: 25 MINUTES (READY IN 3 HOURS 15 MINUTES)
SERVINGS: 12

CRUST

1 Pillsbury® refrigerated pie crust
(from 15-oz. box), softened as
directed on box

FILLING

1 cup fresh or frozen cranberries

1 cup pecan halves

1 cup white vanilla chips

3 eggs

¾ cup packed brown sugar

¾ cup light corn syrup

2 tablespoons all-purpose flour

1 teaspoon grated orange peel

1) Place cookie sheet in oven on middle
oven rack; heat oven to 400°F. Spray
sheet of foil (large enough to cover
pie) with cooking spray. Place pie
crust in 10-inch tart pan with removable
bottom as directed on box for one-crust
filled pie.

2) Layer cranberries, pecans and vanilla
chips in crust-lined pan. In large bowl,
beat eggs with wire whisk. Beat in brown
sugar, corn syrup, flour and orange peel
until well blended. Pour over cranberry
mixture.

3) Place tart on cookie sheet in oven; bake
35 to 45 minutes or until crust is golden
brown and filling is set in center. After 25
minutes of baking, cover pie with foil,
sprayed side down, to prevent excessive
browning. Cool completely, about 2
hours. If desired, serve pie with whipped
cream. Store in refrigerator.

HIGH ALTITUDE (3500-6000 FT.): Bake at 400°F. 35
to 40 minutes.

Nutrition Information Per Serving:
Serving Size: 1/12 of Recipe

Calories:	370	From Fat:	150
Total Fat		17g	
Saturated		6g	
Cholesterol		60mg	
Sodium		125mg	
Total Carbohydrate		50g	
Dietary Fiber		1g	
Sugars		31g	
Protein		4g	

Apple-Cranberry Crisp with Eggnog Sauce

PREP TIME: 25 MINUTES (READY IN 1 HOUR 5 MINUTES)
SERVINGS: 10

SAUCE

- 2 containers (3.5 to 4 oz. each) refrigerated vanilla pudding
- 1 cup eggnog

FRUIT MIXTURE

- 5 cups sliced peeled apples (5 medium)
- 2 cups fresh or frozen cranberries
- ¾ cup granulated sugar
- 2 tablespoons all-purpose flour

TOPPING

- ⅔ cup all-purpose flour
- 1 cup quick-cooking oats
- ¾ cup packed brown sugar
- ½ teaspoon ground cinnamon
- ½ cup butter or margarine, cut into pieces

1) Place pudding in medium bowl. Gradually stir eggnog into pudding until blended. Cover; refrigerate.

2) Heat oven to 375°F. In large bowl, mix all fruit mixture ingredients. Spread evenly in ungreased 12x8-inch (2-quart) glass baking dish.

3) In another medium bowl, stir together ⅔ cup flour, oats, brown sugar and cinnamon. With pastry blender or fork, cut in butter until mixture resembles fine crumbs. Spoon over fruit mixture.

4) Bake 35 to 40 minutes or until deep golden brown and bubbly. Serve warm with chilled sauce. Store sauce in refrigerator.

HIGH ALTITUDE (3500-6000 FT.): Bake at 375°F. 50 to 55 minutes.

Nutrition Information Per Serving:
Serving Size: 1/10 of Recipe

Calories:	370	From Fat:	110
Total Fat			13g
Saturated			7g
Cholesterol			40mg
Sodium			110mg
Total Carbohydrate			62g
Dietary Fiber			3g
Sugars			45g
Protein			4g

tip

Prepare the crisp and sauce a day ahead and store separately in the refrigerator. To warm the crisp, place it in a 325°F. oven for about 15 minutes.

Gingered Apple-Berry Crisp

PREP TIME: 15 MINUTES (READY IN 55 MINUTES)
SERVINGS: 6 (1/2 CUP EACH)

TOPPING

- ¾ cup quick-cooking oats
- ¾ cup crushed gingersnap cookies
- ½ cup all-purpose flour
- ¼ cup packed brown sugar
- ½ cup butter or margarine, cut into small pieces

FRUIT MIXTURE

- 1 cup frozen unsweetened blueberries
- 1 cup frozen unsweetened raspberries
- ½ teaspoon ground ginger
- 1 can (21 oz.) apple pie filling

1) Heat oven to 350°F. Spray 12x8-inch (2-quart) glass baking dish with cooking spray. In large bowl, combine all topping ingredients except butter. With pastry blender or fork, cut in butter until crumbly.

2) In large bowl, mix all fruit mixture ingredients; pour into baking dish. Sprinkle topping evenly over fruit.

3) Bake 35 to 40 minutes or until fruit mixture is bubbly and topping is golden brown. If necessary, cover with foil during last 15 to 20 minutes of baking to prevent excessive browning.

HIGH ALTITUDE (3500-6000 FT.): Heat oven to 375°F. Continue as directed above.

Nutrition Information Per Serving:
Serving Size: 1/2 Cup

Calories:	480	From Fat:	160
Total Fat			18g
Saturated			10g
Cholesterol			40mg
Sodium			200mg
Total Carbohydrate			74g
Dietary Fiber			6g
Sugars			46g
Protein			5g

Mocha-Hazelnut Cream-Filled Cake

PREP TIME: 35 MINUTES (READY IN 3 HOURS)
SERVINGS: 16

1 box (18.25 oz.) butter recipe chocolate cake mix

Butter

Water

Eggs

2 teaspoons instant coffee granules or crystals

2 bags (12 oz. each) semisweet chocolate chips

1 bottle (16 oz.) refrigerated hazelnut-flavor coffee creamer

1 package (8 oz.) cream cheese, softened

2 tablespoons chopped hazelnuts (filberts)

1) Heat oven to 350°F. Grease bottoms only of two 9-inch round pans. Prepare cake mix as directed on box using butter, water and eggs and adding coffee granules; pour batter into pans. Bake as directed on box. Cool 10 minutes; remove from pans and place on wire racks.

2) In 3-quart saucepan, cook chocolate chips and coffee creamer over medium-low heat about 8 minutes, stirring constantly, until melted. Remove from heat; beat in cream cheese with wire whisk until smooth. Cover; refrigerate about 30 minutes.

3) In small microwavable bowl, reserve ½ cup of the chocolate mixture; set aside for topping. Beat remaining mixture on medium-high speed 8 minutes or until it forms a light and fluffy frosting.

4) Place 1 cake layer on serving plate, rounded side down. Spread 1-inch-thick layer of frosting over cake. Top with second cake layer, rounded side up. Spread frosting on side and top of cake.

5) Microwave reserved ½ cup chocolate mixture on High 30 seconds or until soft; spread over top of cake. Sprinkle hazelnuts around top edge. Cover loosely; refrigerate at least 1 hour before serving. Store in refrigerator.

HIGH ALTITUDE (3500-6000 FT.): When making cake, follow High Altitude directions on box. Continue as directed above.

Nutrition Information Per Serving:
Serving Size: 1/16 of Recipe

Calories:	550	From Fat:	280
Total Fat			32g
Saturated			16g
Cholesterol			70mg
Sodium			400mg
Total Carbohydrate			63g
Dietary Fiber			4g
Sugars			45g
Protein			6g

To keep the frosting from sticking to the plastic wrap, poke toothpicks around the outside edge of the frosted cake before covering with plastic wrap. Remove the toothpicks before serving.

Lime-Kiwi Cloud with Strawberry Sauce

PREP TIME: 30 MINUTES (READY IN 3 HOURS 30 MINUTES)
SERVINGS: 15

DESSERT

1 large angel food cake, cut into 1-inch cubes (about 12 cups)

2 containers (6 oz. each) Yoplait® Custard Style® lowfat vanilla yogurt

2 teaspoons grated lime peel

¼ cup lime juice

1 container (8 oz.) frozen light whipped topping, thawed

6 kiwi fruit, peeled, sliced

SAUCE

2 packages (10 oz. each) frozen strawberries in syrup, thawed

2 teaspoons cornstarch

1) In ungreased 13x9-inch (3-quart) glass baking dish, arrange half of cake cubes.

2) In large bowl, mix yogurt, lime peel and lime juice until well blended. Fold in whipped topping.

3) Spoon half of mixture over cake cubes in baking dish; press down to smooth layer. Arrange kiwi fruit slices over mixture. Repeat cake and yogurt layers; press down. Cover; refrigerate 3 hours or until set.

4) Meanwhile, drain strawberries, reserving liquid in 2-quart saucepan; set strawberries aside. Stir cornstarch into liquid until well blended. Heat to boiling over medium heat, stirring constantly. Remove from heat; cool 15 minutes. Stir in strawberries. Refrigerate until chilled, about 30 minutes.

5) To serve, cut dessert into squares; place on individual dessert plates. Spoon sauce over each serving. Store in refrigerator.

HIGH ALTITUDE (3500-6000 FT.): In Step 4, boil 2 to 3 minutes after adding cornstarch. Continue as directed.

Nutrition Information Per Serving:
Serving Size: 1/15 of Recipe

Calories: 190	From Fat: 35
Total Fat	4g
Saturated Fat	4g
Cholesterol	0mg
Sodium	190mg
Total Carbohydrate	35g
Dietary Fiber	2g
Sugars	31g
Protein	3g

Pear and Ginger Cream Tart

PREP TIME: 45 MINUTES (READY IN 1 HOUR 45 MINUTES)
SERVINGS: 8

PASTRY CREAM

1½ cups milk

1 tablespoon grated gingerroot

4 egg yolks

¾ cup sugar

½ cup all-purpose flour

2 tablespoons butter

1½ teaspoons vanilla

CRUST

1 Pillsbury® refrigerated pie crust (from 15-oz. box), softened as directed on box

TOPPING

2 cans (15 oz. each) pear halves in juice, drained

1 oz. white chocolate baking bar (from 6-oz. box)

1 teaspoon shortening

1) In 3-quart saucepan, heat milk and grated gingerroot over low heat about 5 minutes, stirring frequently, until very hot but not boiling.

2) In medium bowl with electric mixer, beat egg yolks and sugar on medium speed 4 to 6 minutes or until pale yellow. Beat in flour. Gradually beat in warm milk mixture until well blended.

3) Return mixture to saucepan; cook over medium-low heat about 5 minutes, stirring constantly, until mixture is very thick and begins to boil. Boil 1 minute, stirring constantly. Remove from heat; stir in butter and vanilla. Pour into medium bowl; place plastic wrap on surface of pastry cream. Refrigerate until completely cooled, about 1 hour.

4) Meanwhile, heat oven to 450°F. Prepare pie crust as directed on package for one-crust baked shell using 9-inch tart pan with removable bottom or 9-inch pie pan. Trim edges if necessary. Bake 9 to 11 minutes or until lightly browned. Cool completely, about 15 minutes.

5) Fill baked shell with pastry cream. Cut pear halves into thin slices; arrange on top of tart.

6) In small microwavable bowl, microwave baking bar and shortening on High 45 to 60 seconds, stirring once halfway through microwaving, until melted. If necessary, continue to microwave on High in 15-second increments, stirring until smooth. Drizzle over tart. Store in refrigerator.

HIGH ALTITUDE (3500-6000 FT.): No change.

Nutrition Information Per Serving:
Serving Size: 1/8 of Recipe

Calories:	380	From Fat:	135
Total Fat			15g
Saturated Fat			7g
Cholesterol			125mg
Sodium			160mg
Total Carbohydrate			56g
Dietary Fiber			1g
Sugars			35g
Protein			5g

Cherry-Almond Torte

PREP TIME: 25 MINUTES (READY IN 3 HOURS 35 MINUTES)
SERVINGS: 12

CHERRY MIXTURE

1 can (21 oz.) cherry pie filling

1 tablespoon cornstarch

CAKE

1 box (1 lb. 2.25 oz.) yellow cake mix

1¼ cups water

⅓ cup vegetable oil

2 teaspoons almond extract

3 eggs

WHIPPED CREAM AND ALMOND CREAM

1½ cups whipping cream

1 container (8 oz.) cream cheese spread, softened

½ cup sliced almonds, toasted

1) Heat oven to 350°F. In 2-quart saucepan, mix pie filling and cornstarch. Cook over medium heat about 7 minutes; stir constantly until mixture comes to a boil.

2) Grease bottoms only of two 9-inch round pans. In large bowl with electric mixer, beat all cake ingredients on low speed just until combined; beat on medium speed 2 minutes. Pour and spread batter evenly into pans.

3) Bake 25 to 30 minutes or until toothpick inserted in center comes out clean. Cool 10 minutes; remove from pans and place on wire racks. Cool completely, about 30 minutes.

4) In medium bowl, beat whipping cream on high speed, until soft peaks form. Beat in cream cheese spread until fluffy. Reserve ½ cup whipped cream mixture for garnish. Stir almonds into remaining cream mixture.

5) With serrated knife, cut each cake layer in half horizontally. To assemble torte, place 1 half cake layer on serving plate; spread with 1 cup almond cream. Top with second half layer; spread with 1 cup cherry mixture. Top with third half layer; spread with 1 cup almond cream. Place remaining half layer on top.

6) Spoon remaining cherry mixture on top of torte, spreading almost to edge. Frost sides of torte with remaining 1¼ cups almond cream. Spoon reserved ½ cup whipped cream mixture into decorating bag with large star tip. Pipe cream around top edge of torte. Refrigerate about 2 hours. Store in refrigerator.

HIGH ALTITUDE (3500-6000 FT.): When making cake, follow High Altitude directions on box. Continue as directed above.

Nutrition Information Per Serving:
Serving Size: 1/12 of Recipe

Calories:	500	From Fat:	270
Total Fat			30g
Saturated			13g
Cholesterol			105mg
Sodium			380mg
Total Carbohydrate			50g
Dietary Fiber			1g
Sugars			39g
Protein			7g

Silky Chocolate-Caramel Sauce

PREP TIME: 10 MINUTES (READY IN 10 MINUTES)
SERVINGS: 16 (2 TABLESPOONS EACH)

 EASY

¾ cup packed brown sugar

⅔ cup whipping cream

10 tablespoons butter

4 oz. semisweet baking chocolate, chopped

Nutrition Information Per Serving:
Serving Size: 2 Tablespoons

Calories: 170	From Fat: 110
Total Fat	12g
Saturated	8g
Cholesterol	30mg
Sodium	55mg
Total Carbohydrate	15g
Dietary Fiber	0g
Sugars	14g
Protein	1g

1) In 2-quart saucepan, cook brown sugar, whipping cream and butter over medium heat 2 to 3 minutes, stirring constantly, until mixture comes to a full boil.

2) Add chocolate; cook about 2 minutes, stirring constantly, until chocolate is melted and sauce is smooth. Serve warm or cover and refrigerate until serving time.

HIGH ALTITUDE (3500-6000 FT.): No change.

Cinnamon Roll-Topped Cobbler

PREP TIME: 10 MINUTES (READY IN 35 MINUTES)
SERVINGS: 8

1 can (29 oz.) pear halves in syrup, drained, sliced

1 can (21 oz.) cherry pie filling

1 can (12.4 oz.) Pillsbury® refrigerated cinnamon rolls with icing

Nutrition Information Per Serving:
Serving Size: 1/8 of Recipe

Calories: 300	From Fat: 55
Total Fat	6g
Saturated	2g
Cholesterol	10mg
Sodium	370mg
Total Carbohydrate	59g
Dietary Fiber	3g
Sugars	37g
Protein	3g

1) Heat oven to 375°F. In 2-quart saucepan, mix pears and pie filling. Cook over medium-high heat, stirring frequently, until mixture boils. Pour into ungreased 11x7-inch (2-quart) glass baking dish.

2) Separate dough into 8 rolls; set icing aside. Place rolls, cinnamon side up, over hot fruit mixture.

3) Bake 15 to 20 minutes or until rolls are deep golden brown and fruit is bubbly. Spread icing over hot rolls. Cool 5 minutes before serving.

HIGH ALTITUDE (3500-6000 FT.): Not recommended.

 tip

Peaches, either halves or slices in syrup, can be substituted for the pear halves, and blueberry pie filling substituted for the cherry pie filling.

Chocolate-Cherry Fantasy Dessert

PREP TIME: 20 MINUTES (READY IN 1 HOUR 10 MINUTES)
SERVINGS: 2

2 cups frozen cherries
(from 16-oz. bag)

2 tablespoons sugar

2 teaspoons cornstarch

2 Pillsbury® Oven Baked frozen
buttermilk biscuits (from 25-oz. bag)

1 teaspoon milk

1 teaspoon sugar

Vanilla ice cream, if desired

2 tablespoons fudge topping, heated

1 tablespoon slivered almonds,
if desired

1) Heat oven to 350°F. Place 2 (1½-cup)
ungreased ovenproof bowls or ramekins
on cookie sheet. Spoon 1 cup frozen
cherries into each bowl. Add 1
tablespoon sugar and 1 teaspoon
cornstarch to each bowl; toss to coat
cherries.

2) Bake 15 minutes. Remove from oven.
Stir cherries well; place 1 frozen biscuit
on top of each bowl of cherries. Brush
biscuits with milk; sprinkle with 1
teaspoon sugar.

3) Return to oven; bake 18 to 22 minutes
longer, adding almonds to cookie sheet
during last 3 minutes of baking time.
Bake until tops of biscuits and almonds
are golden brown. Cool 5 to 10 minutes
before serving. To serve, top with ice
cream, fudge topping and almonds.

HIGH ALTITUDE (3500-6000 FT.): Heat oven to 375°F.
After placing biscuits over cherries, brushing with milk
and sprinkling with sugar, return to oven and bake 22
to 26 minutes longer.

Nutrition Information Per Serving:
Serving Size: 1/2 of Recipe

Calories:	560	From Fat:	120
Total Fat			13g
Saturated			4g
Cholesterol			0mg
Sodium			650mg
Total Carbohydrate			107g
Dietary Fiber			7g
Sugars			78g
Protein			8g

Banana-Chocolate Cream Tarts

PREP TIME: 15 MINUTES (READY IN 3 HOURS 45 MINUTES)
SERVINGS: 6 TARTS

 EASY

1 (3-oz.) pkg. vanilla pudding
and pie filling mix (not instant)

1¾ cups milk

1 medium banana, sliced

1 (4-oz.) pkg. (6) single-serve
graham cracker crusts

6 teaspoons fudge ice cream
topping

6 tablespoons aerosol whipped
cream

Cinnamon, if desired

Nutrition Information Per Serving:
Serving Size: 1 Tart

Calories:	235	From Fat:	80
Total Fat			9g
Saturated			3g
Cholesterol			10mg
Sodium			200mg
Total Carbohydrate			35g
Dietary Fiber			0g
Sugars			27g
Protein			3g

1) In 2-quart saucepan, combine pudding mix and milk; mix well. Bring to a full boil over medium heat, stirring constantly. Remove from heat; place sheet of plastic wrap on top of pudding, pressing out any air. Cool 30 minutes. Refrigerate 1 hour or until slightly firm.

2) Slice banana; arrange slices in bottom of each crust. Spoon ¼ cup pudding evenly over banana in each crust. Refrigerate at least 2 hours or until serving time.

3) Just before serving, drizzle each tart with fudge topping. Garnish tarts with whipped cream; sprinkle with cinnamon. Garnish with additional banana slices, if desired.

HIGH ALTITUDE (ABOVE 3500 FT.): No change.

Strawberry-Rhubarb Sundaes

PREP TIME: 20 MINUTES
SERVINGS: 6 SUNDAES

 EASY

2 cups sliced fresh or frozen rhubarb

½ cup sugar

¼ cup water

1 (10-oz.) pkg. frozen strawberries in syrup

6 individual sponge cake cups

1½ pints (3 cups) vanilla ice cream

Nutrition Information Per Serving:
Serving Size: 1 Sundae

Calories:	350	From Fat:	80
Total Fat			9g
Saturated			5g
Cholesterol			75mg
Sodium			70mg
Total Carbohydrate			62g
Dietary Fiber			1g
Sugars			51g
Protein			5g

1) In medium saucepan, combine rhubarb, sugar and water; mix well. Bring to a boil. Reduce heat to medium-low; simmer 5 minutes, stirring occasionally.

2) Add strawberries; cook and stir 1 to 2 minutes or until berries are thawed. Serve sauce warm or cool.

3) To serve, place sponge cake cups on individual large dessert plates. Place ½ cup ice cream in each cake cup. Spoon about ⅓ cup strawberry-rhubarb sauce over each.

HIGH ALTITUDE (ABOVE 3500 FT.): No change.

White Chocolate Bread Pudding
With Red Berry Sauce

PREP TIME: 30 MINUTES (READY IN 1 HOUR 55 MINUTES)
SERVINGS: 8 (2/3 CUP PUDDING AND 3 TABLESPOONS SAUCE EACH)

BREAD PUDDING

- 1 box (6 oz.) white chocolate baking bar (6 bars), coarsely chopped

- 3 cups milk

- 6 cups cubed (1-inch) French bread (about 6 oz.)

- 2 eggs

- ¼ cup sugar

- 1 teaspoon ground cinnamon

- 1 teaspoon vanilla

SAUCE

- 1 package (10 oz.) frozen sweetened raspberries in syrup, thawed

- ¾ cup cranberry juice cocktail

- 2 tablespoons sugar

- 2 tablespoons cornstarch

1) Heat oven to 350°F. Grease 2-quart casserole with shortening or spray with cooking spray. In 3-quart saucepan, cook white chocolate and milk over medium heat about 5 minutes, stirring frequently, until white chocolate is melted (do not boil). Stir in bread cubes; set aside.

2) In large bowl, beat eggs. Stir in all remaining bread pudding ingredients until well blended. Stir in bread mixture. Pour into casserole.

3) Bake 45 to 55 minutes or until knife inserted in center comes out clean. Cool on wire rack 30 minutes.

4) Meanwhile, in 2-quart saucepan, combine all sauce ingredients. Cook over medium heat about 4 minutes, stirring constantly, until mixture comes to a boil and thickens.

5) Place strainer over 2-cup serving bowl; pour raspberry mixture into strainer. Press mixture with back of spoon through strainer to remove seeds; discard seeds. Serve warm bread pudding with sauce.

HIGH ALTITUDE (3500-6000 FT.): No change.

Nutrition Information Per Serving:
Serving Size: 1/8 of Recipe

Calories:	345	From Fat:	100
Total Fat			11g
Saturated			6g
Cholesterol			65mg
Sodium			240mg
Total Carbohydrate			54g
Dietary Fiber			2g
Sugars			38g
Protein			8g

Pineapple Upside-Down Gingerbread

PREP TIME: 25 MINUTES (READY IN 1 HOUR)
SERVINGS: 8

½ cup butter, melted

⅓ cup packed brown sugar

1 can (8 oz.) pineapple slices in juice, drained, ¼ cup juice reserved

1¼ cups all-purpose flour

½ cup granulated sugar

1 teaspoon ground ginger

½ teaspoon baking soda

½ teaspoon ground cinnamon

¼ teaspoon ground nutmeg

¼ teaspoon salt

¼ cup molasses

¼ cup milk

2 eggs

TOPPING

½ cup whipping cream, whipped

8 maraschino cherries with stems

1) Heat oven to 350°F. In 9-inch round pan, mix 2 tablespoons of the melted butter and the brown sugar; spread evenly to cover bottom of pan. Cut pineapple slices in half; arrange 4 halves over brown sugar mixture in center of pan. Cut remaining halves in half again; arrange pieces around edge of pan.

2) In large bowl, mix flour, sugar, ginger, baking soda, cinnamon, nutmeg and salt. With spoon or wire whisk, beat in remaining 6 tablespoons melted butter, ¼ cup reserved pineapple juice and all remaining gingerbread ingredients until smooth. Spoon batter carefully over pineapple; spread to cover.

3) Bake 30 to 35 minutes or until toothpick inserted in center comes out clean.

4) Run knife around side of pan to loosen. Place heatproof serving plate, upside down, over pan. Turn plate and pan over; remove pan. Cut into wedges. Serve with whipped cream and cherries.

HIGH ALTITUDE (3500-6000 FT.): Bake at 375°F. 30 to 35 minutes.

Nutrition Information Per Serving:
Serving Size: 1/8 of Recipe

Calories:	350	From Fat:	140
Total Fat			15g
Saturated			9g
Cholesterol			90mg
Sodium			260mg
Total Carbohydrate			49g
Dietary Fiber			0g
Sugars			32g
Protein			4g

Spoon the batter carefully over the arranged pineapple pieces so they stay in place.

Chocolate Cream Angel Slices with Cherry-Berry Sauce

PREP TIME: 20 MINUTES (READY IN 20 MINUTES)
SERVINGS: 8

 EASY

SAUCE

1 can (21 oz.) cherry pie filling

1 cup frozen whole raspberries (from 12- to 14-oz. bag)

2 tablespoons amaretto, if desired

ANGEL SLICES

2 oz. semisweet chocolate

1 cup whipping cream

1 tablespoon amaretto, if desired

1 loaf (10.5 oz.) angel food cake (about 7x3x3 inch)

TOPPING

8 teaspoons chocolate-flavored syrup

1) In small bowl, mix all sauce ingredients. Cover; refrigerate until serving time.

2) In 1-quart saucepan, heat chocolate over low heat, stirring occasionally, just until melted. Remove from heat. Stir in $1/4$ cup of the whipping cream.

3) In medium bowl, beat remaining $3/4$ cup whipping cream with electric mixer on high speed until stiff peaks form. Beat in chocolate mixture and amaretto. Serve immediately, or cover and refrigerate up to 2 hours.

4) To serve, cut cake into 8 slices; place on individual dessert plates. Spoon about $1/3$ cup sauce over each slice. Top each with about $1/4$ cup chocolate cream mixture; drizzle with 1 teaspoon chocolate syrup.

HIGH ALTITUDE (ABOVE 3500 FT.): No change.

Nutrition Information Per Serving:		
Serving Size: 1/8 of Recipe		
Calories: 340	From Fat:	110
Total Fat		12g
Saturated		7g
Cholesterol		35mg
Sodium		290mg
Total Carbohydrate		56g
Dietary Fiber		5g
Sugars		47g
Protein		5g

Greek Walnut Pie

MARIA E. IRVINE | SAN LEANDRO, CALIFORNIA

PREP TIME: 25 MINUTES (READY IN 4 HOURS 15 MINUTES)
SERVINGS: 12

PIE

1 (15-oz.) box Pillsbury®
   Refrigerated Pie Crusts,
   softened as directed on box

2½ cups finely chopped walnuts

¼ cup packed brown sugar

2 tablespoons granulated sugar

1½ teaspoons ground cinnamon

¾ cup butter or margarine,
   melted, cooled

¾ cup honey

1 tablespoon lemon juice

TOPPING

½ pint (1 cup) heavy whipping cream

1 teaspoon granulated sugar

1 teaspoon vanilla

1) Heat oven to 325°F. Spray 9-inch glass pie pan with cooking spray. Prepare pie crusts as directed on box for two-crust pie using sprayed pie pan.

2) In medium bowl, mix walnuts, brown sugar, 2 tablespoons granulated sugar and the cinnamon. Pour and evenly spread ¼ cup of the cooled melted butter over bottom of pie crust. Spread walnut mixture evenly over butter. Drizzle another ¼ cup butter over nut mixture.

3) Top with second pie crust; seal edges and flute. Cut large slits in several places in top crust for steam to escape. Drizzle remaining ¼ cup butter evenly over top crust.

4) Bake at 325°F. for 45 to 55 minutes or until golden brown. About 5 minutes before removing pie from oven, in 1-quart saucepan, cook honey and lemon juice over medium heat, stirring frequently, until mixture has a watery consistency.

5) Remove pie from oven; place on wire rack. Slowly pour hot honey mixture evenly over top of hot pie, making sure it seeps into slits in top crust. Cool at least 3 hours before serving.

6) Just before serving, in small bowl, beat all topping ingredients with electric mixer on high speed about 2 minutes or until stiff peaks form. Spoon topping onto individual servings of pie.

HIGH ALTITUDE (ABOVE 3500 FT.): Bake at 325°F. for 55 to 65 minutes.

Nutrition Information Per Serving: Serving Size: 1/12 of Recipe	
Calories: 590	From Fat: 390
Total Fat	43g
Saturated	17g
Cholesterol	60mg
Sodium	230mg
Total Carbohydrate	46g
Dietary Fiber	2g
Sugars	26g
Protein	6g

Big Birthday Cookie

PREP TIME:	15 MINUTES (READY IN 1 HOUR 5 MINUTES)	 EASY
SERVINGS:	12	

1 roll (18 oz.) Pillsbury® refrigerated chocolate chip cookies

Decorating icing in tubes

Candy sprinkles

1) Heat oven to 350°F. Into ungreased 12-inch pizza pan, break up cookie dough. With floured fingers, press dough evenly in pan.

2) Bake 15 to 20 minutes or until golden brown. Cool completely, about 30 minutes. Decorate as desired with decorating icing and candy sprinkles. Cut into wedges or squares to serve.

HIGH ALTITUDE (3500-6500 FT.): Bake at 350°F. 17 to 20 minutes.

Nutrition Information Per Serving:
Serving Size: 1/12 of Recipe

Calories:	200	From Fat:	90
Total Fat			11g
Saturated			3g
Cholesterol			5mg
Sodium			135mg
Total Carbohydrate			26g
Dietary Fiber			0g
Sugars			15g
Protein			2g

Sweet Bunny Cupcakes

PREP TIME:	45 MINUTES (READY IN 45 MINUTES)
SERVINGS:	6 CUPCAKES

½ cup vanilla frosting (from 16-oz. can)

3 drops green food color

6 unfrosted white cupcakes (purchased or made from a mix)

1 package (3 oz.) cream cheese, softened

2 cups powdered sugar

1 tablespoon milk

¼ teaspoon lemon extract

Candy decors

Decorating icing

Nutrition Information Per Serving:
Serving Size: 1 Cupcake

Calories:	490	From Fat:	90
Total Fat			10g
Saturated			7g
Cholesterol			15mg
Sodium			70mg
Total Carbohydrate			99g
Dietary Fiber			0g
Sugars			93g
Protein			1g

1) In small bowl, mix frosting and green food color until well blended. Frost cupcakes.

2) In medium bowl with electric mixer, beat cream cheese, powdered sugar, milk and lemon extract on medium speed until smooth. Shape cream cheese dough into 6 bunnies.

3) Decorate bunnies with candy decors and decorating icing. Place bunnies on frosted cupcakes.

HIGH ALTITUDE (3500-6500 FT.): No change.

Fudge Crostata with Raspberry Sauce

PAULA CASSIDY | BOSTON, MASSACHUSETTS

PREP TIME: 50 MINUTES (READY IN 3 HOURS 10 MINUTES)
SERVINGS: 12

CRUST

1 box (15 oz.) Pillsbury® refrigerated pie crusts, softened as directed on box

FILLING

1 cup semisweet chocolate chips

½ cup butter or margarine, softened

⅔ cup sugar

1 cup ground almonds

1 egg

1 egg yolk

SAUCE

1 package (12 oz.) frozen raspberries without syrup, thawed

¾ cup sugar

1 teaspoon lemon juice

GARNISH, (IF DESIRED)

Sweetened whipped cream

Chocolate curls

Whole raspberries

1) Make pie crusts as directed on box for Two-Crust Pie using 10-inch tart pan with removable bottom or 9-inch glass pie pan. Place 1 pie crust in pan; press in bottom and up sides of pan. Trim edges if necessary.

2) Place cookie sheet on middle oven rack in oven to preheat; heat oven to 375°F. In 1-quart saucepan, melt chocolate chips and 2 tablespoons of the butter over low heat, stirring constantly, until smooth. In medium bowl with electric mixer, beat remaining 6 tablespoons butter and ⅔ cup sugar on medium speed until light and fluffy. Beat in almonds, egg, egg yolk and melted chocolate until well blended. Spread mixture evenly in crust-lined pan.

3) To make lattice top, cut second pie crust into ½-inch-wide strips. Arrange strips in lattice design over chocolate mixture; trim and seal edges.

4) Place tart on preheated cookie sheet; bake 45 to 50 minutes or until crust is golden brown. If necessary, cover edge of crust with strips of foil during last 10 to 15 minutes of baking to prevent excessive browning. Cool completely, about 1½ hours.

5) Meanwhile, in blender or food processor, blend thawed raspberries on high speed until smooth. Place strainer over small saucepan; pour berries into strainer. With back of spoon, press berries through strainer to remove seeds; discard seeds. Stir in ¾ cup sugar and the lemon juice until well blended. Heat to boiling, stirring constantly. Reduce heat to medium-low; boil 3 minutes, stirring constantly. Cool slightly; refrigerate until serving time.

6) At serving time, garnish crostata with whipped cream, chocolate curls and whole raspberries; serve with raspberry sauce. Store in refrigerator.

HIGH ALTITUDE (3500-6500 FT.): Bake tart on preheated cookie sheet at 375°F. 42 to 47 minutes. Continue as directed above.

Nutrition Information Per Serving:
Serving Size: 1/12 of Recipe

Calories:	460	From Fat:	240
Total Fat			27g
Saturated			10g
Cholesterol			60mg
Sodium			210mg
Total Carbohydrate			55g
Dietary Fiber			4g
Sugars			35g
Protein			4g

Chocolate-Peanut Butter Cookie Pie

JENNY MONFRED | WINTERSVILLE , OHIO

PREP TIME: 15 MINUTES (READY IN 1 HOUR 50 MINUTES)
SERVINGS: 16

1 roll (18 oz.) Pillsbury® refrigerated chocolate chip cookies

3 cups powdered sugar

1 cup creamy or crunchy peanut butter

2 tablespoons butter, softened

¼ cup water

1 cup milk chocolate chips, melted

16 pecan halves, if desired

Nutrition Information Per Serving:
Serving Size: 1/16 of Recipe

Calories:	410	From Fat:	190
Total Fat			21g
Saturated			7g
Cholesterol			10mg
Sodium			200mg
Total Carbohydrate			51g
Dietary Fiber			2g
Sugars			40g
Protein			6g

1) Heat oven to 350°F. Cut cookie dough into ½-inch slices; arrange in bottom of ungreased 10- or 9-inch springform pan. With floured fingers, press dough in pan to form crust.

2) Bake 14 to 18 minutes or until golden brown. Cool 15 minutes.

3) In medium bowl, mix powdered sugar, peanut butter, butter and water until smooth (if necessary, add additional water 1 teaspoon at a time). Drop spoonfuls of peanut butter mixture over crust; spread evenly to cover crust.

4) Spread melted chocolate chips over peanut butter mixture (if desired, carefully swirl chocolate with fork). Garnish with pecan halves. Refrigerate until chocolate is set before serving, about 1 hour.

HIGH ALTITUDE (3500-6500 FT.): No change.

Mint Cheesecake Squares

PREP TIME: 30 MINUTES (READY IN 4 HOURS)
SERVINGS: 20

CRUST

1 package (9 oz.) thin chocolate wafer cookies, crushed (1¾ cups)

½ cup butter or margarine, melted

FILLING

2 packages (8 oz. each) cream cheese, softened

½ cup sour cream

4 eggs

⅔ cup sugar

½ cup crème de menthe syrup

¼ teaspoon mint extract

TOPPING

4 oz. semisweet baking chocolate, chopped

½ cup sour cream

Nutrition Information Per Serving:
Serving Size: 1/20 of Recipe

Calories:	300	From Fat:	190
Total Fat			21g
Saturated			12g
Cholesterol			90mg
Sodium			200mg
Total Carbohydrate			25g
Dietary Fiber			1g
Sugars			14g
Protein			5g

1) Heat oven to 350°F. In medium bowl, mix crust ingredients. Press in bottom of ungreased 13x9-inch pan. Freeze crust while preparing filling.

2) In large bowl with electric mixer, beat all filling ingredients on low speed until smooth. Pour into crust-lined pan. Bake 30 to 35 minutes or until knife inserted in center comes out clean. Cool on wire rack.

3) Meanwhile, in 1-quart saucepan, melt chocolate over low heat, stirring constantly. Cool 5 minutes; beat in sour cream with spoon. Spread over warm cheesecake. Refrigerate 3 hours or until firm. Cut into squares. Store in refrigerator.

HIGH ALTITUDE (3500-6000 FT.): Bake at 350°F. 35-40 minutes.

Alphabetical Index

General Recipe Index

This handy index lists every recipe by food category, major ingredient and/or cooking method, so you can easily locate recipes to suit your needs.